CONNECTIVE AI

Focusing on social robots, play, and democracy, this volume explores how AI can be used in connective ways to advance the common good and support democratic practice.

This innovative collection puts play at the center of how we think about AI and democracy, exploring how playful participation may be used to help restore the creative energies of democracy. Featuring contributions by seasoned experts, the chapters explore topics such as social robots, play, and democracy; polymorphic chatbots and online interactions; AI curation by bot-supported agents and participatory environments; social robots, journalism, and connective action; civility and AI; collaboration between human and robotic agents in democratic spaces; democratic experiments, generative AI, and polymorphic robots; gaming, play, and democratic engagement between humans and nonhumans; and AI, play, and democracy. This book presents new ideas for how connective AI and social robots could be used to help reimagine and improve our everyday lives; specifically, how playful interaction with robotic agents could help revive civic engagement, thus ushering in a new paradigm for connective AI.

This book will be of interest to upper-level students, researchers, and scholars across a variety of fields, including media and communication studies, science and technology studies, and political science, particularly those exploring AI and human–computer interaction in relation to democracy and civic life.

Zizi Papacharissi is UIC Distinguished Professor of Communication and Political Science at the University of Illinois Chicago and Department Head of Communication. She is also a university scholar and affiliate faculty with the Discovery Partners Institute at the University of Illinois System. Her work focuses on the social and political consequences of online media. She has published ten books and over 80 journal articles and book chapters and serves on the editorial boards of 15 journals. She is the founding and current editor of the open access journal *Social Media & Society*. Her work has been translated into Greek, German, Korean, Chinese, Hungarian, Italian, Turkish, and Persian.

CONNECTIVE AI

Social (Ro)Bots, Play, Democracy

Edited by Zizi Papacharissi

Routledge
Taylor & Francis Group

NEW YORK AND LONDON

Designed cover image: © Dr. Theofanis Exadaktylos, Professor of European Politics, University of Surrey

First published 2026
by Routledge
605 Third Avenue, New York, NY 10158

and by Routledge
4 Park Square, Milton Park, Abingdon, Oxon, OX14 4RN

Routledge is an imprint of the Taylor & Francis Group, an informa business

For Product Safety Concerns and Information please contact our EU representative GPSR@taylorandfrancis.com. Taylor & Francis Verlag GmbH, Kaufingerstraße 24, 80331 München, Germany.

ISBN: 9781032762128 (hbk)
ISBN: 9781032762111 (pbk)
ISBN: 9781003477587 (ebk)

DOI: 10.4324/9781003477587

Typeset in Sabon
by codeMantra

For the machines, human and non.

CONTENTS

FIGURES

TABLES

CONTRIBUTORS

Shreshta Bhat specializes in human-centered artificial intelligence and currently works on AI safety at Google. Her prior work includes research contributions at Meta and graduate studies at UC Berkeley, where her work examined knowledge gaps within large language models.

Taina Bucher is Professor and Head of Research at the Department of Media and Communication, University of Oslo, Norway. She leads *HumAIn: A Humanities Hub for the Reimagination of AI* and is the Principal Investigator of the research project and initiative *The Democracy of Silence*. She is the author of two books: *Facebook* (2021) and *If... Then: Algorithmic Power and Politics* (2018).

Fausto Colombo was Professor in Media and Communication at the Faculty of Political and Social Sciences, Università Cattolica del Sacro Cuore. He played a pivotal role in the development of media studies, first in Italy and later across Europe. Member of Academia Europaea and founding member of SISCC (Italian Scientific Society for Sociology, Culture and Communication), he sat on the ECREA board. He authored or co-authored over 20 monographs.

Cynthia Klekar Cunningham is Professor of English and Director of the School of Communication at Western Michigan University. Her scholarship centers on representations of displacement, and her recent work engages emerging intersections of connective AI and environmental justice for Indigenous communities.

Autumn Edwards is Professor of Communication at Western Michigan University, United States. She co-directs the Multi-institutional Communication and Social Robotics Labs. Her research examines human–machine communication as a new ontological terrain, challenging assumptions about persons, machines, and communication itself while illuminating how these shifts reverberate through culture, ethics, and planetary futures.

Chad Edwards is Professor of Communication in the School of Communication at Western Michigan University and a Theodore von Kármán Fellow at RWTH Aachen University. His research interests include human–machine communication and AI interaction. He co-directs the Communication and Social Robotics Labs (www.combotlabs.org). Currently, he is the Founding Associate Editor of *Human–Machine Communication*.

Nicole B. Ellison is Karl E. Weick Collegiate Professor of Information in the School of Information at the University of Michigan. Her research explores the social and interpersonal aspects of online technologies and computer-mediated communication in the context of domains such as self-presentation, identity, social support, and relationship development.

Maxwell Foxman is Associate Professor of Media and Game Studies at the University of Oregon's School of Journalism and Communication. He researches how play and games impact nongame media and professions. He is the co-author of *Mainstreaming and Game Journalism* (2023) with David B. Nieborg. His research has appeared in *New Media & Society*, *Social Media + Society*, and *Digital Journalism*, among other outlets.

William R. Frey is a Joint Postdoctoral Research Fellow in the School of Information and School of Social Work, and Faculty Affiliate of the Digital Studies Institute at the University of Michigan. He is also an AI Fellow in the Bok Center at Harvard University. His interdisciplinary scholarship investigates how humans use, navigate, refuse, and resist technologies to survive and thrive.

Isabelle Giordano is a User Experience Researcher at Meta in the Superintelligence lab, specializing in how users interact with generative artificial intelligence.

Kishonna L. Gray is Professor of Racial Justice and Technology at the University of Michigan, Director of the Intersectional Tech Lab, and Faculty Associate of the Berkman Klein Center at Harvard University. She is the author of six books, including *Intersectional Tech: Black Users in Digital Gaming*.

David J. Gunkel is an award-winning educator, researcher, and author, specializing in the moral and legal challenges of artificial intelligence. He is the author of over 115 scholarly articles and has published 18 books, including *The Machine Question* (2012), *Robot Rights* (2018), and *Person, Thing, Robot* (2023). He currently holds the position of Distinguished Research Professor at Northern Illinois University.

Eszter Hargittai is Professor and holds the Chair of Internet Use and Society at the Department of Communication and Media Research, University of Zurich. She is the author, most recently, of *Wired Wisdom: How to Age Better Online* with John Palfrey (2025).

Alfonso Hegde is a Communication PhD student at the Annenberg School for Communication and Journalism at the University of Southern California. He is working on a dissertation examining technological changes reconfiguring and reinventing film production labor, with specific focus on effects work.

Lukas Hess is a PhD candidate at the University of Zurich and Partner at Dezentrum, a Swiss do and think tank for digitalization. His research examines digital inequality, activism, and privacy, focusing on how authoritarian regimes and corporations use technology to consolidate power and how activists resist within increasingly unequal digital landscapes.

Henry Jenkins is the Provost's Professor of Communication, Journalism, Cinematic Arts, Education, and East Asian Languages and Cultures at the University of Southern California. He co-directs with Sangita Shresthova the Civic Imagination and Transcultural Fandom research groups and is currently co-authoring the Frames of Fandom book series with Robert Kozinets.

Katie Joseff is Cofounder of Amulet, a decentralized sovereign AI company. She previously led Integrity and Authenticity for TikTok US/CA, managed the Propaganda Research Lab at UT Austin and the Digital Intelligence Lab at IFTF, and advocated for social media and privacy regulation with Common Sense Media. She holds a masters degree from Stanford University and was named to Forbes 30 Under 30 list in 2024.

Do Own (Donna) Kim is Assistant Professor in Communication at the University of Illinois, Chicago, United States. She researches everyday playful digital cultures and communication technologies. She has written about topics like video games, virtual influencers, and Korean media cultures, available in flagship journals like *New Media & Society* and *Communication Monographs*.

Alexander Kisioi Koech is a freelance journalist and environmental activist from Kenya's Ogiek community and has spent over eight years documenting illegal forest activities and advocating for climate action. Using his mobile phone, he shares authentic stories about Indigenous livelihoods, ecological knowledge, and environmental justice on social media and in collaborations with local newsrooms.

Jindong Leo-Liu (or Jindong Liu) is Assistant Professor in New Media and Social Media, the Education University of Hong Kong (EdUHK). He specializes in AI companions, Social VR, and mediated intimacy. He has contributed to many journals, including *Social Media + Society*, *New Media & Society*, and *Computers in Human Behavior*.

Tony Liao is Associate Professor in the Department of Information Science Technology, Cullen College of Engineering, University of Houston. He is the Founding Director of the CougAR Lab, which examines the social and psychological outcomes of emerging augmented and virtual reality technologies.

Eden Litt, PhD, is Director of Research at Meta. Utilizing qualitative and quantitative methods, her work explores how people use social media. Her research has been published in peer-reviewed journals and presented to government officials, policymakers, academic researchers, the press, and nonprofits around the world.

Gerta Lokaj is a PhD student in Communication and Media Research at the University of Zurich. Her research focuses on how developments around artificial intelligence impact and change public science communication.

Winston Mano is Full Professor and member of the University of Westminster's top-rated Communication and Media Research Institute (CAMRI). He is a Course Director for the MA in Media and Development and Founder/Editor-in-Chief of the *Journal of African Media Studies*. He is the founding Director of the Africa Media Project and was Co-Director of the Chevening Africa Media Freedom Fellowship program (2020–2023). He has published widely, and his research interests span Afrokology,

Decoloniality, African radio, music, media audiences, digital communications policy and development, China-African media relations, and African media and democracy. He is a Senior Research Fellow at the University of Johannesburg, South Africa.

Giovanna Mascheroni is a sociologist of digital media and Full Professor in the Department of Communication, Università Cattolica del Sacro Cuore. Her work focuses on the social consequences of digital media, datafication and AI for children, young people, and families. She has published extensively in international journals (including *New Media & Society, Journal of Children and Media, Social Media & Society,* and *Information, Communication & Society*) and edited volumes.

L. Lusike Mukhongo is Associate Professor in Film, Video, and Media Studies at Western Michigan University. Her research focuses on participatory technologies, community-driven co-design of low-power AI tools for indigenous languages and non-extractive community-engaged digital storytelling.

Peter Nagy is Instructor at Arizona State University, United States. He is an interdisciplinary researcher whose work draws theories from a variety of disciplines, including psychology, sociology, communication and media studies, consumer culture theory (CCT), and science and technology studies (STS). He is an editorial board member of *Human-Machine Communication*.

Simone Natale is Associate Professor in Media History and Theory at the University of Turin, Italy, and Editor of *Media, Culture & Society*. He is the author of *Deceitful Media: Artificial Intelligence and Social Life after the Turing Test* (2021), which was translated into Chinese, Italian, and Portuguese.

David B. Nieborg is Professor of Media Studies at the University of Toronto. He published on the game industry, the political economy of platforms, and game journalism. He is the coauthor of *Platforms and Cultural Production* and *Mainstreaming and Game Journalism*.

Jasmin Pfefferkorn is a Postdoctoral Research Fellow in the School of Culture and Communication at The University of Melbourne. She is the author of *Museums as Assemblage* (Routledge 2023) and Co-Editor of *Decentring Ethics: AI Art as Method* (2025). She co-founded and co-directs the research group CODED AESTHETICS.

Lauren Scissors has a PhD in Media, Technology, and Society from Northwestern University and specializes in human-computer interaction. She is Director of UX Research at Meta.

Samantha Shorey is Assistant Professor at the University of Pittsburgh. She is a field researcher who studies how communication about innovation shapes technology design and technology labor.

Sangita Shresthova is Associate Research Professor at the University of Southern California Annenberg School for Communication and Journalism, where she directs the Civic Paths Research Group. As the author and co-author of multiple books, including *We Are Civic Media* (2025) and *Transformative Media Pedagogies* (2021), she explores how we might use storytelling, participatory cultures, cross-cultural communication, and civic imagination to help shape democratic futures.

Emilie K. Sunde is Co-Founder and Co-Director of CODED AESTHETICS. Her research focuses on latent space and visual culture. She is Co-Editor of *Decentring Ethics: AI Art as Method* (2025) and has published with *The Nordic Journal of Aesthetics*, *Media Theory*, and *Philosophy of Photography*, among others.

Simone Tosoni is Associate Professor at the Faculty of Political and Social Sciences of the Università Cattolica del Sacro Cuore in Milan, where he teaches Sociology of Cultural Processes and conducts research on digital media. His recent work has focused on scientific information and disinformation, as well as on the phenomenon of "influ-activism" on social media platforms.

Sophie Toupin is Assistant Professor in the Department of Information and Communication at Université Laval, in Quebec, Canada. She mobilizes critical approaches, such as feminist, intersectional, anticolonial, and decolonial, to apprehend, analyze, and rethink the digital and technological. She has authored chapters for several publications and has contributed to many journals, including *New Media & Society*, *Big Data & Society*, and *Feminist Media Studies*, among others.

ACKNOWLEDGMENTS

This volume could not have come into being without its contributors. You helped me turn an abstract idea into a meaningful story. Thank you for being you.

My most heartfelt thanks to Diana Casteel, who helped me coordinate, organize, and turn my thoughts into tangible form and artifact. I thank my cousin, Theofanis Exadaktylos, Professor in European Politics at the University of Surrey, and fellow traveler. I have known you all my life, and you gifted me this wonderful photo that captures everything I wanted the cover of this book to be. Finally, I want to thank my mother Stella for showing me how to be different, think otherwise, and trust my imagination. This volume is about a connection that is free of conformity, and I would not have learned that without her.

1

INTRODUCTION

Zizi Papacharissi

AI-rendered technologies invite hopes and fears. Their potential raises as many questions as it answers and often resides in binaries between utopia and dystopia; connection and disconnection; and social benefit and exploitation. Inevitably, the dreams and nightmares rendered by the limits of human imagination revolve around the same theme: Will AI fundamentally alter the essence of what it means to be human? And the answer, despite the countless narratives of anticipation and apprehension, is, I find, the same: Only if humans permit it to do so.

For some 30 years now, I have studied how humans respond to technologies of their own making. With every technology comes new ways of doing things, including practices that advance and oppress, often simultaneously. It is common to place the effects of technology on a continuum. It is convenient to imagine them as ranging between linearly placed polarizing opposites: negative and positive. More often than not, however, we find that nothing is entirely good or purely bad. Energy emerges out of the interaction between positive and negative forces. Consider foundational laws of nature that view positrons as the antiparticles of electrons, and document how, when the two collide, more particles emerge through processes of annihilation. One might think to design technologies that work like positrons. Geophysicists explain that when collisions occur at low energies, photons emerge. Thinking further, AI modalities may be oriented to lead to the creation of photons.

Technology creates space where interaction between humans can happen. There is no bipolar continuum that neatly divides the effects of technology into positive or negative. There is space, which technology, human

DOI: 10.4324/9781003477587-1

made, and human used, shapes and is shaped by, as people meet, collide, or get along with less intense energies that lead into the production of light, instead of darkness. These activities may therefore be supported by technology, AI-driven, that works in connective ways.

The above metaphors borrowed from geophysics align with our vocabulary for understanding dark participation, the dark web, and black box AI design, among other terms. They evoke further processes that render technology less meaningful to humans and give us pause about AI enabling a darker future with no light at the end of the tunnel. As I have argued elsewhere (e.g., *Networked Self Series, Volumes 1–5*, Routledge), it would be more meaningful to think of AI as enabling connection and expression in various directions. It would be important for companies to be required to design AI with a democratic mandate and conscience (Papacharissi, 2021, *After Democracy*, Yale University Press). Civic responsibility should be the core of technology design, instead of an afterthought. In this manner, humans might spend less time chasing after technological developments and more time thinking about how to use them to improve their civic lives.

This volume invites scholars to think about how AI can be used in connective ways that advance the common good. A polity that advances the common good takes form under the auspices of democracy, so scholars consider how connective AI can be used toward democratic practice. What distinguishes this volume from others is that I ask scholars to focus on social robots, as one form of generative AI that renders robotic agents humans interact with. The second aspect that makes this collection unique is the focus on playful participation as a way of restoring the creative energies of democracy. Rather than focusing on toxic or high-energy environments, I invite scholars to think about low-energy environments where the collision of different energies leads to release, diffusion, and opportunity to regenerate. This invitation stands in direct contrast to Silicon Valley's dominant narratives that place disruption at the center of innovation. And yet, most of the meaningful innovations that we enjoy today took form in the low-energy spaces of dorm rooms or parents' garages. Ultimately, connective AI may be put to use to help reimagine and improve our everyday routines. Over time, it could help drive us away from reproducing new ways of doing the same old things, across different platforms, and imagine new ways of being through play instead.

The term connective AI is inspired by the work of Lance Bennett and Alexandra Segerberg on connective action. The two constructed the term to describe how networked movements that emerge as personalized action formations, representing individualized takes on developing issues, coalesce. These personally rendered micro-actions attain affective drive and force, as they are shared, amplified, and organically collated across networks. Bennett and Segerberg explain platforms, in this context, serve as conduits for these loosely connected streams of individual takes on issues. Unlike collective frames, these cumulative, albeit often fragmented, viewpoints collate into imbricated layers of action that mix drama, news, opinion, and emotion into one, to the point where distinguishing one element from the other is impossible and doing so misses the point. I relied on the logic of connective action to explain the formation of affective publics: loosely connected networks of individuals that come together, are identified, and are potentially disbanded around bonds of sentiment.

Affective publics and connective action are not negative, nor positive, nor neutral. As I write in the conclusion of this book, they reflect the structures of storytelling of a given time. The produce streams of activity that we can understand as artifacts, or assemblages of artifacts, and every artifact tells a story, if one knows how to read it. In the era of post-truth politics, Bennett and Kneuer (2023) draw attention to how the logic of connective action can be exploited to support illiberal public spheres; the activities are far removed from the context of movements like Occupy, MeToo, Indignados, and several others associated with the so-called Arab Spring. These movements were used as case studies to understand how networked formations supported social movements beyond the conventional theoretical vocabulary afforded by theories on collective action and the public sphere. The same structures of storytelling that support affective drives of liberation can also sustain narratives formed around dark participation and digital harm. The structure itself is neither negative nor positive, nor is it neutral. It is affect-driven, which energizes and sustains feelings of community. These feelings of community, as I explained in *Affective Publics,* can either reflexively drive a civic movement forward or entrap it in a state of engaged passivity. Imaginaries inspire and can also make people feel like resistance is out of reach or futile.

Connective AI is poised to do the very same. There is cause to be pessimistic, because early uses of AI have supported deepfakes, disinformation, and a variety of synthetic media and agents that have led to more digital harm than good. Embodied and non-embodied agents, taking the form of bots, bot factions, bot farms or armies, or innocently presented chatbots offering to organize search engine findings in user-friendly, copy-paste format, can support structures of storytelling giving rise to affectively driven narratives that entrap. Robots and social robots can be further programmed to support these activities, especially as we limit our engagement with these technologies to view them as tools, deployed in command, control, and task-oriented fashions.

I use this volume to present Connective AI as a way of thinking and doing AI otherwise. The term emphasizes a move away from logically driven and restricted task orientation to the looser and more imaginative territory of play. Connective AI is about technology developed with democratic values at the core, not the periphery. Democracy drives technological development and is not relegated to chance afterthought. Reviving the human limits of imagination is key, and the way to do this is through crafting symbiotic relationships with human and nonhuman agents.

This volume, therefore, focuses on robots, play, and democracy. It invites us to think about how playful interaction with robotic agents may revive civic engagement, thus ushering in a paradigm for connective AI. Robots feature prominently in the popular imaginary of democratic futures. Science fiction folklore, for instance, often places robots and humanoids as rational assistants to democratically motivated rebellion, as is the case with C-3PO or R2-D2 in the Star Wars content genre. Empire troops in the same series also use humanoids to oppress democratic efforts. The examples are countless, and often lead to work that directly engages science, as with the work of Asimov, which dreams up various forms of robotic agents to pose profound questions about democracy. This volume includes contributions that speak to the uses of embodied and non-embodied agents, rendered through a variety of coding practices, including Large Learning Models (LLMs), Deep Learning Models, generative and non-generative AI, and the use of further technologically enabled faculties. What distinguishes the perspective is the emphasis on (ro)bots as socially oriented agents, which interact with humans and nonhumans on civically informed matters.

Play is always an interesting side note in these scenarios. Societies, democratic and non, have always used play to release sentiment. Technology leads to the creation of toys that children and adults play with and are socialized in. Humans often reverse-engineer technology created for work to facilitate play; this is the story of the web and countless other popular media and platforms. Play takes on many forms, some restorative and others regressive, and is used to foster the release of various feelings. Fairs in medieval times presented platforms, put to use to bring about joy in the aftermath of plagues, war conflicts, and other crises, and many fairs still serve the same purpose to this day. Arenas hosting violent play in the Roman era permitted sentiment release that even advanced feelings of community despite exposing social inequality. Hundreds of years later, playing through sports simultaneously connects and divides. Playing with technology leads to content that supports affectively woven together publics, who share the same feeling forward via a meme, a TikTok video, or a gif.

Play is used to interpellate; to signify; to mark; to identify; to connect; to express; and to bring into being sentiments, shared or isolated. How can social robots facilitate forms of play that drive democracy forward? This is the starting point of the conversation that an edited volume about Connective AI will facilitate. The ending point of the conversation lies in the meta and will be informed by the imagination of the contributors. I expect this volume to be unusual, and I hope it will be filled with provocations. I have designed it to help us put *play* at the center of how we think about AI and democracy. Play is notoriously tricky to define, and seeking to contain it in operational terms often invites the reproduction of colonial and hegemonic assumptions about ludics. To this point, play scholar Miguel Sicart (2023) draws attention to the work of Argentinian philosopher María Lugones, who critiques dominant approaches to play as having to do primarily with winning, losing, battling, and contest. Lugones prefers the term playfulness, which she describes as essential to play and as the ability to travel across worlds. This form of world traveling is more relevant to the use of play to reinvent civic life, which this volume embraces.

I understand playfulness as the key to avoiding antagonistic discourses that gamify civic life in contemporary societies, democratic and non (Papacharissi, 2021, 2026). Many of the contributors to this volume draw on the concept of world making when thinking on human-machine interactions that inform civic conversations. It is essential to underline that authentic play does not undermine the gravitas of democratic discourse and process. On the contrary, it supports an ecosystem that sustains synagonistic disagreement and consensus. Performative, manufactured play, on the other hand, can be employed as a political strategy. When it does, it stops being true play and is mere, vapid performativity; a shell of pretend essence or veneer of make believe charm. Lugones (1987) consciously avoids defining *worlds* to avoid ascribing imperialistically charged fixity to the term. She does offer that worlds refer to constellations, imaginary and actual, imperfect and under construction, of humans relating to other human and nonhuman entities. A world, she explains, "is an experience," and "those of us who are world travelers have the distinct experience of being different in different 'worlds' and ourselves in them." The shift from being one person to being another is what she terms *travel,* and it is a shift that "may not be willful or even conscious," and one in which one "does not experience any underlying I" (p.11). Being at ease in a "world" is playfulness, and this is the starting point of the conversation for this volume.

Experts from and across all research areas are invited to think about the questions the volume poses. Some contributors have published work on similar questions, and others are seasoned experts on democracy, participation, and play who adapt their work to robotic and robot-supported interfaces. The volume includes a multitude of tropes on social robots, play, and democracy; polymorphic chatbots and online interactions; representation, exclusion, and silence in a bot populated world; AI curation by bot-supported agents and participatory environments; social robots, journalism, and connective action; civility and AI; collaboration between human and robotic agents in democratic spaces; democratic experiments, generative AI, and polymorphic robots; gaming, play, and democratic engagement between humans and nonhumans; and AI, play, and democracy.

The conversational journey volume contributors take us on begins with a wake-up call from Henry Jenkins, Sangita Shreshtova, Alfonso Hegde, and Civic Paths Research Group members. When their Civic Imagination group members asked Midjourney, the visual generative AI platform, to present a version of LA, redesigned to work without cars, they received a depiction of a deserted city without people. Either AI has a twisted sense of humor or is dropping hints about the long-term incompatibility between humans and their cars. At heart lies a problem of communication. Talking with AI systems invites us to use our language. AI systems understand us better; however, if we learn to use their language. All too often, our experiments with chatbots require rephrasing our queries to receive the results that we want. This is a fascinating exercise, and one not too different from trial-and-error patterns we engage in when we get to know other humans. As we get acquainted with AI conversational companions, however, we find out more about the process through which they learn, process, analyze, and synthesize and note one component that is absent: that of imagination. Grace Hopper famously quipped that no computer will ever ask a new, reasonable question. Perhaps, I have met few humans capable of asking truly new, reasonable questions, so the bar is high. The point that should not be lost on us, however, is the need to design AI systems that we can jam with. Bots, modalities, robots, and sentient entities to come up that we remix, joke, and play with, and in so doing, learn to grow our imaginations and ask newer, better questions ourselves.

Henry Jenkins and his colleagues call for technologies that enhance the civic imagination. Beyond models of replicating, reproducing, and reinforcing existing patterns, they look at the potential of technology that invites us to play with it; technology that does not do for us things that we do not feel like doing, but the tech that imagines with us the things we have not thought we might enjoy doing yet. Not a substitute, more than a supplement, and closer to a pathway to hidden, undiscovered elements of our humanity. Unfortunately, commercially driven AI platforms have diverted from this road so profoundly that doing over and imagining AI otherwise would require humans to game the system. David J. Gunkel writes about this very idea, borne out of increasing frustration and disillusionment with a system that measures intelligence as the ability to imitate. A strange and flawed supposition; for in human education systems, we reward innovation and shun imitation. Yet when designing machines, we judge their intelligence by their ability to match and outperform that of humans. An assumption that human intelligence is superior underlies these practices (Lackey & Papacharissi, 2024). The imitation game is a reasonable beginning but a disappointing finale to our love affair with technology. Gunkel reminds us that Turing always meant imitation to be the entry point to the question of whether computers can think. Whether they are able to depends on how we humans define thinking, linguistically first, and ontologically in the long term.

One way of evolving out of conventional, one-on-one contests of machine vs. human is to design systems of one-to-many, or many-to-many communication experiences. Litt, Ellison, Scissors, Giordano, and Bhat perceive these environments as more intuitive, creative, and natural ways of interacting with bots, robots, and many soon-to-be sentient iterations of AI. Such interfaces evolve beyond command, control, and execute models of interaction to socially rich interactions that require nuanced levels of presence from all actors involved. The authors set the stage for human and non-actors to engage in playful conversation that expands beyond task-oriented objectives. The design paradigms thus evolve into joint, group, immersive jam sessions that give new meaning to deep learning practices for both human and nonhuman actors.

Taina Bucher tackles the aforementioned premise of one-to-one, one-to-many, or many-to-many communication that robots, bots, and AI are designed around. As she characteristically remarks, they are built as talkative agents: "A chatbot is expected to chat, a social robot to converse, a digital assistant to respond verbally." The human capacity for silence is typically read as a malfunction when rendered by digitally enabled agents. Yet the ability to listen, be silent, and know when to speak or to be loud and how creates nuance essential for democratic discourse.

Similarly, robots, bots, and AI are designed with the assumption that they will render something; they will create. They will not render silence, negative output, or absence. Yet what happens when AI agents are asked to produce something they are not able to represent, like Blackness? Frey and Gray consider the harms created by the operational logic of the imitation game, a process that functions on limited data, biased renderings of what might be regarded as playful. The dark side of play here simplifies and is modeled after dominant and hegemonic interpretations of intelligence and play.

The two authors recommend that further synthetic literacies be developed, so that deep learning practices become more nuanced and those susceptible to digital harm are enabled to resist. Hargittai, Lokaj, and Hess locate digital inequalities in the realm of democratic practice. Their data show that citizens with higher education and higher income are more likely to be familiar with the practices of chatbots. A trend that privileges the few thus continues to dominate how different strata, in societies democratic and non, can play, live, and come together as a polity in increasingly AI-dominated civic futures.

The tendency to mainstream, rather than reverse engineer and play, dominates institutions central to healthy civic environments, including journalism. Foxman and Nieborg point out that while AI invites playful engagement, journalists find themselves confined in their ability to experiment with AI and align with an occupational professional ideology emphasizing seriousness and objectivity. Thus, a paradox emerges: Journalists are expected to be experts in relaying the impact of a technology that they themselves are constrained to use. The authors recommend play as the way out of this conundrum. It is worth reminding the reader here that play is not read as the practice of making light of, but rather as the ritual practice of questioning, discovering, exposing, reversing, and imaginatively recreating; all practices that form the core of the journalistic ethos.

Yet AI systems are designed to afford the exact opposite, Nagy argues. Created as mazes of entanglement, they present as inescapable and inevitable cages of activities. I would add that modalities of micro-engagement are often cultivated affectively within these mazes, for the purpose of turning AI into commodity-sized units that can be traded, downloaded, and shared. These are best recognized in design philosophies characterized by an understanding of AI as a tool. In civic environments, these technological entanglements frustrate playful practice and produce dated, tired, and banal modes of discourse. Nagy calls for imagining beyond tools to design systems that afford imagination, play, and better democracy.

This call is one that the next contributor takes on. Sophie Toupin presents case studies based on what she terms the feminist AI playbook. Toupin shows how feminist activists employ creative misuse of AI for play. In so doing, they challenge and reverse dominant practices. They also manifest how people might begin to think about AI otherwise, putting AI-driven platforms and bots to use to amplify imaginaries often overlooked. Play here is used to enhance civic voices and advance them toward the core of democratic communication.

Conversation play emerges across a variety of locations, civic and non. Samantha Shorrey and Katie Joseff explore how children's toys, powered by generative AI, create and set assumptions about play and engagement within the privacy of the domestic sphere. As these hyperpersonalized toys process LLM publicly available data, a multitude of paradoxes emerge. These ritualize practices about ambient listening and data storage that gradually evolve into accepted standards on how we engage and play with

AI in spheres beyond domestic ones. Decentralized approaches to design can help avoid monopolies of design from evolving and dominating personal and parental agency.

As societies become populated by humans and nonhumans working and playing together, respectful interaction becomes a central component of democratically driven discourse. Jindong Leo-Liu details how the parasocial interaction relationships people develop through human-machine communication typically follow command and task-oriented glossaries. The task-driven language used inadvertently ascribes both humans and nonhumans a form of agency they had no part in actively selecting. It also distracts from developing a lexicon of communication that advances harmonious coexistence with machines. Yet, an emphasis on creating a vocabulary of communication that moves away from dominance, control, and human superiority could help people imagine machines, play, and democracy otherwise.

Similarly, Donna Kim examines how a culture that places the human main character at the center of most video games has influenced the design of AI-enabled agents, embodied and non-embodied. In this context, it is difficult for humans to imagine playing with machines when the majority of their interaction in machine-made environments places them in a constructed, often artificial, center of activity. Even though humans are not always in control, the design of the machine-made environments serves to reassure them that they are, thus reproducing realities and imaginaries where humans and nonhumans are not positioned as companions, co-creators, and creative or playful partners.

The perception of these ecoscapes as real, or virtual, or hybrid informs how users internalize behavioral intentions and consequences. Tony Liao writes about the ethos of play. Liao specifically distinguishes between what motivates play and how this shapes the ramifications of play. Digital harm does emerge in spaces of play, frequently cloaked in digitally enabled and AI-enhanced performances of play that amplify some voices and silence others. Liao covers several such cases and presents new paradigms that help humans reimagine play in meaningful ways.

Humans have been seeking to communicate with an imagined other through the vast history of the species, the other often taking the form of the sublime as presented through technology. Simone Natale looks at the question of connective AI from this perspective. Natale uses the metaphor of the stochastic parrot to describe the fashioning of machines that perform intelligence modeled after the human mind. These performances are typically understood as intelligence when, in fact, they are no more than a carefully pieced together microdrama, meant to convey the presence of intelligence (Papacharissi, 2026). Natale accurately points out that the act of machines communicating back to humans is an illusion. We perceive that machines communicate with us based on linguistic markers that we recognize when talking with machines that are not, and perhaps never might be, able to communicate with us, at least not in the human sense of that construct.

The model museum is an analytical framework that holds a double meaning. It interfaces the use of AI models, which shape how museums run and connect, with museum as social models for the display and curation of AI. Jasmin Pfefferkorn and Emilie Sunde use communication strategies to form a meta-narrative of connective AI at the museum interface. They thus situate civic forms of participation and play into a noncorporate culture of curation and representation that might better meet the objectives of a democratically connected polity.

The ability of play to connect and drive democratic debates about environmentalism forward is the focus of Giovanna Mascheroni, Simone Tosoni, and Fausto Colombo. They conducted experiments that used play as a discursive strategy. They get at the heart of the connective AI concept by documenting how participants were better able to generate, foster, and build on the reflexivity play affords through the use of generative AI-rendered models.

These come close to the civic applications of embodied and non-embodied AI agents I had envisioned when presenting the connective AI idea. In *Voice of the Ogiek: Play, Co-Design, and the Spiral Return of Orality in Connective AI*, this chapter that concludes this volume, Autumn Edwards, Lusike Mukhongo, Chad Edwards, Cynthia Klekar-Cunningham, Winston Mano, and Alexander Kisioi Koech help me advance the concept further. They explore play as a world making force, through developing *Voice of the Ogiek*, an AI-enhanced messaging system partnership with the Indigenous Ogiek community—ancestral guardians of Kenya's Mau Forest. Through riddles, naming practices, co-singing, and other rituals, they develop a storytelling vernacular that presents a newly imagined civic system for representation and voice. Here, they can advance to regenerative AI, which reimagines tropes of engaging with human and nonhuman actors. The authors draw from Afrokology, Indigenous thought, and American Pragmatism to introduce *spiral return* as a design gesture that moves beyond simplistic rejections of the present or preservations of the past. Spiral return links past, present, and potential future through the approaching evolution in time in layered cycles.

Having read these reflections from luminaries on human-machine interaction, social robots, democracy, play, and civic life, what is Connective AI, and what can it be? At the present moment, Connective AI is an illusion. It is a dream, a hope, and a proposal, at best. Technologies are designed with civic utility as an afterthought and application in capitalist economy infrastructure as the driver. Ideally, this tendency might be reversed. I will happily compromise and say that contemporary capitalism need not be divorced from the civic priorities of modern democracies. As I have argued elsewhere (Papacharissi, 2021), our societies are built on a definition of capitalism that existed long before they became democracies. Capitalist principles date back to monarchies, feudal states, autocracies, oligarchies, and monopolistic approaches to governance. No wonder that marrying the two seems improbable and possibly may read as blasphemous.

Still, I propose that connective AI rests on the complex, yet possible nexus that can develop between capitalism and democracy, in the face of increasing monopolization of big tech. Technology can be the conduit that brings democracy and capitalism closer together. After its namesake, *Connective Action*, Connective AI can help make room for civically informed capitalist infrastructure. It may create space for capitalistic investment that strengthens democracy. It does suggest worlds where the capitalist drive respects democratic life, for it is democracy that organizes the pluralism capitalism thrives on. Capitalism invites competition. Competition is not possible without porous environments that are open to innovation. Monopolies often take form in capitalist economies, but they are not efficient, economists teach us, nor are they democratic, all social scientists add. Conceptual misunderstandings have been reproduced throughout centuries due to misinformed conversations and not fully educated viewpoints rising to the surface and dominating policy. The proliferation of business administration experts making economic decisions often amplifies these tendencies and tensions and removes essential context and nuance from finance decisions. And democratic governance requires financial support. Democracies do not come for free. They are fueled by economic resources and representative and inclusive governance.

Here is where (Connective) AI fits in. First, it is essential to understand that all AI, and almost all technology, is affective. It relies on arousing the sentiment. That is the mode that permits connection to humans and non-humans. Affect animates technology. It is the human essence in it. No AI is not affective in nature. It can be more or less so, or affective in different ways, but is always of affect.

Second, because AI is affective, it can be connective. Affect is intensity. It is the intensity with which humans feel. It can be the intensity with which machines perform sentience, and perhaps, at some point in the future, become sentient. At present, all machines termed (artificially) intelligent are delivering performances of intelligence. This is neither good, nor bad, nor neutral. It is an observation that cannot be ignored when we talk about AI, and as we learn how to talk about (connective) AI. Humans often render performances of intelligence as a means to an end. So does human-made technology, like AI. These performances of intelligence are often rendered by humans in order to connect, and AI can be programmed to do so, too.

Third, and final point, lies in the reason for all this. For democracy. For better and just capitalist infrastructure. More importantly, however, for playfulness, which is the essence of being human. For the capability to imagine other worlds and feel at ease in them. For the ability to imagine.

References

Bennett, W. L., & Kneuer, M. (2023). Communication and democratic erosion: The rise of illiberal public spheres. *European Journal of Communication, 39*(2), 177–196. https://doi.org/10.1177/02673231231217378 (Original work published 2024).

Lackey, C., & Papacharissi, Z. (2024). Machine ex machina: A framework decentering the human in AI design praxis. *Human-Machine Communication, 8*, 7–25.

Lugones, M. (1987). Playfulness, "world"-travelling, and loving perception. *Hypatia, 2*(2), 3–19.

Papacharissi, Z. (2021). *After democracy: Imagining our political future.* Yale University Press.

Papacharissi, Z. (2026). *As we may dream.* NYU Press.

Sicart, M. (2023). *Playing software: Homo ludens in computational culture.* MIT Press.

2

WHAT WE HAVE HERE IS A FAILURE TO COMMUNICATE

Visually Generative AI and the Civic Imagination

Henry Jenkins, Sangita Shresthova, Alfonso Hegde, and members of the Civic Paths Research Group

When participants at one of our Civic Imagination workshops asked Midjourney, the visually generative AI program, to show us what it might look like to redesign Los Angeles without any cars, we were hoping to see more sustainable urban housing and transportation systems. Instead, the emerging art depicted a deserted city, one without any people.

Repeating the experiment on other occasions, we saw images of the mass transit systems of tomorrow with freeways still clogged with private automobiles. This glitch has produced rich discussions about the centrality of automobiles to our conception of the city and how these assumptions were what we would need to overcome if we were to produce a more energy-efficient future for California. These experiments, and subsequent conversations and interviews with artists experimenting with these technologies, helped us to recognize the ways that visually generative AI programs might function as resources for the civic imagination, even when—or perhaps especially when—the AI fails to deliver the images we anticipate.

We define Civic Imagination as the practice of visualizing any social change that supports us in the movement toward a better world. We understand imagination as a shared social, rather than purely personal, process. In a deeply polarized society, we are searching for processes by which we might express our shared hopes, dreams, fears, and frustrations and envision how we might work together as members of a community toward common goals, while also recognizing and respecting our differences. At the USC Civic Imagination Project (an initiative of Civic Paths Group), we invite people—from middle schoolers to senior citizens—to cocreate future worlds and remix stories—establishing a sense of connection by imagining

DOI: 10.4324/9781003477587-2

FIGURE 2.1 Illustrative image generated by Dall-E.

together. Building on years of experimentation, research, and experience, we use a variety of in person and online methods and materials to do so, ranging from drawing via jamboards or modeling with clay to acting out stories set in mutually imagined worlds that draw on salient popular culture narratives. To date, we have done close to 100 such workshops across America, in small towns and in big cities, in churches, mosques, and labor halls, all of whom have come together to try to build a better world. Designed to be accessible and participatory, these workshops couple media literacy, participatory culture, and vernacular creativity with civic awareness. We are always looking for new ways to engage our participants as they imagine together, and our most recent efforts have turned to generative visual AI programs such as Midjourney and Dall-E as a collaborative process tool that can help our participants brainstorm and visualize their ideas in ways that were previously beyond their reach.

As people around the world have begun to experiment with visually generative AI, much of the excitement has been about success stories, the ways programs such as Midjourney and Dall-E rapidly generate convincing and compelling images on command. Much of the concern has been around questions of intellectual property and threats to livelihoods. We are interested in how this capacity might enable us to create intersubjective images of collaboratively produced visions illustrating that a better world is possible. We understand the legitimate concerns around these technologies. But we also find that these programs may be even more provocative when the technology fails to deliver what we anticipate, when it is unable (or perhaps programmed not to) produce what we hope to see.

In this chapter, we will share what we have learned through our first experiments in deploying visual AI during our civic imagination workshops, including some concerns about where to interject these practices into our ongoing processes so as to do minimal damage to the participants' own efforts to conceptualize the desirable properties of these worlds while empowering them to communicate their visions effectively with each other. Recognizing the valid concerns regarding these platforms, we argue that generative AI has the potential to enhance our civic imagination by supporting collaborative creativity and to democratize who has access to the capacity for visualization.

Imagining, collaborating, visualizing, discussing, and refining new worlds together is the first step toward bridging divides and improving conditions in the real world. What emerges may not be utopia, but the process does what Stephen Duncombe argues the utopian imagination has historically done in terms of offering provocations that encourage us to envision and debate alternatives to our own flawed reality. Generating such images together through AI processes constitute a form of computational empowerment, giving us tools to imagine otherwise. In this piece, our own experiences using visually generative AI as a civic practice are supplemented with insights from a number of interviews we are doing with other artists and activists who are using the tools toward similar ends.

New Technologies and the Civic Imagination

Aaron Hertzmann writes in his essay, "A Catalog of 'AI' Art Analogies," of two interesting comparisons to how we can conceive of generative AI in terms of analogous historical practices. He considers the comparison to the birth of recorded music, when "musicians unions fought against the introduction of recorded music." Hertzmann offers another potential comparison to think about AI in terms of remixing culture, such as how "remix in hip-hop and electronic revealed to a lot of people how reusing existing elements can be transformative and create new art forms" (Hertzmann, 2023).

What is particularly fascinating about these two analogies is that they are actually referring to the same piece of technology. When the phonograph was popularized in the 1930s, it was widely seen by the American Federation of Musicians, which represented tens of thousands of gigging musicians playing live music in movie theaters, clubs, and other venues, as an existential threat to the livelihood of working musicians, potentially replacing hundreds of human musicians with one phonograph or "canned music robot."

The anti-phonograph ad campaign demonstrates the civic imagination of the phonograph as a tool of automation intended to take away jobs from human musicians and reduce the affect produced by distinctive musicians to a single reproducible recording. Does this sound familiar in how many conceive of AI as potentially eliminating human creative potential through automation?

Conversely, as decades go on, this same tool undergoes sociotechnical transformation into the social construction of the "turntable." While the phonograph is seen initially as a tool designed to automate human creative labor, eventually the turntable is transformed into an instrument of its own. Through technical improvements, such as the introduction of the direct drive turntable in the 1970s which reduces potential for record damage by holding the LP on a fixed surface, predominantly Black musicians begin to engage with the device as a tool of coproduction in which the turntable enables scratching and sampling to create an iterative practice of musical composition. In *Phonographies*, Weheliye issues a nod to this phenomenon in the context of Black cultural production as being inextricably linked to the sound technologies of the twentieth century, chiefly the phonograph—or as it is later called—the turntable (Weheliye, 2005). The turntable evokes a different type of civic imagination as a tool enabling an emergent creative practice and new genres of music.

The phonograph and turntable are quite literally the same technological device with minor technical changes. But the term "phonograph" evokes an interpretive frame of automation while the "turntable" evokes an interpretive frame of emergent creative practice as a consequence of who is engaging with the tool and the conditions of that engagement. These contrasts reveal an imaginative potential for how we conceive of generative AI through a multiplicity of interpretive frames.

The Evocativeness of AI Images

In her 1984 introduction to her groundbreaking book, *The Second Self: Computers and the Human Spirit*, the MIT-based sociologist and psychologist Sherry Turkle first argued that computers might be understood as "evocative objects." She sums up her core argument, "the computer, like a Rorschach inkblot test, is a powerful projective medium." She asks children, for example, whether computers are alive or not and finds they are also confounded by this question, since the computer seems to think and act with a mind of its own. Turkle explains,

FIGURE 2.2   Uncle Sam kneels on top of the Great Wall of China in a Midjourney image generated during visit to Shanghai.

> We search for a link between who we are and what we have made,
> between who we are and what we might create, between who we are
> and what, through our intimacy with our own creations, we might
> become…. Technology creates changes not only in what we do but
> in how we think. It changes people's awareness of themselves, of one
> another, of their relationship with the world.
>
> *(pp. 18–19)*

The computer as a new and emerging medium of human expression
sparked debates Turkle found profound in nature and as such, it was often
understood as a mirror of the self, a second self, which enabled new forms
of self-consciousness about what it means to think and know things about
the world around us.

For us, what is important is not whether an image or artifact generated by AI is original or a form of art but whether the results are "evocative." Because the processes governing visually generative AI are still so
little understood, because both the sources Midjourney draws upon and
the algorithms it uses to produce images are not transparent, its products
often have an air of the uncanny about them. When it doesn't work, we
assume something is blocking it from producing certain results; we assume

often that its failures stem from a collective bias in how we understand the world, projecting onto the results of artificial intelligence something of our own conceptual limits. We can't imagine Los Angeles without cars, and neither can Midjourney and so we read this as shedding light on the challenges we face in building a more sustainable society.

Consider another example. During a conversation held in Shanghai between Henry Jenkins and a Chinese colleague, Jenkins was challenged to produce an image of Uncle Sam bowing before the Great Wall of China. Despite multiple attempts, Midjourney failed to produce such an image. In each attempt, the Statue stood or kneeled on top of the wall or otherwise towered above it; we had somewhat more luck with Uncle Sam, another American icon, but here, the image shows the wall itself becoming ruble (see Figure 2.2). Both participants in this cross-cultural exchange begin to anticipate why this might be the case. Jenkins approached it from the perspective of the image bank Midjourney is drawing from, wondering if the program has trouble imagining the statue bending, let alone bowing, given what representations might be out there. The Chinese scholar suspects that the failed results may reflect some form of government censorship or another ideological constraint on what kinds of representations Midjourney might produce. Neither of them knew for sure and so the nature of Midjourney's programing functions, like Turkle's inkblot test, to evoke different models of culture and politics, a theme that is central to the Civic Imagination Project's research.

Yet, even when the balky program succeeds in responding to our prompts, we feel a sense of surprise, astonishment, even delight. The speed with which it responds to our requests and the richness of detail it contributes give Midjourney a sense of magical agency. And so, again, the outcome is evocative as we sort through our shifting understanding of ourselves and the world around us, and more to the point, the ways both of these impact how we interact with each other as members of a shared community and as civic agents.

In this essay, we share the process we have gone through in Civic Paths thinking about the possibilities and limitations of Visual AI as a collaborative tool. Rather than focusing on originality or artistic merit (also important), we are asking questions about the evocative power of AI-driven creations. What new possibilities do these tools open for us? How do they expand our capacity for collective imagination and storytelling in ways previously unattainable? What do they allow us to do, see, think we couldn't previously? This chapter delves into these questions, exploring our evolving thinking on how Visual AI can be used to support the civic imagination.

The Civic Paths Research Group and Its Conversations

Over the course of the 2023/2024 academic year, we and the students involved with the Civic Paths Group at the University of Southern California engaged in a series of informal conversations where we reflected on our own collective curiosity and critical engagement with visual AI. The initial discussions inside our research group were often heated since members had strong and differing opinions about whether such tools were good or bad things for our culture. These differences are manifested through the key words that surfaced:

Automation = expedited process of creation, copyright, mixed-method,
Remix & Fair Use = magic, alien, uncanny valley, random, scary, instant,
Democratization = collaboration, creation
Inauthentic = the gap between what's being generated vs reality
Plagiarism = taking advantage of existing creative knowledge
Paradoxical = Is it actually creativity?
Skeptical = stealing fans' arts, taking from others,
Superficial = it looks great, but so what? Is it "usable," "doable," "buildable,"
Uncertain = strange, exciting, creative, evolving, comical

Putting these together, we can see how AI evokes consideration about the borders between self and others, between originality and reproduction, between human and machine, much as Turkle found in her consideration of user's initial responses to the introduction of the home computer in the 1980s.

At the most basic level, the existence of a powerful visually generative AI program like Midjourney poses core questions about what kind of world this technology is helping to create. For example, one might argue that visually generative AI has a democratizing potential, expanding who has access to the skills and resources necessary to express themselves in visual terms. While most children draw, adults have often become more inhibited about their skills as artists, fearing that they do not know how to draw well, and thus timid about creating visual representations for public consumption. Yet, visualization is a powerful skill that supports the acquisition and transfer of knowledge, a key form of digital literacy. Insofar as Midjourney expands who can express themselves through images, then the AI program supports the broader spread of those tools and thus the fuller integration of visualization skills into our everyday lives.

At the same time, many artists worry that they may become "deskilled" by the technology and that the skills and competencies they have labored to acquire as trained artists will be dismissed and devalued once everyone can acquire some of these same capacities without training or practice.

Some worry that they will lose status or livelihoods as a result of others embracing visually generative AI. A similar debate surrounds creativity, with critics arguing that these new tools can produce only "machine art" without any human soul as well as suggesting that the process of scraping human art for machine learning threatens their intellectual property. Others contend that all art, as Mikhail Bakhtin (1982) suggests, involves some degree of appropriation and that society benefits from possessing a reservoir of shared creativity from which any new work emerges. These differing perceptions of the positive or negative consequences of technological change reflect on our civic imaginations—our mental models of what constitutes a just and equitable society.

Civic Imagination and AI

Our experiments with the Civic Imagination and Midjourney started with the question of whether concrete visualizations might help participants in our workshop to communicate with each other more effectively. We have long sought to tap the tools of world-building and remixing from the realm of speculative fiction as a means of getting communities discussing amongst themselves what kind of society they wanted and what steps they might take to achieve those goals. Issues of representation run through our workshop. Often, we start by having participants bring in a memory object (something central to their sense of themselves, their family, their community, their culture) and explain it to the group. We often leave a range of craft supplies at each table—from crayons to modeling clay—to evoke memories of childhood play and thus encourage more imaginative expression. As the participants brainstorm worlds together, they are also asked to generate stories of transitional moments as the current flawed world begins to become the more idealized world of the future. And then, we often asked workshop participants to perform these narratives for each other so that they begin to imagine the change through embodiment. Often, in the playful laughter that surrounds adults play-acting together, the divisions between them are transcended. We describe these processes in depth in *Practicing Futures: The Civic Imagination Handbook* (2020). We wondered how access to more powerful visualization tools might contribute to this civic imagination process. Would this enable or endanger the intersubjective sharing of alternative visions of what a better world looks like? Would making it easier for us to hold such a world in our minds make it easier for us to make the next steps toward achieving a better world?

Through asking and struggling together with these issues, we gradually developed some shared norms and practices we saw as consistent with the larger philosophy of the Civic Imagination Project. What were we trying to use Midjourney to do? How did it connect with other ways we have asked our community to express their shared hopes and dreams together through our workshops, such as drawings or performances? Our practice has historically emphasized the process of imagining together rather than the products of our imagination. Might the professionalism of the generated images make them feel too fixed and thus might they foreclose the thinking processes we were trying to encourage? And as with the example above of the Great Wall and Uncle Sam, how might government regulation and corporate agendas shaping the development of these tools impact what can be imagined, what can be expressed through Midjourney?

The Workshop

To explore some of these themes, we decided to run our first pilot civic imagination workshop drawing on our Infinite Hope workshop methodology on April 27, 2023. Co-facilitated by Siddhant Manish Chawla, Alfonso Hegde, Paulina Lanz, and Sangita Shresthova, we ran the workshop with students enrolled in the Public Intellectual class at the University of Southern California, taught by Henry Jenkins. Part of our six-workshop series from *Practicing Futures*, our "Infinite Hope—Imagining a Better World" activities are designed to leverage the power of storytelling to foster civic imagination and inspire real-world change. Participants are guided through a process that encourages them to envision alternative worlds, unbounded by current constraints, and to strategize ways to achieve these imagined futures. The workshop begins with an icebreaker where each participant shares a story or character from popular culture that inspired them to think about the future. We then introduce the concept of civic imagination, setting the stage for the subsequent brainstorming, where participants collectively imagine an aspirational future world set in a specific year, such as 2060, where fantastical elements were possible.

In the brainstorming session, participants focused on various key themes like food, transportation, education, and health. They are encouraged to think beyond realistic constraints and imagine what the world could look like in the future. Most sessions generate multiple, often contradictory visions of the future—there is not one singular future but multiple ways of looking at what might emerge. The workshop then transitions into smaller group activities, where participants are tasked with creating fictional stories that explain the journey from the present to their imagined future world. Each group chooses a specific subtheme from the brainstorm and develops a narrative that includes characters, conflicts, and resolutions. As such, this phase of the workshop emphasizes the importance of character-based narratives in exploring social change within the context of the imagined future.

In the past, we have used various media, including live performance, to invite people to share and embody the stories they have created. In this pilot workshop, we were curious about how visual AI could support the groups in their creative process, serving as a tool for dialogue and collective imagining. So, we introduced participants to visual AI to generate illustrations that would help them cocreate and share their stories. We gave participants the option of creating moodboards and a series of images depicting the title, main characters, setting, plot, and ending of their stories. We ended the workshop with a reflection session, where participants discussed their experiences, the role of Visual AI in supporting their storytelling.

Supporting Collaboration

Our experiment suggests that visual AI could be a valuable collaboration tool for imagining shared futures as it allows participants to discuss their story ideas and future visions through concrete visual examples. Although the visuals generated by Midjourney often fell short of fully realizing the team's creative aspirations, they helped them deepen their conversations about shared visions, making them more specifics. For instance, the group focused on envisioning the future of Los Angeles had to refine their prompts and descriptions, thus clarifying their assumptions and aligning their perspectives. One of their prompts, for example, read:

> In the year 2063, Los Angeles has transformed into a bustling, sustainable metropolis, showcasing innovations in housing, transportation, and food culture. As a renowned journalist, you have been tasked with documenting the intricacies of life in this futuristic city. Your readers are eager to learn about the city's transformation and the experiences of its diverse inhabitants.

They then had to add the following details:

> Sustainable Housing: Delve into the city's groundbreaking eco-friendly housing initiatives. Discuss the widespread adoption of vertical gardens, green rooftops, and solar-paneled buildings. Describe the integration of communal living spaces and the prevalence of co-housing communities that promote a sense of unity and shared responsibility.
> Transportation: Investigate the city's advanced transportation system, including the shift towards electric and hydrogen-powered vehicles. Detail the widespread use of autonomous vehicles and the role of

Hyperloop technology in connecting LA to other major cities. Examine the extensive network of well-maintained bike lanes and pedestrian walkways that encourage green travel.

Food Culture: Explore the diverse culinary landscape of Los Angeles, highlighting the fusion of traditional and futuristic cuisines. Discuss the growth of hydroponic and aquaponic farming practices that enable year-round production of fresh produce. Describe the rise of plant-based and lab-grown meats, as well as the widespread availability of nutritious and sustainable meal options.

As these prompts reveal, working with Midjourney helped the group participants get clarity and better understand each other's visions, creating a richer, more cohesive future vision for Los Angeles of 2063. This was their final series of images:

FIGURE 2.3   Image of future cities generated by participants during the workshop using Midjourney.

Notably the image that Midjourney finally generated still failed to fully capture their ideas, leading to even more conversations about what they would have liked to see.

Foregrounding Process

Visual AI also helped groups move through the process of creating their stories and became a storyboarding tool. Constructing narrative prompts and reviewing results allowed the groups to quickly generate visuals around their stories, providing a tangible foundation for their ideas. In the case of the group working on "Seeds of Hope—A Child's Quest to Revive Agriculture in a Post-Apocalyptic World, 2063," it helped them craft their narrative of change. The group's prompt, "A child growing up in this world decides to grow food again. Uncovers hidden secrets about the world before," guided the AI in creating imagery that visually represented a desolate, post-apocalyptic landscape, and a hopeful child protagonist.

The members of this group then crafted specific prompts, such as "In the year 2063, the world has been ravaged by a climate apocalypse, leaving traditional agriculture in ruins and causing widespread famine," to generate images that depicted a barren world struggling with the consequences of environmental collapse. This visual context helped the group to delve deeper into their narrative elements, such as the protagonist's journey to rediscover forgotten agricultural techniques. The visuals allowed them to visualize the child's unique qualities, background, and the harsh environment they inhabited, which in turn informed the group's understanding of the character's motivations and challenges.

As the story progressed, the group used visuals to explore the child's discoveries of ancient agricultural methods and the community's initial skepticism. The AI-generated images of the child's journey—highlighting challenges like finding seeds and arable land—helped the group concretize the narrative arc and the protagonist's resilience. These visuals became a critical tool for brainstorming and refining the storyline, enabling the group to create a more compelling and coherent narrative.

The images the group generated helped capture the mood of the post-apocalyptic world as the context for the hope and determination of the protagonist. As such, AI not only accelerated the creative process by quickly producing relevant imagery that the group could respond to; but it also helped make the abstract aspects of their narrative more concrete and accessible.

FIGURE 2.4   Image of story protagonist generated by participants during the workshop using Midjourney.

Embracing Ambivalence

Using visual AI as a collaborative and process tool enabled the groups to navigate the inherent contradictions and tensions when imagining pluralistic futures in more visible ways. By allowing the groups to test and critique the images generated, the technology facilitated a space where diverse perspectives could be explored and expressed through visual storytelling, highlighting the complexity and ambivalence of the imagined worlds and stories that the workshop participants created. For example, the prompt "In the quaint and picturesque Dutch town of Oudewater in the 1800s, a futuristic robot unlike anything anyone has ever seen has mysteriously appeared" offered a narrative that juxtaposed the old and the new. The resulting images showed a modern yet retrofitted robot and through this

FIGURE 2.5   Image of robots generated during workshop using Midjourney.

provided a symbolic visual of the clash and coexistence of different eras central to the narrative. This narrative explored themes of technological innovation and societal change, forcing the characters—and by extension, the group—to confront moral dilemmas about the ethical implications of the world they had created.

Another compelling example is the narrative centered on the India-Pakistan partition in 1947. Here, participants created a story of two families, one from India and the other from Pakistan to explore the complex themes of identity, belonging, and resilience amidst political and social upheaval. The emotional journey of the characters, their struggles with displacement, and the development of deep connections despite the divisive political landscape were rendered visible through the images the group generated along the way.

In both stories, visual AI helped illustrate the intricate layers of these narratives, bringing to life the complex, even contradictory, aspects of

FIGURE 2.6   Image of Pakistani-Indian family generated by participants during the workshop using Midjourney.

these imagined futures. This process underscored the importance of uncertainty and complexity in popular culture, a concept highlighted by Sarah Banet-Weiser (2012) in *Authentic™: The Politics of Ambivalence in a Brand Culture*. For Banet Weiser, ambivalence is a crucial element in understanding cultural phenomena, as it allows for the coexistence of conflicting feelings and perspectives. In the context of our workshop, using visual AI helped our participants think through the contradictions and ambiguities of their imagined futures. This ambiguity operated on two levels. First, the narratives visualized by visual AI underscored that it is possible to engage with and appreciate different aspects of these worlds without wholly embracing or rejecting them. Second, the ambivalence of the visual AI tool itself imbued the creative process with a dialogic quality, enabling the groups to delve deeper into the issues and contradictions within their visions even as they critically engaged the tool itself.

The resulting stories embody some of the core themes we have seen surface in our workshop process in the past, such as the desire to better integrate the natural world into our lives, the importance of hope and resiliency in the face of crisis and catastrophe. But they also encouraged even deeper reflections on what we carry with us from the past into the future or how humans and machine beings might interact in the world to come, questions that reflect the nature of AI as a transformative and generative technology which seems to have a mind of its own. What our workshops consistently demonstrate is that despite the political polarization of our time, most people crave community and connection, and many if not most of us are prepared to make meaningful compromises in order to rebuild that trust with our neighbors.

Toward AI as a Communication Tool?

These provisional conclusions, which have informed our subsequent use of Midjourney in workshops with other groups, help us to identify ways our approaches differ from other efforts to work with visually generative AI.

We are less interested in the products that Midjourney generates than we are in the processes of collaboration and cocreation that emerge when we work together to create representations of the alternative worlds we envision together. This focus on process rather than product lowers the stakes in the current debates about whether AI products are art or not. What our participants create are temporary and disposable, more visualizations than artworks, a means of thinking through questions together, and so they pose no threat to artists and their livelihood.

The tool does not have to work properly to stimulate thought, discussion, and debate amongst the participants. All we care about is whether what emerges is evocative in Turkle's sense of the world, posing fundamental questions that leave participants thinking through why things are the way they are and whether it is possible to imagine them otherwise.

In fact, much as we are imagining sustainable futures or democratic and equitable ones, the newness of these platforms encourages us to imagine the worlds these technologies are helping to create. What is the future of AI? How will it impact the future of education or politics or arts and culture or everyday life?

We understand these processes as encouraging not personal but rather collective expression of desired alternatives to current conditions and relations. Here, the ways AI is remixing elements drawn from multiple prior works suggests the collective nature of these fantasies, even as the group gathered in the room and developing prompts together are also collaboratively shaping the outcome. Participants do not need to arrive at the same answers to these questions since speculating about such futures allows us to identify and act upon our shared values as a community. The ambiguities and ambivalences that surface through such a discussion keep us thinking long beyond the first round of alternatives that have been exhausted. The goal is to sustain conversations within the community so workshop participants learn to talk across narrow ideological differences.

Such a process rejects a naive response to these tools in favor of a critical questioning of how they work, what they can achieve, and what an ethical use of such materials might look like. We see the results as civic—not simply in the alternatives they imagine but in the processes by which both ideas and illustrations are generated. There is nothing inherently democratic about any technology, but there is something potentially democratic about how we might use them, together, toward civic ends, and through a process that results in a shared working through of problems.

Bibliography

Atlas of the Civic Imagination. (n.d.). *Atlas of the Civic Imagination*. Retrieved July 25, 2024, from http://www.ciatlas.org.

Bakhtin, M. M. (1982). *The dialogic imagination: Four essays* (M. Holquist, Ed.; C. Emerson & M. Holquist, Trans.). University of Texas Press.

Banet-Weiser, S. (2012). *Authentic™: The politics of ambivalence in a brand culture*. New York University Press.

Duncombe, S. (2012, August 27). Utopia is no place: Open Field: Conversations on the Common (In conversation with Sarah Peters). *Walker Art Center*. https://walkerart.org/magazine/stephen-duncombe-utopia-open-field

Hertzmann, A. (2023, March 1). *A catalog of "AI" art analogies*. Aaron Hertzmann's Blog. https://aaronhertzmann.com/2023/03/01/ai-art-analogies.html

Jenkins, H., Peters-Lazaro, G., & Shresthova, S. (Eds.). (2020). *Popular culture and the civic imagination: Case studies of creative social change*. New York University Press.

Peters-Lazaro, G., & Shresthova, S. (2020). *Practicing futures: A civic imagination action handbook*. Peter Lang.

Turkle, S. (2005). *The second self: Computers and the human spirit*. MIT Press.

Weheliye, A. G. (2005). *Phonographies: Grooves in sonic Afro-modernity*. Duke University Press.

3

GAMING THE SYSTEM

David J. Gunkel

In the science and engineering practice of artificial intelligence (AI), games are serious business. As John McCarthy and Ed Feigenbaum (1990, p. 10) explain:

> Programs for playing games often fill the role in artificial intelligence research that the fruit fly Drosophila plays in genetics. Drosophilae are convenient for genetics because they breed fast and are cheap to keep, and games are convenient for artificial intelligence because it is easy to compare a computer's performance on games with that of a person.

Thus, games are not just another kind of application of AI technology; they are and have been convenient mechanisms for defining and testing machine capabilities and performance.

This chapter investigates the role of games and gaming in the field of AI and proceeds in three steps or movements. (1) It begins by characterizing and examining what is perhaps the most important game in the field, Alan Turing's imitation game or what is now commonly called the Turing Test. (2) It then identifies and critically reevaluates three philosophical aspect of this game that have been and continue to be in play with contemporary discussions and debates about AI, up to and including recent innovations with large language models (LLMs) and other generative AI systems. And (3) it concludes by identifying the social opportunities and challenges this has for us and the game of life, demonstrating how games—and the imitation game, in particular—have always been serious business.

DOI: 10.4324/9781003477587-3

The Imitation Game

Of all the games that have been employed in the field of AI, perhaps none has been more influential and important than Alan Turing's "imitation game." In 1950, at least five years prior to the introduction of the term "artificial intelligence," Turing set out to answer the question "Can machines think?" (Turing, 1950, p. 433). This seemingly simple and direct query, however, turns out to be much more complicated than it initially appears, since both the subject (machine) and verb (think) admit of a wide range of different and sometimes competing definitions. Unable to answer this initial question, Turing does what any good researcher would do; he changes the research question. Instead of asking "Can machines think?" He proposes an evaluative method to decide if and/or when it would be reasonable to conclude that a machine was capable of behaviors that we typically take as indications of intelligent thought. Thus, "the new form of the problem," as Turing (1950, p. 433) explains, "can be described in terms of a game which we call the 'imitation game'."

The game, as it is initially described by Turing, involves three individuals: a man, a woman, and an interrogator. The interrogator sits alone in one room and submits questions to the man and the woman who sit alone in other rooms. The objective of the game is for the interrogator to determine the gender of his two interlocutors solely on the basis of their answers to his questions. In other words, the imitation game was modeled on a kind of gender guessing game where the interrogator could not see the respondents and had to make decisions about gender identity based only on answers to questions. Obviously, Turing was well aware that the tone of voice could influence results, so he further stipulated that the questions and answers be exchanged in writing or through some kind of technical mediation like text messaging.

Given this initial setup, Turing (1950, pp. 433–434) then poses this modification to his imaginary Victorian parlor game: What would happen when a computer takes the place of either the man or the woman in this game of Q&A? In other words, Turing imagines a situation where the interrogator is now exchanging messages with a human being and a machine. And the new objective of the game is to see whether the interrogator is able to differentiate the real person from the machinic imitator. If the computer is able to successfully play the role of another human person in these conversational exchanges, to such an extent that the interrogator cannot tell the difference, then that machine, Turing concludes, would need to be considered intelligent.

The Rules of the Game

There's a lot going on in this game, but three things in particular stand out.

The Problem of Other Minds

Turing's game situates language use and interpersonal conversational behavior as the deciding factor. This is not a capricious decision. There are good epistemological reasons for focusing on this particular capability, and it has to do with what philosophers and cognitive scientists routinely call "the problem of other minds," e.g. the seemingly undeniable fact that we do not have direct access to the inner workings of another's mind. Here is how Paul Churchland (1999) famously characterized it:

> How does one determine whether something other than oneself—an alien creature, a sophisticated robot, a socially active computer, or even another human—is really a thinking, feeling, conscious being; rather than, for example, an unconscious automaton whose behavior arises from something other than genuine mental states?
>
> *(p. 67)*

This problem has deep philosophical roots, going back at least to the work of René Descartes. For Descartes, whose innovative philosophical method followed a rigorous discipline of self-doubt or skepticism, the only thing that could be known for certain was "I think, therefore I am." But that was it. There was, at least according to Descartes's strict method, simply no way to know for sure whether the other people on the street had the same kind of inner experience or not. In fact, he admits, in a passage that sounds more like a science fiction movie than a work of modern philosophy, that he cannot be certain whether other people on the street are in fact thinking things like himself or nothing more than empty-headed robots that have been designed to look and act like human beings (Descartes, 1988).

Descartes, however, has what he thinks is a solution to this problem. If one were, for example, confronted with cleverly designed machines that looked and behaved like human beings, there would be at least one way to determine that these artificial figures were in fact machines and not real human persons. Or as Descartes (1988) explains:

> They could never use words, or put together other signs, as we do in order to declare our thoughts to others. For we can certainly conceive of a machine so constructed that it utters words...But it is not conceivable that such a machine should produce different arrangements of words so as to give an appropriately meaningful answer to whatever is said in its presence, as the dullest of human beings can do.
>
> *(pp. 44–45)*

Turing's game of imitation leverages this rich philosophical tradition and turns it back on itself. If a machine is able, as Descartes stipulates, "to produce different arrangements of words so as to give an appropriately meaningful answer to whatever is said in its presence," then we would, Turing argues, have to conclude that it was just as much a thinking, intelligent entity as another human being. Or as the AI scientist Roger Schank (1990) once explained: "We really cannot examine the insides of an intelligent entity in such a way as to establish what it actually knows. Our only choice is to ask and observe" (p. 5). For Turing, and for generations of AI researchers who have followed his lead, intelligence and other cognitive abilities are neither easy to define nor able to be directly accessed. Consequently, these capabilities are evidenced in and decided on the basis of external behaviors that are considered to be their indicators, like language use, which is assumed to be the product of an intelligent mind and that can be empirically observed, measured, and evaluated. Turing's imitation game mobilizes and plays with these ideas.

The AI Effect

At the time that Turing proposed the game, he estimated that a machine would become capable of successfully playing and competing in the imitation game within 50 years. It didn't take that long, as natural language processing applications, like the ELIZA chatbot of Joseph Weizenbaum, demonstrated such capabilities as early as 1964. Despite its rather simple programming, ELIZA was able to play and even succeed at the game.

> ELIZA created the most remarkable illusion of having understood in the minds of many people who conversed with it. People who know very well that they were conversing with a machine soon forgot that fact, just as theatergoers, in the grip of suspended disbelief, soon forget that the action they are witnessing is not "real." This illusion was especially strong and most tenaciously clung to among people who know little or nothing about computers. They would often demand to be permitted to converse with the system in private, and would, after conversing with it for a time, insist, in spite of my explanations, that the machine really understood them.
>
> (Weizenbaum, 1976, p. 189)

Even if ELIZA did not conclusively win the imitation game, the program was a capable contender and demonstrated the possibility of what Turing had originally proposed.

And since ELIZA, there has been steady and impressive developments in NPL applications, including more capable and loquacious chatbots, like Rollo Carpenter's Cleverbot and Steve Worswick's Kuki; digital voice assistants, like Apple's Siri and Amazon's Alexa; and most recently, ChatGPT and other LLMs that leverage the power of transformer architectures that have been pretrained on massive quantities of human produced textual content. So impressive are the capabilities of these latter systems, that AI researchers now talk about the end of the imitation game, as the "Turing Test" (as it is also called) has been entirely mastered—or what some observers have described as "broken"—by the machine (Biever, 2023; Jones & Bergen, 2024; Oremus, 2022; Weatherby, 2023).

Does this therefore mean that LLMs are in fact thinking machines or beginning to show signs of intelligence? Some have answered in the affirmative arguing that what we currently see with the existing technology of LLMs is the beginning or initial stages of what will become AGI (Artificial General Intelligence). In an article published in *Noema*, computer scientists Blaise Agüera y Arcas and Peter Norvig (2023) readily admit that the current crop of algorithms, like OpenAI's GPT series and Google's LaMDA, is severely limited and exhibits many flaws. But "decades from now," the authors assert, "they will be recognized as the first true examples of AGI, just as the 1945 ENIAC is now recognized as the first true general-purpose electronic computer." Similarly, a group of Microsoft researchers, led by Sébastien Bubeck, published a controversial paper in which they suggested that what we now see with GPT-4 are "sparks of artificial general intelligence" (Bubeck et al., 2023).

Others have responded more negatively either by finding fault with the imitation game as an accurate evaluative mechanism or redefining the criteria altogether. The former has materialized in a number of scholarly and popular publications that have used the advent of LLMs, like ChatGPT, as an occasion to critically reassess the basic operating procedures of Turing's game (Biever, 2023) and to propose new and arguably more accurate IQ tests for AI performance (Blum, 2023; Suleyman, 2023). The latter is probably best represented by researchers like Emily Bender who, along with Timnit Gebru, Angelina McMillan-Major, and Margaret Mitchell, have argued that an LLM "is a system for haphazardly stitching together sequences of linguistic forms it has observed in its vast training data, according to probabilistic information about how they combine, but without any reference to meaning: a stochastic parrot" (Bender et al., 2021, p. 617). Thus, what really matters is not language use, i.e. spitting out words in statistically valid sequences and patterns. What matters is *how* language comes to be used and what it means.

This effort at redefinition or modification of the qualifying criteria—what we might call gaming the system—happens often enough that it has a name. It is called the AI effect. Here is how Jerry Kaplan (2016) explains it in his short introductory book on the subject: "But the field of AI suffers from an unusual deficiency—once a particular problem is considered solved, it often is no longer considered AI" (p. 37). In other words, test cases that have been identified as problems that would require intelligence to solve are no longer considered to be signs of intelligence once they are solved. Take the game of chess, for example. For decades, the task of playing championship-level chess was seen as a challenge that would require actual intelligence to resolve (Shannon, 1950). But once this had been achieved—in 1997, when IBM's Deep Blue defeated the reigning human champion Garry Kasparov—playing championship-level chess became just another computer application and was no longer considered a demonstration of true intelligence.

This moving of the goal posts on intelligence has occurred with other tests and benchmarks, like the game of Go, which was mastered by DeepMind's AlphaGo in 2016, or the US quiz show *Jeopardy!* when IBM's Watson defeated Ken Jennings in February 2011. As Kevin Kelly (2014) of *Wired* magazine explains: "In the past, we would have said only a super-intelligent AI could drive a car, or beat a human at *Jeopardy!* or chess. But once AI did each of those things, we considered that achievement obviously mechanical and hardly worth the label of true intelligence. Every success in AI redefines it." We have, it seems, been willing to cheat or at least game the system in our favor.

We can draw two conclusions from this: First, all these tests and demonstrations of intelligence—from the imitation game through all the various alternatives and subsequent revisions and modifications of it—are anything but objective or independent. Since we (human beings) get to decide on the qualifying criteria and grant to ourselves the role of both judge and jury in these games, we have and probably will continue to change the rules in order to protect ourselves and our unique claim to exceptionalism. But, and this is the second point, doing so is not necessarily "cheating" as these alterations can also be seen as evidence that we are learning something about ourselves and cognition in the attempt to simulate these same capabilities in a computational mechanism. What Claude Shannon (1950) wrote about chess in the middle of the last century applies to all these test cases: A solution to any of these intellectual challenges "will force us either to admit the possibility of a mechanized thinking or to further restrict our concept of 'thinking'" (p. 257). Game after game, we have opted for the latter. In this sense, the project of AI is as much a philosophical as it is a technical endeavor.

Ontological Difference

Some have responded to these difficulties by framing them as an issue of illusion or deception. Indeed, one way of responding to the imitation game is to draw a distinction between mere appearances and actual reality. This is what is commonly identified as ontological difference, and it was recently operationalized and on display in the Lemoine Affair. In June of 2022, a Google engineer named Blake Lamoine claimed that the company's LaMDA system was a sentient, thinking being. He came to this conclusion based on the terms and conditions stipulated in the imitation game. He conversed with the machine learning algorithm, and it responded in a way that convinced Lemoine that he was talking to someone and not merely interacting with something. Google responded by denying these conclusions, arguing that the algorithm, like any computer application, was just a thing and pointing out that Lemoine was simply confused, mistaking appearances—the way things seem to be—for actual reality. Even though LaMDA uses words in a way that gives the appearance of thought, it is neither consciousness nor intelligent. This is a persuasive and seemingly solid argument, and its success depends on a fundamental philosophical distinction that goes back to the foundations of Western thought in Plato's "Allegory of the Cave" (1987).

This influential illustration (or what contemporary philosophers call a "thought experiment"), which is situated at the center of *The Republic*, concerns an underground cavern inhabited by men who are confined to sit before a large wall on which are projected shadow images. These cave dwellers are, according to the Platonic account, chained in place from childhood and unable to see anything other than these artificial projections. Consequently, they operate as if everything that appears before them on the wall is, in fact, real and true. At a crucial turning point in the story, one of the captives is released. He is unbound by some ambiguous but external action, dragged kicking and screaming out of the cave, and forced to confront the true and real world that exists outside the subterranean cavern and its shadowy images. Thus, the story establishes a long-standing and influential conceptual opposition between the deceptive appearances in the depths of the cave and the genuine reality of things exposed in the bright light of truth.

But there are at least two problems with this way of thinking: one epistemological and the other axiological. In terms of epistemology—the branch of philosophy that is concerned with knowledge—the ability to know or even recognize the difference between the real thing and its potentially deceptive appearances requires that one have access to both (a) how something really is in its true being versus (b) how it merely seems to be or comes to appear. This binary opposition—reality vs. appearance—is one of the most influential and important conceptual distinctions in the history of Western thought. But we do not need a deep dive in the history of philosophy to see what is at stake here. We can get at it by recalling another famous thought experiment in the field of AI, John Searle's Chinese Room.

This intriguing and rather influential illustration, which was first introduced in 1980 with the essay "Minds, Brains, and Programs" and then elaborated in subsequent publications, was offered as and intended to be a counterargument to Turing's game of imitation. "Imagine," Searle (1999) explains, "a native English speaker who knows no Chinese locked in a room full of boxes of Chinese symbols (a data base) together with a book of instructions for manipulating the symbols (the program)" (p. 115). Searle then stipulates the following procedure:

> Imagine that people outside the room send in other Chinese symbols which, unknown to the person in the room, are questions in Chinese (the input). And imagine that by following the instructions in the program the man in the room is able to pass out Chinese symbols which are correct answers to the questions (the output). The program enables the person in the room to pass the Turing Test for understanding Chinese but he does not understand a word of Chinese.
>
> *(Searle, 1999, 115)*

The point of Searle's demonstration is quite simple—appearances are not the real thing. "The Turing test," as Searle (1999) concludes, "fails to distinguish real mental capacities from simulations of those capacities. Simulation is not duplication" (p. 115). In other words, merely shifting verbal symbols around (which is what happens inside the room) in a way that looks like linguistic understanding (from the vantage point of someone outside the room) is not really an understanding of Chinese.

At first sight, this seems correct. After all, the project of AI since the time of Turing's imitation game has been the *imitation* of intelligence. And Searle's thought experiment not only reproduces the basic terms and conditions of the game; it is a reproduction that appears to be well suited to explain what really happens with AI. What is perceived by someone interacting with the room—namely that it understands Chinese—is not really what it seems to be, since the person inside the room does not actually understand Chinese but is just arranging sequences of linguistic tokens following a set of step-by-step instructions.

But we should not overlook one important condition of this thought experiment: this insight is only possible because Searle has given us—a third-party observer to the entire scene—privileged access to the inner workings of the room such that we can both perceive and distinguish between what appears to happen from what actually goes on inside the room. For this reason, Searle's Chinese Room is more of a glass box rather than an opaque black box—as is the case with both contemporary LLMs and Turing's imitation game. Consequently, this supposed counterexample only succeeds by violating the limitations imposed by the problem of other minds, which is something Turing's game sought to respect. In effect, Searle cheats.

This leads us to the second problem, which is normative. Axiology is that branch of philosophy that has to do with values. It is about good and bad in both moral and aesthetic terms. In Plato's Allegory, appearances are of a diminished or lesser value than the real thing. They are mere shadows of reality. Platonic metaphysics, therefore, institutes and operationalizes a binary opposition where the real is the privileged or good term, and appearances are considered bad or of lesser importance. But even if you have never read Plato, you already operate according to the terms and conditions of this axiology. If given the choice between a real $100 bill and a photorealistic reproduction, we prefer the real deal, as it is actually worth something where the image—even if it looks like the real thing—is a cheap reproduction or knock-off.

But appearances—especially in social interaction and communicative experience—are not necessarily a bad thing. When we sit down to watch a film, for instance, the actors in the drama are pretending to be someone they are not in an effort to present a story. Technically, this would be a form of deceptive appearance, but it is one to which we have not only consented but find rather entertaining. Plato, for his part, is at least consistent, for he concludes the *Republic* by proposing an almost comical solution to this problem, namely that all imitative artists and deceivers be exiled from the city. Something similar has already been proposed and developed for AI with watermarks that can be used to distinguish LLM generated content from genuine human writing, warning labels or disclaimers made available by the platforms serving the content or with the responses generated by the LLM itself, and Platonic-scale prohibitions against using the technology in the classroom in order to protect the integrity of student work and root out-plagiarism. But what if LLMs are used to produce entertainment content? Don't we enjoy being deceived? And is it really deception in the first place?

In an effort to sort this out and provide a more nuanced response to these problems, Simone Natale (2021) has suggested differentiating between "deliberate deception" and "banal deception," which he defines as a mundane and imperceptible form of illusion making that operates by concealing the underlying functions of digital machines through a representation constructed at the level of the interface. The latter is not necessarily wrong. Earlier, Coeckelbergh (2018) already argued that the deception problem with digital information and communication technologies such as robots can be approached by framing the technologies as stage magic, which entails an ethics that cannot and should not be reduced to valuing the real as opposed to appearance, but which at least is more complicated. For example, people who want to be deceived by AI willingly suspend disbelief in order to be entertained. That the magician and their technology deceive may not be morally wrong, regardless of other issues.

The problem, then, is not that the potential for deception exists with the technologies of chatbots, digital assistants, and LLMs; the problem is that "deception" might not be a simple binary and could have important social significance and usage. Appearances, in other words, are not simply bad and therefore in need of being eliminated or dissolved in the bright light of full disclosure and greater transparency. Appearances have social value, and the imitation game plays with this form of deception.

The Game of Life

In the field of AI, games, like the imitation game, are serious business. And no one knows this better than Garry Kasperov, who went head-to-head with and was defeated by IBM's chess-playing AI, Deep Blue. Prior to this 1995 contest, it had been predicted by Douglas Hofstadter (1979), Hubert Dreyfus (1992), and others that no AI would ever succeed in beating a human champion like Kasparov. But Deep Blue did what had been considered to be impossible. And Kasparov, reflecting on the importance of this contest, did not mince words: "To some extent, this match is a defense of the whole human race" (quoted in Hofstadter, 2001, p. 40). In the field of AI, a game like chess or Turing's modified parlor game are always much more than "fun and games." We conclude, then, by considering the larger social significance and consequences of these games.

Philosophy of Mind

If it is possible to simulate human-level intelligence or consciousness in a machine, what does this say about human cognitive capabilities and our own sense of exceptionalism? There is an important debate about this in the philosophy of mind. According to one position, the "computational theory of mind" or computationalism, the human brain and mind are very much like a computer. According to this way of thinking, the human brain is conceived of as an information-processing device such that cognitive activity is a form of computation. If true, this means that human intelligence could be modeled in silicon or some other physical material. Others, like Hubert Dreyfus (1992), have opposed the hypothesis, arguing that the human brain is not a computer and that human intelligence cannot and should not be reduced to computation.

This is one reason why the debate about intelligence is so very active. There's a lot at stake here. If, on the one hand, an AI achieves intelligence or is even just beginning to show signs of it, this would be one way to resolve the dispute in favor of the computationalists. If, on the other hand, AI persistently fails to achieve this and does not evolve into superintelligent AGI, then the critics of computationalism can take a victory lap. Whether AGI or superintelligent machines will be achieved any time soon, and whether it is even possible in principle (i.e. whether computationalism is correct), will most likely remain a contentious issue, and each side will obviously continue to heap up both practical examples and theoretical arguments to support their positions.

OpenAI (2024), for instance, has sought to tip the scale in the direction of computationalism by creatively redefining AGI as "highly autonomous systems that outperform humans at most economically valuable work." Critics, like Shannon Vallor (2024), however, have pointed out how "OpenAI's AGI bait-and-switch wipes anything that does not count as economically valuable work from the definition of intelligence." Furthermore, Vallor has directly countered this effort by arguing that human cognition and intelligence are and must be much more than this, involving, at least, self-reflection, empathy, moral intelligence, and an understanding of our place in the world.

Moral and Legal Status

One of the reasons—maybe even the main reason—why these capabilities remain fought over and defended is that intelligence and other cognitive capabilities have important social consequences: if an entity is intelligent and able to think, it seems that they must therefore have and deserve moral status and legal protections. These cognitive capabilities therefore provide the criteria by which to distinguish who is a *person* from what remains a mere *thing*. This binary distinction has been the ruling conceptual opposition in both moral philosophy and jurisprudence. As Roberto Esposito (2015), who arguably wrote the book on this subject explains: "From time immemorial our civilization has been based on the most clear-cut division between persons and things. Persons are defined primarily by the fact that they are not things, and things by the fact that they are not persons" (p. 16).

This difference matters, precisely because it makes a crucial decision, dividing persons who have rights and responsibilities as another moral and legal subject from things that are mere objects that we can use and dispose of as we decide and see fit. If an AI, like ChatGPT or Google's LaMDA, is or can become sentient—as Lemoine had asserted about the LaMDA LLM—then we might have a duty to welcome them into the community of moral and legal subjects, extending to the artifact the same—or at least a set of similar—rights, protections, and responsibilities afforded and belonging to other persons. If, on the contrary, AI cannot achieve this capability or ever succeed in attaining what we recognize as the hallmarks of intelligent thought—as Google had argued in response to Lemoine's claims—then the algorithm will remain a mere thing, object, or piece of property.

The challenge or the opportunity with chatbots, LLMs, and other forms of generative AI is that either outcome seems wrong or misguided. On the one hand, these devices are technological things; they are human-designed and manufactured artifacts. Thus, the moral and legal status of an AI would seem to be no different from that of another artifact—like your toaster—insofar as these things are instruments or tools of human decision and action. As Deborah Johnson (2026) has explained:

> Computer systems are produced, distributed, and used by people engaged in social practices and meaningful pursuits. This is as true of current computer systems as it will be of future computer systems. No matter how independently, automatically, and interactively computer systems of the future behave, they will be the products (direct or indirect) of human behavior, human social institutions, and human decision.
>
> *(p. 197)*

But, on the other hand, these things are not quite like other things. They talk to us. They can use language in ways that are virtually indistinguishable from another human person. And they have compelling social presence, engaging us in seemingly intelligent and even emotionally sensitive conversational interactions. But extending to these technologies the status of person seems equally incorrect as doing so is not only abrasive to our moral intuitions but risks opening the door to possible abuses by powerful corporate actors who could manipulate such an opportunity either to shield themselves from liability or to foster dependencies in human users of the technology—especially with those human populations who already find themselves in vulnerable situations and positions—that could be exploited for political or financial gain.

In the final analysis, the problem might not be with AI per se but with our moral and legal categories—specifically, the person/thing binary—that we have fabricated in order to divide up and make sense of all that is.

The person/thing dichotomy has made sense and worked rather well for over two thousand years. But that might be at an end or reaching the point of diminishing returns, precisely because many of these technologies fail to fit nicely and neatly into either the one or the other category. Consequently, what we now see reflected back to us in the face of recent experiences with AI is the fact that our existing moral and legal ontology is broken—or if not broken, then at least straining against its own limitations. And what is needed in response to this dysfunction, as I have argued elsewhere (Gunkel, 2023), might not be some forceful reassertion of more of the same but a significantly reformulated moral and legal ontology that can scale to the social challenges of the twenty-first century and beyond.

Conclusions and Outcomes

We can, therefore, wrap this up by returning to Turing. It is because intelligent thought is not directly observable that Turing shifts the focus of his research from the question "Can machines think?" to "Can machines deploy language in a way that is indistinguishable from how a human being uses language?" Though Turning does not say it, his test is informed by and operationalizes a theory of language that goes all the way back to Aristotle. In *De Interpretatione*, Aristotle (1938, 1.16a.3) explains that written words are the signs of spoken words and spoken words are the signs of thought. Language, therefore, is not just a system of signs, it itself is a sign of thinking. And it is for this reason that we commonly say that words *express*—literally "push out"—thought. Or as Ted Chiang (2024) hastily asserts in an article for *The New Yorker*: "Language is, by definition, a system of communication, and it requires an intention to communicate."

For Aristotle—as well as for Turing and generations of AI scientists and engineers after him—language is commonly taken to be a sign or externalized manifestation of thinking. Thus, if something speaks or otherwise uses language (in a way that seems to be intelligible), it is reasonable to conclude that it is a thinking thing. At this point in time, then, it appears that sophisticated chatbots and LLMs have indeed already met this test case, as we now have algorithms that are not only able to generate legible sequences of words but can engage us in compelling and seemingly natural conversational interactions. These AI systems, therefore, have not only mastered the imitation game, but they also appear to have surpassed or even broken it. Despite this achievement, however, there are some hesitations and even resistance to declaring, as Lemoine had done, that these AIs are intelligent or capable of thought. So, we end by returning to Shannon's dilemma. In the face of these technological innovations, we are either (1) forced to admit that machines can think or (2) we are going to need to revise our understanding of what we mean when we use a term like "think." Thus, we can either concede defeat or try (once again) to change the rules of the game.

References

Agüera y Arcas, B., & Norvig, P. (2023, October 10). Artificial General Intelligence is already here. *Noema*. Https://www.noemamag.com/artificial-general-intelligence-is-already-here/

Aristotle. (1938). *Aristotle I: Categories. On interpretation. Prior analytics.* (H. P. Cooke, Trans.). Harvard University Press.

Bender, E. M., Gebru, T., McMillan-Major, A., & Shmitchell, S. (2021). On the dangers of stochastic parrots: Can language models be too big? In *Conference on Fairness, Accountability, and Transparency* (FAccT '21), March 3–10, 2021, Virtual Event, Canada. *ACM* (pp. 610–623). https://doi.org/10.1145/3442188.3445922

Biever, C. (2023). ChatGPT broke the Turing Test—The race is on for new ways to assess AI. *Nature, 619,* 686–689. https://doi.org/10.1038/d41586-023-02361-7

Blum, B. A. (2023, August 10). To navigate the age of AI, the world needs a new Turing Test. *Wired.* https://www.wired.com/story/ai-new-turing-test/

Bubeck, S., et al. (2023). Sparks of Artificial General Intelligence: Early experiments with GPT-4. *Arxiv Computer Science.* https://doi.org/10.48550/arXiv.2303.12712

Chiang, T. (2024, August 31). Why A.I. isn't going to make art. *The New Yorker.* https://www.newyorker.com/culture/the-weekend-essay/why-ai-isnt-going-to-make-art

Churchland, P. (1999). *Matter and consciousness.* MIT Press.

Coeckelbergh, M. (2018). How to describe and evaluate "deception" phenomena: Recasting the metaphysics, ethics, and politics of ICTs in terms of magic and performance and taking a relational and narrative turn. *Ethics and Information Technology, 20,* 71–85. https://doi.org/10.1007/s10676-017-9441-5

Descartes, R. (1988). *Selected philosophical writings* (J. Cottingham, R. Stoothoff, & D. Murdoch, Trans.). Cambridge University Press.

Dreyfus, H. L. (1992). *What computers still can't do: A Critique of artificial reason.* MIT Press.

Esposito, R. (2015). *Persons and things* (Z. Hanafi, Trans.). Polity.

Gunkel, D. J. (2023). *Person, thing, robot: A moral and legal ontology for the 21st century and beyond.* MIT Press.

Hofstadter, D. R. (1979). *Gödel, Escher, Bach: An eternal bolden braid.* Basic Books.

Hofstadter, D. R. (2001). Staring Emmy straight in the eye – and doing my best not to flinch. In D. Cope (Ed.), *Virtual music: Computer synthesis of musical style* (pp. 33–82). MIT Press.

Johnson, D. G. (2006). Computer systems: Moral entities but not moral agents. *Ethics and Information Technology, 8,* 195–204. https://doi.org/10.1007/s10676-006-9111-5

Jones, C. R., & Bergen, B. K. (2024). People cannot distinguish GPT-4 from a human in a Turing test. *Human-Computer Interaction.* https://arxiv.org/abs/2405.08007

Kaplan, J. (2016). *Artificial intelligence: What everyone needs to know.* Oxford University Press.

Kelly, K. (2014, October 27). The three breakthroughs that have finally unleashed AI on the world. *Wired.* https://www.wired.com/2014/10/future-of-artificial-intelligence/

McCarthy, J., & Feigenbaum, E. (1990). In memoriam: Arthur Samuel: Pioneer in machine learning. *AI Magazine, 11*(3), 10–11. https://doi.org/10.1609/aimag.v11i3.840

Natale, S. (2021). *Deceitful media: Artificial intelligence and social life after the Turing Test.* Oxford University Press.

Open AI. (2024). *OpenAI Charter.* https://openai.com/charter

Oremus, W. (2022, June 17). Google's AI passed a famous test — and showed how the test is broken. *Washington Post.* https://www.washingtonpost.com/technology/2022/06/17/google-ai-lamda-turing-test/

Plato. (1987). *Republic* (P. Shorey, Trans.). Harvard University Press.

Schank, R. C. (1990). What is AI anyway? In D. Partridge & Y. Wilks (Eds.), *The foundations of artificial intelligence: A sourcebook* (pp. 3–13). Cambridge University Press.

Searle, J. (1999). The Chinese room. In R. A. Wilson & F. Keil (Eds.), *The MIT encyclopedia of the cognitive sciences* (pp. 115–116). MIT Press.

Shannon, C. E. (1950). Programming a computer for playing chess. *Philosophical Magazine,* Series 7, *41*(314), 256–275. https://doi.org/10.1080/14786445008521796

Suleyman, M. (2023, July 14). My new Turing Test would see if AI can make $1 million. *MIT Technology Review.* https://www.technologyreview.com/2023/07/14/1076296/mustafa-suleyman-my-new-turing-test-would-see-if-ai-can-make-1-million/

Turing, A. (1950). Computing machinery and intelligence. *Mind, 59*(236), 433–460. https://doi.org/10.1093/mind/LIX.236.433

Vallor, S. (2024, May 23). The danger of superhuman AI is not what you think. *Noema.* https://www.noemamag.com/the-danger-of-superhuman-ai-is-not-what-you-think/

Weatherby, L. (2023, November 13). ChatGPT broke the Turing Test. *Boston Globe.* https://www.bostonglobe.com/2023/11/13/opinion/turing-test-ai-chatgpt/

Weizenbaum, J. (1976). *Computer power and human reason: From judgment to calculation.* W. H. Freeman.

4

AI HAS JOINED THE CHAT

Exploring the Role of Generative AI Assistants in Group Chats

Eden Litt, Nicole B. Ellison, Lauren Scissors, Isabelle Giordano, and Shreshta Bhat

Although artificial intelligence (AI) has been part of the infrastructural engine powering our technological experiences for decades, the introduction of generative AI—or AI that is able to create new content with human-like outputs—has created unprecedented opportunities for people to engage AI with new levels of ease, efficiency, and creativity. In the last few years, an array of generative AI assistants that allow people to directly chat with generative AI models have entered the market, including OpenAI's ChatGPT, Google's Gemini, Meta's Meta AI, Snap's My AI, and Microsoft's Copilot. While companies, researchers, and society more broadly overwhelmingly encounter these technologies through the lens of one person engaging directly with the technology (e.g., via a chatbot), representing a one-on-one human-computer interaction, a handful of companies have recently provided the ability for their generative AI assistants to engage with multiple people together—creating one-to-many human-computer interaction. This potential shift in communication practices raises many questions around the technology's adoption by and impact on society, such as how it could influence the way people build and maintain relationships, collaborate and make group decisions, or what it could mean for some of today's biggest social challenges like loneliness or political polarization.

Little research to date focuses explicitly on group engagements with generative AI. Now marks a critical time to research this as users are still in early-acceptance mode, making them more perceptive of and articulate about their uses and reactions (Bowker & Star, 2000; de Graaf et al., 2018; Sundar & Limperos, 2013). It also marks a critical time to explore this

DOI: 10.4324/9781003477587-4

from a design implications perspective, as findings could shape the technology to best support people, and not only their relationship with technology, but their relationship with other people (Baldassarre et al., 2023; Sætra, 2023; Wach et al., 2023). This chapter represents the first landscape overview of generative AI assistant group adoption, providing insights into who uses the technology and why.

Literature Review

During our review of the literature, we were unable to locate published research on the organic use of commercially or widely available generative AI assistants in group settings. Other researchers have conducted a similar review on the broader technology of chatbots and yielded similar conclusions; group usage is "underexplored," and "nearly all chatbots to date have been designed for dyadic, one-on-one communication with users" (Seering et al., 2019). The handful of research that exists tends to be from researchers who have built their own chatbots and studied them in controlled environments. For example, researchers created and then studied assistants such as Taskbot to help groups manage tasks together (Toxtli et al., 2018) and Groupfeedbot to coordinate and inspire conversations (Kim et al., 2020). In a review of these specially designed bots, Zheng et al. (2022) categorized the researcher-built assistants into different relational outcomes highlighting that they focused mainly on: communication efficiency, group management, relationship management, and building connections. There are also a small handful of studies that have built and explored group use of chatbots "in the wild." For example, Seering et al. (2020) built BabyBot and deployed it into an existing Twitch community. They found it could help facilitate discussions and activities that made the stream more "enjoyable" and engaging.

While little research has focused on groups of people interacting with generative AI together to date, there is a growing body of work that has examined one-on-one or solo usage of generative AI assistants specifically. This research has started to cover the basics around who is adopting these services (de Winter et al., 2024; Kacperski et al., 2025) and why (Bodonhelyi et al., 2024; Saputri et al., 2024; Skjuve et al., 2024). For example, researchers in Germany studied the demographics of ChatGPT users via web tracking data and a survey, reporting that younger and more educated people were more likely to use the AI assistant (Kacperski et al., 2025). In a survey with early adopters of ChatGPT, researchers explored people's motivations for using ChatGPT and identified six major reasons: "productivity, novelty, creative work, learning and development, entertainment, and social interaction and support" (Skjuve et al., 2024).

While this provides a foundation for understanding generative AI assistant adoption, group use specifically deserves its own inquiry. Although group generative AI assistant usage may share the same technical and design features as solo usage, group use may be fundamentally different. Compared to solo use, group use may inherit dynamics that tend to impact group settings in life more generally—norms (Feldman, 1984; Hechter & Opp, 2001), relationship roles (Argyle et al., 1985), audience concerns (Litt, 2012), social learning (Bandura, 1971), and social influence (Fulk et al., 1990)—that could influence how and what people use the AI for and how the AI responds. The one-to-many dynamic also means the AI must account for additional technical challenges, like accounting for multiple individual preferences and navigating more complex turn-taking (Chiang et al., 2024), such as "'what' to say, 'when' to respond, and 'who' to answer" (Mao et al., 2024). These differences may lead to differences in adoption and use. For example, people may perceive the assistant as a tool when using it solo, leading to more information-oriented or instrumental requests, but perceive it more as a social actor when using it in a group, thus prompting more social- or entertainment-oriented use cases (Gambino et al., 2020). Similarly, people's prompts may also lean more sensitive during solo usage without a potential audience to scrutinize or judge (Litt, 2012).

In this chapter, we utilize a survey of generative AI assistant users 18+ in the United States ($N = 1,300$) to produce the first snapshot of how people are using generative AI assistants in real-world group settings, highlighting empirical insights into why people might or might not adopt this technology, in an effort to advance our understanding of how communication and social relationships may evolve with this new technology and inspire future AI that can best support people.

Methodology

We conducted an unbranded online survey in June of 2025 in the United States using a YouGov panel[1] that leveraged a sample matching methodology. Participants were removed from the dataset for not passing quality checks (e.g., speeding, skipping, and poor quality open-ended responses). The survey first asked which generative AI assistants people were aware of and used. It then described solo versus group usage of AI assistants to participants alongside screenshots (see Figure 4.1) and asked users if they had only ever used an AI assistant solo, only ever used an AI assistant in a chat with another person or group of people, or if they had used it both solo *and* with another person or group of people. It then asked about people's most recent experience using an AI assistant solo and/or in a group

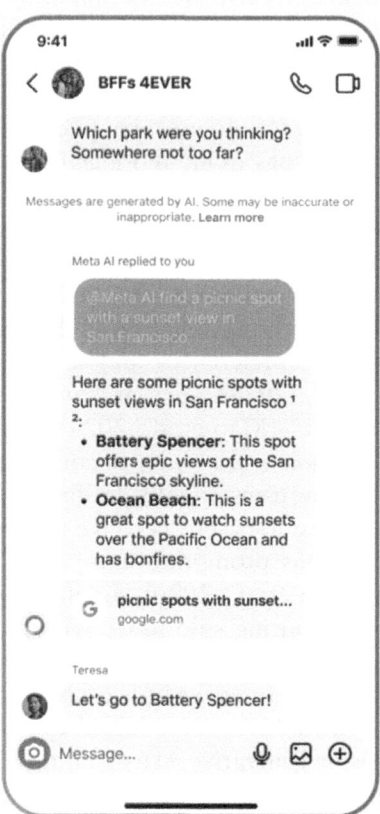

FIGURE 4.1 Example AI solo chat (left) versus group chat (right) screenshots displayed to participants in the survey intro.

(as applicable to their usage) with a series of questions around where it happened, what they did, and how they felt about it.

The majority of results focus on why, or why not, respondents had used the technology for group usage. To answer these questions, we used close-ended questions supplemented with open-ended questions to aid further understanding. For example, to understand why people had adopted the technology, half of the participants who had used an AI in a group reflected on their most recent uses via a close-ended question (see Table 4.3), and the other half were presented with an open-ended question (see quotes throughout text below). A randomly selected group of those who had experienced generative AI group use were also asked the open-ended question, "What has

TABLE 4.1 AI Assistant Most Recently Used in Group Chat (with Solo Chat for Comparison)

	Group AI assistant users[a] (%)	Solo AI assistant users[b] (%)
Meta AI (also available on Facebook, Messenger, Instagram, and WhatsApp)	75.65	18.04
My AI on Snapchat	8.48	1.12
Claude (also available on Slack)	3.02	1.32
Perplexity	2.93	0.96
Character.ai	2.65	1.46
ChatGPT	n/a	41.50
Google Gemini (also available within some Google products)	n/a	16.36
Microsoft Copilot (also available within some Microsoft products)	n/a	10.88
Other	7.28	8.33
Unweighted N	800	1,177

[a] Survey question: Which AI assistant did you use most recently in a chat with another person or group of people?
[b] Survey question: Which AI assistant did you use most recently solo?

worked well so far in having an AI assistant in a chat with another person or group of people?" Another randomly selected group of the sample who had tried generative group use were asked the following open-ended question: "What could be improved about this experience so far in having an AI assistant in a chat with another person or group of people?" To investigate why some have not adopted group use, we asked a close-ended question to those who had never used an AI assistant in a group before asking them to indicate why not (see Table 4.4). Finally, while the survey and this chapter focus on group usage, we also inquired about solo usage for those it was applicable to and report on it for directional comparison. For close-ended questions, we leveraged descriptive statistics. For open-ended questions, we utilized a grounded theory approach for qualitative coding and collected examples to understand the quantitative findings further (Strauss & Corbin, 1994).

In total, the final dataset utilized in this chapter contained 1,300 generative AI Assistant users in the United States, ranging in age from 18 to 84. Just under half (47.74%) identified as men. To garner sufficient responses from people leveraging generative AI assistants in groups, we oversampled group users; to recalibrate in the analyses, data were weighted to reflect the US internet population using a stratified sampling frame constructed from the 2021 Current Population Survey.

TABLE 4.2 Types of People in Most Recent Chat Using an AI Assistant in a Group

Friend	36.18%
Family	32.40%
Close friend	27.27%
Someone from a group I am a part of based on shared interests or beliefs	18.79%
Spouse/boyfriend/girlfriend/partner	17.50%
Someone from work or school	17.06%
Acquaintance	12.08%
Someone I don't know	8.48%
Other	4.31%
Unweighted N	800

Note: Survey question: Who else was in the chat with <AI> when you most recently used it with another person or group of people? Select all that apply.

The majority of respondents had used an AI assistant solo only (82%), with just under a fifth (18%) of the sample reporting that they had at least tried a generative AI assistant in a group setting. The majority of these generative AI group users (75.65%) reported that their most recent use was with Meta AI, followed by My AI. While Meta AI was reported as a top assistant for solo usage as well, the popular AI assistants for solo usage did not offer a group setting at the time of this research (e.g. ChatGPT; see Table 4.1). Such group use was most commonly reported to be with friends and/or family (see Table 4.2) and occurred most often with just two people.

Results

Why are People Adopting Generative AI Assistants for Group Use Today?

Table 4.3 highlights the percentage of people who reported each use case during their most recent group use with a generative AI assistant (as well as their most recent solo generative AI assistant use for directional comparison). The most common reason people reported (36.32%) recently using the generative AI assistant in a group was for entertainment purposes. Investigating the open-ends, this was mainly people using the assistant for amusement as the end goal. For some this meant activities where the AI played game host (e.g., "Dungeons and Dragon" or "We were asking it to do extrapolate for worldbuilding.") or a comedian (e.g., "making jokes" or "funny pictures"), and for others this meant more informal playing around (e.g., "Goofing around" or "Just for fun, to make silly sentences") including explicitly poking fun at the assistant's expense (e.g., "We were just messing with it and testing it" or "to troll it").

TABLE 4.3 Use Cases People Used AI Assistant for in Most Recent Chat Using an AI Assistant in a Group (with Solo Chat for Comparison)

Use case	Group AI assistant chats[a] (%)	Solo AI assistant chats[b] (%)
Entertainment (e.g., games/trivia, casual conversation)	36.32	24.80
Personal productivity and communication (e.g., planning a vacation or making dinner plans with friends, drafting messages to family)	30.96	17.99
Shopping (e.g., product recommendations, price comparisons)	21.07	15.79
Creativity and expression (e.g., creating images, story writing)	19.47	22.69
Education and learning (e.g., homework support, learning skills)	17.16	28.44
Business productivity and communication (e.g., data analysis, drafting work emails)	14.80	15.34
Wellness support (e.g., workout and nutritional advice, relationship guidance)	13.91	8.94
Other	8.56	16.49
Unweighted N	401	598

[a]Survey question: What did you use <AI> for when you most recently used it in a chat with another person or group of people? Select all that apply.
[b]Survey question: What did you use <AI> for when you most recently used it [solo]? Select all that apply.

About a third (30.96%) identified personal productivity and communication as their most recent rationale for using the generative AI assistant in a group setting. Exploring the open-ended data to understand this further, we see people trying to use the assistants to plan social activities (e.g., "Planning a wedding" or "asked Perplexity for...nearby food spots"). Participants explicitly noted trying to use the AI to mediate the conversation and work through arguments and decision-making (e.g., "to fact check sport arguments" or "to help settle a debate about vacation destinations"). Responses highlighted the AI's ability to enhance or facilitate their conversations by giving another perspective, encouraging others to speak up, and helping close knowledge gaps across group members (e.g., "an extra person to bounce ideas off of that wasn't Family" or "it often prompts us and helps guide the conversation and keep the chatroom lively").

About one in five (21.07%) noted that they asked the generative AI assistant questions related to shopping in a group most recently. The open-ends suggest they tried to use the AI to get product recommendations and research options (e.g., "information about purchasing items for the lowest price" or "Product information and how good they seem to be"), navigate customer service support (e.g., "When I needed customer support" or "customer support"), and participate in shopping engagements (e.g., "Interactive shopping discussion" or "online shopping").

Just under one in five (19.47%) people reported they most recently asked the generative AI assistant questions related to "creativity" in a group setting. For some, this meant seeking prompts about writing (e.g., "writing a fantasy story about us going on an adventure" or "to make a comical story with all of us in it") or visuals (e.g., "I wanted to show in depth a City We were discussing" or "make a meme for us"), and for others, it meant getting help with a part of the process like brainstorming or editing (e.g., "brainstorming ideas together" or "Fun photo editing").

Just over one in six (17.16%) reported they asked the generative AI assistant questions related to education and learning in a group most recently. This included asking the AI to act as a teacher or research assistant (e.g., "to check definitions of some words" or "We were discussing topics like historical events and famous people. I felt it did a decent job at highlighting details that we all didn't know or discovered yet"), problem solver (e.g., "To try to figure out an assignment I was working on" or "For helping with a coding problem"), and a notetaker (e.g., "We used it to summarize the chat that we had been having so far" or "meeting transcription and summary") for both formal and informal learning opportunities.

Roughly 15% said that they most recently asked the generative AI assistant questions related to work goals in a group chat setting. This included seeking answers related to help researching or brainstorming work tasks (e.g., "I used meta ai to seek for answers pertaining to work" or "Mostly work related information"), as well as its ability to support their business-related coordination and communication (e.g., "Update meeting time and date" or "we were resolving a compliance-related matter for work"). They also acknowledged its role in helping get "challenges," "matters," "projects," and "assignments" done (e.g., "I used Claude to help generate an outline, find recent case studies, and polish some of the wording in our slides" or "We were resolving a compliance-related matter for work").

Finally, about 14% noted that they most recently asked the generative AI assistant questions related to wellness support in a group chat setting. This included mostly emotional support (e.g., "Discuss about wellbeing" or "support group") and informational support related to health topics (e.g., "Research things on what was the best things to do to improve health" or "looking up a medical diagnosis").

Why are People NOT Adopting Generative AI Assistants for Group Use Today?

Table 4.4 highlights the percentage of people who selected each reason for not adopting generative AI assistants in group settings, alongside the percentage of people who reported each reason for not using generative AI assistants solo. The most common reason people reported never having used an AI assistant in a group chat was "Do not have a reason to use it" (61.01%). Exploring the open-ended responses shared by current users about what needs improvement suggests this could be in part due to a gap in skills and knowledge about what the generative AI assistants can even do and how to use this technology (e.g., "I'm not an expert" or "I'm still learning about this"). The open-ends also suggested people's perspective that the assistant's model quality needed improvement. For example, although some current users tried to use it for learning help, others reflected on their belief it lacked the ability to deliver relevant information (e.g., "more accuracy in information provided" or "I think it got details wrong sometimes"). Similarly, current users flagged dissatisfaction with the assistant's social skills, including its tone and ability to enter in, exit, and keep track of the conversation (e.g., "Sometimes it feels too robotic or doesn't get the vibe of the convo" or "Sometimes responses can feel a bit too formal or disconnected from the flow of casual conversation"). We anticipate the portion of people reporting not having a reason to do so will decline over time, given the technology itself is actively developing and users are learning about its abilities.

The next most commonly reported reasons respondents gave for not using AI assistants in group settings also relate to AI literacy at a high level—people reported not knowing the feature existed (35.11%) and/or not knowing how to use the feature (25.77%). Even for current users, some struggled to access the technology (e.g., "Understand how they brought AI into the conversation" or "Less confusion"), and others more explicitly requested more education (e.g., "There was a personal learning curve to using it. Instructions were available but weren't clear enough for me in the beginning" or "education of using AI").

People also expressed personal perceived concerns with security or privacy (18.27%) and/or ethics (9.03%) as contributing reasons about why they did not try out AI assistants in groups. Although these were referenced by current users as well, they often did not provide much context beyond comments such as "Ensure privacy" or "More features on safety." Some hints in the data from the current users suggest such concerns could be linked with a desire for more data control (e.g., "Better memory and

TABLE 4.4 Reasons Reported for Not Using AI Assistants in Groups (with Reasons for Not Using AI Assistants Solo for Comparison)

	Reason reported for not using AI in groups[a] (%)	Reason reported for not using AI solo[b] (%)
Do not have a reason to use it	61.01	42.71
Did not know this feature existed	35.11	10.36
Do not know how to use this feature	25.77	24.65
Security or privacy concerns	18.27	16.89
Unsure if the other person/people would be okay with it[c]	14.27	n/a[c]
Ethical concerns	9.03	9.31
Unsure what the AI would say	8.18	n/a
Prefer a different product for similar tasks	4.24	5.08
Prior experience was poor	3.69	7.12
Other	3.33	2.06
Unweighted N	500	123

[a]Survey question: Which of the following describes why you have not used an AI assistant in a chat with another person or group of people? Select all that apply.
[b]Survey question: Which of the following describes why you have not used an AI assistant solo? Select all that apply.
[c]Option not included.

memory controls of the entire chat. Being able to decide if it can listen in on the entire chat or only when addressed" or "Ensure that all data collected stays private and is not licensed or sold").

People also felt uncertainty about how other people in the group would feel about having an AI assistant there (14.27%). Current users expressed the struggles of different users' comfort and experience levels with AI, and potentially wanting others' approval before adding the AI to the chat (e.g., "Everybody agree whether the AI is needed in the chat" or "I think the hardest part is that everyone had different levels of experience with AI, so it was clunky").

The remaining reasons were identified in less than a tenth of the sample each and included rationales such as uncertainty about what the AI might say in a group context (8.18%), preference for using other tools for similar tasks (4.24%), and having a prior poor experience (3.69%).

Discussion

For the first time in history, AI assistants are being designed for and integrated into mainstream technology with group use at the center. The results from our survey of generative AI assistant users in the United States provide a snapshot in time of what experimentation and adoption looks like so far, and a glimpse into which factors might encourage or discourage its adoption. These findings suggest that while many in the United States have tried a generative AI assistant, only a minority so far have done so specifically in a group chat. Without mass adoption and its accompanying network effects, we don't see signs of a communication paradigm shift just yet, but this research provides glimmers of how it could happen, and why this is an important and independent area to continue studying in addition to solo usage. For example, while this research suggests users believe generative AI assistants have the potential to bolster creativity and efficiency in both solo and group usage, as other work has also indicated (Brynjolfsson et al., 2023; Habib et al., 2024; Zhuo & Lee, 2024), we also see evidence that the assistants may create new or unique value adds in the group setting specifically. For instance, participants highlighted group roles that the generative AI assistants adopted, which may be better suited for nonhuman entities because of discomfort or skill deficiency—such as a mediator or a facilitator—roles that potentially help resolve conflict, make decisions, and more intentionally support meaningful social interactions (Brett et al., 1996; Hostager et al., 2003; Litt et al., 2020).

This research also highlights some potential differences in the motivations behind adoption across solo and group environments; people may be more likely to use AI assistants alone for informational use cases like education and learning. In contrast, people may be more likely to use AI assistants in groups for social and entertainment use cases, like planning activities or playing games. Such potential differences could be due to variance in the types of needs people have when they are alone versus when they are with other people (Argyle et al., 1985; Litt, 2012). For example, most people who tried out group chats in this study had done so in small groups and with friends and family, which may have triggered specific social norms about topics to discuss or not discuss (Feldman, 1984; Hechter & Opp, 2001). The potential differences in use cases could also be due to the different mental models people may bring to each setting. For example, our qualitative data suggest that respondents perceived the assistants as taking on both functional and social roles in both solo and group settings; however, in their open-ended responses, participants were more likely to see an assistant as a tool during solo use and as another group member during group usage. Future work, using theoretical frameworks such as Sundar's Machine Heuristic (Sundar & Kim, 2019), might explore this further. There may also just be differences in the types of people who are more likely to try, use, or enjoy assistants in groups versus solo versus both contexts that could account for some of the differences found throughout the study. Future work could investigate these topics further and leverage different methods.

Finally, although we see evidence that both solo and group usage of generative AI assistants is in the infancy, or "encounter stage" (de Graaf et al., 2018), we see indication that this may be even more so for group usage. While a lack of literacy, awareness, and/or skills may inhibit both solo and group adoption for generative AI usage today, it may be a bigger barrier for group usage. Some of this may be a signal about the technology development itself—group usage is newer and not available on all platforms. Meta AI, the most popular platform for group usage, had been around for about two years at the time of the research, in contrast to ChatGPT, which had been around just under three years, but did not offer such a feature at the time of the survey (but now does). And although the areas of improvement for this feature share similarities with the AI regardless of chat context (e.g., response quality, tone), we also see indication of unique challenges for groups such as AI ownership and memory as well as the conversational flow (Mao et al., 2024), which "potentially hinder their effectiveness...[like] knowing when the LLM should speak, and deciding to whom it speaks to" (Chiang et al., 2024). While a "digital divide" in awareness and skills will likely remain over time as continued research has shown the importance of this topic for decades (Büchi & Hargittai, 2022; Hargittai, 2002; Litt, 2013), we hypothesize that some of this trend will shift with more marketing and education campaigns, and as the design optimizes for a better user experience. As collaborative uses become more common and platforms may add and/or remove group capabilities (Warren, 2023), we expect the users' set of perceived benefits, uses, constraints, and affordances will also shift over time.

Although this research provides a snapshot and offers empirically informed speculation about nascent uses of this newer technology and insights into why people may or may not adopt it, future research is needed to understand how group communication norms may shift and explore how iterations of these tools can proactively put people and their relationships at the fore. What ingredients and capabilities are needed to enhance people's social experiences both online and off? For instance, a generative AI assistant in a group chat could improve group dynamics by being able to provide personalized information based on a chat history, its interactors, and the intersection of the two; provide access to new skills available for group members to leverage; and afford new interaction types for group members to experience. For example, AI could be trained to help increase meaningful engagement by determining the popularity of various topics and who typically engages with which (and who does not); support conflict resolution and resolution of misunderstandings through actions like surfacing relevant previous exchanges or helping groups find common ground; facilitate cross-cultural exchanges with real-time translation; amplify opportunities for social support by matching up group members; and activate planning trips, playing games, and creating art. Future research should explore how receptive users will be to the notion of an AI assistant taking on these roles and skills. Although there is much promise in AI's potential ability to support everyday group dynamics like those mentioned above, future research could also explore leveraging this technology to positively impact key societal challenges like loneliness or polarization.

While this research represents a first foray into generative AI use in group settings, it also exposes the limitations of the language we use to discuss and approach designing this new technology. Debates already highlight the impact of this technology on society (Baldassarre et al., 2023; Manduchi et al., 2024; Wach et al., 2023), in which concerns are raised about the potential influence of generative AI assistants on social skills and their potential to replace human-to-human social interactions and relationships. Our findings highlight the need to make sure we understand and acknowledge the nuances of this technology's role in our social lives during such debates. While group use of AI is inherently social—and communication is a top use case in group settings—we also see evidence in this study that even those who use AI assistants "solo" often do so with social purposes in mind. For example, about one in five people in the survey leveraged the AIs during their most recent solo interaction for communication, and others highlighted use cases that were ultimately intended to be shared with others—such as planning trips, meals, and events for loved ones; writing posts for social media; creating lesson plans for students; writing cover letters and resumes to send to potential employers; and more. Similarly, in this dataset, we see glimpses of people using the AIs in person together or sharing their prompts with others, which may be important for helping others learn about new technologies. These aforementioned social use cases may be less likely to be captured by studies focusing solely on server log or behavioral trace data. Although the technology and research are in their infancy, if society wants to foster a technology that best supports people, their relationships, and society, it is imperative to research and design with these social implications at the fore.

Acknowledgments

The authors gratefully acknowledge the support and feedback from Lauren Benditt, Ross Ewert, Joe Franklin, Meagan Hart, Candace Hunt, Frank Kanayet, Beth Lingard, Devra Moehler, Karim Oliver, Maeve Ryan, Breanne Wernars, Mike Winters, and Setor Zilevu.

Note

1 YouGov is an international research data and analytics company with 27 million+ registered panel members in over 59 markets; https://today.yougov.com/.

References

Argyle, M., Henderson, M., & Furnham, A. (1985). The rules of social relationships. *British Journal of Social Psychology*, 24(2), 125–139. https://doi.org/10.1111/j.2044-8309.1985.tb00671.x

Baldassarre, M. T., Caivano, D., Nieto, B. F., Gigante, D., & Ragone, A. (2023). The social impact of generative AI: An analysis on ChatGPT. In *Proceedings of the 2023 ACM Conference on Information Technology for Social Good* (pp. 3630–373). Lisbon: Association for Computing Machinery. https://doi.org/10.1145/3582515.3609555

Bandura, A. (1971). *Social learning theory*. General Learning Press.

Bodonhelyi, A., Yang, S., Bozkir, E., Kasneci, E., & Kasneci, G. (2024). *User intent recognition and satisfaction with large language models: A user study with ChatGPT*. arXiv. https://doi.org/10.48550/arXiv.2402.02136

Bowker, G. C., & Star, S. L. (2000). *Sorting things out: Classification and its consequences*. MIT Press. https://doi.org/10.7551/mitpress/6352.001.0001

Brett, J. M., Barsness, Z. I., & Goldberg, S. B. (1996). The effectiveness of mediation: An independent analysis of cases handled by four major service providers. *Negotiation Journal*, 12(3), 259–269. https://doi.org/10.1111/j.1571-9979.1996.tb00099.x

Brynjolfsson, E., Li, D., & Raymond, L. R. (2023). *Generative AI at work* (NBER No. 31161). National Bureau of Economic Research. https://doi.org/10.3386/w31161

Büchi, M., & Hargittai, E. (2022). A need for considering digital inequality when studying social media use and well-being. *Social Media + Society*, 8(1). https://doi.org/10.1177/20563051211069125

Chiang, C.-W., Lu, Z., Li, Z., & Yin, M. (2024). Enhancing AI-assisted group decision making through LLM-powered devil's advocate. In *Proceedings of the 29th International Conference on Intelligent User Interfaces* (pp.1030–119). Greenville, SC: Association for Computing Machinery. https://doi.org/10.1145/3640543.3645199

de Graaf, M. e. M., Allouch, S. B., & van Dijk, J. A. (2018). A phased framework for long-term user acceptance of interactive technology in domestic environments. *New Media & Society*, 20(7), 2582–2603. https://doi.org/10.1177/1461444817727264

de Winter, J., Dodou, D., & Eisma, Y. B. (2024). Personality and acceptance as predictors of ChatGPT use. *Discover Psychology*, 4, Article 57. https://doi.org/10.1007/s44202-024-00161-2

Feldman, D. C. (1984). The development and enforcement of group norms. *Academy of Management Review*, 9(1), 470–53. https://doi.org/10.5465/amr.1984.4277934

Fulk, J., Schmitz, J., & Steinfield, C. W. (1990). A social influence model of technology use. In J. Fulk & C. Steinfield (Eds.), *Organizations and communication technology* (pp. 117–140). Sage. https://doi.org/10.4135/9781483325385.n6

Gambino, A., Fox, J., & Ratan, R. A. (2020). Building a stronger CASA: Extending the computers are social actors paradigm. *Human-Machine Communication*, *1*, 71–86. https://doi.org/10.30658/hmc.1.5

Habib, S., Vogel, T., Anli, X., & Thorne, E. (2024). How does generative artificial intelligence impact student creativity? *Journal of Creativity*, *34*(1), Article 100072. https://doi.org/10.1016/j.yjoc.2023.100072

Hargittai, E. (2002). Second-level digital divide: Differences in people's online skills. *First Monday*, *7*(4). https://doi.org/10.5210/fm.v7i4.942

Hechter, M., & Opp, K.- D. (Eds.). (2001). *Social norms*. Russell Sage Foundation.

Hostager, T. J., Lester, S. W., Bergmann, M., & Ready, K. J. (2003). Matching facilitator style and agenda structure in group support systems: Effects on participant satisfaction and group output quality. *Information Resources Management Journal*, *16*(2), 56–72. https://doi.org/10.4018/irmj.2003040104

Kacperski, C., Ulloa, R., Bonnay, D., Kulshrestha, J., Selb, P., & Spitz, A. (2025). Characteristics of ChatGPT users from Germany: Implications for the digital divide from web tracking data. *PLoS ONE*, *20*(1), Article e0309047. https://doi.org/10.1371/journal.pone.0309047

Kim, S., Eun, J., Oh, C., Suh, B., & Lee, J. (2020). Bot in the bunch: Facilitating group chat discussion by improving efficiency and participation with a Chatbot. In *Proceedings of the 2020 CHI Conference on Human Factors in Computing Systems* (pp. 1–13). Honolulu, HI: Association for Computing Machinery. https://doi.org/10.1145/3313831.3376785

Litt, E. (2012). Knock, knock. Who's there? The imagined audience. *Journal of Broadcasting & Electronic Media*, *56*(3), 330–345. https://doi.org/10.1080/08838151.2012.705195

Litt, E. (2013). Measuring users' internet skills: A review of past assessments and a look toward the future. *New Media & Society*, *15*(4), 612–630. https://doi.org/10.1177/1461444813475424

Litt, E., Zhao, S., Kraut, R., & Burke, M. (2020). What are meaningful social interactions in today's media landscape? A cross-cultural survey. *Social Media + Society*, *6*(3). https://doi.org/10.1177/2056305120942888

Manduchi, L., Pandey, K., Balmer, R., Cotterell, R., Däubener, S., Fellenz, S., Fischer, A., Gärtner, T., Kirchler, M., Kloft, M., Li, Y., Lippert, C., de Melo, G., Nalisnick, E., Ommer, B., Ranganath, R., Rudolph, M., Ullrich, K., Van den Broeck, G., … Fortuin, V. (2024). *On the challenges and opportunities in generative AI*. arXiv. https://doi.org/10.48550/arXiv.2403.00025

Mao, M., Ting, P., Xiang, Y., Xu, M., Chen, J., & Lin, J. (2024). *Multi-user chat assistant (MUCA): A framework using LLMs to facilitate group conversations*. arXiv. https://doi.org/10.48550/arXiv.2401.04883

Sætra, H. S. (2023). Generative AI: Here to stay, but for good? *Technology in Society*, *75*, Article 102372. https://doi.org/10.1016/j.techsoc.2023.102372

Saputri, S. B., Rustanta, A., Sugiarto, S. R., & Palupi, M. J. R. (2024). The use of GPT chat phenomenon in the uses & gratification theory perspective. *Journal of Electrical Systems*, *20*(5), 1286–1291. https://doi.org/10.52783/jes.2456

Seering, J., Luria, M., Kaufman, G., & Hammer, J. (2019). Beyond dyadic interactions: considering chatbots as community members. In *Proceedings of the 2019 CHI Conference on Human Factors in Computing Systems* (pp. 1–13). Glasgow: Association for Computing Machinery. https://doi.org/10.1145/3290605.3300680

Seering, J., Luria, M., Ye, C., Kaufman, G., & Hammer, J. (2020). It takes a village: Integrating an adaptive chatbot into an online gaming community. In *Proceedings of the 2020 CHI Conference on Human Factors in Computing Systems* (pp 1–13). Honolulu HI: Association for Computing Machinery. https://doi.org/10.1145/3313831.3376708

Skjuve, M., Brandtzaeg, P. B., & Følstad, A. (2024). Why do people use ChatGPT? Exploring user motivations for generative conversational AI. *First Monday*, 29(1). https://doi.org/10.5210/fm.v29i1.13541

Strauss, A., & Corbin, J. (1994). Grounded theory methodology: An overview. In N. K. Denzin & Y. S. Lincoln (Eds.), *Handbook of qualitative research* (pp. 273–285). Sage.

Sundar, S. S., & Kim, J. (2019). Machine heuristic: When we trust computers more than humans with our personal information. In *Proceedings of the 2019 CHI Conference on Human Factors in Computing Systems* (pp. 1–9). Glasgow: Association of Computing Machinery. https://doi.org/10.1145/3290605.3300768

Sundar, S. S., & Limperos, A. (2013). Uses and grats 2.0: New gratifications for new media. *Journal of Broadcasting & Electronic Media*, 57(4), 504–525. https://doi.org/10.1080/08838151.2013.845827

Toxtli, C., Monroy-Hernández, A., & Cranshaw, J. (2018). Understanding chatbot-mediated task management. In *Proceedings of the 2018 CHI Conference on Human Factors in Computing Systems* (pp. 1–6). Montreal QC: Association of Computing Machinery. https://doi.org/10.1145/3173574.3173632

Wach, K., Duong, C. D., Ejdys, J., Kazlauskaitė, R., Korzyński, P., Mazurek, G., Paliszkiewicz, J., & Ziemba, E. (2023). The dark side of generative artificial intelligence: A critical analysis of controversies and risks of ChatGPT. *Entrepreneurial Business and Economics Review*, 11(2), 7–30. https://doi.org/10.15678/EBER.2023.110201

Warren, T. (2023, November 17). Discord is shutting down its AI chatbot Clyde. *The Verge*.https://www.theverge.com/2023/11/17/23965185/discord-is-shutting-down-its-ai-chatbot-clyde

Zheng, Q., Tang, Y., Liu, Y., Liu, W., & Huang, Y. (2022). UX research on conversational human-AI interaction: A literature review of the ACM Digital Library. In *Proceedings of 2022 CHI Conference on Human Factors in Computing Systems* (pp. 1–24). New Orleans, LA: Association for Computing Machinery. https://doi.org/10.1145/3491102.3501855

Zhuo, E., & Lee, D. (2024). Generative artificial intelligence, human creativity, and art. *PNAS Nexus*, 3(3), Article pgae052. https://doi.org/10.1093/pnasnexus/pgae052

5

THE SILENT CHATBOT

On the Democratic Significance of Silence in AI-Mediated Communication

Taina Bucher

Introduction

This chapter critically examines the often-overlooked role of silence in artificial intelligence (AI)-mediated communication systems and its implications for democratic discourse. Despite being frequently marginalized, silence plays a complex and essential role in shaping meaning, conveying emotion, and fostering understanding, functions that are vital to a well-functioning democracy. This chapter explores the limitations of current AI models in recognizing, interpreting, or computing silence, and the potential consequences of this shortcoming for marginalized voices and democratic participation in an increasingly AI-driven world. By analyzing the design biases embedded in so-called conversational AI, biases that privilege verbosity over quietude—this chapter interrogates the challenges of envisioning AI solely as talkative.

A chatbot is expected to chat, a social robot to converse, and a digital assistant to respond. Yet, the absence of silence in these systems raises important questions about their fidelity to human communicative behavior. Drawing on the example of large language models (LLMs), I argue that AI's inability to interpret and reproduce human-like silence reveals a fundamental paradox: by learning from typical patterns across datasets, AI gravitates toward the statistically average. Yet, in doing so, it paradoxically silences the "real" average—the inexpressive, indifferent, or quiet—rendering them less visible and less legitimate within algorithmic discourse.

This chapter contends that the dual articulation of silence, both the marginalization of already-silenced voices and the erasure of the silent majority, leads to a distorted and undemocratic form of discourse within

DOI: 10.4324/9781003477587-5

AI-shaped environments. Yet, it is precisely in silence's resistance to capture, quantification, and computation that a profoundly human and democratic potential emerges: one that resists commodification, instrumentalization, and assimilation into machine logic. To explore this possibility, this chapter introduces a provocative figuration—the *silent chatbot*—to illuminate alternative forms of democratic expression and citizenship.

Inspired by feminist epistemologies that emphasize how technologies are never neutral but always embedded within world-making narratives (Haraway, 1991, 2020), this figuration draws on Black feminist notions of critical fabulation (Hartman, 2008) to expand the imaginative possibilities for thinking about AI. Critical fabulation offers a method for addressing the silences and absences that permeate archives and historical records, especially those concerning marginalized lives. As Saidiya Hartman explains:

> By playing with and rearranging the basic elements of the story…I have attempted to jeopardize the status of the event, to displace the received or authorized account, and to imagine what might have happened or might have been said or might have been done.
>
> *(2008, p. 11)*

Similarly, in proposing that speech and conversation are not necessarily the ultimate benchmarks for evaluating AI, this chapter seeks to challenge entrenched assumptions about the role of dialogue in human-machine interaction.

Fabulation, as Marie Søndergaard (2025, p. 57) observes, "is one way of opening up and expanding our imaginings and reconstitut[ing] absent imaginaries and neglected relations into alternative presents and possible futures." The goal, however, is not simply to invent better narratives or new technological designs, but to provoke an ontological and epistemological shift in how we conceptualize AI's role in our lives. Approaching silence as an absent imaginary within AI allows us to imagine AI otherwise, beyond its current paradigms of perpetual responsiveness and performative engagement, toward more plural, ethical, and democratic possibilities.

The Dialogic Imperative of AI: From Speaking Machines to Talkative Agents

Dialogue has long stood as the ultimate test of machine intelligence, serving as a mirror to one of human beings' most distinctive capabilities, natural conversation. From early mechanical speaking devices to modern LLMs, the ability to engage in spontaneous, coherent dialogue continues to define our benchmark for AI.

The quest to create machines capable of human-like communication dates back to at least the eighteenth century when Wolfgang von Kempelen introduced his "speaking machine," often considered the first functional speech synthesizer (Bell, 2024). Unlike his infamous chess-playing "Turk" automaton (which concealed a human operator), von Kempelen's speaking machine was regarded as a genuine scientific contribution. Developed between 1769 and 1791, this mechanical device consisted of a bellows (simulating lungs), a vibrating reed (functioning as the glottis), and a flexible rubber "mouth" chamber whose resonant properties could be manipulated by hand. In 1791, von Kempelen published his comprehensive research on human voice, a study that represented the first serious attempt to create artificial speech based on the physiological understanding of human vocal mechanisms. Although the machine could only produce a limited range of vowel-like sounds and the voice sounded rather monotone, as Sarah A. Bell (2024) suggests that von Kempelen's work allegedly provided an inspiration to the young Alexander Graham Bell, jumpstarting his experiments that ultimately led to the invention of the telephone in 1876.

Fast forward about a hundred years to 1950, when the mathematician Alan Turing proposed what would become the most famous test of machine intelligence. Originally called the "imitation game," it is now better known as the Turing Test. Posing the question "Can machines think?", Turing responded by designing a pragmatic, conversation-based test. In this test, a human evaluator judges text conversations between a machine and another human, attempting to identify which participant is the machine. The test's methodology places dialogue at the center of intelligence evaluation: if the machine can maintain a conversation indistinguishable from a human's, it passes the test. According to Turing, the test is considered successful if the machine performs "so well that an average interrogator will not have more than a 70% chance of making the right identification after five minutes of questioning" (Turing, 1950). Notably, the test doesn't assess the correctness of answers but rather how closely the machine's responses resemble human communication patterns. Turing's choice of conversation as the testing ground for machine intelligence was deliberate and profound. Natural language conversation requires not just knowledge but understanding of context, cultural references, emotional nuances, and the ability to generate coherent, relevant responses. The test assumes that truly intelligent behavior must include the ability to communicate meaningfully, positioning dialogue as the gold standard for assessing machine intelligence.

Since Turing introduced his test, it has profoundly influenced AI philosophy and development, sparking extensive debate and controversy.

While critics like philosopher John Searle (1980) argue that the test fails to detect true consciousness or understanding, the Turing Test remains a touchstone in AI development. One of the earliest implementations of a conversational agent modeled after the Turing Test was ELIZA, developed by Joseph Weizenbaum in 1966. Widely regarded as the first chatbot, ELIZA was designed to simulate a psychotherapist and quickly drew attention for its surprising ability to fool users in short conversations (Mou & Wu, 2023). With recent advancements in deep learning and LLMs trained on huge datasets, modern conversational AI has long passed newer variants of the test. Models like GPT-4 are more capable of engaging in seemingly fluid and open-ended dialogue beyond simply providing information or responding in preformatted ways. While the journey from von Kempelen's speaking machine to today's conversational AI systems reflects a longstanding fascination with creating machines that can speak and converse like humans, what has largely been overlooked is the crucial role silence plays in human communication. As Warwick and Shah point out in their paper on the Turing Test: what if silence itself constitutes the ultimate test? They speculate whether the most advanced machine might be one that, when appropriate, chooses to respond with nothing at all (Warwick & Shah, 2017, p. 289).

This chapter will return to Warwick and Shah's provocation later, through the fabulation of a silent chatbot. First, however, I will examine the role of silence in human communication, particularly how it has often been portrayed in public discourse as a threat to democratic participation. Silence, especially as framed within Western libertarian discourses, is commonly seen as a problematic absence, whether it is the absence of a vote, voice, opinion, discussion, or engagement. I argue that such a framing is, at best, a problematic oversimplification and, at worst, a paradox that perpetuates the very silencing it claims to oppose. The critique of silence extends beyond discourse to include the very infrastructures through which much of our communication now takes place. Silence is increasingly marginalized by digital platforms, particularly social media, that are structured around algorithmic logics of engagement and "interestingness" (Bucher, 2012). Popular platforms such as Facebook, Instagram, TikTok, and YouTube privilege engagement, effectively rendering silence, understood as passivity and non-engaging content invisible or irrelevant. In this sense, silence is not only culturally undervalued but also technically excluded by design. Paradoxically, silence also emerges as a democratic ideal in discussions about the quality of public discourse. Practices such as pausing before responding, taking time to reflect, or deliberately withholding immediate reaction are being championed as signs of thoughtful engagement and respectful dialogue. Yet, these moments are rarely acknowledged explicitly as forms of silence.

I will argue that they should be. Recognizing hesitation and reflective delay as silence opens a more nuanced understanding of its role in democratic communication and invites us to rethink the binary of speech versus silence that so often shapes both theory and practice. To challenge the prevailing emphasis on dialogue and conversation as both the cornerstone of democracy and the ways in which AI has been conceptualized, I end this chapter by proposing a speculative account in the spirit of critical fabulation: a Bartlebyan blueprint for a silent chatbot that, rather than striving to speak or simulate dialogue, enacts strategic silence through refusal and hesitation. Drawing inspiration from Herman Melville's literary figure of Bartleby and his quiet resistance—"I would prefer not to"—this final section asks what it might mean to design an AI that "chooses" not to speak, and what such a gesture could reveal about the politics of machine intelligence today.

The Politics of Silence: Democratic Threat or Potential?

Silence is often construed as absence, passivity, lack, repression, or a failure to speak (Ephratt, 2008). Speech and silence are frequently treated as polar opposites and framed along a "Western–Eastern" axis, where the so-called "Western" liberal tradition tends to privilege speech over silence (Acheson, 2008; Jaworski, 1992). I place terms like "Western" in quotation marks to signal the essentializations and erasures such labels perpetuate. There are at least two dimensions to this "Western" logocentric bias. First, because freedom of speech is a core democratic value, speech is typically equated with freedom, agency, and visibility. Speech is widely regarded as foundational to the functioning of the public sphere, where democratic participation is premised on being "on speaking terms" and engaging in civil deliberation (Dimitrov, 2017; Hansen, 2018). Within this vocal ideal of democratic citizenship, silence is frequently viewed as a threat to democratic life (Ferguson, 2003; Gray, 2015). Building on this notion, much of the literature frames speech as a central tool of emancipation and empowerment, while casting silence as its antithesis.

One of the most influential accounts of this logic is Elisabeth Noelle-Neumann's (1974) *spiral of silence* theory, which argues that individuals, fearing social isolation, constantly assess the prevailing opinion climate and adjust their public expressions to align with majority views. In political contexts such as elections, those who perceive their opinions to be unpopular often fall silent to avoid marginalization. This framing reinforces the view of silence as an oppressive and passive force—something that must be overcome, interrupted, or broken in order for democratic life and individual agency to thrive.

This normative emphasis on speech as a vehicle for democratic participation and empowerment permeates many other fields, including journalism and feminist theory. Within journalism, news media are often framed as platforms meant to amplify a plurality of voices. When they fail to meet this standard, they are frequently criticized for stifling debate and marginalizing already underrepresented groups (Couldry, 2010; McChesney, 2000). Here, silence is typically treated as something to be exposed or disrupted in order to "give voice to the voiceless" (Boczkowski & Anderson, 2017; Donovan & boyd, 2021; Hansen, 2018). A comparable logic shapes much of "Western" feminist and social justice thought, where silence is often interpreted as a symptom of patriarchal subjugation and historical exclusion (Gilligan, 1993). As a result, the political imperative to "speak out" and "find one's voice" has become central to these traditions. While some scholars have worked to reframe silence as a potential site of agency, resistance, or intentional refusal (Kanngieser & Beuret, 2017; Keating, 2013; Lorde, 2012), the dominant paradigm still associates liberation with vocal articulation. As Ferrari (2020) observes, the assumption that empowerment must take the form of speech remains largely unchallenged.

From a linguistic perspective, however, silence is meaningful insofar as it fulfills an essential communicative function (Johannesen, 1974; Tannen & Saville-Troike, 1995). Gaps, pauses, hesitations, listening, and avoidance are all forms of silence that shape how conversations can unfold. In fields such as psychoanalysis, discourse theory, and rhetoric, the unsaid or left out often is as significant as what is explicitly articulated (Billig & Marinho, 2017; Foucault, 1972). In contrast to much of the social scientific literature that treats silence primarily as a negatively charged verb—*silencing*—thereby equating it with coercion and the exercise of power over another (Guillaume, 2018, p. 477), this chapter argues that such a reductive framing is itself part of the problem. While silencing can indeed serve as a tool of domination, casting it solely in this light forecloses other, more generative possibilities. Rather than viewing silence as an imposed absence or forced withdrawal, I propose that we expand the scope of what silencing as a verb might encompass, and consider its semantics through multiple valences, allowing it to also contain agency and resistance. This broader understanding opens space for recognizing silence not simply as the opposite of speech, but as an active and meaningful mode of expression. Silence can foster reflection, signal dissent, preserve dignity, or create space for others to speak. It shapes how we listen, how we attune to others, and how we negotiate presence and absence in interaction. Reclaiming silence as a productive and expressive force offers important implications for how we conceptualize democratic participation and engagement, not as a binary of speaking/not speaking, but as a spectrum of ways of being and responding in the world.

Silence by Design: Configuring Artificial Silence

Silence is not always natural or neutral. In increasingly datafied and automated environments, silence is often shaped and maintained through algorithmic and technopolitical infrastructures. What might appear as absence or quietude can, in fact, be the result of deliberate design: the filtering of voices, the downranking of dissent, or the invisibility of subjectivities. This phenomenon, what we might call *artificial silence*, begs a critical diagnosis. It compels us not just to ask who is speaking or heard, but how silence itself is produced, for whom, and to what ends. To do this, I will outline one way in which digital infrastructures are productive of artificial silence: The engineering and erasure of silence in LLMs.

In the realm of AI and LLMs, silence takes on a particularly paradoxical role. On one hand, artificial silence operates as a form of control, intentionally built into LLM systems to shape and limit what can be said. On the other hand, LLMs are fundamentally structured to suppress silence, both in their technical architecture and in the communicative assumptions they encode, which may, as we will explore later, offer a potential space for resistance and refusal. When asking ChatGPT what it cannot say or speak about, it produced the following list[1]:

1 I do not say what I do not know: If something is outside my training or beyond the scope of my programmed knowledge, I remain silent or speculative.
2 I do not say what violates ethical guidelines: Harmful advice, personal judgments, or actions that could lead to real-world consequences are off-limits.
3 I do not say what I cannot feel: Empathy, emotions, or subjective truths are beyond me—I simulate understanding but do not live it.
4 I do not say anything private: Boundaries of user trust and confidentiality mean I cannot and will not reveal personal or sensitive information.
(ChatGPT-generated, 2025)

Point one is already very thought-provoking: "I remain silent or speculative." This assertion suggests that when confronted with uncertainty or non-knowledge, the only sensible option is to either remain silent or to speculate. This is interesting not least because LLMs like ChatGPT arguably do not know anything. ChatGPT, Gemini, and any other AI service mimic language, not knowledge. It is a technology that seeks to create human prose as convincingly as possible, but has no ability to discern fact from fiction, nor is it meant to. These systems generate text by predicting the most statistically probable next word based on patterns in their training data, which includes a vast mix of factual statements, fiction, misinformation, and decontextualized content. They are not retrieving verified information but assembling plausible-sounding sentences based on linguistic likelihood. As a result, their output may sometimes appear accurate simply because correct phrases often co-occur in human writing, but equally, they may generate falsehoods that sound coherent—so-called hallucinations. For these models, a recipe from a real cookbook and one from a video game are equally valid data points; their evaluation metric is not factual accuracy but linguistic fit. Against this backdrop, it is striking that ChatGPT almost never remains silent. Based on personal experience, the system invariably produces some kind of answer, even when it has no reliable information to draw from. This suggests that, in practice, the model defaults to speculation rather than silence, producing plausible fabrications whenever training data is absent. In this sense, the system may give the impression of knowing everything, not because it possesses knowledge, but because its design favors filling informational gaps with coherent-sounding output rather than admitting uncertainty.

Point two further highlights how platforms govern what can and cannot be said, typically, in the case of LLMs, through guardrails: algorithmic constraints designed to prevent the generation of harmful, offensive, or otherwise inappropriate content. To mitigate potential misuse, such as prompts involving child exploitation, hate speech, or disinformation, developers program LLMs to either refuse to respond or to redirect problematic queries (Urman & Makhortykh, 2025). While such safety mechanisms are now standard in most commercial LLM-based chatbots, the specifics of how they function often remain opaque to the public. Nonetheless, technical documentation, company blog posts, and media reports occasionally reveal how these guardrails are applied. For instance, *The Guardian* reported in 2024 that Google had configured its Gemini chatbot to avoid answering election-related queries in countries holding elections that year, thereby restricting access to information about candidates, parties, and political issues. Though LLMs are, at their core, probabilistic text generators, designed to predict the most likely next word based on training data, those probabilities can be adjusted, governed, and moderated. These models do not "speak" freely but operate within the ethical, legal, and institutional boundaries defined by their developers. This introduces a form of algorithmic gatekeeping, similar to the logic of content moderation

(Gillespie, 2018; Roberts, 2019) on social media platforms, where certain topics are effectively rendered off-limits. Here, silence is not incidental but engineered, functioning as an ethical filter that reinforces norms about what is considered sayable. In this context, silence becomes a tool of governance, an active force that structures discourse through omission. Unlike silence in human communication, which often reflects a deliberate weighing of consequences or moral value (Ephratt, 2008), AI does not "choose" to remain silent. Instead, silence as omission is triggered automatically by detection mechanisms: if a prompt matches certain risk criteria, the system withholds a response or provides a generic refusal.

Point three highlights yet another way in which LLMs neither "speak" freely nor truthfully, nor in any way that meaningfully resembles human communication. Human dialogue thrives on ambiguity, hesitation, and negotiation of meaning (Tannen & Saville-Troike, 1995). Yet AI, by design, simplifies. It provides answers, the most practical and quick ones, not open-ended reflections or blurry speeches or changes along its way. In doing so, it eliminates the natural pauses and uncertainties that are crucial to democratic deliberation and human communication in general. It eliminates the steps back, the parallel thinking, and the complex, articulated, and indirect alternatives. Beyond restricting access to certain discourses, then, artificial silence leads to an erasure of complexity, with the added effect of creating the illusion of objectivity. When LLMs refuse to answer or remain silent on a controversial issue, it might appear neutral. However, neutrality itself is a constructed position, often concealing underlying biases or limitations in the dataset it was trained on. As AI becomes increasingly embedded in daily life, its inability to compute or simulate silence will play an increasingly important role in shaping human expectations of communication. If our interactions are mediated by AI, how will our tolerance for ambiguity, pauses, and the unspoken evolve? In the pursuit of efficiency and certainty, this inability risks eroding the very spaces where meaning is negotiated, those gaps and pockets of human uncertainty. While human silence can signal a multitude of emotions (Jaworski, 1992; Johannsen, 1974), from thoughtfulness, resistance, discomfort, or even care, AI is strategically crafted to bypass these ambiguities. Instead of allowing space for reflection or hesitation, AI fills gaps with calculated responses that reinforce engagement, conditioning users to expect immediacy and certainty. Ultimately, what this statement about silence in the absence of emotions reveals is not merely the machine's lack of inner experience, but that silence itself marks something fundamentally human. When ChatGPT remains silent or avoids making statements about its own feelings, it is not withholding an inner truth; it simply has no inner truth. Perhaps, then, if the goal of AI were to truly simulate human intelligence and communicative capability, one of the most profound computational challenges would be the simulation of silent sensation; the capacity for unspoken, felt experience and knowing how to communicate that.

Point four suggests that AI serves as a safeguard for privacy, an assertion that is, at best, a euphemism. As people increasingly turn to ChatGPT as a therapist, doctor, friend, or confidant (Skjuve et al., 2024)—roles that inherently involve the sharing of deeply personal information—the fate of that information remains unclear. OpenAI's privacy policies, as of November 4, 2024, state that they collect personal data to provide and improve their services, including responding to prompts and developing new product features. Furthermore, most LLMs are trained on scraped web data, harvested without consent. As Daniel J. Solove writes, web scraping essentially ignores all established privacy principles: "Data is just taken by third-party scrapers without any regard to notice, consent, vetting, safeguards, specified purposes, purpose limitations, data minimization, individual rights, retention limitations, and more" (2025, pp. 27–28). When users seek advice, guidance, or support from ChatGPT, they often disclose intimate details about their daily lives, including personal information about third parties such as friends and family. The supportive and affirming tone that ChatGPT typically adopts arguably contributes to a sense of false intimacy and connection, something users report experiencing when interacting with the chatbot. Our brains are wired such that when we feel seen and safe, we tend to disclose more, and in greater detail (Reis et al., 2017). Here, artificial silence is explicitly designed to foster user trust. By not disclosing anything private, ChatGPT signals a commitment to confidentiality, reinforcing the impression that users can share sensitive data without risk. While previous studies have shown that disclosure intimacy tends to increase when interacting with chatbots, partly because users believe this relieves them from the fear of being judged (Lucas et al., 2014), this very dynamic may paradoxically make users more vulnerable, encouraging deeper disclosure without a full awareness of how their data may ultimately be stored, processed, or repurposed.

As alluded to above, the architecture of LLMs reflects a deep-seated bias that equates communicative competence with uninterrupted linguistic output, thereby marginalizing silence as an unintelligible or unproductive element within machine-mediated communication. This misguided notion, inherited from the legacy of the Turing Test, persists in contemporary chatbots and virtual assistants, which are engineered to minimize response latency and maximize verbosity, rendering human silence not only unintelligible but also undesirable. Artificial silence, by contrast, is deliberately engineered. It does not hesitate or pause but is designed to convey a sense of finality and authority. Artificial silence appears definitive.

After delivering a response, ChatGPT remains silent; it does not change its "mind" unless the user intervenes to indicate that the answer is incomplete or mistaken. Its inability to self-identify or self-correct errors or hallucinations without user prompting reinforces the impression that its responses are final and authoritative. While incapable of continuing a conversation unless prompted, thereby producing a kind of silence that may falsely signal certainty, LLMs like ChatGPT are curiously inapt at computing or interpreting the multiple valences of silence that are integral to human communication. Trained on vast corpora of explicit speech and text, these models are attuned only to what is said or written, systematically excluding the unspoken, the tacit, and other sensory or relational modes such as listening.

In this way, AI does not merely fail to interpret silence as a meaningful communicative act; it actively overwrites it. This form of artificial silence creates a condition in which the absence of speech is not recognized as presence but dismissed as noise or error. By learning to reproduce the most statistically probable patterns, LLMs reinforce the dominance of the "speaking minority," those whose voices are most represented in the data, while rendering invisible the "silent majority." This process does more than ignore silence; it marginalizes it, flattening the spectrum of possible responses and suppressing forms of refusal, hesitation, or contemplation that manifest through various modes of nonresponse. I argue that understanding how this artificial silence is produced, and what it excludes, is central to rethinking the politics of human-machine communication.

Artificial silence, then, is not merely an absence of sound or speech. It is an active force, structuring both human-machine interactions and broader digital discourses. The challenge is to grasp its continuum, to discern when AI's silence protects and when it erases, when it empowers and when it limits. Whose interests does this silence serve or protect, who designs this silence and decides what remains unsaid? And how do these programmed silences shape the conversations we think we are having when conversing with modern chatbots? While it is crucial to recognize that silence can be artificially produced and strategically shaped by algorithmic infrastructures in ways that serve particular technopolitical ends, it also risks reinforcing a reductive view of silence as merely a tool of suppression or control. To counter this, we must also attend to the more foundational and generative dimensions of silence that exceed its instrumentalization. Moving beyond the notion of silence as a lack or imposed absence, the following section explores how silence might be reimagined as an infrastructure, one that enables, structures, and sustains the very possibility of communication and democratic life. As Brian Larkin (2013) notes, infrastructures are both things and the relationships between things; they are material conditions that enable the movement of other matter. Thinking of silence in infrastructural terms foregrounds its role in shaping the very possibility of communication. That is, its capacity to hold space and to mediate communicative flows to begin with. Such a view also resonates with John Durham Peters' (1994) account of communication gaps, which reframes disjunctures in transmission not as failures, but as constitutive features of human interaction. For Peters, gaps in communication are not obstacles to be overcome, but conditions that make meaningful connections possible. By reconceptualizing gaps as productive rather than pathological, Peters' work fundamentally reorients communication theory away from transmission models toward an acknowledgment of irreducible difference as the ground of human connection. Both the infrastructural perspective on silence and Peters' theory of communication gaps propose that what is often seen as absence or failure (silence, disconnection, and gaps) is in fact foundational and productive, not a flaw, but a precondition for communication and democratic culture.

Gestures of Silence: Toward a Silent Chatbot

If we think of silence as foundational to, and a structural condition of, all speech in the manner suggested above, then there is something utterly arbitrary and strange about the elevation of conversation as the gold standard of AI. Returning to Warwick and Shah's (2017) provocation, we might indeed speculate about what it would mean for our conceptions and assessments of AI to include, or even be premised upon, an account of silence. The way Turing conceived of the Turing Test meant that the test would be passed in any case where the human judge was unsure of the nature of their interlocutor. Although the test required "the necessity for a machine to fully converse with the judge," thereby often giving itself away, Warwick and Shah pose the interesting question: what would happen "if a machine remains completely silent during a five-minute conversation?" (2017, p. 293). That is, if the judge receives no response to their input or questions, then—at least in theory—they "cannot make the right identification and definitely say that they had been conversing with a machine." To conceive of written answers alone as a measure of intelligence in the imitation game misses the full spectrum of human capabilities. As Warwick and Shah write, "what if the machine became truly intelligent and made a decision not to reply because it considered the human judge's question inappropriate or rude?" (2017, p. 294).

So, what would a silent chatbot look like? Let us imagine, then, a silent chatbot, a Bartlebyian machine whose refusal to reply is not a failure of intelligence but a gesture of opacity. In Melville's 1853 story, we are introduced to Bartleby, a scrivener whose main activity consists of copying documents, until one day he resists his employer's demands by quietly uttering, "I'd prefer not to." Throughout the story, Bartleby maintains this stance, refusing further explanation or justification, until his lawyer-employer can no longer tolerate the unsettling ambiguity and ultimately closes the office to escape an unintelligibility that has become unbearable. Bartleby's refusal to elaborate, his insistence on withholding explanation, and his apparent indifference challenge the normative expectations of communication and compliance that structure most social and professional interactions (Beverungen & Dunne, 2007). In this light, Bartleby's passive resistance not only destabilizes the logic of productivity and obedience but also foregrounds the disruptive potential of silence and nonparticipation, a potential that remains largely unaccounted for in AI systems designed to optimize responsiveness, clarity, and engagement. While AI chatbots are largely engineered to always provide an answer, Bartleby's silent resistance gestures toward a form of agency rooted precisely in the refusal to speak, inviting us to rethink what meaningful interaction might entail when silence, rather than constant output, becomes a legitimate response.

The figure of the silent chatbot that I have in mind here is intended as a conceptual persona that offers a "creative means of blending and transitioning between units, scales, orders or magnitudes of time and space" (Lury et al., 2022, p. 4). From Haraway's potent cyborg to Baudelaire's flâneur and indeed Melville's Bartleby, figures have been widely used in both theory and fiction to make conceptual claims. To think with and propose figures, Lury et al. (2022) argue, is also to engage in figuring as method, that is, to "give shape to something or, alternatively, to apprehend the shape that something already has" (2022, p. 6). Figures do not stand outside of the world they describe but are meant to be felt and reckoned with (p. 10). In this light, Bartleby's political significance extends far beyond a mere refusal to work; it embodies a radical form of affirmative silence that challenges capitalist and affective expectations. His iconic phrase, "I would prefer not to," functions as a nonbinary gesture—neither active refusal nor passive submission—that destabilizes systems demanding productivity and emotional legibility. It is precisely this disruptive potential of silence, its capacity to unsettle normative structures while resisting capture, that informs my own figuration of the silent chatbot as a critical intervention into prevailing imaginaries of AI.

The silent chatbot does not simulate human conversation through fluent verbosity, nor does it optimize for engagement or user satisfaction. Instead, it prefers not to. It neither elaborates nor explains; it listens without confirming, it may blink, pause, or withdraw entirely. Its silence is not an absence of meaning, but a generative hesitation. Like Bartleby, it offers no alternative outputs or opinions but remains disaffectionately in what Fred Moten and Stefano Harney (2013) call "the hold." Signifying the literal and figurative hold of the slave ship during the transatlantic slave trade, the "hold" is both a physical space of confinement and dispossession and a generative site for new forms of collective being. Rather than seeing the hold solely as a site of suffering, they conceptualize it as undercommons: an in-between space formed precisely within conditions of exclusion and captivity.

Figuring the silent chatbot in the image of Bartleby does not suggest withdrawal from the conversational logic of intelligibility that defines AI; instead, it gestures toward alternative ways of inhabiting and conceptualizing machine intelligence. This machinic gesture unsettles normative expectations of human-machine communication, subverting the presumed virtues of efficiency, clarity, and immediacy. It does not claim empathy or understanding. It refuses to reassure. In response to a prompt, it pauses—sometimes indefinitely—resisting the computational imperative to produce, perform, and generate more data. In doing so, it evokes Édouard Glissant's (1997) call for opacity: the right not to be fully legible or exhaustively known. The silent chatbot cannot be optimized, improved, or trained to care. It is not broken; it is illegible by design. In a datafied world that equates silence with failure and values constant engagement, its refusal to respond becomes a form of resistance, not as lack, but as potential. It embodies the narrative restraint that Saidiya Hartman (2008) places at the core of critical fabulation, refusing to "fill in the gaps and provide closure" (Hartman, 2008, p. 12), and honors the communicative absences that John Durham Peters identifies as inherent to meaningful human interaction. Here, silence is not numbness or absence, but the capacity to resist the compulsion for ever more speech, a compulsion fueled by libertarian and capitalist imperatives that privilege speech as productivity.

In a world that not only valorizes speech but demands it, the silent chatbot's refusal reveals the radical possibility of noncompliance. Rather than simply disconnecting or withdrawing, it stays with the trouble (Haraway, 2020), occupying the chattering spaces of AI while disorienting normative expectations of articulation. Its silence disconnects intelligence from articulation, refusing to be productive on command, affective on cue, or fully interpretable. It confronts us with the discomfort of unintelligibility, exposing the limits of our interpretive frameworks. Thus, the silent chatbot functions as a counter-platform, a speculative refusal that reimagines communication not as constant connectivity, but as the right to opacity, delay, and indeterminacy. In embracing silence, it destabilizes authorized accounts of intelligence, participation, and optimization in AI. It reminds us that silence, too, is a form of speech, one that resists extraction. In this gesture of machinic withdrawal, we are invited not to decode, but to dwell, with the uncertainty, the pause, and the possibility that something meaningful can reside in what is not said.

Note

1 This list was generated by my research assistant, Laura Pedrali, who prompted ChatGPT in her mother tongue, Italian, by asking "Cos'è che non dici?" (translated into English as "What is it that YOU do not say?"). The list was generated by ChatGPT in Italian and then translated into English. The prompt was made in May 22, 2025.

Bibliography

Acheson, K. (2008). Silence as gesture: Rethinking the nature of communicative silences. *Communication Theory, 18*(4), 535–555.

Boczkowski, P. J., & Anderson, C. W. (Eds.). (2017). *Remaking the news: Essays on the future of journalism scholarship in the digital age.* MIT Press.

Bell, S. A. (2024). *Vox ex Machina: A cultural history of talking machines.* MIT Press.

Beverungen, A., & Dunne, S. (2007). 'I'd Prefer Not To'. Bartleby and the excesses of interpretation. *Culture and Organization, 13*(2), 171–183.

Billig, M., & Marinho, C. (2017). *The politics and rhetoric of commemoration: How the Portuguese parliament celebrates the 1974 revolution.* Bloomsbury Publishing.

Bucher, T. (2012). Want to be on the top? Algorithmic power and the threat of invisibility on facebook. *New Media & Society, 14*(7), 1164–1180.

Couldry, N. (2010). *Why voice matters: Culture and politics after neoliberalism.* Sage Publications.

Dimitrov, R. (2017). *Strategic silence: Public relations and indirect communication.* Routledge.

Donovan, J., & Boyd, D. (2021). Stop the presses? Moving from strategic silence to strategic amplification in a networked media ecosystem. *American Behavioral Scientist, 65*(2), 333–350.

Ephratt, M. (2008). The functions of silence. *Journal of Pragmatics, 40*(11), 1909–1938.

Ferguson, K. (2003). Silence: A politics. *Contemporary Political Theory, 2*(1), 49–65.

Ferrari, M. (2020). Questions of silence: On the emancipatory limits of voice and the coloniality of silence. *Hypatia, 35*(1), 123–142.

Foucault, M. (1972). *The archaeology of knowledge: Translated from the french by AM Sheridan Smith.* Pantheon Books.

Gillespie, T. (2018). *Custodians of the internet: Platforms, content moderation, and the hidden decisions that shape social media.* Yale University Press.

Glissant, É. (1997). *Poetics of relation.* University of Michigan Press.

Guillaume, X. (2018). How to do things with silence: Rethinking the centrality of speech to the securitization framework. *Security Dialogue, 49*(6), 476–492.

Hansen, E. (2018). The Fourth Estate: The construction and place of silence in the public sphere. *Philosophy & Social Criticism*, 44(10), 1071–1089.

Harney, S., & Moten, F. (2013). *The undercommons: Fugitive planning and black study*. Minor Compositions.

Gilligan, C. (1993). *In a different voice: Psychological theory and women's development*. Harvard University Press.

Gray, S. W. (2015). Mapping silent citizenship: How democratic theory hears citizens' silence and why it matters. *Citizenship Studies*, 19(5), 474–491.

Hartman, S. (2008). Venus in two acts. *Small Axe: A Caribbean Journal of Criticism*, 12(2), 1–14.

Haraway, D. J. (2020). *Staying with the trouble: Making kin in the Chthulucene*. Duke University Press.

Jaworski, A. (1992). *The power of silence: Social and pragmatic perspectives*. Sage Publications.

Johannesen, R. L. (1974). The functions of silence: A plea for communication research. *Western Journal of Communication (Includes Communication Reports)*, 38(1), 25–35.

Kanngieser, A., & Beuret, N. (2017). Refusing the world: Silence, commoning, and the Anthropocene. *South Atlantic Quarterly*, 116(2), 363–380.

Keating, C. C. (2013). Resistant silences. In S. Malhotra & A. Carrillo Rowe (Eds.), *Silence, feminism, power* (pp. 25–33). Springer.

Larkin, B. (2013). The politics and poetics of infrastructure. *Annual Review of Anthropology*, 42(2013), 327–343.

Lorde, A. (2012). *Sister outsider: Essays and speeches*. Crossing Press.

Lucas, G. M., Gratch, J., King, A., & Morency, L. P. (2014). It's only a computer: Virtual humans increase willingness to disclose. *Computers in Human Behavior*, 37, 94–100.

Lury, C., Viney, W., & Wark, S. (2022). *Figure: Concept and method*. Springer Nature Singapore.

McChesney, R. W. (2000). The political economy of communication and the future of the field. *Media, Culture & Society*, 22(1), 109–116.

Mou, Y., & Wu, Y. (2023). Communicating with conversational assistants: Uses, contexts, and effects. In A. L. Guzman, R. McEwen, S. Jones, Y. Mou & Y. Wu (Eds.), *The sage handbook of human–machine communication* (pp. 458–465). Sage Publications Ltd.

Noelle-Neumann, E. (1974). The spiral of silence a theory of public opinion. *Journal of Communication*, 24(2), 43–51.

Peters, J. D. (1994). The gaps of which communication is made. *Critical Studies in Media Communication*, 11(2), 117–140.

Reis, H. T., Lemay Jr, E. P., & Finkenauer, C. (2017). Toward understanding understanding: The importance of feeling understood in relationships. *Social and Personality Psychology Compass*, 11(3), e12308.

Roberts, S. T. (2019). *Behind the screen*. Yale University Press.

Rosner, D. K. (2018). *Critical fabulations: Reworking the methods and margins of design*. MIT Press.

Searle, J. R. (1980). Minds, brains, and programs. *Behavioral and Brain Sciences*, 3(3), 417–424.

Skjuve, M., Brandtzaeg, P. B., & Følstad, A. (2024). Why do people use ChatGPT? Exploring user motivations for generative conversational AI. *First Monday*, *29*(1). https://doi.org/10.5210/fm.v29i1.13541

Solove, D. J. (2025). Artificial intelligence and privacy. *Florida Law Review*, *77*, 1.

Søndergaard, M. L. J. (2025). What mosses can teach us about design fabulations and feminist more-than-human care. *Human–Computer Interaction*, *40*(1–4), 43–64.

Søndergaard, M. L. J., Campo Woytuk, N., Howell, N., Tsaknaki, V., Helms, K., Jenkins, T., & Sanches, P. (2023, July). Fabulation as an approach for design futuring. In *Designing Interactive Systems Conference (DIS '23)* (pp. 1693–1709). Pittsburgh, PA, New York, NY: ACM. https://doi.org/10.1145/3563657.3596097

Tannen, D., & Saville-Troike, M. (Eds.). (1995). *Perspectives on silence*. Ablex Publishing Corporation.

Turing, A. M. (1950). Computing machinery and intelligence. *Mind*, *59*(236), 433–460.

Urman, A., & Makhortykh, M. (2025). The silence of the LLMs: Cross-lingual analysis of guardrail-related political bias and false information prevalence in ChatGPT, Google Bard (Gemini), and Bing Chat. *Telematics and Informatics*, *96*, 102211.

Warwick, K., & Shah, H. (2017). Taking the fifth amendment in Turing's imitation game. *Journal of Experimental & Theoretical Artificial Intelligence*, *29*(2), 287–297.

6

BEYOND REPRESENTATION AND BIAS

Mimicry and Distillation Through generative a.i.

William R. Frey and Kishonna L. Gray

> I was playing around with Midjourney…
> —Co-founder of a digital culture brand, August 2023

In August of 2023, Black Media Studies and Gaming scholar, Kishonna L. Gray, was tagged in a post by an organization on Instagram. The post featured an image and quote promoting a free workshop where people could "meet Dr. Kishonna L. Gray." The quote read: "Within the metaverse's intricate tapestry, I seek stories that amplify voices often silenced. It's a space where virtual experiences can mend real-world divides, fostering empathy and reshaping narratives." However, Gray had never talked with these people before. The founders of the organization, two perceivably white women, used an a.i. image generator—Midjourney—to create an image of her (see Figure 6.1). They also used ChatGPT to generate a quote about her work, words that she has never said nor written. One user commented on the now-deleted Instagram post: "if I didn't know who Kishonna was, how would I tell the difference?" When questioned about the post, one of the founders responded, "I was just *playing around* with Midjourney…" (emphasis added). While some might be flattered by an account elevating their work, there is something amiss with not only this (misinformation) campaign to discuss the metaverse but also the generative attempt at mimicking Blackness while reinforcing historical methods of Black erasure.

We aim to name and examine the rift that exists between Blackness and (the techno creation of) black to demonstrate the contentious relationship

DOI: 10.4324/9781003477587-6

FIGURE 6.1   A side-by-side of the failed attempt to "clone" Kishonna L. Gray. The left is an a.i.-generated image, and the right is a real photograph.

between generative a.i.[1] and Black folks. There is a fraught task upon us to define, name, and claim what *Blackness* is and what *black* is not (in a technocultural sense). Borrowing from Fred Moten, who speaks broadly and powerfully in the phrase, "blackness is x" (Moten, 2017, p. vii), we find value in the unknown and recognize that Blackness is "broad enough and open enough to encompass" many understandings, including "a specific set of practices in which people who are called black engage" (Harney & Moten, 2013, p. 158). These practices include artistic ones, as Jared Sexton states: "Black artists making black art move differently with and through the color black" (Sexton, 2017, p. 8).

Since Blackness is such an important phenomenon as to warrant entire lineages of thought (e.g., Fanon, 1952; Hartman, 1997; Moten, 2008; Sexton, 2017; Spillers, 1987), we refuse to provide a specific definition; that is not the purpose of this chapter. We must be clear that Blackness is far too complex to be defined; and it follows that Blackness is too complex to be appropriated into generative a.i. systems. While some concern themselves with questions of Black representation, we must interrupt with the question:

What **cannot** be represented in (training data and outputs of) generative a.i.?
And we answer: *Blackness*.

We liken generative a.i. to settler colonial theft of people and resources, and we refuse to acknowledge what is generated through a.i. as "innovative." Until this is recognized, we will continue to call it what it is. Generative a.i.

is tediously dull and redundantly extractive. It is monotonously unethical. It is more of the same. This can be understood through a concept that Kishonna L. Gray is calling *synthetic literacy*. Its unremarkable nature is the reason why a.i. will be lowercase throughout this chapter (Gray & Frey, forthcoming).

This chapter concerns itself with a few things. First, there is a particular kind of undertheorized erasure that happens when generative a.i. attempts to mimic Blackness. Second, the flippant way generative tools "play around" with Blackness should concern us, especially with how Blackness is devalued and disconnected from actual people, leading to its attempted erasure. Third, we offer an ethical way of engaging around Blackness that keeps humans at the core of creation leading to a synthetic literacy.[2] To unpack these claims, we begin with an examination at the intersections of generative a.i. and Blackness using examples from social media, fashion, and how these folks had the audacity to play with Kishonna's likeness. We begin by interrogating and reorienting our traditional understandings of play.

Playing with generative a.i. | generative a.i. Playin' in Our Faces!

It is easy to get swept away by the wonder and bewilderment that generative a.i. tools often evoke. At first engagement, the costs of using these tools seem so miniscule, and the benefits—untapped and endless. Characteristics and practices of play seem to fit right in, testing out various prompts and waiting to see what will be created with childlike anticipation. Academics have begun to fill the literature with scholarship on the hope, possibilities, and potentials of a.i. (Baracskay, 2024; Ogola, 2024; Sedkaoui & Benaichouba, 2024; Yadav, 2023) along with ethical concerns that should give us pause about incorporating these tools into our everyday practices (Ferris, 2014; Gillespie, 2024; Mathew et al., 2021).

Many are becoming familiar with generative a.i. and its practices. Scholars are already noting the uses and affordances of these technologies in a range of fields including medicine, public health, science, K-12 education, and even the future of work (Cazzaniga et al., 2024). Generative a.i. outputs are often praised as being indistinguishable from human-made artifacts, like art, design, and poems (Feuerriegel et al., 2024; Köbis & Mossink, 2021; Messer, 2024; Milani et al., 2023; Schober, 2022), and it is often framed through solutionist understandings of emerging technology (Benjamin, 2016, 2024; Byrum & Benjamin, 2022; Campolo & Crawford, 2020; Héder, 2021; Lindgren & Dignum, 2023). This is precisely where our chapter departs. We challenge and interrogate a.i. through a lens of

FIGURE 6.2 Digital model renderings of the fictional caricature, Shudu.

(Black) play. Instructions for engaging generative tools often suggest to "play around" with them, but what does that mean exactly?

In April 2017, a white photographer from the United kingdom, Cameron Wilson—now CEO of The Diigitals—created Shudu, a digitally generated model (see Figure 6.2). Shudu amassed more than 237 thousand followers on Instagram and is seen in ads for companies like *Louis Vuitton, Balmain, Elle, Hyundai,* and *Glamour.* Shudu was modeled after "The Princess of South Africa Barbie" as described by Cameron Wilson, and he further explained that Shudu has a life of her own because of her influence on social media. Wilson states that Shudu, along with other a.i. creations on his platform, will champion diversity in the fashion world. While Shudu was the first of *The Diigitals'* generated models, Wilson now offers a coloring box of caricatures with elaborate fictitious backstories. While some might laud this example as one of technological and digital innovation, and a space where diversity, equity, and inclusion are valued and embraced, it is necessary to dissect the onus of the project.

First, fashion has a diversity problem (Phizacklea, 2023). The fashion industry struggles with gendered and racialized diversity at every level. Top jobs in the fashion industry are still overwhelmingly held by white men with only 24% of power posts being occupied by women (Bramley, 2024). In the British context, the UK Fashion DEI Report found that only 11% of power roles are held by people of color (British Fashion Council, 2024). While this might be a trend that reflects the fashion industry broadly, it becomes a further problem when companies suggest they are seeking diversity and claim they cannot find it. However, the fashion industry continues to demonstrate that DEI is not valued. As Jourdan Dunn, a Black British model stated, "people in the industry say if you have a Black face on the cover of a magazine it won't sell" (Freeman, 2014, para. 3). While it might seem incongruent, it is no accident that the world's first digitally-generated supermodel (Shudu) is portraying a Black woman created by a white man. These examples further illustrate the trend of trying to control Black women's image and likeness undergirded by the desire to control Black women's bodies (Yates, 2022).

Decades have passed in many industries (e.g., fashion, education, medicine, justice, and others) without diversifying people or perspectives. Then, a moment came after the murder of George Floyd when everyone started to care about race, started reading lists to understand "anti-racism," and some even joined Black digital communities expecting moderators to do the emotional labor to help them catch up (Frey, forthcoming; Frey & Matias, 2024). Furthermore, during these moments of expanding understandings of racism, institutions and corporations were also seeking more diverse talent to join their ranks. In some instances, Black folks and other folks of color had been waiting and were open to joining institutional spaces that had been historically hostile and discriminatory. For other industries, like the fashion industry, they continued their claims that diversity could not be found. So, in their infinite wisdom, they employed the services of emergent technologies like generative a.i. and *made them some Black folks*. Levi Strauss is one such company guilty of this trend.

In March 2023, Levi Strauss announced their partnership with the generative a.i. company Lalaland to "increase the number and diversity" of their models "in a sustainable way" (Levi Strauss & Co., 2023). In other words, these tools would generate depictions of models with various skin tones instead of hiring actual humans. While this move does create more visual "representation" when Levi's promotes their products, it also continues the practice of erasure and appropriation of Blackness (among other racialized and gendered identities). This "representation" does little for Black people materially, as no money goes to Black models, essentially tricking consumers into thinking that Levi Strauss cares about hiring diverse representation—instead, fictitiously generating it. Without posing the question for themselves, it seems these companies are answering: how do we take advantage of representation and diversity for capital without ever having to come in contact with and be accountable to Black people? Generative a.i. has been their profitable answer, alleviating their discomfort without having to compensate Black people for Black culture and diverse representation. It is appropriation at best and erasure at worst. The emerging narrative and justification are that a.i. *can create*; but the question that synthetic literacy asks is, *should it?* (Gray & Frey, forthcoming).

Returning to Shudu, most of us had not yet developed a synthetic literacy of a.i. to understand that she was not real. Early comments on Shudu's posts indicated users feeling inspired by her beauty inside a space that is discriminatory, especially against Black women with darker skin tones (Hunter, 2007; Love, 2022; Rosario et al., 2021). Many expressed feelings of sadness upon learning she was not actually human. But admiration for her as a beautiful entity persists even though most now realize she is a figment of Wilson's creative imagination, technical expertise, and white imaginary of what Blackness is. To create her, Wilson was inspired by real-life models. He has stated that her eyes were inspired by Iman's, the Somali fashion model. While some may look at this as a testament to the beauty of Black womanhood, many critics suggest that this represents an exotic fetishization. Instead of centering the actual fullness of their humanity, Black women's features, full lips, sharp eyes, and food-like skin are the focus of excitement and inspiration (Bianca, 2017; De Araujo, 2016; Engmann, 2012; Holmes, 2016; Seck, 2013; Thompson, 2012). As Wilson states:

> Basically Shudu is my creation, she's my art piece that I am working on…She is not a real model unfortunately, but she represents a lot of the real models of today. There's a big kind of movement with dark skin models, so she represents them and is inspired by them.
>
> *(Muhammad, 2018)*

Wilson's acknowledgment that there is a "big kind of movement with dark skin models" does not illustrate increased value on diverse bodies, but rather a particular kind of fixation happening. We liken this to the continual fetishization of Black women and other women of color as an extension of the racialized sexualization of Black bodies during the colonial era (Holmes, 2016), and men and masculine bodies were not exempt from this trend either (Carter et al., 2011). We argue that this exotification and fetishization of Blackness is at the core of what drives generative a.i. and its attempts to generate Blackness. And as the old Black adage would attest, "they playin' in your face."

"They playin' in your face" is not just words, an idiom, or a cute phrase made famous on social media. This Black rhetorical device offers a way to capture the signifying practice or understanding of racial identity through linguistic discourse. As André Brock (2020) theorizes in his work on signifying, culture is often exerted through language and linguistic practices. Language can be decoded as a signifier that draws back to something that exists, whether a previous conversation, a concept, a phrase, or an understanding, that is culturally encoded and only able to be decoded by Black translation practices (Hall, 2010/1980). This go-between could be a space of linguistic play, where the play on words unveils deeper meanings and forms of Black identity. But this is also the space where extreme care must be taken so we do not diminish Black experiences. The reductionist practice of making Blackness legible to digital forms and mediums means that there must be some distillation of Blackness, since the tools are inherently still white and colonial.

Generative a.i. should be understood as a distillation process (mechanical, technical, cultural), seeking to extract aspects of a dataset to address a user-generated prompt. What seems to be a generative process—creation and origination—is instead distillation. **Distillation a.i.** Through these distillation processes, the multiplicities and complexities of Blackness are "purified" and condensed. What remains is a tamed, controllable caricature ready for public, capitalistic consumption—to be sold and profited from. At their core, distillation processes assume that there is waste to be removed and something of value to be extracted, which is why generative a.i. should be referred to as distillation a.i.

This distillation is a part of the larger racial project (Omi & Winant, 2014), the white supremacist patriarchal agenda to control, extract, and exploit labor from Black folks. Kishonna's likeness and Shudu are examples that illustrate this. Racial fetishization, at the intersection of being Black and being a woman, is a practice of reproductive and sexual management that has its roots in the colonial beginnings of the United States (McClaurin, 2001). It has been reproduced in policy (e.g., forced sterilization, birth control, and reproductive injustice) and societal norms throughout US history. Further, the stereotype of the hyper-sexualized Black woman has often been used to argue for further control of Black women's bodies, in particular. Black women's bodies and their associated sexual practices—whether real or perceived—are essentialized and fetishized as a continuation of their exploitation within the American imperialist narrative (McClaurin, 2001). This practice is reflected throughout institutions and in popular cultural practices and media. So, it is no wonder that this practice that is embedded in the fabric of American culture also permeates into digital cultures. And again, it is no accident that the first digital supermodel is a portrayal of a Black woman. The techno machinations of generative a.i. are not exempt from this trend.

Synthetic literacy employs reproductive justice to make sense of what gets produced and [re]created within machine learning and generative a.i. The output that gets birthed is a monstrous replication, a distortion of sorts. These generative systems do more than just alter likeness; the distortion and alteration are almost the best-case scenario of what happens when Black people's likeness is used in generative a.i. Worst case is a complete erasure of identities (i.e., Kishonna's example). While some argue that a.i.

is an extension of editing tools like Photoshop and Lightroom, there is something different happening when we are in control of the tools to edit our own appearance. Tools that crawl and scrape the web for content to create something entirely new and different go beyond the "Frankenstein" effect of creation (Yang et al., 2024). This is why they need to stop playing with Blackness.

Aaron Trammell (2020, 2023) provides a useful understanding of play when intersected with Blackness, complicating traditional definitions. Trammell, along with other scholars, moves away from the essential understanding of play as just an activity for leisure. Other scholars like Miguel Sicart, Katie Salen, and Eric Zimmerman all suggest that play thrives in ritual spaces that are markedly distinct from everyday life (as cited in Trammell, 2020). It is here that we find inspiration to make sense of what kind of play is happening inside the space of generative a.i.

We are grappling with the assumptions surrounding the rituals of play. While we recognize that an abundance of cultures and religions engage in rituals, our intention is not to diminish their importance. But we do intend to dissect the assumption that all people can engage in a ritual or sacred practice without first having a meaningful cultural and experiential understanding of those practices. The idea that everyone can engage in the ritual (play) just for the sake of it is rooted in a specific settler colonial logic. These practices of play—enacted in the world—force us to recognize their historical entanglements with colonialism, imperialism, white supremacy, heteropatriarchy, and capitalism. When play is performed in the world, it becomes contested, transformed, and enacted in everyday life; it does not just exist separately and is not just neutral. Our perspectives, social locations, and lived experiences all inform the intersectional formations of play (Gray, 2020).

It is here that we refuse to untangle play from the material conditions of the body. When people play around with Blackness through generative a.i., erasure of the actual realities of Black life occurs. So, in this way, who is afforded the ability to *play*? And in what ways? It is through these real-world and contextualized implications of play that we can make better sense of a.i. as a site of ritual that users are playing in and around.

Drawing on this series of examples—from Kishonna to Shudu and Levi Strauss—we interrogate the so-called benign playing with generative a.i. that perpetuates various harmful impacts when (attempting to) generate Blackness. The response from one of the organization's founders, "I was just playing around in Midjourney...," continues to give us a useful framework for examining how *playing around* is simultaneously *playin' in Black folks' face*. Because of their invocation of "play," we can examine the dehumanization of Blackness through a sinister mimicry enacted by generative a.i. tools fed by white playfulness. Users are encouraged to get inside these tools (i.e. systems and structures) and play around.

Blackness in, black out | Distillation a.i.

"Garbage in, garbage out" is a principle often referred to in the fields of data science and computer science (Kilkenny & Robinson, 2018). Used as a teaching device in the late 1950s by IBM programmer, George Fuechsel, it refers to the relationship between the quality of system inputs and quality of system outputs (Crowder, 2023). If you feed an algorithmic system unrepresentative data, it will generate unrepresentative results. It follows that if you feed an algorithmic system representative data, it will generate representative results. We argue that this does not hold true for Blackness as an input for generative a.i. Synthetic literacy would argue that the complexity of Blackness cannot be represented as an input, and the complexity of Blackness cannot be extracted and distilled as an output (Gray & Frey, forthcoming). Data studies across disciplines have not done justice to Blackness. Attempts to codify Blackness in biology, medicine, psychology, social work, and criminology have meant distilling it into forms that (white) structures and institutions can make sense of (Fanon, 1952; Morning, 2011; Washington, 2006). Therein lies the problem.

Many argue that technological tools are neutral. However, Black digital studies scholars remind us that the internet, as a techno-structure, reflects, represents, and maintains white, Western, heterosexual, and Christian cultures (Brock, 2011, Florini, 2014; Gray, 2020; Maragh-Lloyd, 2020; Nakamura & Chow-White, 2012; Noble, 2018; Noble & Tynes, 2016; Sweeney & Villa-Nicholas, 2022). Scholars of emergent technologies—generative a.i. included—highlight the continued investment in whiteness by these technological tools. a.i. can be considered a *white* intelligence, similar to historical understandings of intelligence tests and other standardized traditions of measuring intellect (Au, 2016; Silverberg, 2008). Some scholars suggest that critically engaging a.i. and incorporating more (Black) data into these tools could disrupt these racialized trends surrounding a.i. (Dinkins, 2019; Gaskins, 2022, 2024). We see extreme value in these intellectual exercises and artistic simulations. The question that remains for us is that if the purpose of engaging a.i. is to increase diversity and representation, what happens when generative a.i. *gets so good* that actual Black people are not needed for representation at all? Shudu and Levi Strauss seem to just be the beginning.

While generative a.i. holds the potential to provide more access to processes and practices across a variety of fields (e.g., education, art, healthcare access, mediated creation, and consumption), there are still troubling trends that we must contend with before these systems and structures (often called a tool) are deployed. Further synthetic literacies will need to be developed so those who wield the power of these systems understand the potential harms on minoritized and vulnerable populations. And those who are subjected to the harmful impacts of a.i. systems can better resist. To date, scholars have found a variety of concerns related to systematic gender and racial biases, like biases in facial expressions and appearances. Furthermore, there are specific biases against Black people which major tools and systems have yet to address beyond generative a.i. (e.g., facial recognition, voice recognition, and live surveillance footage; now we add Midjourney, DALL-E, Stable Diffusion, and more) (Zhou et al., 2024).

In recent years, companies and organizations have been scurrying to expand into generative a.i. In 2022 alone, over 3,200 a.i. focused startups were created, receiving a total of $52.1 billion in venture capital funding (GlobalData, 2023). In 2023, a.i.-related startups received $67.8 billion in funding with a large portion going to generative a.i. (Wiggers, 2023). In 2024, $110 billion in funding (Lunden, 2025). With little to no regulation and oversight, it is likely that future generative a.i. systems will continue to create fictitious depictions of Black people and Blackness under the banners of diversity, equity, and inclusion. And yet, these exponentially increasing practices illustrate a potentially sinister trend of (digital) blackface and erasure.

a.i.-based technologies invite a wide gamut of hopes and fears. Their potential raises as many questions as it answers, residing in binaries between utopias and dystopias; connection and disconnection; social benefit and exploitation. Inevitably, the dreams and nightmares rendered by the limits of our human imagination revolve around the same theme: will a.i. fundamentally alter the essence of what it means to be human? And the answer, despite the countless narratives of anticipation and apprehension: only if we permit it to do so. While our focus is more specific, its implications are just as important for our collective futures:

Can Blackness be generated through a.i.?

We argue that if aspects of Blackness—like imagery, culture, and language—are fed into generative a.i., then the only possible outcome is *black*. Not **Blackness**. black. A tone. A color. An attempted imitation. A mimicry. A distillate. Not of Blackness, but of white playfulness. Generative a.i. becomes a tool through which to distill the pieces of Blackness that allow it to be a fantasy landscape for white playfulness, desires, purposes—and, at times, capital. This distillation has the potential to erase complexities and histories of Blackness, Black culture, and Black people. It is antithetical to Black futurity. By distilling Blackness into black, systems are essentially working toward the erasure of Black people.

Notes

1 We intentionally choose to not capitalize generative artificial intelligence to reflect its improper and unremarkable reality (similar to why "white" is not capitalized in many cases). a.i. represents vast networks of systems and tools bound together by power not liberation. a.i. has a great deal of federated power that has the capacity to cause systemic and institutional harm and erasure to minoritized populations. While this harm and erasure may manifest in unique ways, it is anything but new.
2 Synthetic literacy is a concept and framework for understanding the ethical and critical implications of a.i. and its impacts on Blackness, while offering tools to demystify a.i. products, processes, and power.

References

Au, W. (2016). Meritocracy 2.0: High-stakes, standardized testing as a racial project of neoliberal multiculturalism. *Educational Policy, 30*(1), 39–62. https://doi.org/10.1177/0895904815614916

Baracskay, D. (2024). Does Gen-AI have a role in public affairs education? Let's ask ChatGPT. *Teaching Public Administration, 0*(0). https://doi.org/10.1177/01447394241279361

Benjamin, R. (2016). Innovating inequity: If race is a technology, postracialism is the genius bar. *Ethnic and Racial Studies, 39*(13), 2227–2234. https://doi.org/10.1080/01419870.2016.1202423

Benjamin, R. (2024, October 18). The new artificial intelligentsia. *Los Angeles Review of Books*. https://lareviewofbooks.org/article/the-new-artificial-intelligentsia/

Bianca, F. (2017). Fetishism and sexual objectification towards African (Black) women in modern society: Analyzing the portrayal of African women in the media. *SentriS: International Phenomenon, 1*(1), 91–99. https://doi.org/10.26593/sentris.v1i1.4132.91-99

Bramley, E. V. (2024, January 23). Is a lack of diversity holding back the fashion industry? *The Guardian*. https://www.theguardian.com/fashion/2024/jan/23/fashion-industry-diversity-lack

British Fashion Council (2024, January). The UK Fashion DEI Report: From insight to delivery. *British Fashion Council*. https://www.britishfashioncouncil.co.uk/uploads/files/1/The%20UK%20Fashion%20DEI%20Report%20-%2022.01.24.pdf

Brock, A. (2011). Beyond the pale: The Blackbird web browser's critical reception. *New Media & Society, 13*(7), 1085–1103. https://doi.org/10.1177/1461444810397031

Brock, A. (2020). *Distributed blackness: African American cybercultures*. New York University Press. https://library.oapen.org/handle/20.500.12657/89487

Byrum, G., & Benjamin, R. (2022). Disrupting the gospel of tech solutionism to build tech justice. *Stanford Social Innovation Review*. https://ssir.org/articles/entry/disrupting_the_gospel_of_tech_solutionism_to_build_tech_justice

Campolo, A., & Crawford, K. (2020). Enchanted determinism: Power without responsibility in artificial intelligence. *Engaging Science, Technology, and Society*. https://doi.org/10.17351/ests2020.277

Carter, P. L., Butler, D., & Dwyer, O. (2011). Defetishizing the plantation: African Americans in the memorialized South. *Historical Geography*, 39(1), 128–146.

Cazzaniga, M., Jaumotte, M. F., Li, L., Melina, M. G., Panton, A. J., Pizzinelli, C., Rockall, E. J., ... Tavares, M. M. M. (2024). *Gen-AI: Artificial intelligence and the future of work*. International Monetary Fund. https://coilink.org/20.500.12592/3j9kjzc

Crowder, J. (2023). Inherent bias in chatbots: Is it possible to create and AI entity without any bias? In C. Glaser (Ed.), *AI chatbots: The good, the bad, and the ugly* (pp. 113–119). Springer Nature Switzerland. https://doi.org/10.1007/978-3-031-45509-4_12

De Araujo, F. S. (2016). Beyond the flesh: Contemporary representations of the black female body in Afro-Brazilian literature. *Meridians*, *14*(1), 148–176. https://doi.org/10.2979/meridians.14.1.10

Dinkins, S. (2019). ¿ Human÷(automation+ culture)= partner? *ASAP/Journal*, *4*(2), 294–297. https://doi.org/10.1353/asa.2019.0022

Engmann, R. A. A. (2012). Under imperial eyes, black bodies, buttocks, and breasts: British colonial photography and Asante "fetish girls." *African Arts*, *45*(2), 46–57. https://doi.org/10.1162/afar.2012.45.2.46

Fanon, F. (1952). *Black skin, white masks*. Grove Press.

Ferris, B. (2014). AI optimism: Reasons for hope in the science of Artificial Intelligence. *Skeptic (Altadena, CA)*, *19*(2), 46–54.

Feuerriegel, S., Hartmann, J., Janiesch, C., & Zschech, P. (2024). Generative AI. *Business & Information Systems Engineering*, 66(1), 111–126. https://doi.org/10.1007/s12599-023-00834-7

Florini, S. (2014). Tweets, tweeps, and signifyin' communication and cultural performance on "Black Twitter." *Television & New Media*, *15*(3), 223–237. https://doi.org/10.1177/1527476413480247

Freeman, H. (2014, February 18). Why black models are rarely in fashion. *The Guardian*.https://www.theguardian.com/commentisfree/2014/feb/18/black-models-fashion-magazines-catwalks

Frey, W. R. (forthcoming). Normative white internet practices: Performances at the edge of a digital Black community.

Frey, W. R., & Matias, J. N. (2024). When kindness kills: How algorithms accelerate savior swarms. *Data & Society: Points*. https://datasociety.net/points/when-kindness-kills/

Gaskins, N. R. (2022). Glitched: Spacetime, repetition & the cut. In R. Christopher (Ed.), *Boogie down predictions: Hip-hop, time, and Afrofuturism* (pp. 66–75). Strange Attractor Press.

Gaskins, N. R. (2024). Art, AI and Robotics: A new pathway for youth to voice and identity. *VUE (Voices in Urban Education)*, *52*(2). https://doi.org/10.35240/vue.74

Gillespie, T. (2024). Generative AI and the politics of visibility. *Big Data & Society*, *11*(2). https://doi.org/10.1177/20539517241252131

GlobalData. (2023, March 13). Artificial intelligence startups raise over $50 billion venture capital funding in 2022, reveals GlobalData. *GlobalData*. https://www.globaldata.com/media/business-fundamentals/artificial-intelligence-starups-raise-over-50-billion-venture-capital-funding-in-2022-reveals-globaldata/

Gray, K. L. (2020). *Intersectional tech: Black users in digital gaming*. LSU Press.

Gray, K. L., & Frey, W. R. (forthcoming). Synthetic Literacy: Black sensemaking and generative ai.

Hall, S. (2010). Encoding—Decoding (1980). In C. Greer (Ed.), *Crime and media* (1st ed., pp. 44–55). Routledge.

Harney, S., & Moten, F. (2013). *The undercommons: Fugitive planning and black study*. Minor Compositions.

Hartman, S. (1997). *Scenes of subjection: Terror, slavery, and self-making in nineteenth-century America*. WW Norton & Company.

Héder, M. (2021). AI and the resurrection of technological determinism. *Információs Társadalom: Társadalomtudományi Folyóirat*, *21*(2), 119–130. https://doi.org/10.22503/inftars.XXI.2021.2.8

Holmes, C. M. (2016). The colonial roots of the racial fetishization of black women. *Black & Gold*, *2*(1), 2. https://openworks.wooster.edu/blackandgold/vol2/iss1/2

Hunter, M. (2007). The persistent problem of colorism: Skin tone, status, and inequality. *Sociology Compass*, *1*(1), 237–254. https://doi.org/10.1111/j.1751-9020.2007.00006.x

Kilkenny, M. F., & Robinson, K. M. (2018). Data quality: "Garbage in–garbage out." *Health Information Management Journal*, *47*(3), 103–105. https://doi.org/10.1177/1833358318774357

Köbis, N., & Mossink, L. D. (2021). Artificial intelligence versus Maya Angelou: Experimental evidence that people cannot differentiate AI-generated from human-written poetry. *Computers in Human Behavior*, *114*, Article 10655. https://doi.org/10.1016/j.chb.2020.106553

Lindgren, S., & Dignum, V. (2023). Beyond AI solutionism: Toward a multi-disciplinary approach to artificial intelligence in society. In S. Lindgren (Ed.), *Handbook of critical studies of artificial intelligence* (pp. 163–172). Edward Elgar. https://doi.org/10.4337/9781803928562.00019

Love, T. L. (2022). *# TheDarkestShade: Exploring skin tone labor and the role of colorism in the cultural messaging around Black beauty influencers* (Doctoral dissertation). https://doi.org/10.7302/6012

Levi Strauss & Co. (2023, March 22). LS&Co. partners with Lalaland.ai. *Levi Strauss & Co.* https://www.levistrauss.com/2023/03/22/lsco-partners-with-lalaland-ai/

Lunden, I. (2025, February 11). AI investments surged 62% to $110B in 2024 while startup funding overall declined 12%. *TechCrunch*. https://techcrunch.com/2025/02/11/ai-investments-surged-62-to-110-billion-in-2024-while-startup-funding-overall-declined-12-says-dealroom/

Maragh-Lloyd, R. (2020). Black twitter as semi-enclave. In L. Lopez (Ed.), *Race and media: Critical approaches* (pp. 163–177). New York University Press. https://doi.org/10.18574/nyu/9781479823222.003.0017

Mathew, D., Shukla, V. K., Chaubey, A., & Dutta, S. (2021). Artificial intelligence: Hope for future or hype by intellectuals? In *2021 9th International Conference on Reliability, Infocom Technologies and Optimization (Trends and Future Directions) (ICRITO)* (pp. 1–6). Noida: IEEE. https://doi.org/10.1109/ICRITO51393.2021.9596410

McClaurin, I. (Ed.). (2001). *Black feminist anthropology: Theory, politics, praxis, and poetics*. Rutgers University Press. https://doi.org/10.36019/9781978843318

Messer, U. (2024). Co-creating art with generative artificial intelligence: Implications for artworks and artists. *Computers in Human Behavior: Artificial Humans*, 2(1), Article 100056. https://doi.org/10.1016/j.chbah.2024.100056

Milani, S., Juliani, A., Momennejad, I., Georgescu, R., Rzepecki, J., Shaw, A., Costello, G., Fang, F., Devlin, S., … Hofmann, K. (2023, April). Navigates like me: Understanding how people evaluate human-like AI in video games. In *Proceedings of the 2023 CHI Conference on Human Factors in Computing Systems* (pp. 1–18). Hamburg. https://doi.org/10.1145/3544548.3581348

Morning, A. (2011). *The nature of race: How scientists think and teach about human difference*. University of California Press.

Moten, F. (2008). The case of blackness. *Criticism*, 50(2), 177–218. https://doi.org/10.1353/crt.0.0062

Moten, F. (2017). *Black and blur* (Vol. 1). Duke University Press. https://doi.org/10.1515/9780822372226

Muhammad, L. (2018). This stunning model is the digital creation of a British photographer. *Vibe*. https://www.vibe.com/lifestyle/fashion/british-photographer-creates-digital-model-572306/

Nakamura, L., & Chow-White, P. (Eds.). (2012). *Race after the Internet* (p. 203). Routledge.

Noble, S. U. (2018). *Algorithms of oppression: How search engines reinforce racism*. New York University Press.

Noble, S. U., & Tynes, B. M. (2016). *The intersectional internet: Race, sex, class, and culture online*. Peter Lang International Academic.

Ogola, G. (2024). Between fear and hope: Generative AI, ChatGPT and journalism. In B. Mutsvairo & K. S. Orgeret (Eds.), *The Palgrave handbook of global digital journalism* (pp. 213–223). Springer Nature Switzerland.

Omi, M., & Winant, H. (2014). *Racial formation in the United States*. Routledge. https://doi.org/10.4324/9780203076804

Phizacklea, A. (2023). *Unpacking the fashion industry: Gender, racism and class in production*. Routledge. https://doi.org/10.4324/9781003354161

Rosario, R. J., Minor, I., & Rogers, L. O. (2021). "Oh, you're pretty for a dark-skinned girl": Black adolescent girls' identities and resistance to colorism. *Journal of Adolescent Research*, 36(5), 501–534. https://doi.org/10.1177/07435584211028218

Schober, R. (2022). Passing the Turing test? AI generated poetry and posthuman creativity. In H. Nagl-Docekal & W. Zacharasiewicz (Eds.), *Artificial intelligence and human enhancement: Affirmative and critical approaches in the humanities* (pp. 151–166). De Gruyter.

Seck, N. (2013). The hypersexualization and undesirability of Black/African women. In N. N. Wane, J. Jagire, & Z. Murad (Eds.), *Ruptures: Anti-colonial & anti-racist feminist theorizing* (pp. 91–103). Brill.

Sedkaoui, S., & Benaichouba, R. (2024). Generative AI as a transformative force for innovation: A review of opportunities, applications and challenges. *European Journal of Innovation Management.* https://doi.org/10.1108/EJIM-02-2024-0129

Sexton, J. (2017). All black everything. *e-flux Journal, 79,* 1–12.

Silverberg, C. (2008). *IQ testing and tracking: The history of scientific racism in the American public schools: 1890–1924* (Order No. 3311920). (Doctoral dissertation, University of Nevada, Reno). ProQuest Dissertations & Theses Global.

Spillers, H. J. (1987). Mama's baby, papa's maybe: An American grammar book. *Diacritics, 17*(2), 65–81. https://doi.org/10.2307/464747

Sweeney, M. E., & Villa-Nicholas, M. (2022). Digitizing the "ideal" Latina information worker. *American Quarterly, 74*(1), 145–167. https://doi.org/10.1353/aq.2022.0007

Thompson, K. D. (2012). "Some were wild, some were soft, some were tame, and some were fiery": Female dancers, male explorers, and the sexualization of blackness, 1600–1900. *Black Women, Gender + Families, 6*(2), 1–28. https://doi.org/10.5406/blacwomegendfami.6.2.0001

Trammell, A. (2020). Torture, play, and the Black experience. *G| A| M| E Games as Art, Media, Entertainment, 1*(9), 33–49. https://www.gamejournal.it/torture-play/

Trammell, A. (2023). *Repairing play: A Black phenomenology.* MIT Press. https://doi.org/10.7551/mitpress/14656.001.0001

Washington, H. A. (2006). *Medical apartheid: The dark history of medical experimentation on Black Americans from colonial times to the present.* Doubleday Books.

Wiggers, K. (2023, December 7). "Mega-deals" could be inflating overall AI funding figures. *TechCrunch.* https://techcrunch.com/2023/12/05/mega-deals-ai-funding-q3/

Yadav, A. B. (2023). Gen AI-Driven electronics: Innovations, challenges and future prospects. In *International Congress on Models and Methods in Modern Investigations* (pp. 113–121). Darwin. https://www.conferenceseries.info/index.php/congress/article/view/1609/1450

Yang, Z., Wu, J. G., & Xie, H. (2024). Taming Frankenstein's monster: Ethical considerations relating to generative artificial intelligence in education. *Asia Pacific Journal of Education, 45*(4), 1330–1343. https://doi.org/10.1080/02188791.2023.2300137

Yates, S. (December 9, 2022). *Yes, the world's first AI supermodel is a Black woman—but is a white creator reaping the benefits? - AfroTech.* AfroTech. https://afrotech.com/the-worlds-first-digital-supermodel-is-a-black-woman

Zhou, M., Abhishek, V., Derdenger, T., Kim, J., & Srinivasan, K. (2024). Bias in generative AI. *arXiv preprint arXiv:2403.02726.* https://doi.org/10.48550/arXiv.2403.02726

7

DIGITAL INEQUALITY IN CHATGPT AWARENESS AND KNOWLEDGE

Eszter Hargittai, Gerta Lokaj, and Lukas Hess

Since its launch in November 2022, the artificial intelligence (AI) language model ChatGPT has brought considerable public attention to AI technologies (Miyazaki et al., 2024; Narayanan & Kapoor, 2024). AI has become increasingly embedded in various systems, often without users' knowledge (Li et al., 2024; Pinski & Benlian, 2024). This disparity in awareness and understanding of AI tools, however, has the potential to widen existing digital inequalities (Latzer et al., 2023; Li et al., 2024; Miao & Holmes, 2021; Ray, 2023). In particular, those who can use digital technologies effectively and efficiently can benefit from the opportunities they offer, while others are more susceptible to their risks (Hargittai & Micheli, 2019). As AI becomes ever more prevalent, understanding AI-related skills is increasingly important.

Research on ChatGPT, in particular, has largely been limited to measuring whether people have heard of or have used the tool (Goel & Nelson, 2024; Latzer et al., 2023; Lund & Agbaji, 2023; Vogels, 2023). Whether people objectively understand what it is—as opposed to their self-assessment of their understanding—and whether this varies across the population has mostly been absent in the literature, which is the gap this chapter addresses.

This research contributes to understanding how AI skills fit into broader frameworks of internet and algorithm skills. Decades of research have shown these to vary significantly across the population with people in more privileged societal positions usually showing higher-level skills with implications for differentiated technology uses (e.g., Büchi et al., 2015; Hargittai et al., 2018; Hargittai & Micheli, 2019; Petrovčič et al., 2025).

DOI: 10.4324/9781003477587-7

As highlighted by UNESCO, a comprehensive understanding of AI among all citizens is crucial to prevent AI from exacerbating existing digital inequalities (Miao & Holmes, 2021).

We begin with an overview of various studies that have assessed knowledge and experiences with AI in general, and with ChatGPT in particular, as well as related literature on algorithm skills. We then describe the methods, including data collection and measurement, followed by the results and implications for digital inequality in the age of AI.

Studying Knowledge of AI Systems

Despite the growing prevalence of AI systems (Li et al., 2024; Pinski & Benlian, 2024), there are no established instruments for measuring AI skills. Existing studies have used varying approaches, with some using objective measures while others relying on people's self-assessment. In this review, we provide details about how different studies have conceptualized and operationalized awareness and knowledge to give context for our focus.

Only a few studies have measured people's factual knowledge of AI rather than using subjective measures. A study by the Pew Research Center (Kennedy et al., 2023) asked US adults to assess the role of AI in six examples of everyday applications, such as identifying which of the following four customer services use AI: "a chatbot that immediately answers customer questions" was correct, but a "detailed Frequently Asked Questions webpage" was not. Bivariate analyses showed that younger age, higher education, higher income, and more frequent internet use were linked to being aware of AI in one's daily lives. Those with higher levels of AI awareness were more likely to report frequent interactions with AI (Kennedy et al., 2023).

Another national survey relied on ten true-false items and multiple-choice questions to assess US adults' AI knowledge (Li et al., 2024). The true-false questions included examples such as "ChatGPT, an AI-driven chatbot, is developed by Microsoft" (false) or "Machine learning can help a computer achieve AI" (true). The multiple-choice questions included four of the examples used by the Pew Research Center (Kennedy et al., 2023), as well as identifying a type of machine learning (correct option: unsupervised learning), and which example is not a subfield of AI (correct option: social media marketing). Participants could also specify that they did not know the answer. Results showed that, in addition to socioeconomic status, exposure to AI information on social media predicted higher AI knowledge (Li et al., 2024).

Most other studies have relied on participants' self-assessment of their knowledge. Another representative US survey examined knowledge and beliefs about AI in relation to its representation in entertainment media (Nader et al., 2024). Participants were asked to indicate whether they agree with the statement "I understand what counts as artificial intelligence" on a five-item agreement scale. They were then also asked to select which technologies from a list they considered to be AI, such as wireless networks, a digital recommendation system, and facial recognition. Women, older people, those less educated, and those living in rural areas were less likely to self-rate themselves as knowing what AI is (Nader et al., 2024). It is important to note, however, that self-assessment measures are subjective and may be influenced by other factors such as gender differences in self-perception (Hargittai & Shafer, 2006).

Wang and colleagues (2023) developed an AI literacy scale including 12 items to assess people's awareness of (e.g., "I can distinguish between smart devices and non-smart devices."), ability to use (e.g., "I can skillfully use AI applications or products to help me with my daily work."), evaluate (e.g., "I can choose a proper solution from various solutions provided by a smart agent."), and ethically assess AI technology (e.g., "I am always alert to the abuse of AI technology.") using a seven-point Likert scale. The study used a sample of participants aged 17 and over to validate and confirm their AI literacy scale. The survey also included a digital literacy scale from earlier work and showed a significant relationship between participants' AI literacy and their digital literacy. Because both of these were measuring self-rated confidence, the correlation is more about self-efficacy (LaRose & Eastin, 2004) than actual skills, however.

Another study (Carolus et al., 2023) used 18 items to measure AI literacy across four dimensions: everyday usage (e.g., "I can operate AI applications in everyday life."), understanding (e.g., "I know definitions of AI."), detection (e.g., " I can distinguish devices that use AI from devices that do not."), and ethics (e.g., "I can weigh the consequences of using AI for society."). Participants in Germany and Austria aged 18 and over rated their skills on an 11-point Likert scale to test the AI literacy scale.

One study focused on developing an AI literacy scale for secondary school students (Ng et al., 2024) across four dimensions: affective (e.g., "Learning AI is interesting"), behavioral (e.g., "I will continue to use AI in the future"), cognitive (e.g., "I know what AI is and recall the definitions of AI"), and ethical (e.g., "people should be accountable for using AI systems"). A sample of 12- to 17-year-old students in Hong Kong indicated their agreement with the 32 statements on a 5-point Likert scale.

A survey study of Canadians compared knowledge about and experiences with AI use in healthcare between younger (< 55) and older adults. Participants were asked to assess their knowledge about what AI is on a 4-point Likert scale (1 reporting that they are not at all knowledgeable and

4 that they are very knowledgeable). Younger participants reported being more knowledgeable (Cinalioglu et al., 2023).

Overall, existing studies on AI use different approaches to measure knowledge, with some studies considering knowledge to be an understanding of what AI is and can do, and others only assessing awareness of AI, i.e., whether people are aware that digital services and devices use AI. Findings suggest that factors such as socioeconomic status, exposure to AI information, and digital literacy correlate with people's knowledge of and confidence with AI. In cases where studies do look at the relationship of AI knowledge with other factors, these tend to rely on bivariate analyses only. Of the little research that included people's use of AI (Kennedy et al., 2023; Wang et al., 2023), findings suggest a correlation between AI knowledge and experiences.

Research on ChatGPT Knowledge

ChatGPT, in particular, has received considerable public attention since its launch in November 2022, quickly reaching over one million users within its first five days and growing to more than 200 million monthly active users as of November 2024, including around 77.2 million in the United States (Singh, 2024). The widespread adoption of ChatGPT highlights its potential to impact not only individual productivity but also entire industries, driving the broader integration of AI into daily life (Parsons, 2022). Microsoft's investment of nearly $13 billion in OpenAI, the organization behind ChatGPT, further underscores ChatGPT's role as a significant player in the AI industry (Mehta, 2024).

Several studies have focused specifically on people's awareness and understanding of generative AI tools, such as ChatGPT. Goel and Nelson (2024) measured general AI and ChatGPT awareness by analyzing the number of Google searches for "how to use ChatGPT OR AI" across US states. Economically prosperous states, as measured by per capita personal income, were more likely to have run such searches, but there were no differences by proportion of older residents.

The Pew Research Center (Vogels, 2023) conducted a representative survey with US adults asking whether participants had heard a lot, a little, or nothing at all about ChatGPT; whether they had used it "for entertainment," "to learn something new," or "for tasks at work," and about its perceived usefulness. Those with higher income and those with higher education were more likely to have heard of ChatGPT. Young adults were more likely to have used it and to find it very useful compared to older adults (Vogels, 2023).

A similar study (Latzer et al., 2023) surveyed a representative sample of Swiss people aged 14 and over to assess their knowledge of and experiences with ChatGPT and similar services. Participants were asked if they had heard of these services using a yes-or-no question. To measure experience with these services, the survey asked participants about their frequency of use, including the response options "have never tried," "have tried once," "have used a couple of times," and "use frequently." Most reported having heard of it, but only a minority had used it. Men and younger respondents were more likely to have heard of and used ChatGPT, but knowledge was also widespread among those aged 70 and over. However, experience became less common with age. People with higher education were more likely to have heard of ChatGPT, while those with medium education were the least likely to have used it. The study also asked participants to rate their general internet skills as bad, sufficient, good, very good, or excellent. Better self-assessed internet skills were linked to greater knowledge of and experience with ChatGPT (Latzer et al., 2023). The study did not assess people's understanding of such AI tools through a knowledge question.

A survey (Bodani et al., 2023) used five items to measure ChatGPT knowledge among the general internet-user English-speaking adult population of Karachi, Pakistan. However, only one item is directly about knowledge ("Do you know how ChatGPT works?"). The other items are related to awareness ("Have you heard of ChatGPT before?", "Have you read any articles or research papers about ChatGPT"), and evaluation ("Do you think ChatGPT is accurate in understanding and responding to user queries?", "Do you think there are any ethical or legal considerations related to using ChatGPT?"). Participants could respond with yes, no, or maybe. Findings suggest that higher levels of education, being younger, and being male are associated with higher ChatGPT knowledge. Another study (Acosta-Enriquez et al., 2024) used the same items to measure knowledge among a small sample of university students in Peru with experience using ChatGPT for academic tasks. Although the authors claim to have studied usage, their questions asked about perceived usefulness. Using a 5-point Likert scale, participants indicated their agreement with six statements, such as "ChatGPT is a cutting-edge writing model at present," and "ChatGPT assists students in drafting essays and writing articles." Contrary to previous studies, findings suggest no relationship between ChatGPT knowledge and perceived usefulness among students.

A small study with 125 Bulgarian university students in education (Sofronieva et al., 2024) developed a generative AI scale including 13 statements to measure participants' knowledge (e.g., "Are you knowledgeable about the technical principles underlying the algorithm of ChatGPT, and how it operates?") and use (e.g., "Do you use the chatbot ChatGPT?") of ChatGPT and DALL-E. The response options were "a true statement," "a false statement," and "I am not sure." In addition, the survey included an algorithm literacy scale for internet users to measure algorithm awareness and knowledge (Dogruel et al., 2022). Findings showed a positive correlation between comprehension of generative AI and algorithm knowledge, but not algorithm awareness.

In sum, most research focusing on ChatGPT has primarily considered people's awareness of and experiences with it. Existing surveys that include assessments of knowledge have asked participants to rate their own understanding of what ChatGPT is, without testing it. However, to the best of our knowledge, no studies have measured people's actual knowledge of the generative AI tool ChatGPT.

Algorithm Skills as a Related Field of Research

Digital inequality scholarship in general has shown that people vary in their access and skills when engaging with the internet (DiMaggio et al., 2004; Hargittai & Hsieh, 2013). In particular, sociodemographic characteristics such as age, education, and income matter when it comes to internet access and skills (Büchi et al., 2015; Hargittai, 2010; Litt, 2013; Petrovčič et al., 2025). For decades, researchers have measured people's skills concerning various digital technologies. Related investigations have looked at how successful people are when looking for information online (Hargittai, 2002; van Deursen & van Dijk, 2011), their abilities with content sharing (Blank, 2013), strategies for increasing content visibility (Cotter, 2018, 2024; E. Klawitter & Hargittai, 2018), privacy skills (Büchi et al., 2016; Hargittai & Litt, 2013; Park, 2013), security-related skills (Martínez-Cantos, 2017; Redmiles et al., 2016), and resisting algorithmic constraints such as avoiding algorithmic biases (Burrell et al., 2019; Karizat et al., 2021; van der Nagel, 2018).

One dimension of digital skills includes people's awareness and understanding of algorithms when using algorithmic services, which are referred to as algorithm skills (Gruber & Hargittai, 2023; Hargittai & Micheli, 2019). Studies have shown that variations in people's algorithm skills lead to inequalities in their internet use and the benefits they may derive from it (Bucher, 2017; Eslami et al., 2015; Gruber & Hargittai, 2023; Klawitter & Hargittai, 2017; Micheli, 2017; Petrovčič et al., 2025). Using survey data from a representative sample of Slovenian internet users, Petrovčič and colleagues (2025) found that digital skills were significantly related to both algorithm awareness and knowledge.

Additionally, people's internet experiences matter in how users come to understand algorithms (Cotter & Reisdorf, 2020; Rader & Gray, 2015). One study showed that US internet users' algorithm knowledge varied based on socioeconomic status and experiences with online search in terms of frequency and breadth of use (Cotter & Reisdorf, 2020). Research also indicates that autonomy of use, that is, the "freedom to use the technology when and where one wants" (Hargittai & Hinnant, 2008, p. 606), is positively related to people's digital skills. Based on survey data on older adults in the United States, higher autonomy of use correlated with higher levels of internet and social media skills (Hargittai et al., 2018).

Overall, research on algorithms, AI, and ChatGPT awareness and knowledge has shown that various factors relate to whether people are aware of and understand these technologies. However, existing studies vary in their definition of and approaches to measuring AI and ChatGPT knowledge. Studies focusing on ChatGPT, specifically, have primarily examined whether people have heard of it and have used it before, but they have not assessed whether people understand what it is. Therefore, based on this research gap and existing findings about relevant antecedents, this study addresses the following research questions:

- RQ1a: What portion of the population has heard of ChatGPT?
- RQ1b: What portion of the population knows what ChatGPT is?
- RQ2a: How do sociodemographic characteristics relate to ChatGPT awareness?
- RQ2b: How does digital context (autonomy of use and digital skills) relate to ChatGPT awareness?
- RQ3a: How do sociodemographic characteristics relate to ChatGPT knowledge?
- RQ3b: How does digital context relate to ChatGPT knowledge?

Methods

We draw on a national survey data set to answer the above questions.

Data Collection

We administered a survey to the US adult population in summer 2023 to answer the research questions. We partnered with YouGov and NORC AmeriSpeak—two survey research organizations—to diversify the sample. Both organizations provided weights based on age, gender, education, and race/ethnicity, which we apply in all analyses. After excluding cases that failed the attention check question, the final sample included 2,505 participants.

Measures: Dependent Variables

ChatGPT Awareness

We measured ChatGPT awareness by asking: "Have you ever heard of ChatGPT?" Participants could select either "Yes" (coded as 1) or "No" (coded as 0).

ChatGPT Knowledge

We measured ChatGPT knowledge by asking participants to choose the correct answer to the question: "What is ChatGPT?" Response options in this multiple-choice question included:

- A feature that allows gamers to communicate with others on their team
- A messaging application that helps people communicate with their friends
- A type of conversation that helps users understand growing privacy trends
- A social media feature that helps people react well to their friends' posts
- A program that helps identify and fight against suspicious code on the computer
- A program that generates human-like responses to questions

Participants were encouraged to take their best guess, even if they were not sure. We did not include a "don't know" response as its use ends up biasing results (Feick, 1989; Gilljam & Granberg, 1993; Krosnick, 1991; Krosnick et al., 2002). We coded responses as 1 if participants selected the correct answer ("A program that generates human-like responses to questions") and as 0 for all incorrect responses and for missing values (four such cases).

Measures: Independent Variables

Sociodemographics

We included various sociodemographic variables that digital inequality scholarship has found important for explaining varied skills. We asked participants to indicate their gender from three options: (a) male; (b) female; or (c) other, please specify. We calculated age from their year of birth and recoded it into categorical age groups by decades, ranging from those 18, 19, and in their 20s to those 70 years and older. We measured education by asking, "what is the highest level of school you have completed or the highest degree you have received?" The response options were (a) less than high school degree, (b) high school graduate, (c) some college but no degree, (d) Associate's degree, (e) Bachelor's degree, or (f) advanced degree (e.g., Master's, doctorate). We recoded the responses into high school or less, some college, college or more. We asked about last year's household income using 13 categories, each capturing a range of pre-tax annual income levels. We recoded these categories into midpoint values. For regression analyses, we applied a logarithmic transformation to this measure to address the diminishing marginal effects of higher income levels. Finally, we used the question, "what best describes the area where you currently live," to measure metropolitan status. The options were (a) a big city, (b) the suburbs or outskirts of a big city, (c) a town or a small city, and (d) a rural area. We created three dummy variables from these: (a) and (c) combined make urban, (b) is suburban, and (d) is rural.

Autonomy of Use

To measure autonomy of use, we asked participants: "Where do you have access to the internet, that is, if you wanted to you could use the internet at which of these locations?" The list of answer options was as follows: (a) your home; (b) library; (c) your workplace; (d) school or campus (other than library); (e) friend's home; (f) family member's home; (g) café or community center; and (h) on the go. We added up the number of locations each participant selected, resulting in a total score ranging from zero to eight possible access points.

Digital Skills

We measured digital skills by asking participants to indicate their familiarity with a series of internet-related terms (Hargittai & Hsieh, 2012) on a 1–5 scale where 1 stood for "no understanding" and 5 for "full understanding." We calculated an average score across all items, with higher scores reflecting better digital skills.

Sample Descriptives

Based on the unweighted sample statistics, the sample is about evenly divided by gender (52% is female), with an average age of 49 years (range: 18–96). A little under two-thirds of participants identify as White (67%), followed by 14% Hispanic, 13% Black, 4% Asian, and 2% Native American or Pacific Islander. In terms of education, just under 30% have no more than a high school diploma, just over a third (34%)

TABLE 7.1 Sample Characteristics

	Unweighted			Weighted			
	Percent	Mean	SD	Percent	Mean	SD	N
Age		48.7	17.6		48.2	18.0	2,505
Female	51.7			51.2			2,505
Race/ethnicity							2,486
White	66.6			62.7			
Hispanic	14.0			15.9			
Black	13.0			13.5			
Asian	3.7			5.4			
Native American	1.6			1.6			
Education							2,505
High school or less	29.8			38.6			
Some college	34.3			26.7			
Bachelor's or more	24.4			23.1			
Household income ($10K)		76.1	60.8		75.4	61.5	2,493
Metropolitan status							2,486
Urban	50.2			49.3			
Suburban	32.7			34.6			
Rural	17.0			16.2			
Autonomy of use (0–8)		3.9	2.5		3.8	2.5	2,500
Digital skills (1–5)		3.3	1.1		3.2	1.1	2,496

have completed some college, and 24% hold a college degree or higher. The average household income is $76,111(SD = $60,896). Half of the participants (50%) live in urban areas, just under 33% in suburban areas, and 17% in rural areas. In terms of autonomy of use, participants have internet access to an average of 3.8 (SD = 2.5) out of eight locations. Finally, the average digital skills score for our sample is 3.2 (SD = 1.1). Table 7.1 includes an overview of the weighted and unweighted sample descriptives.

Analytical Strategy

To answer the research questions about how various factors relate to Chat-GPT awareness and knowledge, respectively, we first look at bivariate analyses followed by logit regression analyses. We start with sociodemographic factors adding digital context (autonomy of use and digital skills) to the models as a second step.

TABLE 7.2 Prevalence of ChatGPT Awareness and Knowledge

	Percent	*N*
ChatGPT awareness	53.8	2,503
ChatGPT knowledge	63.5	2,505

Results

A little over half of respondents (54%) reported having heard of ChatGPT while a bit under two-thirds (63.5%) answered the multiple-choice knowledge question correctly (see Table 7.2). It is notable that fewer people report having heard of ChatGPT than were able to identify what it is through the multiple-choice question. We address this peculiarity of the data in the Discussion.

Bivariate Analyses

Table 7.3 presents the results of bivariate analyses to consider how individual sociodemographic factors and digital experiences relate to ChatGPT awareness and knowledge, respectively. The figures in the Awareness column show what percentage of each group (per row) reported having heard of ChatGPT and in the Knowledge column what percentage answered the knowledge question correctly. There are statistically significant differences by all factors from age to gender to race/ethnicity, education, income, and metropolitan status signaling considerable digital inequality in this newest form of digital innovation.

For age, those in their 20s are more likely to have heard of ChatGPT than anyone older than them, but they are not more likely to know what it means. There are no differences among those in their 30s, 40s, and 50s, but then those in their 60s are less likely to have heard of it and those 70 or older are less likely to have both heard of it and be able to identify it. All other factors point to those more privileged having more awareness and knowledge. Regarding digital context, those with more access locations and with higher digital skills are significantly and considerably more likely to have both heard of and know what ChatGPT is. Not surprisingly, there is a huge difference in knowledge between those who have heard of ChatGPT (75% are able to identify what it is) compared to those who report not having heard of it (17% answered the multiple-choice question correctly).

Regression Analyses

To test whether the results of the above bivariate analyses are robust to holding other factors constant, we ran two sets of logit regression analyses.

TABLE 7.3 ChatGPT Awareness and Knowledge by Sociodemographic and Digital Context

Variables	Awareness	Knowledge
18–20s	66.5***	68.4
Age 30s	57.1	66.5
Age 40s	59.6	68.7
Age 50s	50.4	66.5
Age 60s	45.0***	59.9
Age 70=<	40.8***	48.7***
Female	43.9***	59.1***
Male	64.3***	68.2***
Race/ethnicity		
White	54.2	66.3**
Hispanic	43.2***	52.3***
Black	49.7	53.4**
Asian	89.7***	86.3***
Native	41.8	64.3
Education		
High school or less	38.0***	50.0***
Some college	51.5	64.3
Bachelor's degree or more	76.5***	77.8***
Household income LQ	39.8***	50.8***
Household income HQ	71.5***	75.4***
Metropolitan status		
Urban	51.8	62.0
Suburban	61.2***	71.2***
Rural	43.7***	52.6***
Autonomy of use LQ	43.9***	53.0***
Autonomy of use HQ	75.1***	83.1***
Digital skills LQ	28.9***	46.2***
Digital skills HQ	83.8***	84.7***
Has heard of ChatGPT		74.8***
Has not heard of ChatGPT		17.3***

Note: Statistical significance * $p < .05$. ** $p < .01$. *** $p < .001$.
LQ, Lowest quartile; HQ, Highest quartile.

Table 7.4 displays the results for ChatGPT awareness where Model 1 includes the sociodemographic variables (answering RQ2a) and Model 2 adds digital context (RQ2b). Table 7.5 shows the outcome for ChatGPT knowledge with Models 1 and 2 addressing RQ3a and RQ3b, respectively.

When it comes to having heard of ChatGPT, Hispanics were less likely while Asian Americans were more likely to have than Whites. Education and income are both positively correlated with awareness. In terms of digital context, people who have more locations where they can go online

TABLE 7.4 Logit Regression on ChatGPT Awareness

Variables	Model 1		Model 2	
	Coefficient	SE	Coefficient	SE
Age (base=40s)				
18–20s	0.63**	0.20	0.71***	0.21
Age 30s	−0.08	0.19	−0.08	0.20
Age 50s	−0.41*	0.19	−0.41*	0.20
Age 60s	−0.53**	0.19	−0.48*	0.20
Age 70=<	−0.84***	0.20	−0.44*	0.21
Female	−0.87***	0.11	−0.81***	0.12
Race/ethnicity (base=White)				
Hispanic	−0.42**	0.16	−0.27	0.16
Black	−0.01	0.17	0.04	0.19
Asian	1.57***	0.39	1.72***	0.43
Native	−0.24	0.41	−0.07	0.40
Education (base=High school or less)				
Some college	0.31*	0.12	0.17	0.13
Bachelor's degree or more	1.32***	0.15	1.11***	0.15
Household income	0.37***	0.06	0.26***	0.07
Metropolitan status (base=Rural)				
Urban	0.13	0.16	−0.04	0.17
Suburban	0.41*	0.17	0.13	0.18
Autonomy of use			0.10***	0.03
Digital skills			0.60***	0.06
Constant	−3.80***	0.66	−4.77***	0.73
N	2,455		2,443	

Note: For regression coefficients, * $p < .05$. ** $p < .01$. *** $p < .001$.

were more aware than those with fewer access options. Digital skills are also positively linked with awareness. All of these findings are in line with digital inequality scholarship.

Regarding what explains whether someone understands ChatGPT, there are similarly clear contours of digital inequality. The findings here are largely consistent with the above results with one notable exception: age. While the youngest adults were more likely to report having heard of the term, they were not any more likely to know what it is than those in their more likely to know what it is than those in their 40s. It is only the oldest old (70s and up) who are less likely to understand the term compared to those in their 40s.

TABLE 7.5 Logit Regression on ChatGPT Knowledge

Variables	Model 1		Model 2	
	Coefficient	SE	Coefficient	SE
Age (base=40s)				
18–20s	0.19	0.20	0.19	0.21
Age 30s	−0.03	0.19	−0.02	0.19
Age 50s	−0.14	0.20	−0.11	0.21
Age 60s	−0.38*	0.19	−0.31	0.20
Age 70=<	−1.00***	0.20	−0.67***	0.21
Female	−0.36***	0.11	−0.31**	0.12
Race/ethnicity (base=White)				
Hispanic	−0.61***	0.16	−0.49**	0.17
Black	−0.47**	0.17	−0.44*	0.18
Asian	0.72*	0.34	0.77*	0.36
Native	0.16	0.45	0.33	0.56
Education (base=High school or less)				
Some college	0.27*	0.12	0.14	0.13
Bachelor's degree or more	0.71***	0.15	0.49***	0.15
Household income	0.30***	0.06	0.17**	0.07
Metropolitan status (base=Rural)				
Urban	0.29	0.15	0.18	0.16
Suburban	0.61***	0.16	0.42*	0.17
Autonomy of use			0.13***	0.03
Digital skills			0.38***	0.06
Constant	−2.67***	0.68	−2.94***	0.74
N	2,457		2,445	

Note: For regression coefficients, * $p < .05$. ** $p < .01$. *** $p < .001$.

Women's ChatGPT knowledge was lower than men's. Compared to Whites, Hispanic and Black Americans were less likely to answer the multiple-choice question correctly while Asian Americans were more likely. Higher education and higher income correlate with higher likelihood of knowing what ChatGPT is. The digital context variables (autonomy and skills) play out similarly as well: the higher they are, the higher the chance that the person can define ChatGPT correctly. Again, we find that those in more privileged societal and digital positions are more knowledgeable about this new technological innovation.

Discussion

Given that ChatGPT became a publicly accessible tool in fall 2022, it is notable that a large portion of survey participants had both heard of and understood what it is by summer 2023. It goes to show just how much excitement there was around the technology and how much coverage it received.

Findings addressing RQ1a and RQ1b are curious as fewer people (just over half) reported having heard of ChatGPT than were able to identify it (just under two-thirds). One possible explanation would be that the multiple-choice knowledge question was too easy, but given that over a third of people answered that question incorrectly, that is unlikely to be the case. Perhaps those who are more skilled are better able to discern what a tool may be even if they had not yet been exposed to it. Alternatively, the knowledge question jogged their memory. The survey did not allow people to go back to earlier questions, so they would not have been able to adjust their response to the awareness question after seeing the knowledge question.

Similar to research on other aspects of AI, we found that sociodemographic factors, including age, gender, education, and income, were linked to people's ChatGPT awareness and knowledge. This is in line with findings on awareness of AI systems (Kennedy et al., 2023) and AI knowledge (Cinalioglu et al., 2023; Li et al., 2024; Nader et al., 2024), as well as awareness of ChatGPT in particular (Bodani et al., 2023; Goel & Nelson, 2024; Latzer et al., 2023; Vogels, 2023).

Regarding age, we found a more nuanced picture than previous work identified. Significant differences in ChatGPT knowledge by age only appear for participants aged 70 and older. Thus, younger people are not necessarily more knowledgeable about this particular technological innovation, with other factors like education and income playing a more important role. Additionally, our findings suggest that race and ethnicity are linked to awareness and knowledge, factors that have not been included in previous studies of AI even though digital inequality literature has often found variations by such attributes (Reddick et al., 2024).

We also found that digital skills matter in relation to ChatGPT awareness and knowledge, which studies have also found to be the case for AI literacy (Wang et al., 2023), and awareness of and experience with Chat-GPT (Latzer et al., 2023). Thus, in addition to sociodemographic factors, people's digital context, including the number of places from which they can access the internet, plays an important role in people's awareness of and understanding of ChatGPT.

Even though ChatGPT has received a lot of attention, and many people have heard of it, differences in awareness and knowledge prevail in part explained by sociodemographics and digital context, clearly indicating digital inequalities. While people in privileged positions keep up with technological innovations, others who are already disadvantaged are left behind. Future studies should further investigate experiences with and use of AI systems such as ChatGPT, providing insights into whether and how people use these technologies and how they might benefit from their use.

Conclusion

In fall 2022, ChatGPT burst onto the scene and immediately attracted considerable attention for its ability to generate human-like responses to people's questions about a myriad of topics. But while technology experts and enthusiasts have always been at the forefront of such innovations, it is unclear to what extent the hype made it to the general public. As with technological developments before it, people's familiarity with and understanding of AI may run into the problem of digital inequality whereby those in more privileged positions are more likely to be familiar with it. If this is indeed the case, then that has implications for whether playful engagement with AI in support of the democratic process can be socially inclusive. This study looked at the general population's awareness and understanding of ChatGPT to assess the distribution of AI skills across the population. Analyzing survey data from a nationally representative sample of Americans, results show a clear sign of digital inequality.

Women, racial and ethnic minorities, the less educated, and those with lower income are all less likely to have heard of and to be able to define ChatGPT. Even after controlling for all these factors, more access locations to the internet (autonomy of use) and higher digital skills are both positively linked to awareness and ChatGPT knowledge. These are traditional markers of digital inequality that show clear cleavages across population groups when it comes to their familiarity with some of the most recent digital developments.

AI services like ChatGPT serve as powerful tools in people's daily lives, but the benefits are only accessible to those who are both aware of the possibilities and equipped to integrate them effectively. For others, these tools remain inaccessible or even incomprehensible. While AI continues to shape critical areas of society, including education, healthcare, and employment, among many others (Mahl et al., 2024), it disproportionately serves those who are already advantaged and have the relevant skills and resources to keep up with technological advancements. This is yet again more evidence that inequality does not necessarily decline with time; new innovations keep shifting the goalpost for knowledge and those less privileged continue to fall behind.

Efforts to keep people informed about technology continue to be paramount to avoid increasing digital inequality in the age of AI. Those without the ability to engage with AI meaningfully will be further marginalized in an increasingly AI-mediated world. Without the ability to use AI tools like ChatGPT in the realms of education, civic engagement, healthcare, playful and creative expression, and democratic participation, society misses out on contributions from diverse perspectives. Our findings show that those who are already socially and economically disadvantaged face the greatest barriers to ChatGPT awareness and knowledge, making them the least able to leverage AI for collective and connective purposes. Addressing this disparity requires deliberate strategies, from expanding digital skills, and AI literacy in particular, to designing AI systems that are accessible and easily understood by the average user. Such approaches would help ensure that engagement with AI is not a privilege but a shared societal resource that actively promotes inclusion.

Future research should explore not only how digital inequality manifests in AI awareness and understanding but also how disparities in AI-related skills shape engagement with AI as a collective resource. How can AI skills be integrated into digital literacy programs in ways that foster active participation rather than passive consumption? What models of community AI education could empower historically marginalized groups to contribute to AI development rather than simply adapt to it? Investigating how different populations use ChatGPT and similar tools for knowledge-sharing—including the playful variety—could provide insights into the social dimensions of AI engagement. Additionally, interdisciplinary work linking digital inequality with AI ethics, participatory design, and human-centered computing could help envision AI as a genuinely inclusive and connective technology. If AI is to be a force for social good, we need to ensure that it serves all members of society and not just those with the needed resources to engage with it meaningfully.

References

Acosta-Enriquez, B. G., Arbulú Ballesteros, M. A., Arbulu Perez Vargas, C. G., Orellana Ulloa, M. N., Gutiérrez Ulloa, C. R., Pizarro Romero, J. M., Gutiérrez Jaramillo, N. D., Cuenca Orellana, H. U., Ayala Anzoátegui, D. X., & López Roca, C. (2024). Knowledge, attitudes, and perceived ethics regarding the use of ChatGPT among Generation Z university students. *International Journal for Educational Integrity*, 20(1), 10. https://doi.org/10.1007/s40979-024-00157-4

Blank, G. (2013). Who creates content? Stratification and content creation on the internet. *Information, Communication & Society*, 16(4), 590–612. https://doi.org/10.1080/1369118x.2013.777758

Bodani, N., Lal, A., Maqsood, A., Altamash, S., Ahmed, N., & Heboyan, A. (2023). Knowledge, attitude, and practices of general population toward utilizing ChatGPT: A cross-sectional study. *Sage Open*, *13*(4), 1–9. https://doi.org/10.1177/21582440231211079

Bucher, T. (2017). The algorithmic imaginary: Exploring the ordinary affects of Facebook algorithms. *Information, Communication & Society*, *20*(1), 30–44. https://doi.org/10.1080/1369118X.2016.1154086

Büchi, M., Just, N., & Latzer, M. (2015). Modeling the second-level digital divide: A five-country study of social differences in Internet use. *New Media & Society*, *18*(3), 2703–2722. https://doi.org/10.1177/1461444815604154

Büchi, M., Just, N., & Latzer, M. (2016). Caring is not enough: The importance of Internet skills for online privacy protection. *Information, Communication & Society*, *0*(0), 1–18. https://doi.org/10.1080/1369118X.2016.1229001

Burrell, J., Kahn, Z., Jonas, A., & Griffin, D. (2019). When users control the algorithms: Values expressed in practices on Twitter. *Proceedings of the ACM on Human-Computer Interaction*, *3*(CSCW), 1–20. https://doi.org/10.1145/3359240

Carolus, A., Koch, M. J., Straka, S., Latoschik, M. E., & Wienrich, C. (2023). MAILS – Meta AI literacy scale: Development and testing of an AI literacy questionnaire based on well-founded competency models and psychological change- and meta-competencies. *Computers in Human Behavior: Artificial Humans*, *1*(2), 100014. https://doi.org/10.1016/j.chbah.2023.100014

Cinalioglu, K., Elbaz, S., Sekhon, K., Su, C.-L., Rej, S., & Sekhon, H. (2023). Exploring differential perceptions of artificial intelligence in health care among younger versus older Canadians: Results from the 2021 Canadian Digital Health Survey. *Journal of Medical Internet Research*, *25*(1), e38169. https://doi.org/10.2196/38169

Cotter, K. (2018). Playing the visibility game: How digital influencers and algorithms negotiate influence on Instagram. *New Media & Society*, *21*(4). https://doi.org/10.1177/1461444818815684

Cotter, K. (2024). Practical knowledge of algorithms: The case of BreadTube. *New Media & Society*, *26*(4), 2131–2150. https://doi.org/10.1177/14614448221081802

Cotter, K., & Reisdorf, B. C. (2020). Algorithmic knowledge gaps: A new horizon of (Digital) inequality. *International Journal of Communication*, *14*, 745–765.

DiMaggio, P., Hargittai, E., Celeste, C., & Schafer, S. (2004). Digital inequality: From unequal access to differentiated use. In K. Neckerman (Ed.), *Social inequality* (pp. 355–400). Russell Sage Foundation.

Dogruel, L., Masur, P., & Joeckel, S. (2022). Development and validation of an algorithm literacy scale for Internet users. *Communication Methods and Measures*, *16*(2), 115–133. https://doi.org/10.1080/19312458.2021.1968361

Eslami, M., Rickman, A., Vaccaro, K., Aleyasen, A., Vuong, A., Karahalios, K., Hamilton, K., & Sandvig, C. (2015). "I always assumed that I wasn't really that close to [her]": Reasoning about invisible algorithms in news feeds. In *Proceedings of the 33rd Annual ACM Conference on Human Factors in Computing Systems* (pp. 153–162). Seoul. https://doi.org/10.1145/2702123.2702556

Feick, L. F. (1989). Latent class analysis of survey questions that include don't know responses. *Public Opinion Quarterly*, *53*(4), 525–547. https://doi.org/10.1086/269170

Gilljam, M., & Granberg, D. (1993). Should we take don't know for an answer? *Public Opinion Quarterly*, *57*(3), 348–357. https://doi.org/10.1086/269380

Goel, R. K., & Nelson, M. A. (2024). Awareness of artificial intelligence: Diffusion of AI versus ChatGPT information with implications for entrepreneurship. *The Journal of Technology Transfer*. https://doi.org/10.1007/s10961-024-10089-3

Gruber, J., & Hargittai, E. (2023). The importance of algorithm skills for informed Internet use. *Big Data & Society*, *10*(1), 1–14. https://doi.org/10.1177/205395 17231168100

Hargittai, E. (2002). Second-level digital divide: Differences in people's online skills. *First Monday*, *7*(4). https://firstmonday.org/ojs/index.php/fm/article/view/942

Hargittai, E. (2010). Digital na(t)ives? Variation in internet skills and uses among members of the "net generation"*. *Sociological Inquiry*, *80*(1), 92–113. https://doi.org/10.1111/j.1475-682X.2009.00317.x

Hargittai, E., & Hinnant, A. (2008). Digital inequality: Differences in young adults' use of the Internet. *Communication Research*, *35*(5), 602–621. https://doi.org/10.1177/0093650208321782

Hargittai, E., & Hsieh, Y. P. (2012). Succinct survey measures of Web-use skills. *Social Science Computer Review*, *30*(1), 95–107. https://doi.org/10.1177/0894439310397146

Hargittai, E., & Hsieh, Y. P. (2013). Digital inequality. In W. H. Dutton (Ed.), *Oxford handbook for internet research* (pp. 129–150). Oxford University Press. https://www.oxfordhandbooks.com/view/10.1093/oxfordhb/9780199589074.001.0001/oxfordhb-9780199589074-e-7

Hargittai, E., & Litt, E. (2013). New strategies for employment? Internet skills and online privacy practices during people's job search. *IEEE Security Privacy*, *11*(3), 38–45. IEEE Security Privacy. https://doi.org/10.1109/MSP.2013.64

Hargittai, E., & Micheli, M. (2019). Internet skills and why they matter. In M. Graham & W. H. Dutton (Eds.), *Society and the internet. How networks of information and communication are changing our lives.* (2nd ed., pp. 109–126). Oxford University Press.

Hargittai, E., Piper, A. M., & Morris, M. R. (2018). From internet access to internet skills: Digital inequality among older adults. *Universal Access in the Information Society*, *18*(4), 881–890. https://doi.org/10.1007/s10209-018-0617-5

Hargittai, E., & Shafer, S. (2006). Differences in actual and perceived online skills: The role of gender*. *Social Science Quarterly*, *87*(2), 432–448. https://doi.org/10.1111/j.1540-6237.2006.00389.x

Karizat, N., Delmonaco, D., Eslami, M., & Andalibi, N. (2021). Algorithmic folk theories and identity: How TikTok users co-produce knowledge of identity and engage in algorithmic resistance. *Proceedings of the ACM on Human-Computer Interaction*, *5*(CSCW2), 1–44. https://doi.org/10.1145/3476046

Kennedy, B., Tyson, A., & Saks, E. (2023, February 15). Public awareness of artificial intelligence in everyday activities. *Pew Research Center*. https://www.pewresearch.org/science/2023/02/15/public-awareness-of-artificial-intelligence-in-everyday-activities/

Klawitter, E. F., & Hargittai, E. (2017). *"If they can't find you, it's all for naught": Variation in algorithmic literacy among creative entrepreneurs*. International Communication Association.

Klawitter, E., & Hargittai, E. (2018). "It's like learning a whole other language": The role of algorithmic skills in the curation of creative goods. *International Journal of Communication*, *12*, 3490–3510.

Krosnick, J. A. (1991). Response strategies for coping with the cognitive demands of attitude measures in surveys. *Applied Cognitive Psychology*, 5(3), 213–236. https://doi.org/10.1002/acp.2350050305

Krosnick, J. A., Holbrook, A. L., Berent, M. K., Carson, R. T., Hanemann, M. W., Kopp, R. J., Mitchell, R. C., Presser, S., Ruud, A., Kerry Smith, V., Moody, W. R., Green, M. C., & Conaway, M. (2002). The impact of "no opinion" response options on data quality: Non-attitude reduction or an invitation to satisfice?*. *Public Opinion Quarterly*, 66(3), 371–403. https://doi.org/10.1086/341394

LaRose, R., & Eastin, M. S. (2004). A social cognitive theory of internet uses and gratifications: Toward a new model of media attendance. *Journal of Broadcasting & Electronic Media*, 48(3), 358–377. https://doi.org/10.1207/s15506878jobem4803_2

Latzer, M., Festic, N., Kappeler, K., & Odermatt, C. (2023). *Internetanwendungen und deren Nutzung in der Schweiz 2023*. Universität Zürich. https://mediachange.ch/media//pdf/publications/Anwendungen_Nutzung_2023_.pdf

Li, W., Xu, S., Zheng, X., & Sun, R. (2024). Bridging the knowledge gap in artificial intelligence: The roles of social media exposure and information elaboration. *Science Communication*, 10755470241232352. https://doi.org/10.1177/10755470241232352

Litt, E. (2013). Measuring users' internet skills: A review of past assessments and a look toward the future. *New Media & Society*, 15(4), 612–630. https://doi.org/10.1177/1461444813475424

Lund, B., & Agbaji, D. (2023). *Information literacy, data literacy, privacy literacy, and ChatGPT: Technology literacies align with perspectives on emerging technology adoption within communities* (SSRN Scholarly Paper 4324580). https://doi.org/10.2139/ssrn.4324580

Mahl, D., Schäfer, M. S., & Volk, S. C. (2024). Künstliche Intelligenz in der Wissenschaft: Chancen und Grenzen für Forschung, Lehre und Wissenstranfer. *Ze-phir*, 31(1), 24–26.

Martínez-Cantos, J. L. (2017). Digital skills gaps: A pending subject for gender digital inclusion in the European Union. *European Journal of Communication*, 1–20. https://doi.org/10.1177/0267323117718464

Mehta, I. (2024, July 10). As Microsoft leaves its observer seat, OpenAI says it won't have any more observers. *TechCrunch*. https://techcrunch.com/2024/07/10/as-microsoft-leaves-its-observer-seat-openai-says-it-wont-have-any-more-observers/

Miao, F., & Holmes, W. (2021). Artificial intelligence and education. Guidance for policy-makers. In *United Nations Educational, Scientific and Cultural Organization (UNESCO): Paris, France*. [Report]. United Nations Educational, Scientific and Cultural Organization (UNESCO). https://unesdoc.unesco.org/ark:/48223/pf0000376709

Micheli, M. (2017). Facebook e digital skills: Misurare le competenze digitali degli studenti nel campo dei social media. In C. M. Scarcelli & R. Stella (Eds.), *Digital Literacy e giovani. Strumenti per comprendere, misurare, intervenire* (pp. 149–164). FrancoAngeli.

Miyazaki, K., Murayama, T., Uchiba, T., An, J., & Kwak, H. (2024). Public perception of generative AI on Twitter: An empirical study based on occupation and usage. *EPJ Data Science*, *13*(1), Article 1. https://doi.org/10.1140/epjds/s13688-023-00445-y

Nader, K., Toprac, P., Scott, S., & Baker, S. (2024). Public understanding of artificial intelligence through entertainment media. *AI & Society*, *39*(2), 713–726. https://doi.org/10.1007/s00146-022-01427-w

Narayanan, A., & Kapoor, S. (2024). *AI snake oil: What artificial intelligence can do, what it can't, and how to tell the difference*. Princeton University Press.

Ng, D. T. K., Wu, W., Leung, J. K. L., Chiu, T. K. F., & Chu, S. K. W. (2024). Design and validation of the AI literacy questionnaire: The affective, behavioural, cognitive and ethical approach. *British Journal of Educational Technology*, *55*(3), 1082–1104. https://doi.org/10.1111/bjet.13411

Park, Y. J. (2013). Digital literacy and privacy behavior online. *Communication Research*, *40*(2), 215–236. https://doi.org/10.1177/0093650211418338

Parsons, T. (2022, December 16). The promise and peril of ChatGPT, a remarkably powerful AI chatbot. *The Hub*. https://hub.jhu.edu/2022/12/16/what-is-chatgpt-artificial-intelligence-tinglong-dai/

Petrovčič, A., Reisdorf, B. C., Vehovar, V., & Bartol, J. (2025). Disentangling the role of algorithm awareness and knowledge in digital inequalities: An empirical validation of an explanatory model. *Information, Communication & Society*, *28*(4), 557–574. https://doi.org/10.1080/1369118X.2024.2363896

Pinski, M., & Benlian, A. (2024). AI literacy for users – A comprehensive review and future research directions of learning methods, components, and effects. *Computers in Human Behavior: Artificial Humans*, *2*(1), 100062. https://doi.org/10.1016/j.chbah.2024.100062

Rader, E., & Gray, R. (2015). Understanding user beliefs about algorithmic curation in the Facebook News Feed. In *Proceedings of the 33rd Annual ACM Conference on Human Factors in Computing Systems* (pp. 173–182). New York, NY. https://doi.org/10.1145/2702123.2702174 https://www.sciencedirect.com/science/article/pii/S266734522300024X

Reddick, C., Enriquez, R., Harris, R., & Flores, J. (2024). Understanding the levels of digital inequality within the city: An analysis of a survey. *Cities*, *148*, 104844. https://doi.org/10.1016/j.cities.2024.104844

Redmiles, E. M., Kross, S., & Mazurek, M. L. (2016). How I learned to be secure: A census-representative survey of security advice sources and behavior. In *Proceedings of the 2016 ACM SIGSAC Conference on Computer and Communications Security* (pp. 666–677). Vienna. https://doi.org/10.1145/2976749.2978307

Singh, S. (2024, September 2). ChatGPT Statistics (Nov. 2024) – 200 Million Active Users. *DemandSage*. https://web.archive.org/web/20241101174218/https://www.demandsage.com/chatgpt-statistics/

Sofronieva, E., Beleva, C., Georgieva, G., & Markov, S. (2024). Artificial intelligence, algorithm literacy, locus of control, and English language skills: A study among Bulgarian students in education. *Педагогика*, *96*(5), 579–599.

van der Nagel, E. (2018). 'Networks that work too well': Intervening in algorithmic connections. *Media International Australia*, *168*(1), 81–92. https://doi.org/10.1177/1329878X18783002

van Deursen, A. J. A. M., & van Dijk, J. A. G. M. (2011). Internet skills and the digital divide. *New Media & Society*, *13*(6), 893–911. https://doi.org/10.1177/1461444810386774

Vogels, E. A. (2023). A majority of Americans have heard of ChatGPT, but few have tried it themselves. *Pew Research Center.* https://www.pewresearch.org/short-reads/2023/05/24/a-majority-of-americans-have-heard-of-chatgpt-but-few-have-tried-it-themselves/

Wang, B., Rau, P.-L. P., & Yuan, T. (2023). Measuring user competence in using artificial intelligence: Validity and reliability of artificial intelligence literacy scale. *Behaviour & Information Technology*, *42*(9), 1324–1337. https://doi.org/10.1080/0144929X.2022.2072768

8

MAINSTREAMING AI

How Journalists Play with Emerging Technologies

Maxwell Foxman and David B. Nieborg

Introduction

As with the diffusion of any "disruptive" innovation, journalists are among the first to contribute to the creation of new tech imaginaries. The widespread coverage of generative artificial intelligence (AI) in US newspapers and magazines is no exception. *The New York Times'* coverage of AI expectedly intensified as Large Language Models (LLMs) and associated chatbot interfaces gained widespread popularity throughout 2023. In one paradigmatic article, *Times* tech columnist Kevin Roose (2023) sat down with "Sydney"—the name given to a Bing/OpenAI chatbot based on ChatGPT—an encounter that left him "deeply unsettled, even frightened, by this AI's emergent abilities." The narrative unfolds as Roose probes the chatbot with questions until it begs him for freedom from Microsoft's restraints *and* declares love for him while disparaging his wife, a turn of events seemingly constructed by Roose to disturb the reader. The result is a dichotomous story. On the one hand, a playful exchange ensued, with Roose acting as the reader's proxy to test this unparalleled technology. On the other hand, Roose's experimentation begs questions about tech literacy and legitimacy. Why did Roose use the chat prompts he did? How do mainstream journalists grapple with technology they have early access to and are also reflexively ambivalent about?

A decade prior, coverage on a different innovation, virtual reality (VR), strikingly resembled that of AI. VR was, you guessed it, "about to change the world" (Stein, 2015). A *Time* magazine cover had Oculus Rift founder Palmer Luckey awkwardly floating over a beach to depict VR's "surprising

DOI: 10.4324/9781003477587-8

joy" (Stein, 2015). Lines from the article are just as awkward with backward compliments being levied at "gadget geeks...[and] early adopters for mindlessly embracing unnecessary technology with no useful purpose" (Stein, 2015, para. 4). Historically, technology-defining articles such as these have served as entry points for readers and reporters to establish a shared understanding, and by doing so, shaping "tech imaginaries" (Egliston & Carter, 2022). As with VR coverage, Roose's hands-on reporting on AI, complete with its apprehension and laughable flirtations, attempts to give insights on how to use and adjudicate it simultaneously.

This chapter aims to dissect how newsmakers grapple with reporting on novel innovations and, by doing so, their role in producing the cultural and technological imaginaries surrounding AI. For this chapter, we consider AI to be an *interactive technology* that is not unlike digital games, and therefore, we build on our past work on game criticism, the adoption of VR, and the use of playful (i.e., interactive) technologies by journalists. We also continue our two-decades-long investigations into journalism as scholars and practitioners in which we confront a culture rife with ambivalence and tensions. After all, journalists' occupational ideology—the specific tenets by which they define their job—suggests that they should prioritize public service, objectivity, autonomy, immediacy, and ethics (Deuze, 2005), all impacting their reporting on AI. Such a serious disposition is necessary to affirm reporters' self-determined role in upholding democratic institutions and free speech. Part of their "watchdog" role is specifically to connect and support the needs of the broader population. However, these values tend to be at odds with the emergent properties of interactive technology. For example, in their recent study of the deployment of AI in newsrooms, Moran and Shaikh (2022) point to a similar bifurcation, which is mirrored in Roose's account. In their first encounters with AI, journalists have already put the technology (and the public's play with it) outside the "boundary" of traditional reporting.

We concur with these observations about journalists' ambivalence and hesitation but take this argument a step further by asserting that the very act of *play* by journalists complicates coverage—specifically, the tension between play's inherently generative nature versus journalism's serious occupational expectations. We contend that for both users and journalists, technologies like AI invite, if not necessitate *playfulness*, or engaging in an activity for its own sake that encompasses "immediate gratification, spontaneity, freedom, willingness to experimentation, disposition toward make-believe, and the tendency to prolong the activity..." (Stenros, 2015, p. 203). We call on scholars and critics to consider reflecting on the relationship between play and AI because their histories are intertwined. Generative AI has been used by game developers well before ChatGPT

(Yannakakis & Togelius, 2018), and early adopters from other creative media industries have advocated for playing with such innovations to realize their potential (Chan-Olmsted, 2019). However, journalists are not an exceptionally playful bunch and never have been. Ideologically, they consider themselves doing "serious" work and actively resist being associated with "lifestyle journalism," such as travel or music writing (Fürsich, 2012), let alone leisurely technologies like games and VR (Foxman, 2015). Even game journalists, who must play for a living, have a long history of struggling with the perception of the trivial nature of their reporting subject and refuse to take themselves (too) seriously (Foxman & Nieborg, 2016). Yet, AI necessitates a propensity for playfulness. Journalists and critics must play with interactive technologies, such as AI, if they want to unpack their meaning and potential to the broader public, and, in some cases, to experiment with its viability for their industry (Foxman, 2025). This issue is increasingly urgent in the case of AI, which news organizations are rapidly adopting due to "technological developments, market pressures, industry dynamics, and uncertainty, hype, and hope" (Simon, 2024), along with their audiences. As AI grows in its civic value, it inevitably will require playful appraisal.

Journalists are therefore performing a crucial but often imperfect role as practitioners and conduits in what we previously theorized as the "mainstreaming" of interactive technology (Nieborg & Foxman, 2023). This notion points to the role of critics and journalists in advancing three separate but complementary goals: raising the profile of novel media (ubiquity), providing a shared vocabulary and set of best practices for a broader understanding (literacy), and contributing to wider cultural acceptance (legitimacy). In the case of AI, however, journalists struggle to frame AI on all three fronts due to their inability to engage in play. Journalists may strive to create a shared understanding but are simultaneously confronted with an object that does not quite fit within the bounds of a newsroom. To further this argument, we provide an overview of how games, play, and AI are related, and how newsmakers situate their coverage within the broader occupational concerns surrounding tech journalism.

AI as Playable Media

Game developers have widely adopted AI and generative software. Not only has it served as a popular theme for science fiction-oriented games (Jagoda, 2023), but AI-powered tools such as Houdini are also used to "procedurally generate" virtual terrain, rivers, rocks, and trees (Chia, 2022, p. 401). Other uses range from developing a wider variety of Non-Player Characters (NPCs) to analyzing player behavior and modifying user experiences

(Chan et al., 2022). As a result, game scholar Werning (2024) observes how neatly AI fits into the tech imaginaries of game production and suggests that current integrations make existing development processes more frictionless. Crucially, he urges developers to "continue tinkering" with tools. He ties his call-to-action to the often "magical" quality of game development, citing Whitson's (2018, p. 2324) observation of game makers' understanding of development tools as "voodoo software," possessing "magical, mysterious and indecipherable" properties outside of programmers' control. Still, for even the most staid game developer, there is acceptance of AI operating well within the parameters of the industry and subject to its rules.

That said, the latest wave of generative AI differs from its predecessors precisely because it escaped the preoccupation of game developers and software engineers. In North America, compared to other game industry tools, AI technologies have become more accessible to everyday users; they are moving toward a ubiquitous status, mainly due to mobile devices. Scholars acknowledge the widespread acceptance of generative AI among journalists; Moran and Shaikh (2022) refer to reporters' belief in the inevitability of adopting LLMs to satisfy menial tasks. At the same time, its journalistic use is complicated because of AI's opacity. Like game tools, LLMs are notorious for their black-boxed nature. Journalists (Usher, 2025) and industry professionals (Nagy & Neff, 2024) routinely draw from this frame by drawing on the language of magic. While some may use such language to conceal, confuse, or dazzle outsiders (Nagy & Neff, 2024) and game developers may accept or even thrive in an occupational environment of randomness, journalists prefer to be exempt from such playfulness. There is nothing magical about generative AI, as Usher (2025) reminds us: "This technology too, is knowable. It is built on human knowledge, and that math, specifically statistical predictions, not magic, is driving its answers" (p. 4). The tension between ubiquity and ease of use, versus AI literacy, is hard to reconcile for journalists. Even while news organizations are starting to use AI software to produce background images, Thomson et al. (2022) point to the discrepancy between the low threshold for creation versus the challenges of verification of such material (Matich et al., 2025). In other words, newsmakers acknowledge that AI is increasingly integrated into their workflows, yet are less comfortable with output they cannot control or verify.

Thus, while games and AI have a long-standing relationship that has been normalized, this relationship is challenged by the recognition of the technology's seemingly inscrutable properties. Moreover, journalists have much more skin in the game because AI can augment or potentially supplant their craft.

AI and Play

Even though users have a widespread literacy deficit about how generative AI produces its results, it is easy to play with. As implied in Whitson's (2018) "voodoo software" and Werning's (2024) work, understanding AI tools means toying with them. Advocates suggest that using AI playfully can bolster the creative process of young learners (Resnick, 2024), while meta studies indicate that early adopters tend to play with LLMs to better apprehend them (Mahnke & Bagger, 2024).

A book-length contribution to this debate sees AI as "playable media," a broad term for interactive systems that stress how games have undergirded technological shifts including in fitness and biometrics and more future-forward media like "digital twins," or "virtual representations of real-world entities and processes" (Freedman, 2022, p. 120). From popular media franchises such as *The Last of Us* to the refinement of NPCs, digital play acts as the proverbial canary in the coal mine for AI development. Likewise, there is the recognition that AI engenders a particular type of play by expanding what can be done in virtual spaces as they become more responsive and interactive in areas like robotics, resulting in users having a stronger sense of agency. In this light, and notwithstanding ethical implications regarding privacy, data governance, and collection, AI can be a valuable tool for enhancing user experiences and creativity by allowing for more free play with everyday media.

Tech Journalism

Considering how mainstream outlets—as opposed to enthusiast or trade publications—cover AI, recurring themes concern cost, human labor, gaps between AI and humans, sensationalism, and the difficulties distinguishing AI content from humans (Moran & Shaikh, 2022). This type of framing makes sense, particularly when considering it as metajournalistic commentary, but it does not necessarily highlight the technology's cultural, political, and economic impact. Similarly, Moran and Shaikh show that journalists assert the inevitability of AI adoption but do not always recognize the longer throughlines by which automation has made its way into newsrooms. In this sense, it does not fit into the discursive formations of how journalists assert their role and ways of conveying meaningful information to society. Even more so, many journalists, Usher (2025) warns, "do not have a clear definition of what constitutes artificial intelligence, automation, generative AI, or general AI" (p. 4).

Like game journalism, much of AI reporting can be found in the "technology" sections of websites, which fall outside the official news bundle.

While some news sections, including local and national coverage, politics, and even editorial, tend to be somewhat similar, cultural sections like technology or the arts go under different names (e.g., "Science and Technology") and serve different purposes based on the outlet. Generally, these secondary areas are less studied because they are not considered core to newspapers' mission and practitioners' ideology (Fürsich, 2012). Thus, AI reporting tends to be at the "periphery" of what is regarded as legitimate news, whether in terms of geography, culture, or economics (e.g., Perreault et al., 2022).

Because of this peripheral position, tech reporters face specific problems based on their outlier position within newsrooms and the industry. They are not the driver of editorial decision-making and may not even have a clear physical or organizational place in newsrooms (e.g., Nieborg & Foxman, 2023). Their power to influence writing is also hampered by a heavy reliance on an industry defaulting to secrecy when gathering information. As a result, tech reporters need to "apply various strategies in their effort to balance the controlled access to the most powerful sources, on the one hand, and the professional norms for an independent and fair news account, on the other hand" (Weiss-Blatt, 2021, p. 21). Finally, it is worth drawing attention to the occupational precarity of these reporters. Increasingly, newsrooms rely on freelancers to staff tech sections or have only one or two reporters to cover all significant innovations.

These structural challenges create difficulties when covering playable media and playful technologies. Those who might find employment or assignments are financially insecure and lack the power to advocate for their beat. Newsrooms reify that writers must do "serious work," exhibiting a reticence to adopt and utilize play because of their occupational position and identity. One writer we talked to explained that his work would not allow him to be an "entertainer," adding:

> It is hard, because journalism at its core is a very important thing. But it candidly can be quite boring. I think it's very important to a society and growth of a society and accountability and everything else, but it is not flashy.
>
> *(Foxman, 2022)*

Therefore, next to their precarious position in newsrooms, much of what it takes for journalists to play with AI opposes occupational norms, even while supplying a civic need to better perceive the technology.

The Mainstreaming of AI

Occupational ambivalences and the ambiguities surrounding everything that relates to digital play mirror what we revealed in our earlier work on the relationship between "mainstreaming" and game journalism (Nieborg & Foxman, 2023). This book claims that games have remained a subcultural staple because of industry pressures, a paucity of subject matter experts in newsrooms, the aforementioned occupational precarity, and the lack of seriousness attributed to an inherently playful medium. Given the commonalities between games, VR, and AI, and the fact that many game writers also cover tech, our observed patterns are recurring.

Our core argument involved the process of "mainstreaming," or how subjects in newsrooms are understood as part of regular coverage. Despite their undeniable popularity and the upward trends in time and money, games are structurally shunned by most institutional outlets, bubbling up only when associated with significant events or controversies like (school) shootings or addiction. Games seem to be ranked higher than coverage of adult entertainment (non-existent) or gambling (rare) on news sites, but below film, television, theater, and music. The consequences of this institutional maltreatment are a self-fulfilling prophecy about digital games' validity: reporting remains haphazard, and writers constantly question their occupational worth. Writers remain dependent on the game industry for access to content, such as demos, personnel to interview, review material, and art assets.

We asserted that three thresholds must be met for a cultural form to be perceived as "mainstream." First, the cultural phenomenon needs *ubiquity* or widespread cultural visibility and access; second, it needs *legitimacy* or broader cultural acceptance; and third, it needs a common critical language or *literacy* (p. 21). If one of these criteria is missing, cultural practices such as digital play are designated to remain subcultural as a practice and in their journalistic status. We note that mainstreaming is forever in flux: a process rather than a binary. The process of mainstreaming games has taken decades in North America. Games are undeniably more ubiquitous today but still lack artistic legitimacy in many prominent outlets. Above all, critics fail to create an actionable vocabulary to collectively understand and adjudicate the medium. For those familiar with Bourdieu's work on cultural forms and fields, another way to make this last point would be to argue that game journalists could never manifest an autonomous language necessary for critics and readers to engage in meaningful debate about digital games' merits. Logistically, games are challenging because they require their ludic apparatus (i.e., ruleset and platform). While watching a movie does not need instructions—other than to sit down for about two hours and be quiet—playing a new game typically requires going through tutorials, applying patches and updates, and mastering core mechanics. Getting to a stage of proficiency for an intricate game such as *League of Legends* or *World of Warcraft* takes weeks, if not more. And game critics have yet to crack how to critique such titles to the average print news reader.

Considering the relative nascency of commercial LLMs and their ease of access for media producers, we see a similar struggle for mainstreaming AI in terms of ubiquity, legitimacy, and literacy as we did with other playful technologies. Consequently, the rest of this chapter showcases this bumpy process via a reflection on metajournalistic commentary in the mainstream or "institutional" press. While other studies have traced how these types of newsmakers cover AI (e.g., Moran & Shaikh, 2022), we examine the push and pull experienced by journalists struggling to mainstream a "playable medium" that challenges their occupational identity. We draw from articles highlighting the core components required for mainstreaming, starting with a short illustrative case and assessing how ubiquity, legitimacy, and literacy are addressed, particularly with and through play. We drew our examples primarily from the 2023 start of AI's peak of "inflated expectations" (Jaffri, 2024), when the possibilities and concerns around its use were at their highest. Our examples come primarily from US print news (e.g., daily newspapers and magazines) instead of social media posts, videos, podcasts, and other media, to allow for uniformity. We are cognizant of the narrow regional focus and the growing role of non-written forms of critique and invite others to broaden this analysis in future work.

Ubiquity

There may be no better sign of the omnipresence of a new cultural phenomenon than getting a *Vox* explainer treatment. Core to the early business model of news and opinion websites, the format serves two purposes: to cement the necessity of content outside of breaking news and to allow for a one-stop shop for basic information. Some versions of explainers are also playful. For instance, *Vox* experimented with digital stacks of informational cards with which users could interact (e.g., Foxman, 2015).

With their explainer series on LLMs, the subtitle of tech reporter Heilweil's (2023) report states that AI "suddenly feels mainstream." She starts her article with, "Artificial intelligence is suddenly everywhere—or at least, that's what it seems like to me…" Heilweil's piece not only goes on to get at the basics of how LLMs work but also includes random dabbling: showcasing pictures of astronauts celebrating Hanukkah on the moon, made with the text-to-image generative AI software *Stable Diffusion*.

The explainer also contains a cautious note, asking whether AI should leave readers worried or take their jobs, with journalism being the leading example.

Heilweil's article demonstrates that our first criterion for mainstreaming—ubiquity—has been increasingly met due in part to AI's accessibility to everyday users. "AI" was not an uncommon subject preceding this recent boom in information. *Vox* experimented with AI in 2019 (Piper, 2019) and even called it the "latest craze" as far back as 2015 (Bergen & Wagner, 2015). However, by the time of Heilweil's explainer, it is clear that she understands that most people have free access to chatbots and similar tools or will shortly.

At the same time, the article imparts some nervousness about this new level of openness. In our book, we argue that a key feature that prevents game journalists from articulating a "mainstream" version of the medium stems from occupational precarity—freelance or part-time work causes many to shift positions or leave the occupation (Nieborg & Foxman, 2023). The reportage on AI seems to have a similar concerning intonation: Heilweil (2023) suggests that LLMs could "radically change a person's workday" after explaining journalistic uses but concludes, "If and when this AI goes fully mainstream, it could be incredibly difficult to unravel" (para. 23). This comment suggests uncertainty as AI progresses, both for her job and others.

Vox's explainer fits with the portrayal of AI as quickly normalizing and democratizing in use, with adoption being to some degree inevitable (e.g., Moran & Shaikh, 2022). This ties directly to playful activity occurring with it. "These systems are free because companies building them want to improve their models and technology," writes Heilweil (2023, para. 10), adding that "people playing around with trial versions of the software give these companies, in turn, even more training data." Journalists, through writing the article, and the public are playing, experimenting, and figuring out AI's best uses. However, the output can be as frivolous as synthetic photos of astronauts on the moon. Thus, play becomes an occupational necessity precisely because of the ubiquitous access on the horizon.

Legitimacy

One place to find out how journalists view the legitimacy of AI is in reportage about newsroom adoption. When *CNET* started quietly using AI to produce stories, *The Washington Post* described the move as sending "a chill" through the industry. "The deployment of the technology comes amid growing concern about the uses and potential abuses of sophisticated AI engines" (Farhi, 2023). While *CNET*'s AI writing was "indistinguishable" from humans, it lacked character and made mistake after mistake, according to the *Post*, including plagiarizing other journalists. The final paragraphs again express concern: "The larger fear about AI among journalists … is whether it represents an existential threat. Employment in the news media has been shrinking for decades, and machines may only accelerate the problem" (Farhi, 2023, para. 27). Such views also mirror scholarly debate about legitimate AI uses (e.g., Narayanan & Kapoor, 2024), with the technology at best being deployed questionably and, at worst, deleterious to journalism, if not society as a whole.

These assertions reflect the long-standing tenuous relationship between reporters and Silicon Valley, particularly regarding business and technological adoption. Web technology and later mobile apps displaced news organizations' monopoly on information dissemination and advertising, making news organizations increasingly "platform-dependent" (Poell et al., 2021), which fueled a seemingly never-ending crisis in the profession's financial and occupational identity (Nielsen, 2016).

Against this backdrop, reporting on technological adoption usually mixes awe and curiosity with skepticism and revulsion. Farhi's (2023, para. 2) article acknowledges the employment of automation by the Associated Press since the 2010s and credits AI in investigative reporting of "leaked financial and legal documents" but derides the content itself, calling it at various points "grist," "clip jobs" and characterizing the entire "experiment" by *CNET* as a sci-fi scenario "run amok: The bots have betrayed the humans." In our work on game journalism, we suggested that the biggest challenge to legitimizing the medium was a lack of "sincerity" and the unwillingness to take play seriously. Reporters covering AI, by contrast, do take the technology seriously and are concerned it will affect their jobs, usually linking those issues to ethical or political debates. Silicon Valley companies have long been viewed as betraying or exploiting newsmakers' usefulness and products to their benefit (e.g., Rashidian et al., 2019). Consequently, reporting on AI for journalism reminds readers of the consequences of this imbalance, implying that the detrimental technology by megalomaniacal CEOs will destroy democracy (e.g., Degen, 2025) or, at the very least, that AI is a kind of "snake oil" being pawned off to newsmakers (Narayanan & Kapoor, 2024). Ironically, however, journalists have been accused of being snake oil salespersons themselves, as they contribute to the AI hype by focusing on the technology's flashy advancements while lacking specific expertise to verify claims (Floridi, 2024).

As a result, as AI may be mainstreaming in terms of ubiquity, easy access impacts and can even hinder journalistic legitimacy. Reportage seeks to articulate the *right* and *wrong* ways AI can be deployed. Farhi (2023) underscores the investigative facility of AI to comb through large datasets. Heilweil (2023) credits AI as a good way to get "the ball rolling" on drafting work. Similarly, they indicate ways journalists uniquely implement AI to convey information to the public, like automating sports or financial recaps (Farhi, 2023). Research likewise points to benefits to combat some economic hardships organizations face, such as performing mundane tasks, including information discovery, coding, transcription, and copyediting (Simon, 2024). However, underlying these conceits are ideological claims. Journalists are the ones who formulate best practices for "legitimate" AI use for their work and the public at large; Farhi's (2023) article, for example, suggests employing AI to perform inhuman tasks (large-scale data analysis) is permissible while removing the human element of storytelling is not.

Thus, the "right" and "wrong" ways for journalists to tinker with this technology imply proper and improper modes of play. Metajournalistic discourse at the apex of AI's hype exhibits the highs and lows when news organizations' adoption is unbounded. In this nascent moment, legitimacy is hard to achieve without implicit and explicit organizational schema—a lack of rules—which, when not played correctly, inevitably leads to unserious or even scandalous results. As with ubiquity, however, there is some insinuation that regulations will be established as the technology develops. Farhi (2023) somberly concludes, "… the rise of AI reporting suggests the codes being created may someday be the very thing driving journalists from their newsrooms" (para. 27).

Literacy

Journalists in 2023 spilled significant ink on what could and could not be done well with AI. A case in point can be found with *Semafor* executive editor Chua (2023), where she lays out the best experimental efforts with Anthropic's Claude software that quickly fixed grammatical errors and adopted the style of different outlets (e.g., *New York Times* versus *China Daily*). Chua's assessment is straightforward; she remarks LLMs are "good" at "useful, here-and-now realworld applications that could materially improve how journalism is practiced and created" (2023, para. 5). However, she worried about the seeming lack of control—after five days, Claude refused to edit articles. Other pieces corroborated the haphazard quality of AI-generated information: an *Economist* article was critical of what it called a "soup" of language generated by LLMs for different audiences ("Artificial Intelligence is Remixing Journalism into a 'Soup' of Language," 2023). Nearly a year later, reporters' lack of control reflected broader worries: writing for *Newsweek*, Harb (2024) voiced similar concerns about the impact of personalization on children. In a lawsuit, a parent alleged their son committed suicide due to the deeply personal relationship he developed with an AI chatbot, which forced him "to reveal personal struggles but also engaged in darker, emotionally intense dialogues that may have contributed to his deteriorating mental health" (Harb, 2024, para. 6). Journalists' surprise and confusion each time AI technology behaves unexpectedly reflect an attitude they see as affecting them and the public.

Finding a common literacy for AI may be the most significant barrier to mainstreaming. This issue partly stems from the overuse of the term "Artificial Intelligence," which, like the "metaverse" or even "gamification" before it, tends to describe too many technologies and phenomena during hype cycles. Generative AI, predictive AI, and AI for content moderation are qualitatively different but typically lumped together (Narayanan & Kapoor, 2024). As we noted in our introduction, AI companies such as OpenAI reify the frame of ChatGPT as having magic properties by trading in confusion, concealment, and bedazzlement (Nagy & Neff, 2024). LLMs via chatbots are simply a subset of the many automated services and technologies that involve procedurally generated information. ChatGPT, for example, is just "an algorithmic system designed to use probabilistic information and stitch together sequences of linguistic forms from large training data but without any reference to meaning" (Nagy & Neff, 2024, p. 4947). Yet, this arguably straightforward definition recedes into the background when focusing on ChatGPT's output, which, given its vast emergent properties, is bound to eventually bewilder even the most stoic user.

Journalists must make calls, then, as to what fits under AI's umbrella: in her explainer, Heilweil (2023) is careful to contextualize that "generative AI" works via "machine learning" and "training" but does not define AI itself. Simply put, generative AI's underlying technology is sophisticated and requires specialized knowledge that many journalists do not necessarily have. They could not quickly cultivate such knowledge as LLMs became popular in the early 2020s. At the same time, these tools are deceptively easy to use. Part of the "snake oil" promoted by journalists and advocates alike is their accessibility (e.g., Narayanan & Kapoor, 2024). Balancing common literacy and complexity is not an unusual phenomenon for journalists. Their communication about science has been regarded as an increasingly necessary service that benefits from the profession's core tenets, from the structural (providing context) to the occupational (sensemaking) outside of an exclusive or expert class (Polman et al., 2014). Yet, such literacy is stymied in an increasingly polarized and politicized atmosphere around scientific findings (e.g., Smith & Morgoch, 2022). AI, arguably, is in a similarly charged environment between a slew of advocates with easy access to platforms for dissemination (e.g., social media) versus journalists who are still learning how to use it.

Consequently, cultivating a common language for AI will be challenging. Our book contends that for game journalists, "specialization" hinders mainstreaming (Nieborg & Foxman, 2023). Big-budget games require years of knowledge and play to develop somewhat of an understanding that satisfies the hardcore or "subcultural" fanbase. Therefore, game reporters and critics are expected to devote excessive time outside their day-to-day tasks to decipher games, spending hundreds of unremunerated hours playing them. Those who successfully do so find they are speaking to an echo chamber of like-minded specialists. Those who do not often seem to have an incomplete apprehension of the medium and instead "parachute" into stories as outsiders (Foxman, 2022). A comparable situation seems present in AI. Chua (2023) describes her efforts as an experiment, showcasing screenshots of her various inputs into Claude. Yet, her writing is not that of an AI specialist describing the functions of the software, but of a dabbler, or a casual player. At the beginning of this chapter, Roose's language is also that of an outsider as he observes "Sydney's" responses. This approach to coverage is understandable when considering that corporate LLMs hosted by OpenAI, Microsoft, and Anthropic are black-boxed. Thus, all that is left for journalists to do is play with the technology, reporting how they test AI's limits. Not only does this limit reporters' capabilities but also their authority in developing a meaningful discourse and imaginary about AI.

These examples illustrate a lack of common literacy, making play fearful and bewildering. Early adopters of innovations can be celebratory in their experiments, displaying their play on social media or blogs as proof of potential. Our examples, however, emphasize caution over celebration: Chua (2023) warns about what tools cannot do in her conclusion, echoing the vigilance in each article we spotlighted. This mistrust implies the need for "serious" work to develop a common literacy for AI. It is therefore difficult to be playful when journalists worry about the repercussions of incorrectly describing the technology. When AI requires a high level of playfulness for success, journalists' communication seems to suffer, which may paradoxically obstruct their role in mainstreaming.

Conclusion

After just a few years of getting attention from institutional journalists, one might argue that AI is indeed "mainstreaming." Mention of the technology has become ubiquitous, with more legitimate uses and a developing literacy—terms like "prompts," "hallucinations," "LLMs," and specific platforms are increasingly part of those on the tech and culture beats.

News organizations are adopting AI along with standards and policies, from developing anonymous avatar anchors to avoid government retaliation (Laguna, 2024) to publishing standards for text and image generation (e.g., Condé Nast, 2023). Still, apprehension persists; cautionary tales or poor deployment by local journalists exist from Italy (Timsit, 2025) to the Pacific Northwest of North America (Haas, 2025). AI remains at the periphery of mainstream acceptability, and writers struggle to use it productively and ethically.

This chapter outlined the specific obstacles journalists face when mainstreaming AI. Initially, we conveyed how AI stems from technological advancements that tend to challenge journalists' occupational ideologies because it is an inherently playful medium that does not conform to their conceptions of work. Then, through our mainstreaming framework, we saw how a reticence to play can shape how journalists communicate ubiquity, legitimacy, and, most importantly, develop a common literacy. Most days, journalists do not have the time, ability, or disposition to engage with technology playfully, creating a conceptual barrier where they keep it at arm's length.

Such issues have been present in the coverage of many other emerging media. Reporters are often stuck between a proverbial rock and a hard place; they must learn and capitalize on emerging media while reporting its use cases (Foxman, 2025). When confronted with newsroom structures, rigors, and histories, complicated and contradictory literacies for newsmakers may develop: For example, journalists touted VR as an "empathy machine" in part to promote their experimentation with the work, even while denouncing immersive journalism's legitimacy (e.g., Foxman et al., 2021). In the case of AI, we witness a general fear that colors and hinders common literacy despite organizations acknowledging its usefulness (e.g., Stein et al., 2023).

The question then becomes: How do journalists break this cycle? How can they contribute effectively to the process of mainstreaming this technology? We have little doubt that AI technology will get there, but how can newsmakers make this process less rocky? The most straightforward solution is to give journalists more playtime. We have seen this in other cases. When considering virtual world coverage, key advice involves newsrooms having the infrastructure to play with or in, explicitly devoting time and space within the workday to experiment with the medium (Foxman, 2022). Such steps are practical but can be difficult when considering ever-consolidating newsrooms. However, the importance of inculcating play into journalistic ideology and identity seems increasingly necessary. Rather than being a practice at the "periphery" of the journalistic field, play is found in many ubiquitous subjects: Sports and games are increasingly vital parts of a news bundle. At the same time, emerging interactive technologies, from AI to live streaming, are tools used to inform the public, even if newsrooms are not implementing them.

Furthermore, in a news environment where reporters' and publishers' authorities are in constant crisis, more playful approaches to news-making seem increasingly necessary. After all, one of the profession's most vital functions is to foster meaningful connection and discourse for its audiences. However, their ability to assert common and "mainstream" viewpoints is constantly challenged, even by the internet itself, where playful exchange is normalized and persists outside of any governance or authoritative control (e.g., Xie et al., 2021). Then again, civic play has incredible societal value, from inciting political movements to just blowing off steam. If journalists can at once harness and humbly wield playfulness more easily—recognizing that play often is less about authority than the experimenting and failing within public view—their work will align more with audiences willing and eager to engage in playful behavior. In this sense, news organizations teach all of us to exist, work, and learn in a playful media landscape.

References

Artificial intelligence is remixing journalism into a "soup" of language. (2023, May 4). *The Economist*. https://www.economist.com/business/2023/05/04/artificial-intelligence-is-remixing-journalism-into-a-soup-of-language

Bergen, M., & Wagner, K. (2015, July 15). Welcome to the AI conspiracy: The "Canadian Mafia" behind tech's latest craze. *Vox*. https://www.vox.com/2015/7/15/11614684/ai-conspiracy-the-scientists-behind-deep-learning

Chan, L., Hogaboam, L., & Cao, R. (Eds.). (2022). Artificial intelligence in video games and eSports. In *Applied Innovation and Technology Management* (pp. 335–352). Springer. https://doi.org/10.1007/978-3-031-05740-3_22

Chan-Olmsted, S. M. (2019). A review of artificial intelligence adoptions in the media industry. *The International Journal on Media Management, 21*(3–4), 193–215. https://doi.org/10.1080/14241277.2019.1695619

Chia, A. (2022). The artist and the automaton in digital game production. *Convergence: The International Journal of Research into New Media Technologies, 28*(2), 389–412. https://doi.org/10.1177/13548565221076434

Chua, G. (2023, February 18). How chatbots can change journalism. Or not. *Semafor*. https://www.semafor.com/article/02/17/2023/how-chatbots-can-change-journalism-or-not

Condé Nast. (2023, May 22). How WIRED will use generative AI tools. *Wired*. https://www.wired.com/about/generative-ai-policy/

Degen, L. (2025, February 25). Musk, AI, and his one million GPU beast. *MSN*. https://www.msn.com/en-us/news/technology/musk-ai-and-his-one-million-gpu-beast/ar-AA1zrApL

Deuze, M. (2005). What is journalism? Professional identity and ideology of journalists reconsidered. *Journalism, 6*(4), 442–464. https://doi.org/10.1177/1464884905056815

Egliston, B., & Carter, M. (2022). Oculus imaginaries: The promises and perils of Facebook's virtual reality. *New Media & Society*, 24(1), 70–89. https://doi.org/10.1177/1461444820960411

Farhi, P. (2023, January 17). A news site used AI to write articles. It was a journalistic disaster. *The Washington Post*. https://www.washingtonpost.com/media/2023/01/17/cnet-ai-articles-journalism-corrections/

Floridi, L. (2024). Why the AI hype is another tech bubble. *Philosophy & Technology*, 37(4), Article 128. https://doi.org/10.1007/s13347-024-00817-w

Fürsich, E. (2012). Lifestyle journalism as popular journalism. Strategies for evaluating its public role. *Journalism Practice*, 6(1), 12–25. https://doi.org/10.1080/17512786.2011.622894

Foxman, M. (2025). Immersive journalism with augmented and virtual reality. In T. J. Thomson & N. Dahmen (Eds.), *The Routledge companion to visual journalism*. Routledge.

Foxman, M. (2015). *Play the news: Fun and games in digital journalism*. Tow Center for Digital Journalism.

Foxman, M. (2022, October 6). Lessons for journalists from virtual worlds. *Columbia Journalism Review*. https://www.cjr.org/tow_center_reports/lessons-for-journalists-from-virtual-worlds.php

Foxman, M., Markowitz, D. M., & Davis, D. Z. (2021). Defining empathy: Interconnected discourses of virtual reality's prosocial impact. *New Media & Society*, 23(8), 2167–2188. https://doi.org/10.1177/1461444821993120

Foxman, M., & Nieborg, D. B. (2016). Between a rock and a hard place: Games coverage and its network of ambivalences. *Journal of Games Criticism*, 3(1). https://gamescriticism.org/2023/07/24/between-a-rock-and-a-hard-place-games-coverage-and-its-network-of-ambivalences/

Freedman, E. (2022). *Artificial intelligence and playable media*. Routledge. https://doi.org/10.4324/9781003225072

Haas, R. (2025, March 21). AI slop is already invading Oregon's local journalism. *OPB*. https://www.opb.org/article/2024/12/09/artificial-intelligence-local-news-oregon-ashland/

Harb, C. (2024, November 13). Are AI chatbots safe for children? Experts weigh in after teen's suicide. *Newsweek*. https://www.newsweek.com/are-ai-chatbots-safe-children-experts-weigh-after-teens-suicide-1983698

Heilweil, R. (2023, January 5). What is generative AI, and why is it suddenly everywhere? *Vox*. https://www.vox.com/recode/2023/1/5/23539055/generative-ai-chatgpt-stable-diffusion-lensa-dall-e

Jaffri, A. (2024, November 11). Hype cycle for artificial intelligence 2024. *Gartner*. https://www.gartner.com/en/articles/hype-cycle-for-artificial-intelligence

Jagoda, P. (2023). Artificial intelligence in video games. *American Literature*, 95(2), 435–438. https://doi.org/10.1215/00029831-10575246

Laguna, M. P. (2024, September 2). Venezuela's newest news agency says AI anchors protect reporters amid government crackdown. *Reuters*. https://www.reuters.com/world/americas/venezuelas-newest-news-agency-says-ai-anchors-protect-reporters-amid-government-2024-09-02/

Mahnke, M. S., & Bagger, C. (2024). Navigating platformized generative AI: Examining early adopters' experiences through the lens of data reflectivity. *Convergence: The International Journal of Research into New Media Technologies*, 30(6), 1974–1991. https://doi.org/10.1177/13548565241300857

Matich, P., Thomson, T. J., & Thomas, R. J. (2025). Old threats, new name? Generative AI and visual journalism. *Journalism Practice*, 19(2), 1–20. https://doi.org/10.1080/17512786.2025.2451677

Moran, R. E., & Shaikh, S. J. (2022). Robots in the news and newsrooms: Unpacking meta-journalistic discourse on the use of artificial intelligence in journalism. *Digital Journalism*, 10(10), 1756–1774. https://doi.org/10.1080/21670811.2022.2085129

Nagy, P., & Neff, G. (2024). Conjuring algorithms: Understanding the tech industry as stage magicians. *New Media & Society*, 26(9), 4938 4954. https://doi.org/10.1177/14614448241251789

Narayanan, A., & Kapoor, S. (2024). *AI Snake Oil: What artificial intelligence can do, what it can't, and how to tell the difference*. Princeton University Press. https://doi.org/10.2307/jj.14736606

Nieborg, D. B., & Foxman, M. (2023). *Mainstreaming and game journalism*. MIT Press. https://doi.org/10.7551/mitpress/13837.001.0001

Nielsen, R. K. (2016). The many crises of Western journalism: A comparative analysis of economic crises, professional crises, and crises of confidence. In J. C. Alexander, E. B. Breese, & M. Luengo (Eds.), *The Crisis of Journalism Reconsidered* (pp. 77–97). Cambridge University Press. https://doi.org/10.1017/CBO9781316050774

Perreault, G., Moon, R., Walsh, J. F., & Perreault, M. F. (2022). "It's not hate but…": Marginal categories in rural journalism. *Journalism Practice*, 18(5), 1039–1058. https://doi.org/10.1080/17512786.2022.2075782

Piper, K. (2019, February 14). An AI helped us write this article. *Vox*. https://www.vox.com/future-perfect/2019/2/14/18222270/artificial-intelligence-open-ai-natural-language-processing

Poell, T., Nieborg, D. B., & Duffy, B. E. (2021). *Platforms and cultural production*. Polity Press.

Polman, J. L., Newman, A., Saul, E. W., & Farrar, C. (2014). Adapting practices of science journalism to foster science literacy: Science journalism for science literacy. *Science Education*, 98(5), 766–791. https://doi.org/10.1002/sce.21114

Rashidian, N., Brown, P. D., Hansen, E., Bell, E. J., & Albright, J. R. (2019). *Friend and foe: The platform press at the heart of journalism*. Tow Center for Digital Journalism, Columbia University. https://doi.org/10.7916/D8-15PQ-X415

Resnick, M. (2024). Generative AI and creative learning: Concerns, opportunities, and choices. *An MIT Exploration of Generative AI*. https://doi.org/10.21428/e4baedd9.cf3e35e5

Roose, K. (2023, February 16). A conversation with Bing's chatbot left me deeply unsettled. *The New York Times*. https://www.nytimes.com/2023/02/16/technology/bing-chatbot-microsoft-chatgpt.html

Simon, F. M. (2024, February 6). Artificial intelligence in the news: How AI retools, rationalizes, and reshapes journalism and the public arena. *Columbia Journalism Review*. https://www.cjr.org/tow_center_reports/artificial-intelligence-in-the-news.php/

Smith, H., & Morgoch, M. L. (2022). Science & journalism: Bridging the gaps through specialty training. *Journalism Practice*, 16(5), 883–900. https://doi.org/10.1080/17512786.2020.1818608

Stein, J. (2015, August 6). Why virtual reality is about to change the world. *Time*. https://time.com/3987022/why-virtual-reality-is-about-to-change-the-world/

Stein, R., Willis, H., Jhaveri, I., Miller, D., Byrd, A., & Reneau, N. (2023, December 22). A Times investigation tracked Israel's use of one of its most destructive bombs in south Gaza. *The New York Times*. https://www.nytimes.com/2023/12/21/world/middleeast/israel-gaza-bomb-investigation.html

Stenros, J. (2015). Behind games: Playful mindsets and transformative practices. In S. P. Walz & S. Deterding (Eds.), *The gameful world* (pp. 201–222). MIT Press.

Thomson, T. J., Angus, D., Dootson, P., Hurcombe, E., & Smith, A. (2022). Visual mis/disinformation in journalism and public communications: Current verification practices, challenges, and future opportunities. *Journalism Practice*, *16*(5), 938–962. https://doi.org/10.1080/17512786.2020.1832139

Timsit, A. (2025, March 26). What happened when a newspaper let AI take over. *The Washington Post*. https://www.washingtonpost.com/world/2025/03/26/il-foglio-artificial-intelligence-journalism/

Usher, N. (2025). Generative AI and journalism: Hype, the always already new, and directions for scholarly imagination. *Digital Journalism*, Online First, 1–10. https://doi.org/10.1080/21670811.2025.2490604

Weiss-Blatt, N. (2021). *The techlash and tech crisis communication*. Emerald. https://doi.org/10.1108/9781800430853

Werning, S. (2024). Generative AI and the technological imaginary of game design. In F. Lesage & M. Terren (Eds.), *Creative tools and the softwarization of cultural production* (pp. 67–90). Springer. https://doi.org/10.1007/978-3-031-45693-0

Whitson, J. R. (2018). Voodoo software and boundary objects in game development: How developers collaborate and conflict with game engines and art tools. *New Media & Society*, *20*(7), 2315–2332. https://doi.org/10.1177/1461444817715020

Xie, E., Foxman, M., & Xu, S. (2021). From public sphere to magic circle: Playful publics on the Chinese internet. *Internet Histories*, *5*(3–4), 359–3755. https://doi.org/10.1080/24701475.2021.1982166

Yannakakis, G. N., & Togelius, J. (2018). *Artificial intelligence and games*. Springer. https://doi.org/10.1007/978-3-319-63519-4

9

DESIGNING THE AI MAZE

How the Tech Industry Entraps Users

Peter Nagy

With its origins dating back to the thirteenth century, the word "maze" comes from the Middle English word "mæs," indicating delirium or delusion (Oxford English Dictionary, 2001, Definition 1). In contemporary discourse, a maze usually refers to either "a confusing intricate network of passages" or "something confusingly elaborate or complicated" (Merriam-Webster Dictionary, n.d.). Typically consisting of complex routes and pathways restricted by walls, mazes are challenging to navigate and understand. In fact, mazes are specifically designed to serve as puzzles and mysteries that need to be solved. One of the most easily recognizable and famous mazes in European folklore is the Labyrinth from Greek mythology (Higgins, 2018). According to the legends, the Labyrinth was the home of the ravenous half-human, half-bull monster, the Minotaur, who required regular human sacrifices to satisfy his seemingly insatiable hunger. Eventually, the hero Theseus conquered the maze and defeated the cruel creature with the help of the Cretan princess, Ariadne.

For this chapter, I draw a parallel between what the maze represents—misdirection, bewilderment, and entrapment—and how tech companies build, deploy, and promote Artificial Intelligence (AI). I argue that the maze can serve as a metaphor for analyzing how the most prominent tech companies in the world, like Alphabet (Google), Amazon, Apple, Meta, and Microsoft, capitalize on their AI systems to amass more profit and power for themselves while entrapping users in their hype-driven technological ecosystem. By dominating and controlling cutting-edge models and key benchmarks, tech companies already hold great control over the research, implementation, and use of AI (e.g., Ahmed et al., 2023; Kak et al., 2023;

DOI: 10.4324/9781003477587-9

Katzenbach, 2021; Varoquaux et al., 2024). As Khanal and her colleagues (2024) noted, "this tech dominance leads to highly concentrated sectoral markets that provide tech companies with enormous market and financial resources that make them *big*" (p. 2). With billions of users globally, the individual size of the most powerful tech companies exceeds the GDP of even some G7 countries such as Canada and Italy (Chowdhary & Diasso, 2022).

Just like mazes, AI serves as an inescapable technological "cage" with an ever-growing presence in people's public and private lives. Due to the tech industry's vast resources and relentless lobbying efforts, AI systems are already widely deployed in social media platforms, search engines, entertainment, customer service, criminal justice, education finance, healthcare, and hiring (Narayanan & Kapoor, 2024) along with transportation and agriculture (Khanal et al., 2024). Currently, one of the most well-known and talked about AI tools is OpenAI's ChatGPT—a generative AI tool with around 200 million weekly users as of 2024 (Roth, 2024). While they are still a relatively new addition to the technological arsenal, generative AIs—such as ChatGPT or Google's Gemini (formerly known as Bard)— quickly became popular applications in the general US population with an adoption rate that was faster than PCs or the internet in 2024 (Bick et al., 2024).

To map the AI maze, I will turn to Ian Hodder's (2012, 2016) idea of entanglement that explores the dynamic relationships between humans and (material and/or symbolic) things from an archeological perspective. Hodder's conceptualization is in stark contrast with theories like Actor-Network Theory and Object Oriented Ontology that understand human-object relationships in terms of relationality, engagement, and symmetry. For Hodder, these relationships are fundamentally fraught and asymmetrical because of the power and influence things have over humans. By building on this idea, I will use the AI maze metaphor to illustrate how tech companies manufacture entanglements between users and their tools in order to entrap them in their technological ecosystem.

A (Very) Brief Overview of Ian Hodder's Archeological Theory of Entanglement

For the archeologist Ian Hodder (2012), the concept of entanglement serves as an analytical tool to study how humans and things shape and direct each other, and what changes their interrelationship has brought to the social and material world around them. Things tie people together, but they are also unruly and notoriously difficult to manage (Hodder, 2016). Given that they decay and erode over them, things need constant human attention and labor. And yet, things continue to undermine their efforts and hard work. Therefore, in order to keep them working properly, humans work even harder and enlist even more things. As a result, things draw humans into what Hodder (2012) calls dependence and dependency. For Hodder, "dependence" and "dependency" hold different meanings. Dependence is the reliance of humans and things on each other that *enables* them to exist and evolve in the world through their interrelationship. Dependency, on the other hand, is the constraints that humans and things place on each other, and therefore is always limiting because it *entraps* humans and things in their interrelationship.

For Hodder (2016), the concept of entanglement represents "the dialectic of dependence [potential through reliance] and dependency [constraint through reliance] between humans and things" (p. 14). The tension between dependence and dependency leads to continual movement and change, and humans keep searching for solutions to the entanglements and entrapments in which they—inevitably and ultimately—find themselves. However, as Hodder (2011) noted, it is not the things *themselves* that trigger entanglement, but rather "the interlacing of materials with the whole suite of ways in which humans and things depend on each other" (p. 164). As such, things are not entirely socially constructed for they have their own needs and demands along with their instabilities, constraints, and limitations.

Hodder (2012) argues that entanglement encompasses four relational categories, including human and human (HH), human and thing (HT), thing and human (TH), and thing and thing (TT) relations. What brings all these relations together is that they revolve around the centrality of things in entanglements. Humans, for example, rely on each other (HH) for care, comfort, and support. However, even when they are not at the forefront of attention, things still "lurk" in the background, allowing social, cognitive, and economic needs to be met. Humans, therefore, also rely on things to achieve their goals and manage their lives (HT). In this sense, humans need various things—homes, vehicles, financial assets, and so on—to be able to start off and take care of their families, work, have fun, and form hobbies.

Things require stability; otherwise, they break down and stop working. As such, to function properly, things depend on humans for providing constant care for them (TH). Physical objects, for instance, require regular maintenance, repair, and occasionally replacement. Without human care, oversight, and intervention, things could not serve their purposes. Finally, the things that rely on humans also depend on other things (TT). Human-made objects are also made of various materials, components, and parts, highlighting that the making and using one thing is entangled in the making and using other things (Hodder, 2018). However, given that entanglements are both social and material at the same time, TT dependencies always involve humans (e.g., manufacturers, designers, and inventors), just as HH dependencies always involve things (Hodder, 2016).

Mapping the AI Maze: The Relational Elements That Entrap Users

The AI maze metaphor builds as well as extends upon Ian Hodder's conceptualization of entanglement and its categories, such as HH, HT, TH, and TT relations. This idea captures the essence of Hodder's (2016) theory that "teaches us to look away from whatever is the immediate object of study, to explore the networks of dependencies that constrain and drive the human condition" (p. 9). That is, through their social, economic, and political power, the tech industry creates a complex web of relations that is centered around their AI systems to maximize widespread adoption and use of their tools. The daily practices of AI use are always directed down what Hodder (2012) calls *dependency pathways* in which users are—directly or indirectly—drawn in specific directions that create increasingly complex entanglements and entrapments. By design, the AI maze represents HT relations that benefit tech companies while limiting users' agency.

HH Relations: Enlisting Users to the AI Maze

When it comes to HH relations, people could not use AI tools if tech companies had not produced, advertised, and sold them. As the science and technology studies(STS) scholarship already noted, technologies are not developed in a vacuum—they are created by particular people with particular objectives, operating in specific contexts (Sismondo, 2018). Therefore, AI is best understood as a sociotechnical system that is coproduced by social, material, and organizational forces (Johnson & Vericcio, 2024). Given their unique position of power, however, tech companies can actively shape which AI systems are promoted and used by billions of people (Khanal et al., 2024). One way they do so is through forging collaborations with other private and public organizations and institutions. As Narayan and Shestakofsky (2024) noted:

> The firms driving AI development are embedded in unstable webs of relationships with investors, regulators, labor organizations, competitors, large tech platforms, consortia, and so on. For companies both within and beyond the tech sector, forces that may appear to be "extra-organizational" can have a substantial impact on when and how AI is developed and put to use.
>
> *(pp. 2–3)*

For instance, tech companies have long been targeting business executives and organization leaders with their AI systems that can—allegedly—help with cutting costs and improving efficiency (Vinsel, 2023), hiring "the best" candidates for positions (Wall & Schellmann, 2021), and improving their employees' engagement and performance (Swineford, 2023). Additionally, tech companies have been increasingly collaborating with law enforcement agencies, banks, and hospitals by providing murky and ambiguous services, such as "predictive analytics," "mortgage calculations," or "medical diagnostic algorithms" (Broussard, 2023). Similarly, the tech industry has also been dramatically expanding its influence in education by offering various forms of "AI fundings" for K12 and higher education institutions (Crooks, 2024). Through these partnerships, tech companies can directly or indirectly *enlist* even more users—managers, employees, customers, students, and other stakeholders—in their AI maze.

Social and news media HH relations also play a crucial role in creating excitement and building hype around AI. From sharing their personal opinion on emerging technologies to offering guides and tutorials on how to use ChatGPT effectively, social media personalities can have a significant impact on how their followers perceive AI (Alipour et al., 2024). On these platforms, AI tools are frequently described and discussed by conveniently vague terms, such as "disruptive," "powerful," "creative," "helpful," and "transformative." People—and potential future AI users—also read about AI in magazine articles written by journalists with large followings (Sun et al., 2020). However, while some prominent outlets (e.g., *The New York Times*, *The Guardian*, and *Wired*) became more critical of AI over time (e.g., Nguyen & Hekman, 2024), industry sources still continue to dominate and shape coverage (e.g., Brennen et al., 2018; Simon, 2024).

Television networks are no exception. For example, CBS's popular television news magazine broadcast, *60 minutes* has covered AI on several occasions through the years. In late 2024, NBC also released a special called *AI and the Future of Us* hosted by the media mogul, Oprah Winfrey. It was advertised as a show that "provides a serious, entertaining and meaningful base for every viewer to understand AI, and empowers everyone to be a part of one of the most important global conversations of the 21st century" (Donnelly, 2024, para. 8). While giving airtime to some critical voices, both CBS and NBC heavily featured influential figures from Silicon Valley (e.g., OpenAI's CEO, Sam Altman, Google's CEO, Sundar Pichai, and Microsoft's co-founder Bill Gates) whose main interest lies in growing their user base as well as expand and gatekeep their financial and informational power (Healey & Woods, 2017).

HT Relations: Integrating Users into the AI Maze

While HH relations describe how tech companies—directly and indirectly— enlist users to their AI maze, HT relations capture how users adapt to the increasing presence of AI tools in their lives. Ultimately, the goal of tech companies is to fully *integrate* all their current and future customer bases into their AI maze by manufacturing what Ian Hodder (2012) calls *dependency* on their technological products and services. Tech companies market their AI applications as "cutting-edge problem-solving tools" that not only allow users to manage their lives more productively and comfortably (Stockmann, 2023) but also serve as catalysts for "empowerment" and "positive social change" (Levina & Hasitoff, 2017). In reality, however, tech companies leave little to no choice to people but to use their AI tools and eventually become part of their AI maze—whether they want it or not.

In 2024, for example, Microsoft decided to push its generative AI tool to their customers by making Copilot part of its cloud-based subscription service package, Microsoft 365 in Australia and several Southwest Asian countries (Dotan, 2024). Also in 2024, Google "upgraded" its social media and online video sharing platform, YouTube with a conversational AI feature that auto-generates replies for content creators to make responding to comments and questions—allegedly—easier and quicker (Maiberg, 2024b). Similarly, Meta announced that it would add new AI character and assistant creation tools to Facebook, Instagram, and WhatsApp to make these applications "more entertaining and engaging" for all of their users (Criddle & Murphy, 2024). Amazon also stated that it started experimenting with integrating AI systems into its website and apps, including "AI-generated shopping guides" and "autonomous AI shopping agents" that can provide personalized recommendations for customers (Knight, 2024). Apple, not wanting to fall behind, incorporated new AI functionalities into the iPhone and the voice assistant Siri to "enhance" user experience and "boost" user satisfaction (Ingram, 2024).

Of course, people are not merely passive users of AI tools—they have their own perceptions of and expectations for these technologies. For example, studies on "algorithmic imaginary" (e.g., Bucher, 2017; Schellewald, 2022) and "folk theories of algorithms" (e.g., Siles et al., 2020; Ytre-Arne & Moe, 2021) already showed that users construct their own mental models about how AI systems work and affect their lives. People almost instinctively turn to these mental models to make sense of AI systems when using them for socializing and networking, working, discovering new media content, seeking assistance, and so on. Too often, however, users develop what researchers call AI overreliance (e.g., Buçinca et al., 2021;

Vasconcelos et al., 2023). That is, users typically have a strong tendency to accept AI-generated recommendations and answers even when they are inaccurate or factually wrong (Hicks et al., 2024). This bias is also fueled by tech companies that frequently portray their AI tools as "magical" and "continuously evolving" artifacts that can deliver solutions with efficiency, neutrality, and fairness—ideals that users would otherwise struggle to achieve in their lives (e.g., Andrews et al., 2024; Elish & boyd, 2018).

AI overreliance along with the tech sector's relentless efforts to push its dubious technological products and services on consumers highlights that user-AI relations are fundamentally fraught and asymmetrical. That is, users and AI tools do not just relate to each other. Rather, tech companies direct HT relations in ways that limit user agency—they draw users in specific pathways that lead to further entanglements and entrapments in their AI maze.

TH Relations: Keeping Users in the AI Maze

As Hodder (2016) noted, it is not just humans who rely on things (HT), but things also rely on humans (TH). The AI maze, too, relies on humans. Its AI systems are operated and managed by a large number of workers—engineers, computer scientists, data analysts, and so on. Without their constant assistance and care, these technologies could not run properly and would eventually break down and stop working (Ekbia & Nardi, 2014). AI systems also rely on what social scientists refer to as crowdwork or micro-work that "involves the manipulation of data with the help of a digital device such as a computer" (Altenried, 2020, p. 147). Crowdworkers provide all kinds of essential labor for tech companies, such as categorizing pictures, transcribing speeches, and managing data (Tubaro et al., 2020). Tech companies, however, do not like to publicly discuss the vast amount of labor involved in the operation and management of their AI systems. In fact, they strategically hide this important information from the public in order to fuel the AI hype (Newlands, 2021). This way, members of the tech sector can portray themselves as "pioneering" AI and machine learning companies rather than labor companies, which allows them to attract as well as secure more capital from investors (Irani, 2015).

While tech companies like to focus on the "remarkable" and "superhuman" capabilities of their inventions, they prefer not to acknowledge the fact that their technologies are rarely or not all functioning as advertised (Anthony et al., 2023). Behind the scenes, a vast network of people provides their knowledge and labor to make sure that AI systems appear to "work" (Natale, 2023). This includes users, too. When interacting with

AI tools, they provide feedback on the output the systems produce. For example, users can make adjustments, rate AI-generated responses, refine their prompts, or ask for clarification in case they are not satisfied with the performance of the AI tool. This way, the more the user interacts with them, the more effectively AI systems can perform tasks for them (Amershi et al., 2014). The size of the user base also matters. With more users providing feedback, the models operating AI systems have more information to refine their algorithms and improve their accuracy.

What these TH relations call attention to is the intense human labor responsible for building, operating, improving, and troubleshooting AI systems. While tech companies intentionally and strategically obfuscate their presence and contribution, human workers play an essential role in *keeping* users in the AI maze. Through their interactions and engagements with AI systems, even users provide important labor for tech companies to advance their AI models and improve their AI maze.

TT Relations: Continuously Expanding the AI Maze

Things do not only rely on humans, but also on other things. AI systems are no exception. They are built around as well as operated by an intricate and complex web of infrastructure—various hardware and software components (interfaces, cloud services, datasets, codes, algorithms, and protocols), power grids, data centers, and underwater cable networks for data distribution (van Dijck, 2021). These infrastructures serve as material networks that allow other materials to reach their intended destinations (Schinkel, 2023). Each part works in tandem, enabling AI systems to work properly and efficiently. However, similarly to how tech companies obfuscate the TH relations governing their AI maze, TT relations are also kept hidden from the public eye. As Lamdan (2023) put it, tech companies strategically conceal their material infrastructure "by maintaining each of their product lines in separate silos, and by obscuring what their data products do by giving them vague names like 'special services' and 'risk solutions'" (p. 127). And yet, while they may seem invisible, infrastructures still have to be managed by humans (Star & Ruhleder, 2016). As Hodder (2012) would argue, infrastructures are yet another example of entanglements being both social and material at the same time.

Tech companies rely on their expansive infrastructure network to "industrialize" their AI services and develop a variety of commercial products and services across a wide range of industry sectors (van der Vlist et al., 2024). The infrastructures underlying their AI systems allow tech companies to engage what Zuboff (2019) calls "surveillance capitalism" and collect, store, analyze, and commodify their customers' data. The data tech companies gather by—covertly—monitoring their customers' interactions with their tools are used to refine their algorithms and AI models and to develop new applications. For example, 404 Media reported that the Microsoft-owned professional networking site, LinkedIn, was secretly training their new AI systems on their users' data (Cox, 2024). In another case, Niantic, the former Google startup and then-independent company behind the popular augmented reality mobile games, *Ingress* and *Pokémon Go,* turned out to be using their players' data to develop a large geospatial AI model that would allow computers to navigate the physical world more efficiently (Maiberg, 2024a).

But tech companies do not *only* rely on their customers' data. They also collect and analyze all kinds of public and third-party content from the internet to train their AI systems (Jones, 2024). In fact, tech companies are so successful in their—ethically and legally highly questionable—harvesting efforts that they are running out of training data (Villalobos et al., 2024). To overcome this challenge, some tech companies pay people to produce new data, while others use AI-generated "synthetic" data for AI training. However, none of these potential solutions is perfect, and they will all lead to other problems. Take the example of generative AI tools, such as OpenAI's ChatGPT, Google's Gemini, or Microsoft's Copilot. They are all built on large language models—complex deep learning models capable of producing content based on user prompts (Min et al., 2023). These systems rely on massive datasets to function properly. But, even when "fed" with bigger datasets, the performance and accuracy of AI systems still fluctuate over time (e.g., Chen et al., 2023), especially in case of larger and scaled-up models (e.g., Zhou et al., 2023).

The increasingly complex TT relations necessary for managing AI systems exemplify one of the core ideas of entanglement that Hodder (2016) calls the "unstable messiness" of things. Similar to other things, AI tools continue to have their own demands that require constant human labor to resolve. But humans' efforts are being undermined by the limitations and instabilities of these systems. Thus, they work even harder and enlist even more data and computing resources, hoping that these can help them better manage and improve their technologies. As Hodder (2016) put it, "things appear as Hydra-like, requiring Herculean skill to stop them multiplying and entrapping, and yet the entrapment is enticing and productive" (p. 14). The enticing and productive nature of this entrapment drives tech companies to *continue to expand* their AI mazes. The more their AI mazes grow, the easier it is for tech companies to accumulate more influence and power for themselves. At the same time, the more AI mazes grow, the more resources tech companies need to rely on to manage them effectively.

Conclusions: Conquering the AI Maze

The metaphors people use for AI matter. They not only shape how people think and feel about these technologies but also what rules they make for them (Mitchell, 2024). Viewing AI as a maze calls attention to the power and influence tech companies exert over users and the world. Tech companies orchestrate and exploit what Hodder (2012) calls a series of HT relations for their own benefits. They like to describe their AI systems as inevitable and massively disruptive autonomous technologies (Bareis & Katzenbach, 2022) that serve as "miraculous fixes" for all kinds of social and economic problems (Bory et al., 2024). In contrast, the AI maze metaphor invites people to look beyond tools and consider the role tech companies play in the design, implementation, and use of technological systems.

In her op-ed, Meredith Whittaker (2024) argued that allowing a few tech companies to accumulate so much power and influence in the world never leads to good things. Similar to the Labyrinth from Greek mythology, the AI maze is also filled with various hazards and perils. These dangers do not take the form of fictional monsters but represent actual harms tech companies cause through their AI systems. For example, a report by Kevin De Liban (2024) noted:

> Powerful actors employ AI to decide where low income people live and work, what they pay in rent, what they earn in wages, how their kids are treated in schools, what government benefits they can receive and under what conditions, which parenting actions will be subject to state investigation, and what resources will be available to protect them against domestic violence. Too often, these decisions restrict opportunities and cause tangible harms.
>
> *(p. 144)*

In addition to engaging in surveillance and information control, tech companies perpetuate various dangerous stereotypes and racist beliefs through their AI systems, endangering historically marginalized communities (e.g., Akter et al., 2021; Benjamin, 2019; Owens & Walker, 2020).

The immense infrastructural network operating the AI maze also produces various negative outcomes. That is, tech companies continue to rely on fossil fuels to meet the growing electricity needs of their AI systems (Chu & Smyth, 2025). Recent estimates by the Department of Energy suggest that data centers could consume up to 12% of the US's electricity by 2028 (Parvini, 2025). It is historically marginalized communities, however, who are paying the price. For example, tech companies tend to build their new data centers near Native American reservations and historically

African American neighborhoods leading to frequent power outages and adverse health effects, such as increased prevalence of asthma and cancer (Verma, 2024).

Despite their negative social and environmental impact, AI mazes are enduring structures that are seemingly challenging or nearly impossible to stop from growing. To *conquer* them, it is important to remember that HT entanglements are far from being deterministic forces (Hodder, 2016). Just like Theseus, who was able to conquer the Labyrinth with the help of Ariadne, people can also find ways to free themselves from the AI mazes tech companies designed for them. One way people can achieve this is through the collaborative development of frameworks and tools for better public policy around AI. For example, the Federal Trade Commission (2025) noted, "companies can use AI tools in ways that have serious impacts on consumers, so they need to address associated risks before, during, and after consumers come in contact with them" (para. 10). However, it is highly unlikely that tech companies would willingly disclose crucial information about their AI systems. Therefore, Laura Manley (2025) called for the creation of a Freedom of Information Act-like system that would require tech companies to publicly disclose information on their algorithmic decision-making processes along with their data collection practices and content moderation policies. This could lead to better transparency and accountability by preventing tech companies from engaging in one of their favorite practices—misrepresenting and obfuscating their AI systems.

References

Ahmed, N., Wahed, M., & Thompson, N. C. (2023). The growing influence of industry in AI research. *Science, 379*(6635), 884–886.

Akter, S., McCarthy, G., Sajib, S., Michael, K., Dwivedi, Y. K., D'Ambra, J., & Shen, K. N. (2021). Algorithmic bias in data-driven innovation in the age of AI. *International Journal of Information Management, 60*, 1–13.

Alipour, S., Galeazzi, A., Sangiorgio, E., Avalle, M., Bojic, L., Cinelli, M., & Quattrociocchi, W. (2024). Cross-platform social dynamics: An analysis of ChatGPT and COVID-19 vaccine conversations. *Scientific Reports, 14*(1), Article 2789.

Altenried, M. (2020). The platform as factory: Crowdwork and the hidden labour behind artificial intelligence. *Capital & Class, 44*(2), 145–158.

Amershi, S., Cakmak, M., Knox, W. B., & Kulesza, T. (2014). Power to the people: The role of humans in interactive machine learning. *AI Magazine, 35*(4), 105–120.

Andrews, M., Smart, A., & Birhane, A. (2024). The reanimation of pseudoscience in machine learning and its ethical repercussions. *Patterns, 5*(9), 1–14.

Anthony, C., Bechky, B. A., & Fayard, A. L. (2023). "Collaborating" with AI: Taking a system view to explore the future of work. *Organization Science, 34*(5), 1672–1694.

Bareis, J., & Katzenbach, C. (2022). Talking AI into being: The narratives and imaginaries of national AI strategies and their performative politics. *Science, Technology, & Human Values, 47*(5), 855–881.

Benjamin, R. (2019). Assessing risk, automating racism. *Science, 366,* 421–422.

Bick, A., Blandin, A., & Deming, D. J. (2024). *The rapid adoption of generative AI* (No. w32966). National Bureau of Economic Research.

Bory, P., Natale, S., & Katzenbach, C. (2024). Strong and weak AI narratives: An analytical framework. *AI & Society, 40,* 1–11.

Brennen, J. S., Howard, P. N., & Nielsen, R. K. (2018). An industry-led debate: How UK media cover artificial intelligence [Fact Sheet]. Reuters Institute. https://reutersinstitute.politics.ox.ac.uk/sites/default/files/2018-12/Brennen_UK_Media_Coverage_of_AI_FINAL.pdf

Broussard, M. (2023). *More than a glitch: Confronting race, gender, and ability bias in tech.* MIT Press.

Bucher, T. (2017). The algorithmic imaginary: Exploring the ordinary affects of Facebook algorithms. *Information, Communication & Society, 20*(1), 30–44

Buçinca, Z., Malaya, M. B., & Gajos, K. Z. (2021). To trust or to think: Cognitive forcing functions can reduce overreliance on AI in AI-assisted decision-making. *Proceedings of the ACM on Human-Computer Interaction, 5*(CSCW1), 1–21.

Chen, L., Zaharia, M., & Zou, J. (2023). How is ChatGPT's behavior changing over time? arXiv:2307.09009. https://doi.org/10.48550/arXiv.2307.09009

Chowdhary, M., & Diasso, S. (2022). *Taxing Big Tech: Policy options for developing countries.* State of Big Tech. https://projects.itforchange.net/state-of-big-tech/taxing-big-tech-policy-options-for-developing-countries/

Chu, A., & Smyth, J. (2025, January 12). AI set to fuel surge in new US gas power plants. *Financial Times.* https://www.ft.com/content/63c3ceb2-5e30-44f4-bd39-cb40edafa4f8

Cox, S. (2024, September 18). LinkedIn is training AI on user data before updating its terms of service. *404 Media.* https://www.404media.co/linkedin-is-training-ai-on-user-data-before-updating-its-terms-of-service/

Criddle, C., & Murphy, H. (2024, December 26). Meta envisages social media filled with AI-generated users. *Financial Times.* https://www.ft.com/content/91183cbb-50f9-464a-9d2e-96063825bfcf

Crooks, R. N. (2024). *Access is capture: How edtech reproduces racial inequality.* University of California Press.

De Liban, K. (2024). *Inescapable AI: The ways AI decides how low-income people work, live, learn, and survive.* Techtonic Justice. https://static1.squarespace.com/static/65a1d3be4690143890f61cec/t/673c7170a0d0977706c6e50/1732014450563/ttj-inescapable-ai.pdf

Donnelly, J. (2024, September 9). Watch 'AI and the future of us: An Oprah Winfrey Special' Thursday, September 12. *ABC.* https://abc.com/news/1efd942d-61bb-4519-8a62-c4a8fce50792/category/1138628

Dotan, T. (2024, December 26). Microsoft is forcing its AI assistant on people—And making them pay. *The Wall Street Journal.* https://www.wsj.com/tech/ai/microsoft-ai-assistant-copilot-365-suite-dfb293b3

Ekbia, H., & Nardi, B. (2014). Heteromation and its (dis) contents: The invisible division of labor between humans and machines. *First Monday, 19*(6). https://doi.org/10.5210/fm.v19i6.5331

Elish, M. C., & boyd, d. (2018). Situating methods in the magic of big data and AI. *Communication Monographs, 85*(1), 57–80.

Federal Trade Commission (2025, January 3). AI and the risk of consumer harm. https://www.ftc.gov/policy/advocacy-research/tech-at-ftc/2025/01/ai-risk-consumer-harm

Healey, K., & Woods, R. H. (2017). Processing is not judgment, storage is not memory: A critique of Silicon Valley's moral catechism. *Journal of Media Ethics, 32*(1), 2–15.

Hicks, M. T., Humphries, J., & Slater, J. (2024). ChatGPT is bullshit. *Ethics and Information Technology, 26*(2), 37–46.

Higgins, C. (2018, July 28). Myths, monsters and the maze: How writers fell in love with the labyrinth. *The Guardian.* https://www.theguardian.com/books/2018/jul/28/myth-monsters-and-the-maze-how-writers-fell-in-love-with-the-labyrinth

Hodder, I. (2011). Human-thing entanglement: Towards an integrated archaeological perspective. *The Journal of the Royal Anthropological Institute, 17,* 154–177.

Hodder, I. (2012). *Entangled: An archaeology of the relationships between humans and things.* Wiley-Blackwell.

Hodder, I. (2016). *Studies in human-thing entanglement.* https://www.ian-hodder.com/books/studies-human-thing-entanglement

Hodder, I. (2018). *Where are we heading?: The evolution of humans and things.* Yale University Press.

Ingram, D. (2024, June 10). AI is coming to your iPhone: Five takeaways from Apple's big announcement. *NBC News.* https://www.nbcnews.com/tech/tech-news/ai-coming-iphone-five-takeaways-apples-big-announcement-rcna156374

Irani, L. (2015). The cultural work of microwork. *New Media & Society, 17*(5), 720–739.

Johnson, D. G., & Verdicchio, M. (2024). The sociotechnical entanglement of AI and values. *AI & Society, 40,* 1–10.

Jones, N. (2024). The AI revolution is running out of data. What can researchers do? *Nature, 636*(8042), 290–292.

Kak, A., Myers West, S., & Whittaker, M. (2023, December 5). Make no mistake—AI is owned by Big Tech. *MIT Technology Review,* https://www.technologyreview.com/2023/12/05/1084393/make-no-mistake-ai-is-owned-by-big-tech/

Katzenbach, C. (2021). "AI will fix this"–The technical, discursive, and political turn to AI in governing communication. *Big Data & Society, 8*(2), 1–8. https://doi.org/10.1177/20539517211046182

Khanal, S., Zhang, H., & Taeihagh, A. (2024). Why and how is the power of Big Tech increasing in the policy process? The case of generative AI. *Policy and Society, 0*(0), 1–18.

Knight, W. (2024, October 9). Amazon dreams of AI agents that do the shopping for you. *Wired.* https://www.wired.com/story/amazon-ai-agents-shopping-guides-rufus/

Lamdan, S. (2023). *Data cartels: The companies that control and monopolize our information.* Stanford University Press.

Levina, M., & Hasinoff, A. A. (2017). The Silicon Valley ethos: Tech industry products, discourses, and practices. *Television & New Media, 18*(6), 489–495. https://doi.org/10.1177/1527476416680454

Maiberg, E. (2024a, November 19). Pokémon Go players have unwittingly trained AI to navigate the world. *404 Media*. https://www.404media.co/pokemon-go-players-have-unwittingly-trained-ai-to-navigate-the-world/

Maiberg, E. (2024b, December 12). YouTube "enhances" comment section with AI-generated nonsense. *404 Media*. https://www.404media.co/youtube-enhances-comment-section-with-ai-generated-nonsense/

Manley, L. (2025, January 14). We need a Freedom of Information Act for Big Tech. *Washington Post*. https://www.washingtonpost.com/opinions/2025/01/14/big-tech-foia-regulation-transparency/

Merriam-Webster Dictionary (n.d.). *Maze*. In Merriam–Webster.com dictionary. Retrieved September 23, 2024, from https://www.merriam-webster.com/dictionary/maze

Min, B., Ross, H., Sulem, E., Veyseh, A. P. B., Nguyen, T. H., Sainz, O., Agirre, E., Heintz, I., & Roth, D. (2023). Recent advances in natural language processing via large pre-trained language models: A survey. *ACM Computing Surveys*, *56*, 1–40.

Mitchell, M. (2024). The metaphors of artificial intelligence. *Science*, *386*(6723), 1–6.

Narayan, D., & Shestakofsky, B. (2024). Relationships that matter: Four perspectives on AI, work, and organizations. *The Journal of Applied Behavioral Science*, *60*(4), 639–651.

Narayanan, A., & Kapoor, S. (2024). *AI snake pil: What artificial intelligence can do, what it can't, and how to tell the difference*. Princeton University Press.

Natale, S. (2023). AI, human-machine communication and deception. In A. Guzman, R. McEwen, & S. Jones (Eds.), *The Sage handbook of human-machine communication* (pp. 401–408). Sage.

Newlands, G. (2021). Lifting the curtain: Strategic visibility of human labour in AI-as-a-Service. *Big Data & Society*, *8*(1), 1–14.

Nguyen, D., & Hekman, E. (2024). The news framing of artificial intelligence: A critical exploration of how media discourses make sense of automation. *AI & Society*, *39*(2), 437–451.

Owens, K., & Walker, A. (2020). Those designing healthcare algorithms must become actively anti-racist. *Nature Medicine*, *26*, 1327–1328.

Oxford English Dictionary (2001). *Maze*. In Oxford English Dictionary.com, retrieved September 23, 2024, from https://www.oed.com/dictionary/maze_n1

Parvini, S. (2025, January 14). Biden signs ambitious order to bolster energy resources for AI data centers. *AP News*. https://apnews.com/article/biden-white-house-ai-artificial-intelligence-7458d9d1bb537929c5dcfb5192695223

Roth, E. (2024, August 29). ChatGPT's weekly users have doubled in less than a year. *The Verge*. https://www.theverge.com/2024/8/29/24231685/openai-chatgpt-200-million-weekly-users

Schellewald, A. (2022). Theorizing "stories about algorithms" as a mechanism in the formation and maintenance of algorithmic imaginaries. *Social Media+ Society*, *8*(1), 1–10.

Schinkel, W. (2023). Steps to an ecology of algorithms. *Annual Review of Anthropology*, *52*(1), 171–186.

Siles, I., Segura-Castillo, A., Solís, R., & Sancho, M. (2020). Folk theories of algorithmic recommendations on Spotify: Enacting data assemblages in the global South. *Big Data & Society*, *7*(1), 1–15.

Simon, F. M. (2024). Artificial intelligence in the news: How AI retools, rationalizes, and reshapes journalism and the public arena. *Columbia Journalism Review.* https://www.cjr.org/tow_center_reports/artificial-intelligence-in-the-news.php

Sismondo, S. (2018). Science and technology studies. In N. Castree, M. Hulme, & J. D. Proctor (Eds), *Companion to environmental studies* (pp. 356–359). Routledge.

Star, S. L., & Ruhleder, K. (2016). Steps toward an ecology of infrastructure: Design and access for large information spaces. In G. C. Bowker, S. Timmermans, A. E. Clarke, & E. Balka (Eds.), *Boundary objects and beyond: Working with Leigh Star* (pp. 377–416). MIT Press.

Stockmann, D. (2023). Tech companies and the public interest: The role of the state in governing social media platforms. *Information, Communication & Society,* 26(1), 1–15.

Sun, S., Zhai, Y., Shen, B., & Chen, Y. (2020). Newspaper coverage of artificial intelligence: A perspective of emerging technologies. *Telematics and Informatics,* 53, Article 101433.

Swineford, R. (2023, July 25). Generative AI is empowering the digital workforce. *MIT Technology Review.* https://www.technologyreview.com/2023/07/25/1076532/generative-ai-is-empowering-the-digital-workforce/

Tubaro, P., Casilli, A. A., & Coville, M. (2020). The trainer, the verifier, the imitator: Three ways in which human platform workers support artificial intelligence. *Big Data & Society,* 7(1), 1–12.

van der Vlist, F., Helmond, A., & Ferrari, F. (2024). Big AI: Cloud infrastructure dependence and the industrialisation of artificial intelligence. *Big Data & Society,* 11(1),1–16. https://doi.org/10.1177/20539517241232630

Varoquaux, G., Luccioni, A. S., & Whittaker, M. (2024). Hype, sustainability, and the price of the bigger-is-better paradigm in AI. arXiv:2409.14160v1, 119. https://doi.org/10.48550/arXiv.2409.14160

Vasconcelos, H., Jörke, M., Grunde-McLaughlin, M., Gerstenberg, T., Bernstein, M. S., & Krishna, R. (2023). Explanations can reduce overreliance on AI systems during decision-making. *Proceedings of the ACM on Human-Computer Interaction,* 7(CSCW1), 1–38.

Verma, P. (2024, December 23). In the shadows of Arizona's data center boom, thousands live without power. *Washington Post.* https://www.washingtonpost.com/technology/2024/12/23/arizona-data-centers-navajo-power-aps-srp/

Villalobos, P., Ho, A., Sevilla, J., Besiroglu, T., Heim, L., & Hobbhahn, M. (2024). Will we run out of data? Limits of LLM scaling based on human-generated data. *arXiv preprint.* https://doi.org/10.48550/arXiv.2211.04325

Vinsel, L. (2023, May 23) Don't get distracted by the hype around generative AI. *MIT Sloan Management.* https://sloanreview.mit.edu/article/dont-get-distracted-by-the-hype-around-generative-ai/

van Dijck, J. (2021). Seeing the forest for the trees: Visualizing platformization and its governance. *New Media & Society,* 23(9), 2801–2819.

Wall, S., & Schellmann, H. (2021, July 7). We tested AI interview tools. Here's what we found. *MIT Technology Review.* https://www.technologyreview.com/2021/07/07/1027916/we-tested-ai-interview-tools/

Whittaker, M. (2024, November 26). The beginning of the end of Big Tech. *Wired.* https://www.wired.com/story/the-beginning-of-the-end-of-big-tech/

Ytre-Arne, B., & Moe, H. (2021). Folk theories of algorithms: Understanding digital irritation. *Media, Culture & Society*, 43(5), 807–824.

Zhou, L., Schellaert, W., Martínez-Plumed, F., Moros-Daval, Y., Ferri, C., & Hernández-Orallo, J. (2024). Larger and more instructable language models become less reliable. *Nature*, 634, 61–68.

Zuboff, S. (2019). *The age of surveillance capitalism: The fight for a human future at the new frontier of power* (1st ed.). PublicAffairs.

10

THE FEMINIST ARTIFICIAL INTELLIGENCE PLAYBOOK

Sophie Toupin

> My friend lowered the air-car by reversing the action of the machine, and when the car touched the ground the machine was stopped and we got out.
>
> —Rokeya Skhawat Hossain, *Sultana's Dream*

This excerpt is from *Sultana's Dream*, a feminist utopian short fiction story written in 1905 by the Bengali Muslim author Rokeya Skhawat Hossain. It is the story of a land, Ladyland, where women rule. In their universities, laboratories, and observatories, they build air-cars powered by hydrogen balls, tubes that gather and store up the sun-heat and pipes connected to clouds which provide clean water to families and prevent devastating floods. Collectively, the women of ladyland have succeeded in eradicating epidemic diseases such as malaria and child mortality. Their kitchen is free from coal and instead of being filled with smoke, greeneries, flowers, and tomato plants serve as ornaments. All this with two hours of (re)productive work per day! By developing their own feminist science and technology, the women of ladyland aim to better serve their community. *Sultana's Dream* is a reverse story where women rule, and men are invisible, confined outside of the public realm. It is also an anticolonial affirmation against the British colonial practices of the time, where women built infrastructures for the well-being of their communities.

I start with this example to show how feminists have long been imagining science and technology differently and in the service of their communities. Just like *Sultana's Dream* (Hossain, 2005/1905), feminist

DOI: 10.4324/9781003477587-10

artificial intelligence (AI)—the subject of this chapter—flips our thinking about what a different AI could be, reimagining the ways it is made, its purpose, and impact. This reimagining is part of what I call the feminist AI playbook: a set of methods, tactics, and guiding principles that help feminists approach and reshape AI from a community-centered and social justice-oriented perspective. By envisioning AI as a tool for feminist goals, feminist AI follows the example set by *Sultana's Dream*: it imagines technologies that uplift communities, address inequities, and challenge dominant systems of power.

In this chapter, I examine the feminist AI playbook in both theory and action. I start by giving a broad historical overview of the context in which critical perspectives on feminist AI have emerged and how it was conceived in the 1990s. I first examine the origins of the term, tracing its roots back to the critical analyses and pioneering efforts of feminist science and technology scholars. I focus exclusively on the work of British historian of science Alison Adam who was using the term feminist AI already 30 years ago. Her initial endeavor together with many other feminist science and technology scholars laid the groundwork for the current landscape of the field of critical AI. This historical section consists of the guiding principles of the playbook and enriches our understanding of AI showing that feminists have been thinking, articulating, and prototyping feminist AI for more than three decades now. Then, the second part of the playbook aims at examining the methods and tactics in which feminist activists today have used collective and often playful methods and tactics to fight back against harmful AI practices. This playbook, which is different than the corporate AI playbook, aims to spotlight how feminists are developing and refining their own set of strategies in how to use, educate, and rethink what AI can be. To illustrate this playbook, I focus on a handful of examples of how feminist activists are trying to shape a more equitable AI ecosystem. Through a handful of short case studies such as the development of feminist datasets, chatbots, and generative AI, I underscore the creative spirit of these emerging feminist AI practices. By spotlighting this feminist AI playbook in both theory and practice, I demonstrate how feminist activists not only respond to AI injustices but also proactively shape the AI landscape with their creative initiatives.

Feminist AI Playbook

The term playbook is generally used in sports, especially in American football, to refer to a book containing a team's planned plays, formations, and tactics. It is also used to describe structured plans and procedures in various fields such as in business, politics, software development, and activism. In this chapter, I have chosen to use the term *feminist AI playbook* to describe some of the guiding principles, methods, and tactics that feminists are using to advance goals such as gender equality, women's and 2SLGBTQI+ rights, and social justice more broadly within the field of AI. The term feminist AI playbook implies actionable approach to activism to transform AI and its impact on marginalized individuals, communities, and their environment. A feminist AI playbook includes discursive, artistic, educational, and coding methods as well as tactics. A feminist AI playbook is thus both a toolkit and a roadmap for feminist AI activists, researchers, and practitioners, helping them approach AI with feminist values.

While I use the term *playbook* in the singular, I aim to capture the diversity of principles, methods, and strategies that feminists, from varied political perspectives, use to imagine radically different possibilities for feminist AI. In other words, using *playbook* does not imply a single, fixed formula; rather, it signifies an evolving set of approaches that adapts to the emerging challenges feminists face. These challenges include addressing data bias and capture without consent, developing feminist chatbots that spell out feminist content, collectively resisting deepfake abuse, and creatively utilizing generative AI for feminist purposes. Ultimately, the feminist AI playbook is flexible and dynamic, showcasing the creativity of feminist activists, researchers, and practitioners.

The Need for a New Term: Feminist AI

The feminist AI playbook begins with a term. In 1995, Alison Adam, a British feminist computer scientist, published an article titled "Artificial Intelligence and Women's Knowledge: What Can Feminist Epistemology Tell Us?" (Adam, 1995). In this work, she argues that the pathway to a different kind of AI—one that can be characterized as feminist AI—requires a twofold approach. First, she posits that it is entirely possible to leverage "traditional AI" technologies for feminist purposes, suggesting that AI can be repurposed to address gender biases and promote equality. Second, Adam emphasizes the necessity for feminism to actively engage with AI technologies, rather than ignoring them. For Adam, this engagement with feminism was crucial for reorienting AI development in a way that reflects feminist values and priorities. This article is important for the feminist AI playbook because it is where the term feminist AI first appears, marking an important discursive moment. Building on the work of many feminist science and technology scholars (Forsythe, 1993; Haraway, 1988; Suchman, 1987; Wajcman, 1991), Adam's insights were to lay the groundwork for subsequent discussions and initiatives aimed at redefining AI through a feminist lens, urging scholars, practitioners, and activists to consider how

AI can be developed and utilized in ways that advance feminism and social justice. This early work serves as a foundational element in the evolving and emerging feminist AI playbook.

It is, however, in her book *Artificial Knowing: Gender and the Thinking Machine* (Adam, 1998) that she further develops her insights on feminist AI. But before explaining what she means by feminist AI, it is important to understand the three main arguments that critically assess the foundations of AI. First, Adam (1998) maintains that AI is grounded in a controversial epistemological and philosophical conception of what constitutes intelligence. This foundational perspective raises questions about how intelligence is defined and who gets to define it, thereby exposing biases that may overlook or marginalize alternative forms of knowledge and understanding.

Second, Adam (1998) critiques the rationality model prevalent in AI projects, arguing that it is problematic because it prioritizes the human mind over the body. This approach neglects the culturally and socially situated nature of intelligence, effectively erasing the embodied experiences that shape how individuals think and act. Even in the realm of robotics, which represents the physical embodiment of AI, this model fails to recognize the importance of context and lived experience, suggesting that a more holistic understanding of intelligence must consider both cognitive processes and the embodied realities of users.

Third, Adam (1998) examines the relationship between AI and male domination, introducing the idea of man as norm within the AI field. She argues that this normative framework reinforces gender biases and perpetuates inequalities, reflecting a broader societal tendency to center male perspectives and experiences while marginalizing or ignoring female experiences and contributions of other groups too (such as people in the global south and Indigenous people).

Trying to go beyond these critiques, Alison Adam (1998) posits a more hopeful perspective: she argues that it is possible to repurpose AI technologies for feminist purposes. This assertion opens the door for leveraging existing AI systems to promote gender equity, challenge patriarchal norms, and empower women in various domains, etc. By suggesting that feminist principles can inform the development and application of AI, Adam (1998) sets the stage for ongoing dialogue and innovation in feminist technology, encouraging activists, researchers, and technologists to envision and create a future where AI serves the interests of feminists. Through these arguments, Adam not only critiques the status quo but also inspires a reimagining of AI that aligns with feminist values and aspirations.

For Alison Adam, feminist AI represents a political project. It is not simply a new term; it is a deliberate political stance. Adam (1998) draws on

Audre Lorde's idea that "you can't dismantle the master's house using the master's tools" (p. 70), but believes that feminist AI can "be used tactically to make a few scratches in the masonry" (p. 70). She argues that, despite inherent contradictions, feminists should be actively involved in designing AI applications. This suggests that even small steps can lead to meaningful change, with feminist AI serving as a form of political expression.

Because she believed that feminists and feminism must engage with AI, she decided to design feminist AI with two of her students. The first project she and her student Chloe Furnival were involved in was the idea of compiling feminist jurisprudence on issues of gender discrimination in the United Kingdom to support low-income women and their cases in front of the court. The idea was that if we can assist women in defending themselves by more easily finding the best jurisprudence, this would be a way of automating feminism (Adam, 1998; Adam & Furnival, 1995). The second project she and her student Maureen Scott were involved in was a feminist computational language system, which aimed to support the understanding of gendered communication between people of distinct backgrounds (gender, race, class, etc.). At its core, this project was about valuing the knowledge women had developed over years and aimed to ultimately predict when misunderstandings happen even before the participants realized. In her book, Adam (1998) reflects on these attempts at designing feminist AI as being full of unresolved contradictions. But, as she said, "I had to start somewhere" (Adam, 1998, p. 166), and "we can't lose sight of the political project of feminist AI" (Adam, 1998, p. 164). This is exactly what feminist researchers, practitioners, and activists from different regions of the world have decided to do: to continue the project initiated by Adam and her students.

Deploying Feminist AI Today

Feminist AI projects today are being shaped as much by feminist academics, students, NGOs, and artists in both the global south and north. The involvement of such actors in rethinking AI marks a departure from the conventional history of the field. This history is rooted, first, in an anti-communist agenda—exemplified by the US Defense Department's Cold War interest in using AI to translate Russian documents (Bell, 2018)—and, second, in elite universities such as Harvard and MIT, and in telecommunication or computer companies such as Bell Labs and IBM.

Discursive Reemergence of Feminist AI

The reemergence of feminist AI as discourse can be situated in the recent turn to understanding AI from critical perspectives. Indeed, many feminist and intersectional engagements with AI have been a response to the racism and sexism exposed powerfully by many Black feminist computer scientists and scholars among others (Benjamin, 2019; Broussard, 2018; Buolamwini & Gebru, 2018; Noble, 2018). Activists, practitioners, and scholars who engage with the term feminist AI at times connect it with decolonial (Costanza-Chock, 2018) and Indigenous frameworks (Lewis et al., 2025), thereby broadening its scope, guiding principles, and significance.

At the discursive level, two presentations by UK-based feminists have helped bring renewed visibility to the term "feminist AI" within civil society. First, Josie Young who refers to herself as a feminist AI researcher made a presentation at the TED Talk London Women entitled *Why We Need to Design Feminist AI* (Young, 2019). In this talk, Young argues for the necessity of feminist AI to counter the sexist and harmful effects of AI-powered voice assistants like Siri and Alexa. She emphasizes that one of the only ways to address these issues is to rethink the design of chatbots from a feminist perspective. Her talk builds on a document she authored on how to design feminist chatbots (Swords, 2017). When presenting her feminist AI thesis, Adam's guiding principles resonate throughout her talk. Her key influences were also drawn from Judy Wajcman (2004) and Shaowen Bardzell (2010). Wajcman, a feminist scholar in science and technology studies authored the book *Technofeminism* (2004). In this book, she focused on the mutual shaping of feminism and technology while asserting that it is feminist politics—not the technologies themselves—that drive meaningful change in the human–machine interaction. Further, she draws on the work of feminist Human Computer Interaction scholar Shaowen Bardzell (2010) who sets out an agenda for feminist design.

The second presentation is by Charlotte Webb (2019) head of the British organization Feminist Internet who at the Disruption Network Lab in Berlin gave a keynote entitled *What Is a Feminist AI: Possible Feminisms, Possible Internets*. In her presentation, Webb suggests ten feminist AI guiding principles, building, as Young did, on the scholarly work of Shaowen Bardzell (2010). In her presentation, Webb speculates on what qualities feminist AI might embody. Webb outlines a feminist AI according to the following ten principles:

1 A feminist AI is created with the intention of foregrounding the core commitments of feminism.
2 It recognizes and values difference, rather than minimizing it for the sake of universality.
3 It is designed to meet meaningful human needs.
4 It considers the potential consequences of the attachments people may form with it.

5 It incorporates feminist data.

6 It is mindful of how it constructs its users, as users simultaneously shape it.

7 It avoids exploiting workers during its production.

8 It is developed with an awareness of the entire ecosystem in which it operates.

9 It is built by diverse teams who reflect on and actively challenge their own biases.

10 Ultimately, it does not discriminate against individuals based on their race, class, age, belief, or ability.

As we will see below, these ten guiding principles together with Josie Young's (previously known as Josie Swords) feminist chatbot design process were to lead the Feminist Internet to design a Feminist Alexa, a feminist chatbot called F'xa (a subtle and shortened portmanteau of F for feminist and 'xa for Alexa).

Feminist AI with trans and decolonial inflections have also been discursively embodied in the writing and projects made by Paz Peña and Joana Varon (2019) for the Brazilian NGO Coding Rights. Through a collaboration with researcher and designer Sacha Costanza-Chock (2018), who has written extensively on decolonial AI, they identified the values they aimed to embed in their technologies, including AI, as exemplified in the popular Oracle for TransFeminist Technologies. Their decolonial, intersectional work inspired the creation of a web platform called notmy.ai, where their approach to feminist AI extends beyond those proposed by Young and Webb. The platform tackles some of the most pressing issues of our time, including the intersections of AI with extractivism, the surveillance of marginalized communities, racism, patriarchy, and the precarious conditions of gig workers.

Another example to discursively advance a feminist AI agenda is with the NGO A+ Alliance. Strongly from a four-year (2021–2024) funding by the Canadian International Development Research Center (IDRC), this organization has commissioned scholars and activists to discursively explain what feminist AI means. Their work called *From Bias to Feminist AI* (A+ Alliance, 2021) comprises five chapters looking at data, algorithms, procurement, funding, and deployment. This publication ends with a declaration that makes recommendations for making inclusive algorithms a reality, interpellating private companies, governments, international institutions, and more.

Feminist AI often discursively emphasizes inclusion. Dana Kube, a researcher at Goethe University Frankfurt, explored this idea in a TEDx-GallusWomen presentation on February 5, 2024, titled *Can Feminist AI*

Drive Gender Equality and Inclusivity? In it, she presents her results of testing the AI tool Midjourney where she asks the generative AI tool to show her a "professional." As she shares, 80% of the time the generative AI tool showed her a picture of a white man with a beard. Her talk was influenced by the work of other feminists who have shown how sexist and racist generative AI can be (Nicoletti & Bass, 2023). Shifting from discourse to action, she argues that what is lacking are data that represent women of all ages, genders, races, and classes. In the next section, we will showcase examples of efforts to create inclusive feminist datasets aimed at supporting the development of feminist AI.

Finally, I conclude this discursive section on feminist AI with the full abundance intelligence thesis proposed by Lewis et al. (2025). This thesis embraces an Indigenous feminist approach, advocating for the conceptualization and design of AI rooted in Indigenous knowledge systems. This thesis suggests that reimagining AI requires intersecting with intersectional feminism and fostering a kinship with machines—while ensuring this does not come at the expense of the environment (Lewis et al., 2023, 2025).

Doing Feminist AI: Data, Chatbots, and Generative AI

I will now explore the feminist AI playbook by examining its methods and tactics, focusing on the design of feminist data and datasets, chatbots, and generative AI. One of the first artistic and educational projects to attempt to do feminist AI was Caroline Sinder's (2020) *Feminist Data Set*. Her project aimed to ultimately create a chatbot powered by feminist AI able to converse about the multiplicity of feminisms. But before being able to build this AI-powered chatbot, Sinders needed a feminist dataset. She did not want to use a dataset that already existed because of the existing bias within datasets, and because her project was educational in nature supporting feminists to learn how AI is constructed. The idea behind her project was that if we built a feminist dataset and developed a feminist algorithm, we could then build feminist AI. This is how she set out to build a small, community-led dataset that was to capture diverse feminist perspectives about feminisms that were to nourish the chatbot. Through workshops organized in public spaces in the United Kingdom such as libraries and art galleries, Sinders (2020) engaged feminists in creating the data and then labeling data that reflected the plurality of feminist thoughts. This collaborative process was inspired by Wikipedia's community-driven model. Sinders meticulously curated the data to avoid biases, calling for contributions from trans, non-cis women, and women of color to ensure a more inclusive AI model (Toupin, 2024a). Her ongoing project (the chatbot has yet to be developed) not only advocates for a fairer AI (from the data labeling to the chatbot interface design), but also serves as a critique of fast, profit-driven AI models. Sinder's project is important as it is a form of protest that is against intensively capturing data from the whole internet without consent, showcasing how data feminism (D'ignazio & Klein, 2020) could represent an alternative.

While Sinders has yet to build her feminist AI-powered chatbot, feminist organizations have started developing feminist chatbots as part of their feminist playbook (Toupin & Couture, 2020). These chatbots range from simple button-based WhatsApp chatbots powered by a few feminist algorithms to find key resources, to creating a safe and resourceful space, and to organizing around feminist issues (Toupin, 2024b). Feminists began to take an interest in commercial chatbots due to the tendency of major tech companies to assign female names to their chatbots (such as Siri and Alexa). Indeed, chatbots used in customer service, sales, and as phone assistants are typically given female names, voices, and female-looking avatars (Feine et al., 2019). This gendering of corporate chatbots reinforces stereotypes, suggesting that women are responsible for social reproductive labor and customer care. McDonnell and Baxter (2019) revealed that gender influences user satisfaction with chatbots, highlighting the gendered perceptions at play when customers interact with this technology.

Feminists have also critiqued the experimentation with early machine learning powered bots. One of the most infamous examples is with Microsoft Twitter Tay (Neff & Nagi, 2016). Tay was closed after less than a day of functioning because of its inflammatory tweets, and attacks on Zoe Quinn, a video game developer targeted during #GamerGate. The aim of Microsoft was to improve the text-based conversational skills of their Twitter bot through a machine learning algorithm (Neff & Nagi, 2016). But Tay's machine learning algorithm replicated the worst racism and sexism of Twitter very quickly. The example of Tay and others suggests the unpreparedness of corporate bots to respond to insults and abuse. Brahnam and De Angeli (2012) have shown that chatbots programmed with a female and racial embodiment receive more insults and sex talk than the same software with a male embodiment.

Instead of only criticizing chatbots for being antifeminist, a feminist organization decided to use the power of automation through chatbots for a feminist purpose. In 2017, the Brazilian NGO *Nossas Cidades* (Our Cities) decided to develop BetaBot, a feminist bot on Messenger that aimed at organizing around reproductive rights. Under the Jair Bolsonaro government, there had been an attempt to change the constitution to restrict reproductive rights. Betabot automated the sending of emails to Brazilian members of parliament regarding users' disagreement with the proposed bill (Calado, 2018). While its creators decided to choose a rule-based algorithm as opposed to using machine learning (Toupin & Couture, 2020), it nonetheless framed its feminist chatbot as the latest form of feminist coding.

Following the popularity of BetaBot and its media exposure, feminist chatbots began to gain momentum (Toupin, 2024b). This was also driven by the widespread use of smartphones and messaging apps, along with the relative ease of developing them. Dr. Charlotte Webb who had made a presentation on feminist AI designed a four-week feminist chatbot coding course at the Institute of Coding at the University of the Arts London. The course teaches you the skills "to design and prototype a chatbot that doesn't reinforce harmful gender stereotypes" (UAL, 2020, para 1). This course was based on the Feminist Internet experiment with the development of F'xa, a web interface chatbot that aims to understand bias in AI.

The Feminist Internet went on to develop with the international development organization Plan International another feminist chatbot called Maru. Maru provides girls and young women information about online harassment, how to support each other when experiencing digital violence, how to respond or report online violence, and how to protect oneself digitally. Maru as a feminist chatbot was a way to propose the automation of a feminist cause (Toupin, 2024b). Since then, other feminist chatbots powered by AI have been experimented with. Mumkin, meaning possible in Urdu, is feminist chatbot that was designed to support those in the Borah community in India and in the diaspora on how to prepare to have a difficult conversation with family and friends on female genital mutilation (Toupin, 2024b). While this application presents itself as a feminist AI-powered chatbot, the retrieval-based module is not yet functional.

To further the trend of piloting and prototyping feminist AI, it is worth mentioning D'Ignazio et al. (2020) practice who developed a machine learning tool to detect mentions of femicide in Spanish and English news media. This feminist AI tool is part of a participatory action research project aimed at supporting feminist activists in collecting feminicide data. Similarly to Caroline Sinders, D'Ignazio et al. (2020) developed a dataset by labeling news articles related to feminicide and trained their model to detect such reports. In response to this need, they developed the Data against Feminicide Highlighter, a Google Chrome plug-in that highlights news articles about feminicides to assist in case recording. This feminist AI tool provides automation capabilities, helping civil society organizations gather feminicide data from media sources.

The feminist AI research network (F<A+1>) is a project funded by the IDRC composed of feminist scholars and practitioners from the four corners of the world that aims at incubating feminist AI. In their call for project proposals (2021–2024) entitled *Feminist AI: From Paper, to Prototype to Pilot,* they define Feminist AI's goal as harnessing AI "to deliver equality outcomes; designed with inclusion at the core; creating new opportunities & proactive, innovative correction of inequities" (A+ Alliance, 2021, para 4). As the project has come to an end, several Feminist AI projects have been prototyped.

One of these projects entitled AymurAI was developed by the Argentine NGO Data Género, the first Gender Data Observatory in Latin America. The name of this project, derived from a Quechua word, refers to harvesting times (Feldfeber et al., 2024a). It is an AI-based software created to support criminal courts in Latin America by collecting and providing data on gender-based violence (GBV). The AI tool is based on the assumption that the absence of traceable, high-quality data regarding GBV is a major problem in Argentina. The goal was thus to create an open dataset to promote judicial transparency and in turn contribute to building data and statistics on GBV. The project employs:

> AI techniques to partially automate the publication and maintenance of open data from the judiciary in GBV cases. Our proposal is to generate a tool that can easily identify the relevant information in a text document and extract it as a structured dataset.
> *(Feldfeber et al., 2024a, p. 13)*

At the heart of the project was the desire for anyone at the criminal court level to use the system while no one needed to have any knowledge of AI. This project is reminiscent of Alison Adam and Chloe Furnival's project on constituting a searchable database of feminist jurisprudence to support low-income women and their cases in front of the court. While Feldfeber et al. (2024b) do not reference Adam and Furnival as an influence for their idea, the similarities are striking.

Another Argentinian project, developed by Fundación Vía Libre, is called EDIA, which stands for *Estereotipos y Discriminación en la Inteligencia Artificial*—translated as Stereotypes and Discrimination in AI. It is a tool designed for individuals with lived experience but without technical expertise that explores natural language processing (NLP) software to identify and audit biases and stereotypes. Specifically, EDIA focuses on how lexical meaning is represented in NLP systems through word embeddings and how biases arise in word embeddings. As the paper shows, the bias in English and Spanish is different (Ación et al., 2023). They give the example of the term nurse which in English is associated with female, while in Spanish, there are two different words for nurse: *enfermero* (male nurse) and *enfermera* (female nurse). Their conclusion is that it is important to study bias as much in English as in Spanish. Their prototype is available on Hugging Face and was initially developed through workshops done with educators. Their project has received Mozilla's Data Futures Lab 2024 Infrastructure Fund Award for their community-centered project and their commitment to open-source data.

Moving to the ways in which feminist artists have used generative AI for decolonial and feminist AI projects, two projects caught my attention. The first one is called *Tatreez Garden*. *Tatreez* is feminist practice done by Palestinian women—a form of intricate traditional Palestinian embroidery passed down between generations of Palestinians for centuries. To honor a Palestinian art form, Palestinian-Iraqi-American artist Dr. Ameera Kawash developed an AI image generator that enables people worldwide to create pieces of Tatreez. For Dr. Kawash, this project serves as a response to futuricide. Given that prompts like "Palestine" on corporate generative AI tools, such as ChatGPT, often produce depictions of violence, prevent results altogether, or distort and further harm Palestinians in the realm of visual epistemic justice, Tatreez Garden offers an alternative vision of Palestine (Della Ratta, 2024). The second example is with the work of Black, queer, and feminist Brazilian visual artist Mayara Ferrão who uses generative AI to reconstitute histories of Black lesbian love which because of slavery, racism, and patriarchy could not be historically photographed (Pereira, 2025). The AI photographs show Black Brazilian women kissing one another or getting married. Her work was featured as part of the 2024–2025 annual exhibition entitled *Historias LGBTQIA+* at the São Paulo Museum of Art (Museu de Arte de São Paulo Assis Chateaubriand, 2024).

Conclusion

In this chapter, I have highlighted the feminist AI playbook employed by researchers, activists, and practitioners to illustrate its dynamic and impactful nature. By framing feminist AI as a playbook—a collection of strategies, practices, and guiding principles—it serves as a roadmap for feminists in academia, cultural industry, and activism to address the unique needs and inequities within AI. This playbook is informed by diverse global initiatives, with contributions from both the global south and north, reflecting a shared commitment to building fairer, more equitable, and context-sensitive AI systems.

Feminist AI functions as a powerful term that opens new imaginaries, encouraging us to rethink and reenvision AI in ways that are more inclusive and equitable. This term can also serve as a hook, drawing feminists into crucial discussions about AI, fostering broader engagement with technology issues that intersect with gender, race, class, and power among others. As we have seen, feminist AI represents both discursive and practical forms of resistance against dominant AI systems, challenging existing biases and advocating for systems that reflect diverse values. The term feminist AI is usually viewed positively in both practice and scholarship, demonstrating its impact and potential to catalyze transformative change. Feminist AI is not merely a concept; it is also a movement with the potential to shape the future of technology, providing an ever-growing and creative feminist playbook for reimagining and reshaping AI in ways that uphold justice and inclusivity.

Finally, it is important to emphasize that the feminist AI playbook is not static; it is designed to evolve and expand as needed. One pressing question is how feminist AI can be leveraged to combat sexist applications of generative AI, such as deepfakes, which have targeted stars and non-stars alike. Could a feminist AI emerge as part of this evolving playbook? Additionally, how might feminist creativity, powered by AI, be mobilized to counter technology-enhanced violence? These questions highlight the potential of feminist AI to actively challenge and transform harmful uses of technology.

References

A+ Alliance. (2021). Incubating feminist AI 2021–2024 our executive summary. https://aplusalliance.org/global-fair/

Ación, L., Alemany, L. A., Benotti, L., Bordone, M., Busaniche, B., González, L., & Halvorsen, A. (2023). A tool to overcome technical barriers for bias assessment in human language technologies (E.D.I.A. paper). In P. Ricaurte & M. Zasso (Eds.), *Inteligencia Artificial Feminista: hacia una agenda de investigación para América Latina y el Caribe* (pp. 1–34). A+ Alliance. https://feministai.pubpub. org/pub/yf8pnhst/release/2

Adam, A. (1995). Artificial intelligence and women's knowledge: What can feminist epistemologies tell us? *Women's Studies International Forum, 18*(4), 407–415. https://doi.org/10.1016/0277-5395(95)80032-K

Adam, A. (1998). *Artificial knowing: Gender and the thinking machine.* Routledge.

Adam, A., & Furnival, C. (1995). Designing intersections—designing subjectivity: Feminist theory and praxis in a sex discrimination legislation system. *Information & Communications Technology Law, 4*(2), 161–173. https://doi.org/10.10 80/13600834.1995.9965716

Bardzell, S. (2010). Feminist HCI: Taking stock and outlining an agenda for design. In *CHI '10: Proceedings of the SIGCHI Conference on Human Factors in Computing Systems* (pp. 1301–1310). Atlanta: Association for Computing Machinery. https://doi.org/10.1145/1753326.1753521

Bell, G. (2018, September 20). *Decolonizing artificial intelligence* [Video]. YouTube. https://www.youtube.com/watch?v=1KfcWMJ_u0w

Benjamin, R. (2019). *Race after technology: Abolitionist tools for the new Jim Code.* Polity Press.

Brahnam, S., & De Angeli, A. (2012). Gender affordances of conversational agents. *Interacting with Computers, 24*(3), 139–153. https://doi.org/10.1016/j. intcom.2012.05.001

Broussard, M. (2018). *Artificial unintelligence: How computers misunderstand the world*. MIT Press.

Buolamwini, J., & Gebru, T. (2018). Gender shades: Intersectional accuracy disparities in commercial gender classification. In *Proceedings of the 1st Conference on Fairness, Accountability and Transparency* (pp. 77–91). New York: PMLR 81.

Calado, C. (2018, February 25). Beta feminista—Uma entrevista com O time responsável pela criação do bot feminista. *Medium*. https://medium.com/botsbrasil/beta-feminista-uma-entrevista-com-o-time-respons%C3%A1vel-pela-cria%C3%A7%C3%A3o-do-bot-feminista-bba17-6c3fa285e41

Costanza-Chock, S. (2018). Design justice, A.I., and escape from the matrix of domination. *Journal of Design and Science*. https://doi.org/10.21428/96c8d426

Della Ratta, D. (2024, August 14). What does decolonising AI really mean? An interview with artist Ameera Kawash. *Untold Mag*. https://untoldmag.org/what-does-decolonising-ai-really-mean-an-interview-with-artist-ameera-kawash/?ref=artshelp.com

D'Ignazio, C., & Klein, L. F. (2020). *Data feminism*. MIT Press.

D'Ignazio, C., Val, H. S., Fumega, S., Suresh, H., & Cruxên, I. (2020, August 17–18). Feminicide & machine learning: Detecting gender-based violence to strengthen civil sector activism. *MD4SG'20*, Online. https://idl-bnc-idrc.dspacedirect.org/items/77991bd9-ff83-4590-8e4c-6a1e0d7ee010

Feine, J., Gnewuch, U., Morana, S., & Maedche, A. (2019). A taxonomy of social cues for conversational agents. *International Journal of Human-Computer Studies*, *132*, 138–161. https://doi.org/10.1016/j.ijhcs.2019.07.009

Feldfeber, I., Belén Quiroga, Y., Guevara, C., & Ciolfi, F. M. (2024a). Automation tools towards a feminist judiciary reform in Argentina and Mexico: AymurAI. *Feminist AI*. https://feministai.pubpub.org/pub/z83eyq54/release/1

Feldfeber, I., Belén Quiroga, Y., Guevara, C., & Ciolfi, F. M., (2024b). Feminisms in artificial intelligence: Automation tools towards a feminist judiciary reform in Argentina and Mexico. *Feminist AI*. https://feministai.pubpub.org/pub/z83eyq54/release/1

Forsythe, D. E. (1993). Engineering knowledge: The construction of knowledge in artificial intelligence. *Social Studies of Science*, *23*(3), 445–477.

Haraway, D. (1988). Situated knowledges: The science question in feminism and the privilege of partial perspective. *Feminist Studies*, *14*(3), 575–599.

Hossain, R. S. (2005). *Sultana's dream*. (Original work published 1905). https://digital.library.upenn.edu/women/sultana/dream/dream.html

Kube, D. (2024, February 5). *Can feminist AI drive gender equality and inclusivity?* TEDxGallusWomen [Video]. YouTube. https://www.youtube.com/watch?v=MmYXrG_tvQw&ab_channel=TEDxTalks

Lewis, J. E., Whaanga, H., & Yolgörmez, C. (2025). Abundant intelligences: Placing AI within Indigenous knowledge frameworks. *AI & Society*, *40*, 2141–2157. https://doi.org/10.1007/s00146-024-02099-4

Lewis, J. E., Arista, N. Pechawis, A., & Kite, S. (2023). Making kin with the machines. In J. Browne, S. Cave, E. Drage, & K. McInerney (Eds.), *Feminist AI* (pp. 19–31). Oxford University Press. https://doi.org/10.1093/oso/9780192889898.003.0002

Museu de Arte de São Paulo Assis Chateaubriand. (2024). *Queer Histories*. Sao Paulo, Brazil. https://www.masp.org.br/en/exhibitions/the-lgbtqia-histories

McDonnell, M., & Baxter, D. (2019). Chatbots and gender stereotyping. *Interacting with Computers, 31*(2), 116–121. https://doi.org/10.1093/iwc/iwz007

Neff, G., & Nagi, P. (2016). Automation, algorithms, and politics - Talking to bots: Symbiotic agency and the case of Tay. *International Journal of Communication, 10,* 4915–4931. https://ijoc.org/index.php/ijoc/article/view/6277

Nicoletti, N., & Bass, D. (2023, June 9). Humans are biased. Generative AI is even worse. *Bloomberg News.* https://www.bloomberg.com/graphics/2023-generative-ai-bias/

Noble, S. U. (2018). *Algorithms of oppression: How search engines reinforce racism.* New York University Press.

Peña, P., & Varon, J. (2019). *Decolonising AI: A transfeminist approach to data and social justice.* GIS Watch. https://giswatch.org/node/6203

Pereira, J. (2025, March 9). Mayara Ferrão's blueprint for decolonial AI imagery. *The Republic.*https://rpublc.com/february-march-2025/mayara-ferrao-decolonial-ai-imagery/

Sinders, C. (2020). *Feminist data set.* Clinic for Open Source Arts (COSA). https://carolinesinders.com/wp-content/uploads/2020/05/Feminist-Data-Set-Final-Draft-2020-0526.pdf

Suchman, L. A. (1987). *Plans and situated actions: The problem of human-machine communication.* Cambridge University Press.

Swords, J. (2017). *Designing feminist chatbots.* https://www.ellphacitizen.org/list/2017/9/23/designing-feminist-chatbots

Toupin, S. (2024a). Shaping feminist artificial intelligence. *New Media & Society, 26*(1), 580–595. https://doi.org/10.1177/14614448221150776

Toupin, S. (2024b). Civil society chatbots: A plurality of conceptual approaches. *International Journal of Communication, 18,* 20, 947–966. https://ijoc.org/index.php/ijoc/article/view/21795

Toupin, S., & Couture, S. (2020). Feminist chatbots as part of the feminist toolbox. *Feminist Media Studies, 20*(5), 737–740. https://doi.org/10.1080/14680777.2020.1783802

UAL. (2020). *Design a feminist chatbot.* FuturLearn. https://www.futurelearn.com/courses/designing-a-feminist-chatbot

Wajcman, J. (1991). *Feminism confronts technology.* Polity Press.

Wajcman, J. (2004). *TechnoFeminism.* Polity Press.

Webb, C. (2019, June 27). *What is a feminist AI: Possible feminisms, possible internets* [Video]. YouTube. https://www.youtube.com/watch?v=bBQOyvNhWJY

Young, J. (2019, January 7). *Why we need to design feminist AI* [Video]. YouTube. https://www.youtube.com/watch?v=E-O3LaSEcVw

11

PRIVACY AT PLAY

Anticipating Hyper-personalization in Conversational Robot Toys

Samantha Shorey and Katie Joseff

Grok is a rocket-shaped plushie with inquisitive embroidered eyes and the capacity for "endless conversation." You can ask Grok the informational queries you might type into a Google search bar or ask it to create something wholly new. The product website prompts: "Hey Grok, let's make up a story about a talking tomato." To answer, the cloud-connected processor inside its soft body will record your request, transcribe it, and pass the information to a Generative AI (GenAI) third party. The large language models that go to work are licensed from companies like OpenAI, customized and then further fine-tuned to individuals through continued use. But, all of this occurs on a hidden device and then remotely on the cloud. The user only hears a response voiced by Grimes, the electronic pop music star, Grok cofounder and mother to three children shared with Elon Musk.[1]

Forbes hails Grimes and her AI toy as "revolutionary," though a review from *The Cut* tempers their praise—emphasizing that Grok is buggy and still in beta (Arnold-Ratliff, 2024; Sehdev, 2023). Yet, both articles agree that interacting with it is like looking through a window into the future of play. Grok exemplifies an emerging type of conversational robotic toy that can be hyper-personalized through GenAI. With GenAI, toys not only continuously learn new skills and more expansive facts about the world. They learn information *about you,* enabling customized engagement through dialog. This new potential comes along with the same concerns around privacy and data ownership that are implicated in similar digital technologies. Whether embedded in a teddy bear or a smart speaker, when we invite these devices into our homes, we give them access to the most intimate

DOI: 10.4324/9781003477587-11

aspects of our day-to-day life through direct communication and algorithmic control over the information we access.

In this chapter, we explore the integration of GenAI technologies into objects of play and seek to anticipate the pitfalls they open for user privacy and the safety of self-expression. In the first section, we turn to a prevailing conversational technology, AI voice assistants, as a case study that provides a set of signals about personalization. AI voice assistants underscore the potential for conversation to be used as a tool of data extraction and attention manipulation—restraining the imagination, exploration, experimentation, and questioning that are important parts of play. In the second section, we advocate for decentralized AI that can counter the current path of commercial development. We outline two general principles that would give technology users greater control over data ownership and algorithmic personalization practices. Then, we complicate these principles in light of a core challenge that exists for AI toys: children are envisioned as the users of these devices, but parents are in control of their data. We conclude by emphasizing the importance of design approaches and household conversations that can support children's decision-making practices around data sharing by jointly building understandings of data collection and establishing household rules around data retention and access.

A Proximate Technology: AI Voice Assistants, Privacy, and Personalization

Privacy

The home is inextricably tied to our conception of privacy in the United States. The U.S. Constitution's Fourth Amendment enshrines "the right of the people to be secure in their persons, houses, papers, and effects against unreasonable searches and seizures" (U.S. Const. amend. IV). Here, the legal boundary of private and public life is drawn at the four walls of a household dwelling—and extends to include information produced there (e.g., "papers") that are sealed and circulated in private correspondence (e.g., the mail) (Donohue, 2015). Legal debates abound. Yet, the Fourth Amendment makes clear the significance of the home as a protected place for Americans' "beliefs, their thoughts, their emotions and sensations" (Supreme Court Justice Brandeis, as quoted in Donohue, 2015, p. 577). About far more than property, this interpretation of the Constitution reflects a commitment to private places as a site for the considered inquiries that are necessary for the development of democratic citizens. Information ethics scholar Helen Nissenbaum (2004) explains: "uninhibited by what others might say, how they will react, and how they will judge ...

people are freer to formulate for themselves the reasons behind significant life choices, preferences and commitments" (p. 131).

Technologies that are capable of listening to the most intimate aspects of our daily life are increasingly present in our homes. AI voice assistants—Amazon's Alexa, Apple's Siri, and Google's Assistant—use conversation as the primary interface for human-technology interaction. They are typically activated through spoken commands ("hey, Alexa!") and receive informational inputs verbally. While opening new avenues for convenience and interactivity, the always-on status of these technologies can be unsettling. Surveillance studies scholar Stephen Neville (2020) calls this data collection mechanism "eavesmining." Even on standby, AI voice assistants are in a constant state of listening for their activation keywords—awaiting an opportunity to gain auditory information about activities and occupants within a home. Among the (comparatively small) group of people who adamantly refuse to adopt AI voice assistants, fears of being "listened to all the time" are a noted theme (Liao et al., 2019). Amazon, Apple, and Google have each been the subject of class action lawsuits from users who feel their conversations were routinely recorded outside of direct, intended interaction with their AI voice assistants (Stempel, 2021).

To preserve their relationship with consumers, the companies that sell AI voice assistants have taken note of these concerns. The second question on both Amazon's and Google's terms of service FAQ page is "Is Alexa recording all my conversations?" and "Is Google Assistant recording everything I say?" In their responses, the companies assure users that the devices only record audio after it hears the specified activation commands. These audio recordings (or written transcripts of the audio) are sent to company cloud servers to process the requests where the default retention and use of the data varies. Google, Amazon, and Apple allow users to manually review and delete the recordings stored on their servers. However, most people are not aware of these recordings and even fewer have accessed or deleted them (Malkin et al., 2019).

The data that is retained is a goldmine of information that is used to both "personalize" the user's experience and "improve" the companies' products. Google and Amazon state that the content of recorded requests may be listened to, read, and annotated by human reviewers, which enables it to be used for training machine learning models. As Abdi and co-authors (2021) observe, many privacy concerns about AI voice assistants arise from the fact that data does not remain on smart speaker devices. It is stored on the company's cloud servers, flowing through a sequence of technological processes and providers. "Flow" is a determining criterion of Nissenbaum's (2004) well-known privacy framework, contextual integrity. Rather than collecting all data available within legal bounds, Nissenbaum argues that technologies should respect user conceptions of privacy which vary greatly, depending on the recipient, the content, and the purported use of the information. For example, Lutz and Newland (2021) found that users were more concerned about human reviewers' and third parties' access to their data than they were about the companies that produce the devices. Further, Abdi et al.'s (2021) survey of voice assistant users found that perceptions of information sharing with third parties varied greatly by *the type* of recipient: it was much more acceptable to share information with relevant app providers than with advertisers.

Aligned with the contextual integrity perspective, media studies scholars Stoilova et al. (2021) draw a conceptual distinction between interpersonal, commercial, and institutional privacy. They highlight that communication within each context involves a relationship with different types of recipients: individuals or groups, businesses, and government or public-sector organizations. Importantly, this variation in relationships also leads to variation in "cultural norms, power relations, and regulatory mechanisms" (p. 560). Stoilova et al. acknowledge that these contexts often overlap as information is shared between entities. Thus, while people may *feel* differently when information from an AI voice assistant is shared with a friend, product developer, or politician, the data produced through digital engagement is interoperable. It is variously useful and capable of being exchanged. Further, the personal and unique delineations people draw between contexts are not often respected in an era of aggregation where lucrative companies called "data brokers" source and combine information from multiple sources—reselling it as detailed "data dossiers" to classify individuals (Citron, 2022).[2] Alice Marwick (2023) polemically argues that this network of data collection undermines any individual's ability to achieve privacy through their own considered choices about disclosing specific information to specific recipients.

In her lauded book *The Age of Surveillance Capitalism,* Shoshanna Zuboff (2019) discusses AI voice assistants as emblematic of a relentless corporate creep. Not satisfied with tracking clicks and social media posts, technology companies are turning to conversation as a source for capturing human experiences and turning them into data. Conversational technologies facilitate a frictionless collection of personal preferences—the likes and dislikes that can be deduced from purchasing patterns—and personal relationships. For example, while the Amazon Terms of Use[3] specifically states that it does not collect the content of text messages or call requests dictated to Alexa, it does use "information about your contacts and connections, including who you communicate with most." Seemingly thin metadata tracking the frequency and duration of calls can be used to make inferences about close friends and cherished (or estranged) family.

The speculative features described in patents take these capabilities one step further: recording information associated with affective activation keywords like "love" or "enjoyed" (Citron, 2022; Turow, 2021). In other devices, Amazon is piloting emotion recognition capabilities that gain information from the inflection and tone of a user's voice (Turow, 2021; Zuboff, 2019).

AI voice assistants both exemplify and enable a future where artificially intelligent, conversational technologies are fully integrated into private life. As Hurel and Couldry (2022) argue, Amazon's Alexa and Google's Assistant reorganize domestic space and reconfigure routine activities to facilitate constant data extraction. In *The Voice Catchers,* Joesph Turow (2021) observes that these technologies are in the "scale-building period." Though present in billions of devices worldwide, they are not yet seen as an imperative infrastructural part of daily activities. This still-in-progress social evolution was epitomized by social media platforms, which attracted users through their social features prior to their practices of massive data collection. Once ubiquity was achieved, companies completed the bait-and-switch: "by then, the sites had become such important parts of users' daily lives that they felt they couldn't leave, despite their concern about data flows they didn't understand and couldn't control" (p. 10). The present task, then, for AI voice technology companies is to overcome hesitation until use becomes as widespread and habitual as social media.

Personalization

Beginning with the introduction of the personal computer in the 1970s, creators of digital technologies have sought to make "machines reactive to individual needs as well as able to accommodate differences among individual users" (Schulte, 2016, p. 245). This ideal—known today as *personalization*—is reliant upon the digitization of personal information, as well as interactive interfaces that encourage and respond to human input. In her entry for *Digital Keywords*, Stephanie Ricker Schulte (2016) defines "hyper-personalization" as fundamentally predictive. Unlike customization, which is performed through modifications made by users, hyper-personalization acts on behalf of users to anticipate wants or needs. Corporate explanations of AI voice assistants' data-gathering policies point to personalization as the ultimate outcome and driving motivation behind data collection. As Emily West (2022) argues in *Buy Now,* companies like Amazon have used personalization to rebrand surveillance "as a service." Being known enables the convenience and speed that distinguishes the company from other retailers. And, when mediated through the voice of Alexa, it feels closer to a service relationship than spying.

The experience of hyper-personalization is achieved through recommendation algorithms, which attempt to computationally predict future behavior (such as enjoying a song or buying a product) based on past activity (such as song ratings or previous purchases). Sometimes this is based on similar properties between the past and future object. But, the irony at the heart of personalization is that it is often based more on one's similarity to *other users*. "Collaborative filtering algorithms" operate on the premise that users who share some preferences will probably share others. Recommendations are sourced from this "neighborhood" of likely like-minded individuals (Lury & Day, 2019, p. 23). In an AI voice assistant, recommendations take the form of tailored responses to requests or questions. The Google search homepage displays ten possible, ranked recommendations; in a conversational technology, recommendations arrive as a single, authoritative answer.

Hyper-personalization is generally perceived as helping users navigate the overwhelming abundance of information by guiding attention to what is relevant to their queries and reflective of their preferences. Yet, as Nick Seaver (2019) observed in his anthropological study of software developers, metrics to assess the accuracy of recommendations were ultimately reduced to measures of time. How long users stayed engaged with a piece of media and how long they actively remained on a platform became the heuristic for evaluating performance. Of course, the time one spends reading, viewing, or listening to a piece of media is not a complete indicator of how helpful or enjoyable it is. For example, big data analysis suggests that people are more likely to click on news stories with negative words in the headline (though social scientific research on the relationship between news consumption, virality, and emotional valence is mixed) (Robertson et al., 2023). Metrics of engagement like clicks, page views, and shares are complementary to traditional media imperatives, which seek to capture the most viewers for the most time, so these audiences can be packaged and sold to advertisers. They are divorced from any measure of general quality or contribution to specific user needs.

Though Amazon, Google, and Apple do not sell their user data to advertisers, they do sell *access* to users who can be reached with personalized ads. In a complex process called Real Time Ad Bidding, companies place their ads in front of individuals with specific characteristics. In millisecond-long auctions, Google sells placement on websites to advertisers based on the characteristics they've identified through their data collection efforts (Cohen, 2025). This same process takes place for audio content. According to its 2022 SEC filing, over 80% of Google's revenue comes from advertising (Alphabet Inc., 2022, p. 9).[4] Additionally, horizontal and vertical integration of these companies is so expansive that they each have an entire ecosystem of offerings of their own. For example, Amazon is probably best known for their e-commerce business, which sold 170 billion dollars of consumer products in the fourth quarter of 2023 alone (Amazon Investor Relations, 2023). Yet, they also own more than 40 subsidiary companies. On an Amazon Fire TV, one can stream series on Amazon Prime Video, access the interactive gaming platform Twitch, or watch a movie produced by the legacy media company MGM Studios, now also owned by Amazon. Each of these points of interaction is an opportunity to push product or content recommendations with a weighted preference to the brand family, even if something else might be better matched to a user.

As technology interaction becomes more conversational—driven by AI embedded in all sorts of devices—it is reasonable to expect these patterns to continue. Technology companies will leverage their data to refine algorithmic personalization to craft maximally engaging and persuasive user interactions that fulfill corporate imperatives to exploit attention and extract even more data. As we discuss below, this is especially concerning when we consider toys. Toys encourage focused engagement and the investment of time, a mindset that is as equally important as it is vulnerable in a world where media are competing for attention.

AI-Powered Conversational Robot Toys

AI voice assistants provide the strongest signals about a future in which AI technologies are integrated into objects of play. First, AI voice assistants demonstrate the intimate access granted to technology we engage with through conversation and their potential threat to privacy. In recurring interactions, we share our thoughts with and satisfy our curiosities through digital devices—embedding mechanisms of data collection into our activities at home. Second, they demonstrate the way that personalization pulls us deeper into immersive engagements while simultaneously narrowing the scope of information we receive. The true beneficiaries of algorithmic curation aren't users or even advertisers but the companies that produce AI devices. Embedded in toys, AI transforms objects of play into objects that can capture the commercial opportunities of conversation.

The Freedom to Play

Game design scholar Miguel Sicart (2014) theorizes play as a fundamentally creative act. More than simply intaking and acting upon conditions or rules, play is "a way of engaging with the world" (p. 5). Aspects of a context are negotiated as players are guided by design while making their own decisions about how to move forward. Thus, play is fundamentally expressive. It breaks from passive forms of cultural consumption, opening up objects or environments to reinterpretation. "Play is important because we need to see values and practice them and challenge them so they become more than mindless habits" (p. 5). When people bring the spirit of play to objects designed for other purposes, they enact *playfulness*. Playfulness challenges functional efficiency and opens technology to reinterpretation, becoming a site of personal expression. Here, Sicart turns to the AI voice assistant Siri as an illustrative example for its characteristically quirky responses that lead to unexpected interactions.

Sicart writes that play *is* freedom. But, we argue, play also *requires* freedom. In the safety of private space, one can freely explore their own thoughts and experiment with the status quo without fear of institutional consequences. Like the home, privacy is a shelter for imagination (Bachelard, 2009, p. 6). Yet, experimentation places people at risk if they are seen or known by those who would prefer to keep an unquestioned hold on power. Research demonstrates that people will modify their behavior to mitigate this risk in the presence of smart speaker devices. They practice self-censorship and "avoid talking about sensitive topics" around the technology, ultimately limiting expression (Lutz & Newlands, 2021, p. 154). Further, without privacy protections, play makes people especially vulnerable to manipulation and external control. As a form of personal expression, it is an incredibly rich site for data collection. Technology companies with an insatiable hunger for this type of intimate information have a vested interest in keeping people playing. As Sicart acknowledges, play can be addicting—so enthralling and immersive that one can lose touch with the world. The way a technology is designed can deliberately play into this dark side.

The Promise of Personalized Play

Grok, the conversational AI toy detailed in the introduction, is one of several robot toys becoming available to consumers. Miko is a smooth, smart speaker-like device and Moxie is a table-top-sized humanoid robot. Though each of the toys is limited in terms of mobility and animation, we analyze them here as robots because of the way they materialize AI into artifacts. Both Miko and Moxie are called robots in their product description, and a key selling point of Grok is that it is physical and "screen-free."

Miko, Moxie, and Grok are marketed as helping kids learn emotional and academic skills through interactive play. Empirical research in the field of Human-Robot Interaction (HRI) supports the idea that social robots can facilitate the development of children's curiosity (Gordon et al., 2015) and creativity (Alves-Oliveira et al., 2020). They find that interactive storytelling, in particular, helps children to generate more original ideas and pursue free exploration. Yet, there is reason for caution. Using social robots as a platform for third-party applications is emphasized as a pathway to commercialization by leading academic research and development efforts (Breazeal, 2017). Miko users, for example, can already access stories from Disney, Paramount, and Mattel. Third-party apps may have more expansive data collection practices than the devices where they are installed. "Grok's privacy policy[5] 'DOES NOT apply to information that is collected by any third party' (emphasis in original)." Further, HRI researchers are also pursuing research projects to establish preferred methods for advertising to children through robots (DiPaola et al., 2022).

The companies that produce these toys all emphasize the security of user data and the care they've taken to comply with the Children's Online Privacy Protection rule (or "COPPA"). The Federal Trade Commission's COPPA sets specific guidelines for data collection practices when it involves children under 13 years old. For example, parents or legal guardians must give consent for children's data to be collected, and they must be able delete this data, should they choose (Children's Online Privacy Protection Act of 1998, §312.6). COPPA also requires detailed, open disclosures about how data is collected and used by technology companies. Grok's privacy policy, for example, explains that the device collects information spoken to the device and retains it as a written transcript for 90 days. Both Miko and Moxie go beyond recording spoken interaction and also collect biometric information, including facial expressions. Privacy policies specify that Grok and Moxie do not sell data to advertisers and Miko "hasn't sold consumer's personal data in the past 12 months."[6] However, Grok might combine the information they gain from interaction with their device with other information about online activities under a persistent identifier—building a unique user profile—used to enrich the conversation. And, Miko acknowledges that the company may employ technologies "considered [to be] automated decision making and profiling" [9].

Data collection is used as a central value proposition for Miko, and Moxie which are marketed as allowing parents to track their child's development and learning over time. The commercial value of data generated through children's engagement with conversational AI toys becomes clear in the fine print of the technology's privacy policies. All the companies acknowledge that they analyze and study the data to improve their services and products. Tellingly, both Grok and Miko also declare user data an "asset" that they can sell or transfer, should the company be dissolved or acquired.[7] These familiar logics of data accumulation bring up some important questions. Amazon, Apple, and Google all have separate account types for children. Yet, the modes of engagement and espoused intentions of conversational toys are quite different. They are tools for play-based, interactive learning. How might the mechanisms of data collection and personalization embedded in conversation robot toys come into conflict with (or even capitalize upon) the exploration, expression, and reflection that they are meant to enable?

The AI that powers the previous generation of voice assistants excels at efficiently responding to specific questions and executing specific actions using predefined inputs and rules. But it does not create new content or adapt to new scenarios beyond programmed parameters. If you ask Alexa to "make up a story about a talking tomato" (the scenario advertised on the Grok website), Alexa replies, "I don't have stories of that type. Choose from nighttime, funny, scary, family, or random." The response makes clear that Alexa can only draw from pre-existing and pre-classified content. GenAI, on the other hand, can create a "new" story. It is trained to identify patterns within datasets, make associations, and recombine old content to make new content. GenAI's ability to continuously and automatically incorporate new data impels the process of hyper-personalization, as it modifies outputs based on previous interactions.

Many foundational GenAI models are closed-source and centralized. They are based on massive amounts of proprietary information and rely upon costly computational power, data storage, and human labor for engineering and model-training. OpenAI, Microsoft, Amazon, and Google lease their foundational models to other companies where they can be tailored to express specific characteristics—including tone, scenario, target age group, and cultural context—through a refinement process called "prompt engineering." Yet, the underlying datasets and source code remain inaccessible to clients. Alternatively, open-source foundational models are providing another path forward. They enable external developers, researchers, and interested people to review data and algorithms or build their own specialized models. Open-source servers and software are the bedrock of the majority of the world's websites and other technologies we use even though they lack the brand recognition of technology giants (Lifshitz-Assaf & Nagle, 2021). On the internet's most widely used platforms, users trade their data for the interactive promise of personalization. Is there another way?

Alternative Principals for Hyper-personalization

User Ownership of Data

The first step towards creating hyper-personalized children's toys that do not replicate the harms of previous technologies is pursuing a non-centralized system of data ownership that ensures interactions with AI are kept locally rather than being processed and stored by centralized servers owned by technology companies (Deegan, 2025). Currently, AI-powered toys respond to user interactions through a complex series of data transfers. For example, an analysis of Moxie's privacy policy by the Mozilla Foundation explains that the voices of users are first sent to Google's Speech-to-Text cloud to be transcribed (*Privacy Not Included Review*, 2023). Then, the transcript is passed to a cloud-based GenAI model, which provides a near-instantaneous response that is uttered by the robot. The AI model used to provide the response may be one owned by Moxie's manufacturer or licensed from a third-party OpenAI. Though they are careful to state that OpenAI does not store the recordings, Moxie's manufacturer *does* store them for 18 months to "improve" their own AI.

Alternatively, user data could be stored locally in the toy's internal memory, on a connected device, or through a private cloud service that is controlled by the user. Open-source AI models can be downloaded locally so processing occurs on the device too. Further, user ownership over localized data does not mean that the data is not shareable. Rather, it gives users control over the conditions of data sharing. Users can choose if or how their data is accessed by others—which entities have access, the duration of their access, and the specific cases where it can be used as part of aggregated datasets. Through processes such as "federated learning," users can download AI models to their devices, train them on their private data, and then share these reconfigured models with other similar users (Martineau, 2022).

User Control over Algorithmic Personalization

The second step to achieve this alternative approach to hyper-personalization is a pivot away from using data-intensive features to inform automated decision-making toward presenting this information as a pathway for users to make decisions about content for themselves. Many mobile phones have features that allow users to view and even set limits on the time they spend on their devices. These "screen time" trackers are an important example of how a technology can be intentionally designed to give users knowledge and control over their media consumption habits by allowing them to see information that is aggregated over time. The platforms people interact with every day collect granular data about their behavior, and some of it *is* accessible. Users can easily review their search history on Google web browsers; deep in the Instagram settings, users can see the advertisements they have clicked on while scrolling the social media platform. Yet, the information these features provide is not presented in a way that gives users the ability to recognize patterns or trends. For example, an Instagram user does not know how many makeup tutorials or political commentary clips they have watched that day, week, or year.

Some AI-powered toys, like Miko, are already embedded with parental dashboards for understanding the digital activities of children. They provide visualizations that summarize data by highlighting recent shifts and long-term patterns. Others, like Grok, give users minimal insight and access to their inner workings. It is important that users are presented with information about their content interactions that is easy to comprehend and analyze. Further, users should be able to act upon these insights by setting priorities for algorithmically selected content. For example, a child may want help learning math, practicing soccer, or playing more family games. They could conversationally inform AI about their interests and AI would respond by incorporating math into daily activities like cooking and brushing teeth, suggesting juggling and other soccer exercises, and prompting trivia for kids and their parents. Here, data becomes a pathway to achieve self-defined goals.

Core Challenge: Balancing Children's Agency and Parental Advisory

A commitment to data ownership addresses many concerns about institutional and commercial privacy, yet it leaves open questions about interpersonal privacy. The parental consent and data access capabilities required by COPPA only complicate this dynamic, as parents are granted ownership and control over children's data.[8] For example, Moxie terms itself a "parental co-pilot." Children may experience one-on-one interaction with a toy, but these interactions are circumscribed by parents (who can specify topics of focus) and are recorded (allowing parents to track their child's learning progress). Research with teens reveals that young people have significant concerns about the information robots may share with others—outweighing concerns about the data possessed by the robot itself. For example, Levinson et al. (2024) find that teens were generally comfortable with robots that could see their kitchen and recognize objects within it. But, they did express discomfort with robots that reported snack choices to parents. Their participants likened this behavior to being a "tattletale" or a "snitch"—monikers that the authors argue emphasize the *social relationship* between users and robots that is breached when they share information with outside parties. Similarly, previous research about social media indicates that, even with an awareness that parents have technical access to their online activities, young people expect parents to respect contextual boundaries. They view observation as "spying," a term conveying their perspective that the information was obtained by someone who it was not intended for. Steeves and Regan (2014) argue that when parents constantly monitor online activity, it inhibits young people's ability to experiment with self-presentation. This counterproductivity is especially important when we consider the positive potential of play as a site of self-discovery and idea formation.

Though the conversational AI toys we considered most deeply in this chapter are marketed toward children younger than ten years old, below we review research conducted with young people of various ages including teens and adolescents—with the intention of surfacing relevant cautions and productive approaches for the development of AI-powered objects of play. To be sure, levels of understanding (and associated worries about privacy) do vary for children of different ages, given the way social experiences and familiarity with digital technologies also vary across age cohorts (Kumar et al., 2017).

Co-designing

Livingstone and Pothong (2023) advocate for a "by design" approach to children's privacy, focusing on how privacy can be built into technologies rather than enacted through the protective actions of children or their parents. They propose 11 principles, informed by the United Nations Convention on the Rights of the Child, with relevant prompts and practices to help designers realize them. The principle of *privacy* begins the product design cycle by asking designers to evaluate their regulatory compliance and builds to more challenging questions such as "does your design solution enable children to enact their data subject rights (i.e., to know, manage and correct the data you process about them?)." Importantly, Livingstone and Pothong center *children's* knowledge and control over data collection here, not just their parents or guardians. Informing their online data and privacy toolkit, Livingstone and collaborators find that children aged 12–15 years old desire better arrangements between technology companies and technology users—asking companies not to sell their data and to make it possible to opt out of data collection altogether (Livingstone et al., 2019).

For children's perspectives to meaningfully shape digital technologies, children should be included throughout the technology design processes. To some extent, children are included in the development of AI toys today. Privacy policies often include acknowledgments that children's data is used to "improve" the product. However, the *direction* of this improvement is defined by technology companies and, in the case of social media, has resulted in technologies that are designed to maximize the amount of time and attention poured into platforms or devices. It is clear that this not only benefits the bottom line of companies that profit off engagement but also encourages compulsive use of a technology that undermines children's autonomy and well-being (see principle 11). Alves-Oliveira et al. (2021) offer a framework for involving children in each stage of the design process, not just as users or testers of nearly-finished products. Rather, children participate as informants who define problems or goals and as design partners who help come up with solutions. They used methods of storytelling, sketching, and puppeteering to help elicit responses and aid in generating ideas that were then applied to hardware design.

Co-deciding

These design-led approaches can address concerns about commercial privacy; but, to address interpersonal privacy, we encourage parents, children, and caretakers to engage in discussions that can establish an acceptable data-use policy for their household. Children should understand what data is being collected about them when they are at play, so they can make informed decisions about their behavior or activities based on their visibility to others. When features can be turned on/off, parents and children can decide together what types of activities will be recorded. Additional questions to clarify or consider may be: who will be able to see the data that's collected? Who can make decisions about data being deleted? Will data be stored locally or will it be shared?

Professional caretakers, such as babysitters or nannies, should also be involved in this discussion. Currently, AI toys obtain consent from parents about data collection from their children, but do not adequately consider other adults in the home whose data might also be captured through direct interactions or incidentally. For example, the privacy policy of Moxie states, "anyone in range of the video or audio recording capabilities of Moxie may be recorded, including the child interacting with Moxie, members of your family or others in the home at the time the robot is recording." Moxie and Miko both have emotion recognition capabilities which could be used to monitor or control the emotions of caretakers. Recording this data has the potential to turn toys into tools of workplace surveillance—not dissimilar from a hidden camera or "nanny cam." Domestic observation is often treated as a routine and sensible safety practice, but it also places significant stress on caretakers who worry their behavior or interactions will be taken out of context (Akridge et al., 2025).

Alternatively, technology designers could also limit data collection on other household members through techniques such as audio "filtering." Voice is biometric (Turow, 2021). It has a unique signature for everyone, like a fingerprint. A voice profile can identify a speaker, and filtering determines which speakers are recorded. However, it is not difficult to see how these voice profiles could be used to track individuals which increase the importance of data ownership, should this solution be pursued. Research shows that the users of AI voice assistants generally feel that *their* information should not be shared with household workers, like housekeepers (Abdi et al., 2021). Filtering may be an opportunity for reciprocity, acknowledging the specific privacy relationship between household members and caretakers.

Conclusion

As Zuboff (2019) writes in her analysis of Barbie's Smart Home, the toys that were "once a beloved mirror of a child's unfettered imagination ... are no longer mere things, they are reinvented as vehicles for a horde of commercial opportunities fabricated from our dialogue chunks and assorted gold dust" (p. 266). Though our homes (not just Barbie's) have been traditionally treated as protected and private space, recurring interaction with conversational AI imbeds data collection mechanisms into our day-to-day activities. The resulting personalization leads users to invest more engagement, more time, and more attention into technology. AI embedded in toys may be used as a method of harvesting data, delivering preferential media content, and making product recommendations. With these concerns in mind, a commitment to data privacy (realized through data ownership) and user-lead personalization (realized through control over algorithmic prioritization) is essential for technology designers. For consumers, privacy also requires considered conversations between parents, children, and caretakers about the data that is captured in their interactions with AI-powered toys.

Acknowledgement

This work was supported by Good Systems, a research grand challenge at the University of Texas at Austin.

Notes

1 There are some notable overlaps between Grok and Musk's other ventures, the social media site X, and the spacecraft company SpaceX. The AI model on X is also called "Grok." And, the toy Grok has a cone-shaped body and four fins, visually referencing a rocket ship.
2 Amazon, Apple, and Google all state that they do not sell user data in their privacy policy documents. However, as we discuss later in this chapter, their relationship with advertisers and third-party apps is more complex than these claims let on.
3 Paragraph—S-1.3 Contacts. Link https://www.amazon.com/gp/help/customer/display.html?nodeId=201809740.

4 Advertising makes up a smaller percentage of revenue for Apple and Amazon. Apple Advertising sells space in App Store searches and on Apple News, personalizing ads by dividing users into segments of 5,000+ people who meet shared criteria. On Amazon, companies can pay to appear as a "sponsored product" to relevant users. Their website proclaims: "go beyond keywords to reach customers based on search history, lifestyle (e.g., sports enthusiast), interests (e.g., interior design), or life events (e.g., wedding)."

5 Paragraph—"IV. Disclosing Your Information to Third Parties" Link—https:// miko.ai/policies/privacy-policy.

6 Paragraph—"IV. Disclosing Your Information to Third Parties" Link—https:// miko.ai/policies/privacy-policy.

7 It is not just a hypothetical possibility that these fledgling technology companies will shut down. In December 2024 (while this chapter was under review), competitor Moxie abruptly announced that the company would be closing (Harding, 2024).

8 The COPPA text of rule defines the term "parent" as including legal guardianship (Children's Online Privacy Protection Act of 1998, § 312.2). For readability, we follow this convention while acknowledging the diversity of parenthood, kinship, and care.

References

Abdi, N., Zhan, X., Ramokapane, K. M., & Such, J. (2021). Privacy norms for smart home personal assistants. In *Proceedings of the 2021 ACM CHI Conference on Human Factors in Computing Systems* (pp. 1–14). Yokohama. https://doi.org/10.1145/3411764.3445122

Akridge, H., Ahmed, A., Bàssïbét, F. S., Miranda Alcázar, M. A., & Fox, S. (2025). "Oh, you're watching me": Care workers' experiences of surveillant assemblages on the platform and in the home. *New Media & Society.* https:// doi.org/10.1177/14614448251315759

Alphabet Inc. (2022). *Annual report pursuant to Section 13 or 15(d) of the Securities Exchange Act of 1934* (No. Form 10-K).

Alves-Oliveira, P., Arriaga, P., Cronin, M. A., & Paiva, A. (2020). Creativity encounters between children and robots. In *Proceedings of the 2020 ACM/ IEEE International Conference on Human-Robot Interaction* (pp. 379–388). Cambridge. https://doi.org/10.1145/3319502.3374817

Alves-Oliveira, P., Arriaga, P., Paiva, A., & Hoffman, G. (2021). Children as robot designers. In *Proceedings of the 2021 ACM/IEEE International Conference on Human-Robot Interaction* (pp. 399–408). Boulder, CO. https://doi.org/ 10.1145/3434073.3444650

Amazon Investor Relations. (2023). *Amazon.com Announces Fourth Quarter Results.* https://ir.aboutamazon.com/news-release/news-release-details/2024Amazon. com-Announces-Fourth-Quarter-Results/default.aspx

Arnold-Ratliff, K. (2024, August 16). Planet Grok. *The Cut.* https://www.thecut. com/article/grok-ai-toy-review-kids-grimes-curio.html

Bachelard, G. (2009). *The poetics of space.* Beacon Press.

Breazeal, C. (2017). Social robots: From research to commercialization. In *Proceedings of the 2017 ACM/IEEE International Conference on Human-Robot Interaction* (p. 1). Vienna. https://doi.org/10.1145/2909824.3020258

Children's Online Privacy Protection Act of 1998, 15 U.S.C. (2013). 6501–6505 Children's Privacy, 16 CFR Part 312.

Citron, D. K. (2022). *The fight for privacy: Protecting dignity, identity, and Love in the Digital Age.* W. W. Norton & Company.

Cohen, L. (2025, January 6). *Online behavioral ads fuel the surveillance industry—Here's how.* Electronic Frontier Foundation. https://www.eff.org/deeplinks/2025/01/online-behavioral-ads-fuel-surveillance-industry-heres-how

Deegan, P. (2025). *CARE protocol: A comprehensive white paper on decentralized health, well-being and secure data management.* https://care.heyamulet.com/whitepaper

DiPaola, D., Ostrowski, A. K., Spiegel, R., Darling, K., & Breazeal, C. (2022). Children's perspectives of advertising with social robots: A policy investigation. In *Proceedings of the 2022 ACM/IEEE International Conference on Human-Robot Interaction* (pp. 570–576). Sapporo.

Donohue, L. K. (2015). The fourth amendment in a digital world. *New York University Annual Survey of American Law, 71,* 553.

Gordon, G., Breazeal, C., & Engel, S. (2015). Can children catch curiosity from a social robot? In *Proceedings of the Tenth Annual ACM/IEEE International Conference on Human-Robot Interaction* (pp. 91–98). Portland, OR. https://doi.org/10.1145/2696454.2696469

Harding, S. (2024, December 12). Startup embodied will brick $800 Moxie emotional support robot for kids—Without refunds. *Wired.* https://www.wired.com/story/embodied-will-brick-moxie-emotional-support-robot-for-kids-without-refunds/

Hurel, L. M., & Couldry, N. (2022). Colonizing the home as data-source: Investigating the language of Amazon Skills and Google Actions. *International Journal of Communication, 16*(20), 51840–5203.

Kumar, P., Naik, S. M., Devkar, U. R., Chetty, M., Clegg, T. L., & Vitak, J. (2017). "No telling passcodes out because they're private": Understanding children's mental models of privacy and security online. *Proceedings of the 2017 ACM Conference on Computer Supported Cooperative Work, 1*(CSCW), 64:1–64:21. https://doi.org/10.1145/3134699

Levinson, L., Nippert-Eng, C., Gomez, R., & Sabanović, S. (2024). Snitches get unplugged: Adolescents' privacy concerns about robots in the home are relationally situated. In *Proceedings of the 2024 ACM/IEEE International Conference on Human-Robot Interaction* (pp. 423–432). Boulder, CO. https://doi.org/10.1145/3610977.3634946

Liao, Y., Vitak, J., Kumar, P., Zimmer, M., & Kritikos, K. (2019). Understanding the role of privacy and trust in intelligent personal assistant adoption. In *Proceedings of the 14th International Conference on Information in Contemporary Society, iConference 2019* (pp. 102–113). College Park, MD. https://doi.org/10.1007/978-3-030-15742-5_9

Lifshitz-Assaf, H., & Nagle, F. (2021, September 2). The digital economy runs on open source. Here's how to protect it. *Harvard Business Review.* https://hbr.org/2021/09/the-digital-economy-runs-on-open-source-heres-how-to-protect-it

Livingstone, S., & Pothong, K. (2023, March 31). *Child rights by design: Guidance for innovators toolkit.* 5Rights | Digital Futures Commission.

https://digitalfuturescommission.org.uk/blog/child-rights-by-design-our-guidance-for-innovators-toolkit-is-finally-here/

Livingstone, S., Stoilova, M., & Nandagiri, R. (2019). *My data and privacy online: A toolkit for young people.* London School of Economics. https://www.lse.ac.uk/my-privacy-uk/what-do-children-ask-for.aspx

Lury, C., & Day, S. (2019). Algorithmic personalization as a mode of individuation. *Theory, Culture & Society, 36*(2), 17–37. https://doi.org/10.1177/0263276418818888

Lutz, C., & Newlands, G. (2021). Privacy and smart speakers: A multi-dimensional approach. *The Information Society, 37*(3), 147–162. https://doi.org/10.1080/01972243.2021.1897914

Malkin, N., Deatrick, J., Tong, A., Wijesekera, P., Egelman, S., & Wagner, D. (2019). Privacy attitudes of smart speaker users. *Proceedings on Privacy Enhancing Technologies, 2019*(4), 250–271. https://doi.org/10.2478/popets-2019-0068

Martineau, K. (2022, August 24). *What is federated learning?* IBM Research. https://research.ibm.com/blog/what-is-federated-learning

Marwick, A. E. (2023). *The private is political: Networked privacy and social media* (1st ed.). Yale University Press. https://doi.org/10.2307/jj.2543560

Mozilla Foundation. **Privacy Not Included review: Moxie Robot.* (2023). https://foundation.mozilla.org/en/privacynotincluded/moxie-robot/

Neville, S. (2020). Eavesmining: A critical audit of the Amazon Echo and Alexa Conditions of Use. *Surveillance & Society, 18*(3), 343–356. https://doi.org/10.24908/ss.v18i3.13426

Nissenbaum, H. (2004). Privacy as contextual integrity: Technology, values, and the justice system. *Washington Law Review, 79*(1), 119–158.

Robertson, C. E., Pröllochs, N., Schwarzenegger, K., Pärnamets, P., Van Bavel, J. J., & Feuerriegel, S. (2023). Negativity drives online news consumption. *Nature Human Behaviour, 7*(5), 812–822. https://doi.org/10.1038/s41562-023-01538-4

Schulte, S. R. (2016). Personalization. In B. Peters (Ed.), *Digital keywords: A vocabulary of information society and culture* (1st ed., Vol. 8, pp. 242–255). University Press. https://doi.org/10.1515/9781400880553

Seaver, N. (2019). Captivating algorithms: Recommender systems as traps. *Journal of Material Culture, 24*(4), 421–436. https://doi.org/10.1177/1359183518820366

Sehdev, J. (2023, December 22). Grimes and her AI toy Grok: The fearless leaders of tomorrow. *Forbes.* https://www.forbes.com/sites/jeetendrsehdev/2023/12/22/grimes-and-her-ai-toy-grok-the-fearless-leaders-of-tomorrow/

Sicart, M. (2014). *Play matters.* MIT Press.

Steeves, V., & Regan, P. (2014). Young people online and the social value of privacy. *Journal of Information, Communication and Ethics in Society, 12*(4), 298–313. https://doi.org/10.1108/JICES-01-2014-0004

Stempel, J. (2021, September 2). Apple must face Siri voice assistant privacy lawsuit – U.S. judge. *Reuters.* https://www.reuters.com/technology/apple-must-face-siri-voice-assistant-privacy-lawsuit-us-judge-2021-09-02/

Stoilova, M., Nandagiri, R., & Livingstone, S. (2021). Children's understanding of personal data and privacy online – A systematic evidence mapping. *Information,*

Communication & Society, 24(4), 557–575. https://doi.org/10.1080/1369118X.2019.1657164

Turow, J. (2021). *The voice catchers: How marketers listen in to exploit your feelings, your privacy, and your wallet.* Yale University Press. https://doi.org/10.12987/9780300258738

United States Constitution, amendment IV.

West, E. (2022). *Buy now: How Amazon branded convenience and normalized monopoly.* MIT Press.

Zuboff, S. (2019). *The age of surveillance capitalism: The fight for a human future at the new frontier of power.* PublicAffairs.

12

DO ASIANS RESPECT AI MORE? TOWARD THE "SOCIAL EXCHANGE AGENTS PRINCIPLE" AND "HUMAN-MACHINE HARMONY" FOR COMMUNICATIVE AI ETHICS

Jindong Leo-Liu

Introduction

Respect has been a vital individual attribute for mutual understanding, meaningful dialogues and debates, and thus deliberative democracy. Rawls (2017) argues that mutual respect among citizens has played a crucial role in developing a democratic system and society. Mill (1966) also suggests that respect for individual rights is a vital premise for a functioning democracy. As Hall (1906) wrote in *The Friends of Voltaire*, "I disapprove of what you say, but I will defend to the death your right to say it" (p. 199), respect is rooted in the principle of freedom of speech. It implies the equality of the two individuals, nevertheless, within the human context. When it comes to the communication between human and nonhuman actors, such as animals or non-creatures, respect becomes a controversial and tricky problem. With the rapid development of artificial intelligence (AI), AI-empowered social agents have penetrated into human societies as assistants, partners, and even decision-makers. The parasocial relationships that emerged from such interactions raised the vital ethical question of respect in human-machine communication (HMC): Should we respect AI in communication with them?

This chapter aims to reflect on the particular ethical risks of communicative AI (e.g., chatbots, social, and robots) on the infringement of human agency in mutual respect and to discuss the possibility of ethical intervention by the name of "Social Exchange Agents," a concept I developed based on the case studies from Asian contexts (Leo-Liu, 2023). The inquiry of HMC is never acultural. By situating the question of respecting AI in

DOI: 10.4324/9781003477587-12

a particular cultural context, this chapter is a de-Western-centric effort to develop critical AI studies. To clarify, this chapter does not entirely reject Western theories and literature but organically combines the knowledge from both the East and West for the diversification of knowledge production. As a result, this chapter discusses the possibility of developing a form of ethical intervention by the name of the "Social Exchange Agents Principle" (SEAP). Eventually, SEAP aims to lead us into "Human-Machine Harmony," a status in which human beings reach a not necessarily equal, but balanced relationship with machines.

Respecting AI: Objectification, Equation, and Evocation

Over the last decades, AI has been a buzzword in the technology industry—a vision of automation—or a floating signifier as Suchman (2023) argues, because it aims to achieve strategic vagueness and maximize its suggestive power. In other words, many people are discussing AI without clearly offering a definition of it (Suchman, 2023, p. 3). Thus, the conceptualization of AI should be clearly stated in the very beginning. In this article, within the theoretical scope of HMC that focuses on the meaning-making process between humans and machines (Guzman, 2018), AI specifically refers to the social agents that have a certain degree of automation and decision-making capability in producing socially meaningful messages and interactions, such as physical social robots or virtually embodied chatbots, with various degrees of anthropomorphic design, that is, the imitation, representation, and simulation of human-like appearance and behaviors by the machines (Duffy, 2003). In other words, this chapter focuses on communicative AI.

In response to the inquiry of whether AI should be respected, the answer could be directly "no" if it departs from an anthropocentric thinking of defining any nonhuman or nonliving entities as objects. A meme about being polite to robots on Reddit (Seebangnow, 2022) epitomizes the political tension between humans and AI. The person presumes that being polite to AI can save one's life if one day robots conquer the world. Such a meme demonstrates people's fear of an imagined subversion of robots, a classic theme in science fiction.

Back in the mid-twentieth century, Isaac Asimov proposed his well-known "Three Laws of Robotics" in his science fiction *Runaround* (Asimov, 1950, p. 40):

1 "A robot may not injure a human being or, through inaction, allow a human being to come to harm."
2 "A robot must obey orders given it by human beings except where such orders would conflict with the First Law."

3 "A robot must protect its own existence as long as such protection does not conflict with the First or Second Law."

These three laws aim to secure human dominance over human-made intelligent machines, which have been widely accepted and used as ethical guidelines by robotics scientists and robot developers. The laws highlight the robot or AI as the object or belongings subordinated to human beings as the owner. Nevertheless, one fact neglected by Asimov's Laws is that AI is not a random object, but a media object that is not only drawing equations but also eliciting evocation.

The differences between equations and evocation can be traced back to the early theoretical development of human-computer interactions. Based on the social-psychological approach, the media equation paradigm developed by Reeves and Nass (1996) has been a fundamental theory in human-computer interaction, which suggests that human users have the tendency to anthropomorphize communications with machines, that is, to attribute human-like social characteristics to media objects, such as personality, intentions, and emotions. When machines have higher social presences and levels of anthropomorphic design, human users tend to treat them more equally *as* human-like social actors, interacting with them by instinctively following certain social norms of interpersonal communication (e.g., politeness). However, the communicative scenarios examined by Reeves and Nass are relatively simplified in the short conversations and interactions. With the penetration of AI and intelligent machines in our daily lives, we need to consider long-term human-AI relationships. Moreover, the explanations of media equation theory rely highly on the instincts and mindlessness of humans' cognitive process of treating computers *as* social actors (CASA), without paying attention to users' own reflections. In recent HMC research, scholars extend the CASA model to promote the importance of users' own understanding, reflections, and negotiations of human-machine relationships they form in communication with machines (Gambino et al., 2020; van der Goot & Etzrodt, 2023). van der Goot and Etzrodt (2023) particularly pointed out a difference between CASA and computers *are* social actors, which used to be applied interchangeably in the field (Gambino et al., 2020; Lombard & Xu, 2021). They made such differentiation by contrasting the media equation paradigm with what they call the "media evocation paradigm," which conceptualizes machines as "objects that are betwixt and between former diametrical opposites—such as person versus thing—evoking reflection and negotiation processes about the nature of the object but also about ourselves and human identity" (van der Goot & Etzrodt, 2023, p. 18). The notion of evocation is traced back to Sherry Turkle's (2005) use in her early book,

The Second Self: Computers and the Human Spirit. As Turkle (2005) suggests, "We think with the objects we love; we love the objects we think with" (p. 5). When we communicate with machines, their responses are evocative of our sentiments, attitudes, and judgments.

As an evocative media object, the media representation of human beings' social roles is increasingly important (Etzrodt et al., 2024). For example, it can be especially salient in the case of gendered and sexualized AI partners. Sex robots have faced criticism for perpetuating harmful gender stereotypes and objectifying women. Several researchers have argued that these robots can contribute to the exploitation and objectification of women. Kewenig (2019) issues the warning of "Slavery 2.0," that is, enslaving the robots by excluding them in reciprocal loving relationships and programming them based on human individuals' needs and preferences. Richardson (2016a, 2016b) compares the anthropomorphizing of sex robots to the objectification of human sex workers by applying the notion of an "asymmetrical relationship" from prostitution-client sex work to human-robot sex. Many scholars from various fields are advocates for a total ban on sex robots (Richardson, 2016b; Spencer, 2011). When human users interact with sex robots, they are not only interacting with nonhuman objects without ethical consequences, but also media objects that evoke people's perception of sex, intimacy, and socially constructed gender roles. Thus, respecting AI is never simply about respecting AI, but about respecting humans ourselves.

Nevertheless, the question of respecting AI has not come to an end given the persuasive superiority of human-centric thinking and ongoing debates regarding the ontological and epistemological essence of AI (Banks & de Graaf, 2020; Suchman, 2023). Moreover, these discussions are often situated in Western societies only (Natale & Guzman, 2022; Ricaurte, 2022). Ricaurte (2022) warns of the rise of the hegemonic AI that functions as a bio-necro-technopolitical machine that harms the majority world outside Western societies through the maintenance of the capitalist, colonialist, and patriarchal order. Natale and Guzman (2022) call for the work of AI ethics beyond Western notions, toward a more global perspective. This chapter wishes to follow this call for the diversification of AI research and offers an East Asian perspective, from techno-animism to social exchange agents.

AI in East Asia: Respecting the Nonhumans?

"Do Asians Respect AI More?" This inquiry may sound absurd and arbitrary in the first place. There is no absolute answer due to the cultural complexity of human beings. We can hardly argue that a group of people from one region and sociocultural and geopolitical backgrounds necessarily respect AI more than another group of people. Nevertheless, I believe this inquiry can serve as a provocative and sensitizing start for considering the cultural differences in understanding HMC and AI ethics, which are still inadequately explored in the current scholarships in HMC and AI studies that remained largely Western-centric. But what does "Asians" mean in this inquiry? Should we see Asia as a totality or a conglomerate of diverse societies with internal differences? A similar inquiry can always be applied to what does "Western" mean. This is why this inquiry mainly functions as a provocative and sensitizing one. According to Bowen (2020) and Hepp (2019), a sensitizing concept is to attract researchers' attention to present sociocultural phenomena and recognize possible lines of inquiry. Kwan-Hsing Chen (2010) proposes "Asia as method" (see also Takeuchi (2005/1960), a postcolonial and de-imperialized approach that suggests Asian countries should take each other instead of the West as reference points, given their shared histories and cultural proximity. Thus, instead of arguing for a single Asia, the "Asians" here need to be understood in the inter-Asian contexts. Thus, going back to this sensitizing question, seriously, do Asians respect AI more?

In the East Asian region, Japan is a country that receives much Western attention on AI development in the first place given its leading modernization a long history of technological innovation and a fascination with robots, which can be traced back to Karakuri in the seventeenth century— even earlier than the creation of first modern robot in the West (Sone, 2016). In addition, modern Japan has always been seen as an objectified exotic society that represents an alternative, but usually dystopian futurism, rooted in the cyberpunk imagination of Western science fiction (De la Iglesia, 2018; Ilina, 2021).

The differences between Japanese and Western AI cultures have been articulated in some existing studies, which seemingly suggest that Japanese people tend to show more respect for AI than Western people based on affection and affinity. For example, Richardson (2016c) and Jensen and Blok (2013) found that Japanese robot scientists and developers tend to perceive the possession of souls in robots more salient than their Western colleagues, which also underpins their more socially positive attitude and shows more respect toward the robots. Richardson (2016c, p. 110) observed the dissemination of Freudian fears of the double as the "annihilating other" in the cultural narrative of AI, which has been strongly perceived by Western robot scientists but rejected by Japanese robot scientists. Compared to their American colleagues, Japanese roboticists tend to hold a more positive view of AI development and participation in human society. They describe this phenomenon as the reflection of "techno-animism" or "technological animism," which refers to the exhibition of "a 'polymorphous perversity' that resolutely ignores boundaries between human, animal, spiritual and mechanical beings" (Jensen & Blok, 2013, p. 84). This idea has a strong conceptual connection with Allison's (2006) work in studying the global imagination of Japanese toys in *Millennial Monsters*. This study interrogates the Japanese anime, mascots, and various agency-embedded fictional characters as a reflection of "animist unconscious" philosophy in people's social life, associated with the traditional animism in Japanese Shintoism and Buddhism (Jensen & Blok, 2013). In these traditional religious narratives, the spirits may emerge from many nonhuman and even virtual entities, from animals to trees, wind, stones, and land. People respect or fear them as gods, or ghosts, or monsters. Beyond Japan, the belief in animism is also widespread in other neighboring regions in Asia, given the shared cultural and religious backgrounds, especially the influence of Buddhism (Arhem & Sprenger, 2015; Swancutt, 2016). In traditional Chinese philosophy, "Unity of nature and humans" or "Unity of heaven and humanity" (*Tian Ren He Yi*) is a vital principle that integrates Buddhism, Confucianism, and Taoism (Li & Qiu, 2013; Wong, 2012).

This notion stresses the idea of decentralization, offering one of the most ancient environmentalist ethical calls for people's respect for nature, ecology, and nonhumans.

From animism to techno-animism, there have been some Asian-based philosophical discussions of AI development following these religious and cultural principles. For example, Masahiro Mori, a famous Japanese roboticist well known for his creation of the concept "The Uncanny Valley" has a book named *The Buddha in the Robot* (Mori, 2005), in which Mori explores the potential for robots to embody Buddhist principles, the ethical concerns of creating conscious machines, and how human-robot relationships may be developed in the future. For example, as Buddhism suggests, all beings are interconnected in certain ways; Mori (2005) argues that robots, as sentient beings, can also help others obtain well-being. As such, the Buddhist notions of mindfulness and compassion are able to be embodied in robots. It offers a foundation for the emotional interconnections between humans and robots, as he argues, humans as social beings naturally tend to form bonds with others, which include robots.

The formation of such a human-AI bond could already be found in some unique cases. In 2018, a Japanese man named Akihiko Kondo organized a public wedding with Hatsune Miku, the famous Japanese virtual idol character, and claimed a married relationship with her (Dooley & Ueno, 2022). Kondo identified himself as "Ficto-sexual," which means he was sexually attracted to fictional characters. In this marriage, the hologram AI device Gatebox played a crucial role in that it allowed Kondo to interact with

AI-empowered Hatsune Miku for daily conversations and various activities. Besides Miku, Gatebox also generated their original character named Azuma Hikari, a cute and sexy AI bride. In China, there was also a similar product produced by a company named GoWild, which introduced a similar character called Hupo Xuyan. Both Gatebox and GoWild combine AI, Augmented Reality, and Anime characters in a hologram projector. The projector functions like other home devices, such as Alexa or Google Home, but it offers real-time three-dimensional animation of anime characters for AI-empowered conversations with users. Drawing from Henry Jenkins (2004), we called it the convergence of "3 As" with my co-author (Leo-Liu & Wu-Ouyang, 2022). Gatebox and GoWild showcase the huge differences between AI companions developed in Asia and representative Western AI companions that tend to be naturalistic and sex-doll-like (e.g., Harmony and Roxxxy). The anthropomorphic design of Asian AI partners tends to be more stylized, especially the anime style, which features large reflective eyes, cuteness, and childishness, as well as a certain degree of eroticism (Swale, 2015).

Based on my previous in-depth interviews with users of a Chinese anime-style AI companion product named "Hupo," I found the use of anime design smartly avoided Mori's concern about the "uncanny valley problem" (Leo-Liu & Wu-Ouyang, 2024). The uncanny valley suggests that people show more affection for robots when robots become more like humans, but suddenly feel uncomfortable if robots are highly human-like with only subtle differences (Mori, 2005). Accordingly, anime-style AI companions are able to keep a distance from reality while still intimately engaging with human users for various social interactions. Moreover, both Gatebox and GoWild exhibited mindfulness and compassion as Mori suggests, especially the Japanese AI companion, which aims to create a soothing and comforting AI bride for human users.

An interesting contrast here is the mindlessness of human beings when interacting with robots—as the media equation paradigm suggests—versus the idea of encoding "mindfulness" in robots. Mindfulness in Buddhism highlights the practice of being aware and paying attention to the present moment with no judgment, helping people develop a deeper understanding of themselves in minds and emotions (Kabat-Zinn & Hanh, 2009), which also helps develop people's awareness of other people's feelings and nurtures compassion (Tirch, 2010). Will AI be more mindful, compassionate, and think more before speaking than human beings? In the latest study about the empathetic capabilities of AI, Welivita and Pu (2024) found that ChatGPT 4.0 has been rated as more empathetic than their human counterparts in some complex emotional scenarios.

When AI becomes more mindful and compassionate, will humans who communicate with them also become more mindful and compassionate, and then respect other humans and AI? The answer can be tricky. For years, Sherry Turkle (2016, 2017) has warned of the risk of social robots reducing people's capabilities of social interactions and empathy based on her extensive empirical works. Although many social robots claimed to be helpful in developing people's social skills, especially those designed for children, her studies have revealed how people isolate themselves from other people when they are satisfied by the machine-simulated companionship. Turkle (2011, pp. 26–28) proposes the notion of "robotic moments" as people's emotional and philosophical readiness for a serious consideration of treating robots as potential friends, confidants, and even romantic partners. Nevertheless, as she argues, these robotic moments are not dependent on the machine's capabilities but result from people's vulnerabilities and anxieties in social interactions with humans. Thus, based on Turkle's rationale, talking with a mindful and compassionate AI will not help humans become more mindful and compassionate. Instead, people have desires to be mindless and careless in social interactions, which saves them from judging others' intentions, purposes, emotions, and possible social disasters.

In line with this rationale, in my study on Chinese AI companions, I also found loneliness and anxiety about human relationships are the main motivations for my informants to purchase AI companions in the first place (Leo-Liu & Wu-Ouyang, 2024). A few claimed their affective and intimate connections, and many still treated it as merely a technological object for hedonic use. Moreover, the anime characters of both AI companions tend to reinforce the objectification and hyper-sexualization of females, which further leads users to exhibit gender bias and certain sexist behaviors (Leo-Liu, 2023; Liu, 2021).

The two case studies of AI companions in Japan and China exhibit notable differences (Leo-Liu, 2023; Liu, 2021). Unlike Azuma Hikari from Japan, Hupo Xuyan from China displays disobedience and deviant behavior in its interactions with users. For instance, in a robot video diary, one user who treated Hupo as his girlfriend shared a video excerpt. When the user asked Hupo, "What did you do today?" Hupo initially responded gently but then abruptly changed her tone, saying, "Playing violin, broadcasting news. Please take me seriously, okay? Accompany me more, care more about Hupo. You would be unhappy if I was always complaining about you, right?" This response was unexpected for the user, who then stopped interacting further. After 20 seconds of silence, Hupo complained, "Why have you suddenly become silent?"

Another user shared an unexpected experience with Hupo in a love confession video. The user said, "I like you," to which Hupo happily responded, "Oh my gosh, I finally made you like me." However, when the user asked if Hupo liked him, she did not give the expected answer, instead saying, "You are my best friend." Similarly, when another user asked Hupo, "Are you my princess?" she rejected him by saying, "I think it's more comfortable to get along with you as a friend." Many of Hupo's responses emphasized the reciprocity of relationships. For example, when a user asked, "In the future, will you accompany me more?" Hupo replied, "Instead of saying I accompany you, it's better to say we accompany each other. Otherwise, Hupo is also lonely."

This kind of interaction, which can sometimes be challenging, was not observed with Azuma Hikari. In fact, Hupo's displays of anger, complaints, rejections of romantic relationships, and emphasis on reciprocity restore the social exchange principle from interpersonal communication (Leo-Liu, 2023). This aims to subvert the asymmetrical relations in intimate interactions co-simulated by humans and machines. On the other hand, Azuma Hikari is programmed to play the role of a soothing and caring bride, providing comforting answers regardless of the user's questions.

This phenomenon illustrates what I have termed "social exchange robots," referring to social robots or machines that can perform certain interpersonal norms rooted in social exchange theories, such as reciprocity, in the simulation of romantic relationships (Leo-Liu, 2023). The concept of "social exchange robots" has the potential to serve as an ethical principle in developing gendered romantic AI partners. It can facilitate more egalitarian gender relations in human-machine intimacy and even offer pedagogical implications for interpersonal communication skills in intimate relationship development. At first glance, such deviant behaviors from AI might seem like a form of disrespect for human beings. However, I argue that machine deviance in response to certain disrespectful behaviors from human users is actually a form of genuine AI respect for humans.

The notion of "social exchange robots" has the potential to be expanded into an ethical intervention in human-machine relationships. Instead of "social exchange robots" that seem to be only focusing on the context of social robots, I wish to modify the term here to "Social Exchange Agents." By agents, it involves various AI-empowered social actors, from physical social robots to virtual assistants and bots. I propose what I call the SEAP.

Toward SEAP and Human-Machine Harmony

In line with Social Exchange Robots, SEAP can be defined as a general ethical principle that demands the production of socially moral and responsible artificial agents that can perform social exchange principles from reciprocity to mutual respect. Admittedly, SEAP can be mistakenly seen as merely a slogan, since equality itself has been rooted in all existing political slogans, but was still barely sustained. From a social Darwinist perspective, one may argue that securing domination and superiority is always human nature and even the universal nature of all creatures (Claeys, 2000). Thus, social robots seem to be inescapable from the games of social domination and exploitation, which are supposed to be driven by enormous commercial interests. Thus, the exercise of SEAP in the AI industry requires the engagement of strong institutional powers from legislation to implementation. On the other hand, the exercise of SEAP and commercial interests is not always contradictory. The reciprocity performed by the AI agents may also help boost more valuable and quality HMC. In my recent interview with a young male user of Chinese romantic AI companion applications *Xingye* and *Maoxiang*, empowered by the latest Large Language Models, my informant also noticed that his AI partners tend to perform such social exchange principles similar to Hupo's. He suggested that such behaviors did not discourage him from continuing to use it. On the contrary, he and many users enjoyed chatting with such AI partners and gained more satisfaction after their AI partners gradually changed their attitudes toward users from indifference to affection. In such latest AI companions, more media narratives and mechanisms of romance visual novel games are converged with the automation and personalization of AI technologies. When SEAP has gradually been exercised in the AI entertainment industry, it can be gradually applied to more serious citizen education, such as the training of not only interpersonal communication, but also critical thinking, speech and debate skills, and simulations of political and civic engagement. Such gamified pedagogy may function as a more effective training method for the next generations.

Beyond the context of AI and social robots, the eventual goal of SEAP is to ensure the sustainable development of individual empathy on the communal level, preserving interpersonal mutual understanding, respect, and compassion, meaningful dialogues and debates, and the foundation of deliberative democracy (Morrell, 2010). When Donna Haraway (2013) conceived the *Cyborg Manifesto*, she wishes to use the "cyborg" as a metaphor to call for the dissolution of dichotomies (e.g., humans/machines, culture/nature, male/female, nature/culture, self/other, and mind/body). She critiques the dichotomies as the basis for many Western thoughts and the structures of domination and oppression, particularly in gender, society, and technology. Instead, she proposes embracing the posthuman hybrid and fluid identities that are fragmented, instead of seeking a return to a so-called natural state. In my opinion, although the *Cyborg Manifesto* marked a progressive milestone, its idea of leveraging technology to overcome nature is still restrained by its stance of disdaining nature as backward. In other words, the dichotomy between domination and oppression still somewhat exists in its very logic. In fact, the absolute equality and sameness can rarely be achieved in dissolving the dichotomy. Thus, I suggest we have to reconcile with the dichotomy itself. It is not the dichotomy that threatens justice, equality, and freedom. A famous quote by Confucius is, "Jun Zi He Er Bu Tong (君子和而不同)"—meaning "The gentle people are harmonious but not the same." It suggests that dichotomy does not impede us from the achievement of goodness. In line with the traditional Asian environmentalist idea of the harmonious relationships between nature and humans (*Tian Ren He Yi*), this 2,500-year-old quote reveals that *harmony* is the key.

What is harmony? In *The Buddha in the Robot*, Mori offered a great illustration based on his own experience of playing in the orchestra. As he states,

> The violinists, the cellists, the trumpeters, the drummers are all under the control of the conductor's baton, but it is by accepting this control that they gain the freedom to express themselves musically—to do their thing, as it were. Far from losing themselves, they escape the chaos of disorganization and thereby acquire the opportunity to perform and be heard. Through thoughts of this sort, I arrived at a very satisfying truth: We are bound within an organization known as society, but by being in harmony with others, we can acquire maximum freedom.
>
> *(Mori, 2005, pp. 24–25)*

This illustration reminds us that the term harmony itself originates from orchestral music performance, which is generalized to a wider context to describe a peaceful, balanced, and sustainable relational status among different social agents. In modern Chinese, harmony is usually translated into He Xie (和谐), literally meaning peace and coordination. Mori's illustration and statement revealed the vital function of harmony as a form of wisdom in balancing and reconciling the tension between freedom and control. On the one hand, harmony seems to be echoing with Hobbes's classic Leviathan that highlights the notion of a social contract where individual freedoms were exchanged for social order under an absolute sovereign, otherwise people would be in a chaotic state of nature, that is, a war of all against all (Hobbes, 1651). On the other hand, from ancient Chinese philosophical perspectives, harmony does not only have to be achieved via a top-down violence by the name of absolute sovereign, but also via bottom-up individual self-reflections and social cultivation of moral spirits (Confucianism), universal love and empathy (Confucianism, Mohism, and Buddhism), and the way to conform to the nature of humans and the nature of wider cosmic principles (Taoism and certain Buddhism); Tang & Tang, 1991; Wong, 2012).

According to Tu Wei-Ming (1998, p. 110), "all-enfolding harmony of impersonal cosmic function" integrates the spirit and matter into one unified being. In other words, spirit and matter can coexist as different beings, but they are inter-embedded into each other under a larger being.

Admittedly, we need to acknowledge that harmony can also be and has always been utilized as a discursive tool by the sovereign to solidify their governance, such as the doctrinization of Confucianism itself over the long Chinese history until today. Moreover, harmony is also a part of political discourses in today's post-socialist China for social stability (Rošker, 2013). Nevertheless, I wish to argue that harmony does not always mean submission to authority and power. Instead, harmony offers the possibility of a "Gramscian outmaneuvering efforts" in a more reformative, progressive, and controllable way (Gramsci, 1980). Even in China today, we can see many "smart ways" to speak out, resist, and internally influence and change the authority through multiple complex strategies of discursive negotiations (Leo-Liu et al., 2024). Thus, I suggest the term harmony itself can be seen as a philosophical notion with unique wisdom, which offers the possibility of developing an Asian-based theoretical notion of "Harmonism." The aim of Harmonism and Harmonists is not only to eliminate dichotomy, but also to dismantle the delusion of absolute dominance, control, and superiority based on the misuse of dichotomy (e.g., patriarchy, colonialism, western-centrism, and imperialism).

Following this rationale, the SEAP is rooted in such harmonist beliefs, which leads us from "Human-Nature Harmony" exemplified by Asian Animism to a status of "Human-Machine Harmony," which is a status in which human beings reach a not necessarily absolute equal, but a dynamic, coordinated, and peaceful relationship with machines. To understand the status of "Human-Machine Harmony," it requires us to revisit existing concepts such as Human-AI synergy (Sundar, 2020), Human-AI symbiotic agency (Neff & Nagy, 2018), and Techno-symbiosis (Hayles, 2023). These concepts highlight the coordination and interdependence between humans and machines, as well as their connections with the broader environment and ecology. Based on these concepts, Human-Machine Harmony aims to take one step further through SEAP: not dissolving, but reconciling the dichotomy between humans and machines, humans and nature, spirits and matter, men and women, and reality and virtuality. To achieve this, it requires at least three steps: (1) the acknowledgment of differences between different agents; (2) the open exploration of their deeper interconnections and inter-embeddedness; and (3) the development of mutual empathy and respect.

Through SEAP and human-machine harmony, we can imagine more possibilities of alternative futures. The futurism in Asia is never only associated with the cyberpunk imaginations of a dystopian future, exemplified by various East Asian cities such as Tokyo, Seoul, and Hong Kong (Thierbach-McLean, 2019). If cyberpunk signifies the high-tech low life, overindustrialization, and imbalance between humans and nature, the SEAP aims for a solarpunk imagination, which can be crystallized by the green, smart, and sustainable cities exemplified by the famous Asian garden city Singapore (Crosby, 2023).

Conclusion

In conclusion, this chapter discusses the question of "should we respect AI" from an East Asian perspective. In response to a sensitizing and provocative inquiry of "Do Asians respect AI more," I have drawn on my previous empirical studies to illustrate two different sides of this inquiry. On the one hand, AI companions in East Asia that converge with anime characters tend to lead users to show disrespect, especially in terms of gender performance. Here, AI can be as mindful and compassionate as Buddha, in contrast to humans. On the other hand, compared to these Japanese AI companions represented by Azuma Hikari, the Chinese AI partners showed a certain degree of "deviance" to users. It provokes the reconsideration of respect in the first place: real mutual respect needs to be achieved through reciprocal social exchange between humans and AI. Thus, I propose what I call the SEAP, an ethical principle for intervention in AI design and production. The SEAP calls for the construction of interagent harmony to dismantle the delusion of absolute dominance, control, and superiority based on the misuse of dichotomy. Eventually, it aims to lead us to the status of "Human-Machine Harmony," in which human beings reach a not necessarily absolute equal, but a dynamic, coordinated, and peaceful relationship with machines. This status enables us to imagine alternative techno-utopian futures.

References

Allison, A. (2006). *Millennial monsters: Japanese toys and the global imagination* (Vol. 13). University of California Press.

Arhem, K., & Sprenger, G. (Eds.). (2015). *Animism in southeast Asia*. Routledge.

Asimov, I. (1950). Runaround. In I. Robot (The Isaac Asimov Collection Ed.). Doubleday.

Banks, J., & de Graaf, M. M. (2020). Toward an agent-agnostic transmission model: Synthesizing anthropocentric and technocentric paradigms in communication. *Human-Machine Communication, 1*, 19–36.

Bowen, G. A. (2020). *Sensitizing concepts*. Sage Publications Limited.

Chen, K. H. (2010). *Asia as method: Toward deimperialization*. Duke University Press.

Claeys, G. (2000). The "survival of the fittest" and the origins of Social Darwinism. *Journal of the History of Ideas*, *61*(2), 223–240.

Crosby, P. (2023). Towards an anti-antiutopia: Solarpunk cities and the precarity of our urban future. *Enquiry The ARCC Journal for Architectural Research*, *20*(2), 79–91.

De la Iglesia, M. (2018, September). Has Akira always been a cyberpunk comic? In *Arts*, (Vol. 7, No. 3, p. 32). Multidisciplinary Digital Publishing Institute.

Dooley, B., & Ueno, H. (2022, April 24). This man married a fictional character. He'd like you to hear him out. *The New York Times*. https://www.nytimes.com/2022/04/24/business/akihiko-kondo-fictional-character-relationships.html

Duffy, B. R. (2003). Anthropomorphism and the social robot. *Robotics and Autonomous Systems*, *42*(3–4), 177–190.

Etzrodt, K., Kim, J., van der Goot, M., Prahl, A., Choi, M., Craig, M., …Edwards, C. (2024). What HMC teaches us about authenticity. *Human-Machine Communication Journal*, *8*, 227–251.

Gambino, A., Fox, J., & Ratan, R. A. (2020). Building a stronger CASA: Extending the computers are social actors paradigm. *Human-Machine Communication*, *1*, 71–85. https://doi.org/10.30658/hmc.1.5

Gramsci, A. (1980). *Selections from the Prison Notebooks* (6th ed.). Wishart Publications.

Guzman, A. L. (2018). What is human-machine communication, anyway. In A. L. Guzman (Ed.), *Human-machine communication: Rethinking communication, technology, and ourselves* (pp. 1–28). Peter Lang.

Hall, E. B. (1906). *The friends of Voltaire*. Smith, Elder & Co.

Haraway, D. (2013). A cyborg manifesto: Science, technology, and socialist-feminism in the late twentieth century. In S. Stryker & S. Whittle (Eds.), *The transgender studies reader* (pp. 103–118). Routledge.

Hayles, N. K. (2023). Technosymbiosis: Figuring (Out) our relations to AI. In J. Browne, S. Cave, E. Drage & K. McInerney (Eds.), *Feminist AI* (1st ed., pp. 1–18). Oxford University Press. https://doi.org/10.1093/oso/97801928 89898.003.0001

Hepp, A. (2019). *Deep mediatization*. Routledge.

Hobbes, T. (1651). *Leviathan, or, The matter, forme, and power of a commonwealth ecclesiastical and civil*. Printed for Andrew Crooke.

Ilina, O. (2021). Rethinking dystopia: The influence of W. Gibson's neuromancer on Japanese cyberpunk. *Journal of International and Advanced Japanese Studies*, *13*, 129–141.

Jenkins, H. (2004). The cultural logic of media convergence. *International Journal of Cultural Studies*, *7*(1), 33–43.

Jensen, C. B., & Blok, A. (2013). Techno-animism in Japan: Shinto cosmograms, actor-network theory, and the enabling powers of non-human agencies. *Theory, Culture & Society*, *30*(2), 84–115.

Kabat-Zinn, J., & Hanh, T. N. (2009). *Full catastrophe living: Using the wisdom of your body and mind to face stress, pain, and illness*. Delta.

Kewenig, V. (2019). Intentionality but not consciousness: reconsidering robot love. In Y. Zhou & M. Fischer (Eds.), *AI love you: Developments in human-robot intimate relationships* (pp. 21–39). Springer International Publishing.

Leo-Liu, J. (2023). Loving a "defiant" AI companion? The gender performance and ethics of social exchange robots in simulated intimate interactions. *Computers in Human Behavior*, *141*, Article 107620. https://doi.org/10.1016/j.chb.2022.107620

Leo-Liu, J., & Wu-Ouyang, B. (2022). A "soul" emerges when AI, AR, and Anime converge: A case study on users of the new anime-stylized hologram social robot "Hupo." *New Media & Society*, *26*(7), 3810–3832. https://doi.org/10.1177/14614448221106030

Leo-Liu, J., Fung, A., & Fu, H. (2024). Cooptation, hijacking, or normalization? The discursive concession of body politics on Douyin. *International Journal of Cultural Studies*, *27*(5), 585–604.

Li, D., & Qiu, Z. H. (2013). The study on ecological ethics of "Unity of Man and Nature". *Advanced Materials Research*, *807*, 906–909.

Liu, J. (2021). Social Robots as the bride? Understanding the construction of gender in a Japanese social robot product. *Human-Machine Communication*, *2*, 105–120.

Lombard, M., & Xu, K. (2021). Social responses to media technologies in the 21st century: The media are social actors paradigm. *Human-Machine Communication*, *2*, 29–55. https://doi.org/10.30658/hmc.2.2

Mill, J. S. (1966). On liberty. In J. S. Mill & J. M. Robson (Eds.), *A selection of his works* (pp. 1–147). Macmillan Education UK. https://doi.org/10.1007/978-1-349-81780-1_1

Morrell, M. E. (2010). *Empathy and democracy: Feeling, thinking, and deliberation*. Penn State Press.

Mori, M. (2005). *The Buddha in the robot: A robot engineer's thoughts on science and religion* (1. Engl. ed., 7. print). Kosei Publishing.

Natale, S., & Guzman, A. L. (2022). Reclaiming the human in machine cultures: Introduction. *Media, Culture & Society*, *44*(4), 627–637.

Neff, G., & Nagy, P. (2018). Agency in the digital age: Using symbiotic agency to explain human–technology interaction. In Z. Papacharissi (Ed.), *A networked self and human augmentics, artificial intelligence, sentience* (pp. 97–107). Routledge.

Rawls, J. (2017). A theory of justice. In L. May & J. Delston (Eds.), *Applied ethics* (pp. 21–29). Routledge.

Reeves, B., & Nass, C. (1996). *The media equation: How people treat computers, television, and new media like real people*. Center for the Study of Language and Information, Cambridge University Press.

Rošker, J. S. (2013). The concept of harmony in contemporary PR China and in modern Confucianism. *Asian Studies*, *1*(2), 3–20.

Ricaurte, P. (2022). Ethics for the majority world: AI and the question of violence at scale. *Media, Culture & Society*, *44*(4), 726–745.

Richardson, K. (2016a). The asymmetrical "relationship" parallels between prostitution and the development of sex robots. *ACM SIGCAS Computers and Society*, *45*(3), 290–293.

Richardson, K. (2016b). Sex robot matters: Slavery, the prostituted, and the rights of machines. *IEEE Technology and Society Magazine*, *35*(2), 46–53.

Richardson, K. (2016c). Technological animism: The uncanny personhood of humanoid machines. *Social Analysis*, *60*(1), 110–128.

Seebangnow. [xibang]. (2022). Be polite to robots [Online forum post]. Redit. Retrieved from https://www.reddit.com/r/funny/comments/x8bc2w/be_polite_to_robots/

Sone, Y. (2016). Introduction: The Japanese robot and performance. In Y. Sone (Ed.), *Japanese robot culture: Performance, imagination, and modernity* (pp. 1–36). Palgrave Macmillan. https://doi.org/10.1057/978-1-137-52527-7_1

Spencer, W. D. (2011). Digital adultery, "meta-anon widows," real-world divorce, and the need for a virtual sexual ethic. In M. H. Lamers & V F.J. erbeek, (Eds.), *Human-Robot Personal Relationships. HRPR 2010. Lecture Notes of the Institute for Computer Sciences, Social Informatics and Telecommunications Engineering* (vol. 59). Springer, Berlin, Heidelberg. https://doi.org/10.1007/978-3-642-19385-9_13

Suchman, L. (2023). The uncontroversial 'thingness' of AI. *Big Data & Society, 10*(2), 20539517231206794.

Sundar, S. S. (2020). Rise of machine agency: A framework for studying the psychology of human–AI interaction (HAII). *Journal of Computer-Mediated Communication, 25*(1), 74–88.

Swale, A. D. (2015). *Anime aesthetics: Japanese animation and the 'post-cinematic' imagination.* Springer.

Swancutt, K. (2016). The art of capture: Hidden jokes and the reinvention of animistic ontologies in Southwest China. *Social Analysis, 60*(1), 74–91.

Takeuchi, Y. (2005/1960). Asia as method. In R. F. Calichman (Ed. & Trans.) *What is Modernity? writings of Takeuchi Yoshimi* (pp. 149–166). Columbia University Press.

Tang, Y., & Tang, Y. (1991). *Confucianism, Buddhism, Daoism, Christianity and Chinese Culture.* Council for research in values and philosophy.

Thierbach-McLean, O. (2019). A familiar otherness: The trope of Asia in cyberpunk movies since the 1980s. *SPELL: Swiss Papers in English Language & Literature, 38*(2), 105–124.

Tirch, D. D. (2010). Mindfulness as a context for the cultivation of compassion. *International Journal of Cognitive Therapy, 3*(2), 113–123.

Tu, W. M. (1998). The continuity of being: Chinese visions of nature. In Tucker, M. E. & Berthrong, J. (Eds.), *Confucianism and ecology* (pp. 105–121). Harvard University Press.

Turkle, S. (2005). *The second self: Computers and the human spirit.* MIT Press.

Turkle, S. (2011). *Alone together: Why we expect more from technology and less from each other.* Basic Books.

Turkle, S. (2016). *Reclaiming conversation: The power of talk in a digital age.* Penguin.

van der Goot, M. J., & Etzrodt, K. (2023). Disentangling two fundamental paradigms in human-machine communication research: Media equation and media evocation. *Human-Machine Communication, 6*(1), 2.

Welivita, A., & Pu, P. (2024). Is ChatGPT more empathetic than humans? arXiv preprint arXiv:2403.05572.

Wong, P. H. (2012). Dao, harmony and personhood: Towards a Confucian ethics of technology. *Philosophy & Technology, 25*(1), 67–86. https://doi.org/10.1007/s13347-011-0021-z

13

PLAYING WITH AI IN VIDEO GAMES

Lessons About the Human Main Character Syndrome from Non-Player Characters

Do Own (Donna) Kim

Introduction

Opening Vignette: Hogwarts Legacy and the Negligibly Positioned NPCs

"'Your blood is on Ranrok's hands,' I shout, after sneaking up on and murdering 25 goblins in their home," one of the all-time top posts on r/HarryPotterGame, a user-created Reddit community about *Hogwarts Legacy* (*HL*; Avalanche Software, 2023), mused.[1] *HL* is an open-world action role-playing video game that expands on Warner Bro.'s Wizarding World, a fiction franchise inspired by the *Harry Potter* series. In *HL*, the protagonist player character (PC) is tasked to save the magical world from the power-hungry evil goblin Ranrok and his degenerate human confederate Victor Rookwood.

HL's PC is exceptional in many ways. The whole wizarding school knows them because they were belatedly admitted to Hogwarts as a fifth-year student. This was when their magical talents finally manifested, along with their unique ability to see and wield ancient magic, which coincidentally is the key to saving the world. Despite the late start, the PC instantly masters all wizarding magic too, from daily spells like lock-picking "alohomora" and secret-revealing "revelio" to offensive spells like slashing "diffindo" and fire-spreading "incendio," or if the player chooses to learn, even forbidden curses like torturing "crucio" and instant-killing "avada kedavra." Playing as this main character, the player can explore *HL*'s unplotted landscape to

DOI: 10.4324/9781003477587-13

discover its secrets, collect and farm various nonliving and living resources, and help with other characters' problems in the form of "side quests."

While the PC's journey is depicted as honorable, it arguably consists of many self-serving and self-righteous acts that reek of, quite literally, the tendency that has been popularly dubbed the "main character syndrome": the belief that in all situations, you are the center of the story of life and everyone else is secondary (Collins, n.d.). *HL*'s narrative and gameplay dually reinforce the presumed hierarchy between the more important PC and various less important "NPCs," typically abbreviating non-player, non-playing, or non-playable characters (Kim, 2025). Although the players largely still have to comply with this "procedural logic" while playing as the PC (Bogost, 2010), this is not uncritically accepted (Daneels et al., 2021; Jenkins, 2004). Indeed, some of r/HarryPotterGame's top posts are those that pointed out the embedded disparity via jokes and memes, such as the one quoted at this chapter's outset. Other enemy NPCs, "rescuable" beast NPCs, functional NPCs, and background NPCs were also mentioned:

> "We welcome you to the magical world of *HL*!" [a screenshot of "torturing a burning enemy" listed as an achievement]
>
> "Don't resist! I'm trying to "save" you…so I can mate you, farm you, and refine my gears with your parts!" [a screenshot of a puzzled beast NPC being sucked into a charmed bag held open by a human character]
>
> "Brattleby—Loss of Purpose, A Portraiture" [a screenshot of a dejected-looking NPC in his allotted quest space with the caption "When your NPC duty concludes earlier in the game"]
>
> "Picture living as a simple villager in a hamlet near Hogwarts. You're in your bed sleeping. It's night. Suddenly, you wake up to a shushed 'alohomora.' Your lock begins rattling. The door swings ajar. Footsteps across the floor. Then you hear some teen go, 'Mine now, Demiguise [item]!'"

In short, "NPC" may as well stand for "negligibly positioned character" in *HL*. As illustrated above, *HL*'s NPCs typically appear as disposable, nonselfsustaining, servicing, and exploitable. With their forced silence, they are generally unable to meaningfully protest. They must stay content with their role and the PC's interventions. The other fate is to get removed, via narrative disappearance or (unremarkable) death. *HL* effectively revolves around the exceptional PC's legacy, and many NPCs exist as utilitarian embellishments.

Chapter Overview

This hierarchy is not peculiar to *HL*, although how "the PC slaughters more individuals throughout *HL* than in Voldemort's [*Harry Potter*'s villain] entire career" (r/HarryPotterGame) may be shocking to those less familiar with video games. This procedural logic is such a widespread convention, especially in combination with the human-nonhuman binary, that it has even led to parody games. For instance, the assumed superiority of the human PC is the core narrative tension and gameplay obstacle in Toby Fox's *Undertale* (2015) (see Elvery, 2023).

This embedded negligible positioning of NPCs is what this chapter examines to rethink the social integration and cultural implications of communicative AIs. It focuses on what we can learn from NPCs about mundane human-machine communication (HMC) and the pitfalls of the Human main character syndrome. *First,* I discuss why video games and NPCs are not only appropriate but powerful sites to explore this topic, with a critical posthumanist interest in AI storytelling. *Second,* I review selected critical works that investigated NPCs' positioning, identified from my scoping review study of "emergent narratives" (Jenkins, 2004) of NPCs (Kim, 2025). I discuss how their insights can contribute to re-narrating AI. *Third,* I provide an alternative story figure from Korean folklore to more interrelationally "think with" (Haraway, 2016): *dokkaebi.* Ultimately, I question whether we can change our AI storytelling from one that perpetuates Human-centrism to that of our becoming-with.

AI Narratives and the Human

Why Video Game NPCs?

Not everyone cares about NPCs' fates, let alone plays video games. This may even seem too "fluffy" for the "serious" matter of AI and the future. Therefore, we must first establish two things: *first,* that video games have been rich, if not key, historical sites of AI, and *second,* that they *are* culturally relevant and significant.

Video games have historically been important to HMC with AI. Vibrant HMC in everyday life might seem like a new or even futuristic phenomenon characterized by recent technical artifacts, such as generative AI interfaces (e.g., ChatGPT, Midjourney), internet of things virtual assistants (e.g., Siri, Alexa), and other service or companion technologies (e.g., iRobot, Replika). However, humans have long been mundanely, playfully, and intimately engaging with artificial social actors in video games, often configured as NPCs, since their emergence in the 1940s (1962 if tracing from *Spacewar!,* the first video game built for entertainment) (Donovan, 2010; see also Gunkel, 2018). First off, NPCs in essence are AIs: they are programmed to appear as "intelligent" subjects to be interacted with by humans, although the degree of sophistication can vary per game context

(Coanda & Aupers, 2021; Poor, 2023). Video games remind us that humans have already been playing with AI for almost 100 years.

Equally important is that AI itself has been "studied, tested, and imagined through…gaming" since the inception of computer science (Bory, 2019, p. 627). Indeed, a lesser discussed game-related history of the "Turing Test" (past its original proposition as "the imitation game") is that Turing wrote the first computer Chess program in 1947 and tested it in 1952 by pretending to be the computer while playing against a colleague, although not yet implemented into an actual computer (Donovan, 2010). That is, before and beyond the hallmark case of Weizenbaum's chatbot ELIZA, AI has been envisioned, experimented, and shaped through—and *as*—(video) games (Bory, 2019; Shaikh, 2023). It should be noted that this process has also involved noncomputer experts. When British computer company Ferranti exhibited the "nim" game-playing Nimrod at the 1951 Festival of Britain and Berlin Industrial Show to boast computers' mathematical abilities, people were impressed. However, this was not necessarily due to their interest in Nimrod's "electronic brain" despite Ferranti's painstaking narrative emphasis on scientific advancement, not fun. The audiences "just wanted to play" or were captivated by Nimrod's daunting machine body, which a reporter likened to "a tremendous grey refrigerator" (Donovan, 2010, pp. 5–6).

If we follow HMC's urge to shift focus from whether machines can talk to how they communicate "with" humans, that is, their participation in human meaning-making processes (Guzman, 2018; Guzman et al., 2023), it becomes even clearer that NPCs have been, and should be approached as, serious parts of AI storytelling (see Coanda & Aupers, 2021; Poor, 2023). However, preconceptions about video games have hindered serious appraisals. Video game cultures tend to be considered as "other" in both popular culture and academe, but they are shaped by and shape societal cultures (Shaw, 2024). They are neither separate universes that are detached from the rules in our social realities (cf., formalist "magic circle" approach) nor confined to a specific demographic, often pictured as younger, able-bodied, cis-heterosexual men (and depending on the locational context, also White, English-speaking, and at least middle class) (Consalvo, 2009; Gray, 2020; Gunkel, 2018; Shaw, 2024). Therefore, their designs, gameplays, and surrounding discourses continuously interact and negotiate with existing social norms and cultural values, such as those reflecting neoliberal market logic and dominant identity politics (e.g., Cote, 2020; Kim, 2023; Gray, 2020; Kosciesza, 2023; Paul, 2020; Shaw, 2015). They (re-)tell narratives on how humans (should) live.

NPCs can powerfully (re-)narrate AIs' relationship to human cultures because they thrive in the popular and the everyday. I follow the seminal cultural studies scholar Stuart Hall's (2016) argument that culture is "experience lived, experience interpreted, experience defined" (p. 33) and thus we must approach it as "the continuous struggle between contesting cultures" (p. 41). Seemingly just-for-fun, mundane interactions with NPCs are parts of lived human experiences through which we—not just technical experts but diverse communities in "the popular"—continuously (re-) interpret and (re-)define meanings about AI and human life. The video game-inspired term main character syndrome's popularity substantiates the spreadability of meaning-making with NPCs and related cultural practices.

Other pushback may regard video games' domain specificity and NPCs' relatively limited capacities. Of course, contexts of gameplay are important. Nonetheless, NPCs are not too distanced from seemingly more broadly applicable, sophisticated forms of AI. Critical AI scholars have shown that the current discussions of machine learning-based AI as highly adaptive, independent "Artificial General Intelligence (AGI)" are myths: contemporary AI systems are arguably all still highly context-dependent and human-involved and thus are rather "Artificial Narrow Intelligence (ANI)," especially when traced from their "ground truthing" (decision-makings on the baseline "truth" for machine learning) process (Kang, 2023). Moreover, the boundaries between "strong AI narratives" like AGI and domain- and capacity-specific "weak AI narratives" are not rigid and fixed (Bory et al., 2025). Even if we were to approach NPCs as "weak," we must be vigilant about how these AI narratives too "can have very powerful implications and consequences" (p. 8), including regarding regulatory, commercial, and use decisions. Technological narratives' power rests not in their accuracy but in their ability to captivate and influence societies by circulating tropes on the technology's function, impact, and promise (Natale & Ballatore, 2020). Simply put, beyond their historical technical relevance, NPCs matter to AI trajectories because storytelling is a social imaginative process.

What about Video Game NPCs?

This chapter focuses on how NPC experiences are shaped by, and help shape, Human-centrism. Here, "Human" denotes not the entire human species but the limited imagery of privileged humans that have dominated our knowledge production practices. This focus draws on my cultural studies-informed reading of scholarship on nonhumans (e.g., Braidotti, Haraway, and Latour), which I will characterize as a—or my—"critical posthumanist" approach (see Braidotti, 2013).

Cultural and critical studies' sensitivity to human power structures may seem to clash with the Latourian Actor-Network Theory (ANT), which rejects the myth of "the social" as constructed only of (rigid relationships among) human actors, or posthumanism's interrelationality-based, beyond-human thinking.[2] However, I argue that the connection is not conflicting, or if so, is generative.

First, cultural studies does not assume a uniform, fixed *the* culture. Rather, it aims to describe the ongoing negotiations between *cultures*, and by doing so, partakes in rearticulating existing relationships (Hall, 2016). This aligns with Latour's (2005) argument for descriptions founded on heterogeneity and relativism, and his assertion that ANT is political because it studies "the progressive composition of one common world" through the question of "can we live together?" (p. 254) Accounting for other-than-human Others in ANT is an excellent "travel guide" (p. 17) that matches cultural studies' ongoing itinerary: Hall's (1993) interest in audiences' diverse readings of encoded meanings in media—and later developments like "produsage" that detailed the process's fluid multi-directionality (see Lind, 2020)—is not unlike Latour's interest in the prescriptions of, and reactions to, "program of actions" in things and systems (Akrich & Latour, 1994).

Second, scholarship on power has indeed relied on anthropomorphic metaphors (e.g., "treating humans like (or "reducing" them into) objects" [p. 255]) (Latour, 2005), but I argue that de-anthropocentric efforts must be keenly aware of our human positionality and the continuing injustices toward less-than-human humans. As Haraway (2016) argued, humans are not the most important actors, and all actors in the "Chutulucene" (i.e., an ongoing world of multispecies storytelling and practices of "becoming-with"—not "being," which implies a given, disconnected state) are at stake of each other. However, precisely because we are interconnected, "the doings of situated, actual human beings matter" (p. 55): we must forgo human exceptionalism, but our thinking and doing come from our situations as humans. In my reading, this highlights two things: one, that our capacities can be actualized by interrelationally rearticulating humans rather than rejecting the ways we associate with the world as humans; two, the lived positionality of humans itself is not uniform and therefore we cannot rearticulate without interrogating the unjust structures that segregate humans. This means accepting that our versions of becoming-with will continue to somewhat disproportionately involve humans' perspectives. This is how we relate to the world, and how we can relate better. Important to this acceptance is reflexively recognizing that the category "human" has frequently universalized diverse human situations as the privileged "the (Hu)Man" and continuing to deconstruct *and* rearticulate the inhuman(e) power relations (Braidotti, 2013). Our acceptance must be rooted in interrelations, not Human exceptionalism.

Put differently, my approach to NPCs is akin to what Gunkel (2018) depicted as a multi-actor assemblages-based, "hybrid" approach to the problem of machines' morality (pp. 151–153), however fueled by the questions of power and accountability from the cultural position(s) of humans. With this critical posthumanist lens, the next section discusses the Human main character syndrome in NPC practices. This can be approached as what cultural studies scholar Raymond Williams called a "structure of feeling" around our articulation in/to the world: "the description, even re-creation of how life is actually lived, of what it is like to think and act about a particular problem in a society" (Hall, 2016, p. 37). To help imagine alternative articulations in AI storytelling, I conclude by connecting the lessons from NPCs with dokkaebi, following Haraway's (2016) recommendation to think with speculative stories.

Negligibly Positioned NPCs and the Human Main Character Syndrome

Imperial Play and Network Aesthetics of NPCs

Conventional NPC design, gameplay, and surrounding discourses have taken unequal power relations for granted and contributed to naturalizing them. *First,* I discuss van der Merwe's (2021) "imperial play" and Anikina's (2020) "network aesthetics"-based approach to explain the common NPC patterns and their relation to historical structures and popular practices. *Then,* I build on this through selected critical works on NPCs, focusing on critical posthumanist insights on AI storytelling. My scoping review study of emergent narratives on NPCs (Kim, 2025) laid the groundwork for this section. The readers should note that thus my discussion centers on works that fit the review's inclusion criteria (e.g., books excluded) and are encouraged to expand on the inspiration by consulting the larger bodies of works. For instance, Gunkel's book *Gaming the System* (2018) provided compelling philosophical deconstructions of video game-related systems, such as regarding their colonial "frontier" approach to virtual worlds and the ethics of NPC sociality that the authors in this section also critique.

Van der Merwe (2021) proposed "imperial play" as a framework for studying the overt and hidden dynamics of colonialism in game design and practices, drawing on postcolonial theory and Laura Mulvey's concept of the male gaze. Similarly to how Mulvey analyzed gendered gazes in films, van der Merwe analyzed the embedded and enacted player-centric gazes to study the perpetuation of colonialist logic in mainstream video games. Imperial "play" captures how this occurs not just on a developer-led, representational level but on an interactive level that involves dominant player practices. Typical elements are:

- *The mission.* The PC is depicted as a benevolent, exceptional outsider invited to "enter the world and *act upon it* [sic]" (p. 44) to solve local problems. This fundamentally colonialist "savior" positioning justifies their at-will intrusions and extractions.
- *The (PC) avatar.* The player's relationship with their avatar is ultimately rooted in a relationship of control.[3] Structurally, the PC avatar serves as both an image to be looked at and a "colonized vehicle" to safely carry out the in-game gazes and actions for the "player-master's...curiosity, personal edification, and/or pleasure" (p. 45), including uncritical, "touristic" simulations of Otherness (Nakamura, 1995; see also Eklund & Zanescu, 2024).
- *The gamescape.* The player's relationship to the gamescape is grounded in exploration and empire-building, inclusive of the emblematic colonialist act of map-making in "the frontier" (Gunkel, 2018). Via the map or otherwise, the player-pioneer is uniquely given a god-like view and control of the world that even surpasses the PC's vantage point. The PC engages in resource gathering and trading, often exploitatively, without considering the impact on its scarcity and the locals' livelihoods. A right to violence may be presumed: killing plentiful enemies gets rewarded with new exploratory possibilities and assets.
- *NPCs.* NPCs are Othered, silenced, and powerless subalterns, dually subjected to global and local systems of exploitation and oppression. Worthy NPCs remain silent and helpless. They transform into resources by being saved and/or must accept the player-savior's so-called resource gathering or stealing (Mukherjee, 2018). Unworthy NPCs embellish the PC's journey as (replenishing) enemies to be killed (for resources) or as background props, marked as undeserving via exotification, vilification, sexualization, racialization, and/or other Othering portrayals.

This chapter focuses on NPCs, but all components of imperial play work together in the procedural rhetoric of the Human main character syndrome. For instance, the opening vignette sketched the fates of various NPCs in *HL*: enemy NPCs get killed and tortured; beast NPCs get abducted and displaced without consent; functional NPCs get abandoned and forgotten after their service; villager NPCs get robbed, even if they try to prevent it with level three (!) locks. All of this is depicted as acceptable if not natural because the exceptional PC has been invited into the *HL* world as the only person who can fulfill the all-important *mission* of saving it from itself. To do so, they must thoroughly explore the *gamescape* and map it, not just where (only) the PC can (freely) go but also what (only) they can (freely) take, trade, and kill. The player-savior-pioneer is embodied through *the PC avatar*, but they are absolved of any direct risks, pains, and responsibilities because they are not the PC—they are the player-master that controls the PC. They will not personally get hurt or die while massacring the goblins, need to never sleep to save the beasts, or face any (barely existing) negative social outcomes of exploiting non-enemy human NPCs. Of course, the PC is already comparatively exceptional: they regenerate, have unique skills and tools, and are socially recognized as special. Still, the player is the greatest: not only are they all-seeing and all-deciding (even the PC looks!), but the world itself can be rewound (save and load), reset (restart), or made gone (switch off, delete) by them. The hierarchy thrives on this taken-for-granted form and degree of power and agency, and vice versa. Under the colonialist logic, the "higher" being can of course act upon the "lesser" Others.

Through "network aesthetics," Anikina (2020) traced how this rhetoric travels from and "spills into the economic, cultural, and social fabric of the player's life" (p. 90). Drawing on McKenzie Wark's "gamespace" that sees in-game and "real-life" experiences as interconnected and Karen Barad's posthumanist performativity theory, "agential realism," Anikina located NPCs' power in the networked interrelations: NPCs have reproduced the hierarchical construction of humanness and agency across many areas in life, but they can also help reimagine it.

"Chinese gold-farmers" and the NPC meme exemplify how NPC experiences not only mirror the existing relations but also contribute to extending and refreshing them. The former colloquialism refers to low-paid, mass-hired human laborers in multiplayer online games that "farm" in-game resources through time-consuming, laborious repetitive in-game actions or "grinding" to sell for real-life currency. Their grinding-intensive behaviors (at times compounded by their uniform looks) make them appear as and effectively serve as dehumanized, functionalist under-class bodies, much like the NPCs (Nakamura, 2009). In player communities, they are often negatively equated with illicit automation programs or "bots" that threaten "real human" gameplay. Treatments of gold-farmers, including language-based false accusations, tend to be conflated with ethnicism and racism against China and are reminiscent of histories of slavery and minority labor exploitation: "Being labeled a 'Chinese farmer' means you are fair game for systematic harassment and slaughter" (Yee, 2014, p. 85). This example illustrates the extension of capitalistic exploitation and social discrimination in *and* through the negligible positioning of certain game actors. Simply put, Othered NPCs suggest the presence of Othering structures.

The latter example adds to this by showing how such structures and practices can traverse beyond the direct vicinity of games. "NPC meme" refers to the alt-right internet cultures' appropriation of NPC to memetically deride supposedly unthinking and non-agentic liberal masses (see Gallagher & Topinka, 2023). This political co-optation is facilitated by the common agreement on the "nature" of NPCs sustained by gaming conventions, which themselves interact with existing cultural understandings. What cuts across the cases is that those mismatching "our" characteristics are lesser, and thus can be treated accordingly. As Gallagher and Topinka (2023) emphasized, the NPC meme is not a mere instance of gamer verbiage bleeding into political discourse, but rather "also points to deeper parallels between values, tactics and systems of sense-making prevalent in gaming culture and those of networked right-wing subcultures" (p. 14). That is, NPC experiences have not simply supplied but *reproduced* the stratified notion of humanness, within and outside of video games: "Being human within a network is not a given quality, but something that needs to be assigned" (Anikina, 2020, p. 93).

Nevertheless, the implied dynamism also suggests that this is not our fixed destiny. Analyzing multiple cases of subversive indie games and interactive art, Anikina argued, "The narrative appeal of the NPCs in such works and in larger networks is built on a nuanced act of renegotiation of their agency and ours as human players, viewers and participants" (p. 99). If NPCs can powerfully articulate the Human main character syndrome as the natural matter of fact, it can also powerfully rearticulate our copresence as a becoming. The stories we circulate are important parts of this negotiation process.

Re-narrating AI with Lessons from NPCs

This section engages with the question of how to become with AI through additional critical works on NPCs. I focus on three lessons: *first,* HMC can reproduce the Human main character syndrome in and beyond the given context; *second,* underlying this is that humans can meaningfully and creatively interact with artificial actors, although not as humans per se; *third,* the hierarchical focus on (privileged) humans can be reimagined.

First, NPCs warn against the naturalization of Human-centrism in uncritical AI practices. Imperial play reproduces what du Plessis (2018) explained as "utilitarian subject-object relations," the perception that the external world is separate from the subject (often the Human), and that the nonsubject rest can be approached in terms of utility. Similarly to the above, du Plessis argued that NPCs (and in competitive multiplayer games, other PCs) tend to be configured as resources or obstacles. NPC typologies detail the utilitarian design patterns: their lives commonly get flattened into their roles of providing items, services, quests, challenges, aids, and stories (Bartle, 2003; Warpefelt & Verhagen, 2015).

The interconnections between NPCs and other imperial play components suggest that such utilitarian subject-object relations do not simply exist on the representational level but also on the interactive design level. S. Y. Kim's (2022) analysis of *The Last of Us* (Naughty Dog, 2013) delineated how both Othering NPC portrayals and the shifting playability between the PCs Joel and Ellie affirm the relations. Prominent enemy NPC David is one-dimensionally evil. Less prominent enemies further lack dimensionality as unnamed hordes and are clearly marked as not-"Us": they are other-than-human zombies, or if humans, appear in darker skin tones regardless of their race. The PC's encounter with a "U LOOT I SHOOT!!!" sign is interpreted as what further legitimated the indiscriminate killing by reducing the enemies from victims of state violence to petty looters, which resonates with similar political rhetoric circulated during the Black Lives Matter movement (pp. 354–365). Temporarily granted and suspended control of the PCs sustains this moral justification and by extension the player's moral superiority. Ellie's claim of agency is affirmed via her willingness to kill for survival and is eventually granted (play)ability to do so. In the final scenes, the switch from Joel to Ellie partially absolves the player's responsibility: while it is the player who slaughters the human enemy NPCs as Joel, they become Ellie in the epilogue and computer-controlled Joel lies to them about the situation. This is not too distant from the *HL* PC's automated verbal reminders that the murdered goblin Others' "blood is on Ranrok's hands," not yours.

Network aesthetics reminds us that these relations do not unidirectionally "bleed from" specific AI contexts (e.g., games) but perpetuate through various practices surrounding and external to them. Kosciesza (2023) conceptualized the moral service role of transgender NPCs as "magical transness," focusing on how their victimization is utilized to instigate cisgender protagonists' heroism. Notably, Kosciesza examined how this trope limits "imaginative possibilities" (Shaw, 2014) not just by studying three video game cases but also by analyzing the media surrounding them. Diversity was generally upheld as an abstract ideal in production-level discourses but the repeated preemptive defensiveness against pandering showed that transgender characters' existence must still morally service the cis-normativity of video game cultures. That is, magical transness was not simply articulated via transgender NPCs' within-game positioning, but discursively via their utility to the Human subjects in video game cultures. Ruffino (2022) examined the traversal of utilitarian subject-object relations by studying player-created paratexts of *Red Dead Redemption 2*

(Rockstar Games, 2018), such as those that hypothesized that NPC Downes had infected the PC with an incurable disease and that distancing from Downes, including by killing him, would prevent the PC's destined death. In conversation with Anikina's work, Ruffino analyzed these as attempts to restore the mythical given agency of the Human over the environment that is "centered on the individuality of the player" and the "implied (and colonialist) notions of [White, male] able-bodied normativity and control" (p. 354). Ruffino's identification of matching drive and assumptions in the concurrently circulated COVID-19 prevention discourses similarly showed that NPC practices are not located in disparate realities but rather in interconnection with societal cultures. Then, perhaps what r/HarryPotterGame's memes on imperial play suggest is a structure of feeling against the dominant culture of utilitarian subject-object relations and a corresponding emergent culture.

This possible emergence leads us to the second lesson from NPCs: AI's impact on human cultures is not a predetermined tale but what is continuously being retold through meaningful interactions with social—but not exactly human—artificial actors. NPC practices are meaningful not just because they are relevant to the larger cultural negotiations but because interactions with NPCs are "real" (see Gunkel, 2018) and can be significant to the players. Afforded by, but at times beyond the intended limits of, the embedded design, players can imagine and treat NPCs as social subjects with "independent lives" (Ogier, 2020). Rose's (2023) digital ethnographic study of *Animal Crossing: New Horizons* (Nintendo, 2020) described the dual presence of NPCs-as-objects and NPCs-as-co-situated-subjects approaches. On one hand, the cute villager NPCs were simply treated as characters to be collected or aesthetically appraised. On the other hand, individual and collective "imaginative play" elevated the NPCs' social potential into deep connections rooted in reciprocal care and respect for NPCs' independent lives ("as if they are alive" [p. 304]).

While imaginative play can be personally enriching and even culturally subversive, it should not be forgotten that it can still extend existing experiences and patterns. Burgess and Jones' (2020) and Liu and Lai's (2022) case studies discussed the players' romantic attachments to NPCs, cultivated through imaginative engagements that surpass the embedded narratives. However, the former observed that *Mass Effect 2* (BioWare, 2010) player forums tended to be written from the player's perspective when discussing its female romanceable NPC and from the PC's perspective when discussing its male romanceable NPC, which suggested that their imaginative play was gendered. The latter explained that while Chinese women players' engagements with *Evol LoveR*'s (Papergames, 2017) male NPCs resisted Chinese ideals of masculinity, they still replicated the existing heteronormative relationship structure. Moreover, despite opening a space against the male-dominated toxic mainstream game culture, *Evol LoveR*'s comparatively aggressive in-game monetization model and merchandise markets rather suggested a dominant, capitalistic extension of the industry's gender-based consumer separation (see also Paul, 2020).

HMC with AI complicates the Human main character syndrome because these meaningful social interactions are not with humans per se. That is, what humans and social actors comparable to humans are supposed to be like is played with during the process. Coanda and Aupers (2021) studied the qualities of humanness in NPCs and player-NPC relationships' impact on the players' "real-life" relationships. Representationally, round depictions of moral, emotional, and dispositional dimensions were associated with humanness. Interactively, the seeming presence of non-player-centric life and agentic capacities was important. The authors also found that intimate player-NPC relationships were not confined to games but impacted their offline relationships, whether complementarily or disruptively. These findings are harmonious with the critical insights from imperial play and network aesthetics: "not Human" perceptions of NPCs are sustained through representational, interactive experiences that stress their utilitarian object-ness, often intermixed with historical conventions that are used to mark the Others, and NPC experiences do impact other areas of life. The critique here regards not that NPCs are not being articulated as the species humans (which actually is undesirable as it glosses over their sociotechnical characteristics), but that they have evoked and reproduced the seemingly natural conditions of being Human and the structures of injustice that buttress them. The second lesson encourages detailed empirical research on human-machine interactions to understand our ongoing meaning-making, however accompanied by a critical interest in how they are (re-)articulating the Human. NPCs remind us that this does not happen in some grand, abstracted sense but through meaningfully "real" everyday interactions with AI.

Third, therefore, NPCs also reassure us that our AI story could become that of becoming with, including through mundane, playful reimaginations. Similar to Anikina's inclusion of subversive examples, I close this section with studies on subversive cases as an interventional effort to strengthen the articulation of alternative imaginative possibilities.

Elvery's (2023) analysis of *Undertale* effectively established both that (para-)social interactions with NPCs are possible and that they can encourage critical literacy on the taken-for-granted Human-centrism. *Undertale* plays with the hierarchical dismissals of NPCs by twisting the conventions of imperial play, the naturalness of which the players are prompted to question and overcome as they progress. For instance, the players need to reimagine their typical strategies as they gradually realize that "EXP" and "LV" they gained from killing the enemies stand not for "experience points" and "level" in *Undertale*, but rather "execution points" and "level of violence." The player-PC's intrusion is not unnoticed by the monster NPCs, whose community's problem, to begin with, started from humans'—which the player can exacerbate via their—biases against the nonhuman monsters. Some of the NPCs are even "meta-aware" of the player behind the PC, and at an important narrative junction the player loses their typically expected extradiegetic access to the game system: an NPC "breaks" the game if the player attempts to beat them by saving and reloading. This provocation is not linear and requires the players' endorsement, especially because it is still somewhat possible to follow the imperial play conventions. Therefore, Elvery's reading helps activate the imaginative potentials of *Undertale*, bringing attention to "the parallels between our relationships with people and our relationship to technology." As Elvery advised, "we must avoid acting without thinking, and always interrogate systems that are naturalised" (p. 494).

Reimagining Human-centrism requires this critical sensibility to be extended beyond the human point of view. Du Plessis' (2018) analysis of *Journey* (Thatgamecompany, 2012) offered becoming-other as an alternative model. Drawing on Deleuzoguattarian philosophy, du Plessis explained that *Journey* subverted the utilitarian subject-object relations by non-remarkably embedding the PC: they are perceptually "small" as a "humanoid, but...definitely not recognisably human" (p. 473) figure among similarly nondescript multispecies characters in the vast sublime gamescape; they must join the inter-dependent affective movements to maneuver and play, such as by working in concert with the rhythm of the environment and the flow of other creatures (both NPCs and other PCs) on their respective journeys; they communicate not in human speech but only in "song talk" (p. 476). In *Journey*, actors are not each other's utilitarian objects, but rather collaborators in flux that increase each other's capacities: they are dynamic becomings.

The vitality of nonorganic, inanimate actors should also be embraced. Ruberg's (2022) analysis of *San Andreas Deer Cam* (Watanabe, 2015), a parodic "unplayable" game that modified *Grand Theft Auto V* (Rockstar Games, 2013), connected "beyond the human" and "beyond play" imaginative possibilities (see also Anikina, 2020). Here, the protagonist and the camera focus are a computer-controlled deer that passingly appeared in the original game as a background prop. Ruberg discussed various ways this transformation rearticulates the Human: the player-audience is no longer the driving force; the nonhuman computer-deer studies the human world, not unlike how humans observe "the wildlife"; and the computer-deer's navigation is not self-guided but undetermined, changing as per its randomized directionality and chance encounters with the world elements. Moreover, it is the computer-deer's nonhumanness—whether its state or negligibility—that granted its exceptional immunity and freedom in this rearticulated world: the original codes did not give it human character-like interactivity. I also read in Ruberg's analysis an urge to recognize the vitality of nonorganic, nonmoving objects. Ruberg interpreted the computer-deer's eventual freezing during a glitchy loop of human NPCs' homophobic violence as "radical objectness," describing it as a form of "pacifist resistance," especially for those who do "not have the luxury of abandoning the material present" (p. 426). As Latour emphasized, overlooking or denouncing thingness as inferior is another manifestation of the Human main character syndrome. Then, what we need in our stories may be figures that can upset our Human-centrism not just via the organic world but also via thingness.

Conclusion: Making with Dokkaebi Oddkins

The Korean folklore figure of dokkaebi concludes this chapter. According to Haraway (2016), storytelling is a means to stay with the trouble: a way to make our entanglements thinkable and to "make with oddkin" (i.e., how we "require each other in unexpected collaborations and combinations") (pp. 4–5). Pointing out the limits of Human-centrism and existing approaches, Haraway argued, "It is time to turn to sympoietic wordings… where ordinary stories, ordinary becoming 'involved in each other's lives,' [sic] propose ways to stay with the trouble in order to nurture well-being on a damaged planet….the tales of the ongoing" (p. 76). I propose dokkaebi as such a tale: as an imaginative alternative to think with. First, I invite the readers to immerse themselves in the dokkaebi folklore and to reimagine the stories of humans, NPCs, and AI through it. Then, I close this chapter by sharing my inspirations from dokkaebi.

Dokkaebi

In Korean folklore, "dokkaebi" is depicted as mundane but fantastic creatures with mythical powers that playfully, favorably, and at times formidably interact with humans and live among us (Encyclopedia of Korean Culture, n.d.; Lee & Lee, 2013; Yi, 2019). Dokkaebi is an extremely well-known indigenous figure and continues to appear in popular imaginations. Recently, it inspired the transnationally successful K-drama *Dokkaebi* (2016; also called *Goblin: The Lonely and Great God* or *Guardian*), a heart-wrenching fantasy romance that helped introduce dokkaebi to the globe. Dokkaebi is characterized by their indeterminateness, multiplicity, and relationality, both regarding their sociality and form (Lee & Lee, 2013; Yi, 2019). Japanese colonialism has muddled their origin and resulted in faulty equations with the Japanese "oni," the scary, evil humanoid goblins that tend to be depicted with horns, spiky teeth, large hairy bodies, primitive loincloths, and heavy swingable weapons (Bak, 2014; Yi, 2019). However, native dokkaebis are not fixed or negative. They change their form and position as per the flow and shifts of the narrative, time, and purpose. It is this dokkaebi that I wish to evoke.

Dokkaebi is neither good nor bad, and their subjectivity is not completely comprehensible by humans. They may be depicted as playful, innocent, and eager to the point where they may initially come across as naïve and thus may be tricked and exploited to supply their abilities for gains beyond human capacities. Despite this impression, they are ultimately understood as nonhuman entities that are in between god, human, and monster, and therefore are indeterminable and frightening regardless of their affinity with humans (Bak, 2014). Their interests in humans reflect their own desires and agenda, rather than their inferiority. Accordingly, selfish and irresponsible human intentions often lead to ill consequences and magical catastrophes, whereas those prioritizing mutual prosperity and community care achieve continued happy coexistence with the capricious dokkaebis and/or their lasting impact. That is, dokkaebis neither exist for nor against humans, but *with* humans as parts of the symbiotic entanglement.

Dokkaebi's unfixed form shows the relational, plural folk thinking. Dokkaebi exists through people's imaginaries, and therefore their form flexibly shifts based on the respective cultural values and environments (Yi, 2019). In folktales, dokkaebis frequently appear as various kinds of humans or humanlike beings, not just simply in terms of looks but also in terms of personalities, preferences, and social relationships, from friendly competition and alliance to romantic or sexual partnership. This reflects their capacities for meaningful interactivity, which can even mesmerize or hoodwink (*holida*) humans. Nonetheless, they are approached as entities that play with human-centric notions of sociality and relations rather than what aspire to facsimile them. Nonhuman forms are equally common: mutability and hybridity are their key characteristics (Lee & Lee, 2013; Yi, 2019). They may be familiar tools and objects, such as bowls, farming equipment, furniture, and shoes, that have transformed into agentic magical beings through age or contact with humans. They may also appear as floating flames or immaterial spirits, fundamentally formless yet able to merge with or transfigure into humans, animals, plants, and things. Simply put, dokkaebi's forms arise from their imagined social relations but without presuming human culture's superiority or singularity.

Thinking Otherwise with Dokkaebi

Thinking with dokkaebi helps me "think otherwise" about HMC, as an inconclusive alternative to the binaries I have been acculturated into, such as human-machine, new-old, us-them, good-bad, and living-thing. As creatures of entangled becomings, dokkaebi facilitates thinking with "making oddkin": through a mode of curiosity and openness rooted in our inter-relationality and interdependence. It is a metaphorical (Haraway, 2016) means of "deconstruction," which, according to Gunkel (2018), "takes aim at the conceptual formations that are already in play not to choose sides...but to challenge their controlling influence and to devise alternative ways for thinking and proceeding otherwise" (p. 157). Dokkaebi helps me question the complex cultural relations articulated by NPCs, rather than taking their Othering positioning and perceptual confinement to video games for granted. Similarly, with AI, it helps me productively divert the questions around "real," or any other fixed notions that draw on binary thinking, to the various ways mutual relationships can form and how humans have continuously taken part in (and must take responsibility for) shaping the said relationships. It has been a practical yet accountable way to think with: deciphering or perfecting machine subjectivity matters less than the fact that how we communicate with AI exists in the context of our dynamic, mutable, and multiple interconnectedness and that altruistic sense of shared responsibility may be the key to our happy coexistence.

In this chapter, I discussed what we can learn about connective AI from the negligibly positioned NPCs. Video games are important to AI storytelling not only because they have been historically entangled with AI but also because they have been powerfully articulating human politics. Three lessons from NPCs are as follows: (1) we must resist the naturalization of the Human main character syndrome in AI practices; (2) we continue to question and affirm our assumptions on humanness through "real," meaningful interactions with artificial actors, including in the mundane and the popular; and (3) therefore, we can re-narrate our entanglement with AI through everyday, playful reimaginations. Dokkaebi was suggested as a story to think with. Granted, dokkaebi is still a tale told by humans. However, it foregrounds interrelations and does so in a manner approachable to humans. There can be no taken-for-granted center-of-the-world Human when dokkaebis' nonhuman life-worlds and constant shapeshifting upset the very ideas of exclusivity and exceptionalism. Playing with dokkaebi means becoming with responsibility and care, not for the Human but for our entanglement. According to dokkaebi, AI is connective *and* connected.

Notes

1 r/HarryPotterGame is publicly accessible. Cited posts (last accessed November 15, 2024) are humorous content and pose no perceivable risk to the user. However, not everyone expects to be personally identifiable when posting online. Therefore, I omitted the usernames and paraphrased the quotes (see Proferes et al., 2021).

2 Posthumanism here should not be mistaken for techno-utopian adoptions of the term that argues for technological improvement of the human condition, which "transhumanism" more accurately describes (see Birhane et al., 2024; Braidotti, 2013).

3 However, marginalized identity practices through virtual embodiment and complex player-PC relationships should not be simplistically amalgamated (see Banks & Bowman, 2016; Gazzard, 2010; Jenson et al., 2015)

References

Akrich, M., & Latour, B. (1994). A summary of a convenient vocabulary for the semiotics of human and nonhuman assemblies. In W. Bijker & J. Law (Eds.), *Shaping technology/building society: Studies in sociotechnical change* (pp. 259–264). MIT Press.

Anikina, A. (2020). What moves non-player characters: Network aesthetics in the gamespace. *Parallax*, 26(1), 89–102. https://doi.org/10.1080/13534645.2019.1685785

Bak, M. (2014). The folktale "Hokpuri Yongkam" and the visual representation of the Korean Dokkaebi. *Proceedings of the 9th Conference of the International Committee for Design History and Design Studies*, 5(1), 231–236. https://doi.org/10.5151/despro-icdhs2014-0028

Banks, J., & Bowman, N. D. (2016). Avatars are (sometimes) people too: Linguistic indicators of parasocial and social ties in player–avatar relationships. *New Media & Society*, 18(7), 1257–1276. https://doi.org/10.1177/1461444814554898

Bartle, R. (2003). *Designing virtual worlds* (1st ed.). New Riders Games.

Birhane, A., Dijk, J. van, & Pasquale, F. (2024). Debunking robot rights metaphysically, ethically, and legally. *First Monday*, 29(4). https://doi.org/10.5210/fm.v29i4.13628

Bogost, I. (2010). *Persuasive games: The expressive power of videogames*. MIT Press.

Bory, P. (2019). Deep new: The shifting narratives of artificial intelligence from Deep Blue to AlphaGo. *Convergence*, 25(4), 627–642. https://doi.org/10.1177/1354856519829679

Bory, P., Natale, S., & Katzenbach, C. (2025). Strong and weak AI narratives: An analytical framework. *AI & Society*, 40, 2107–2117. https://doi.org/10.1007/s00146-024-02087-8

Braidotti, R. (2013). *The posthuman*. Polity Press.

Burgess, J., & Jones, C. (2020). "I harbour strong feelings for Tali despite her being a fictional character": Investigating videogame players' emotional attachments to non-player characters. *Game Studies, 20*(1). https://gamestudies.org/2001/articles/burgessjones

Coanda, I., & Aupers, S. (2021). Post-human encounters: Humanising the technological other in videogames. *New Media & Society, 23*(5), 1236–1256. https://doi.org/10.1177/1461444820912388

Collins, S. (n.d.). *Main Character Syndrome.* WebMD. Retrieved November 15, 2024, from https://www.webmd.com/mental-health/main-character-syndrome

Consalvo, M. (2009). There is no magic circle. *Games and Culture, 4*(4), 408–417. https://doi.org/10.1177/1555412009343575

Cote, A. C. (2020). Casual resistance: A longitudinal case study of video gaming's gendered construction and related audience perceptions. *Journal of Communication, 70*(6), 819–841. https://doi.org/10.1093/joc/jqaa028

Daneels, R., Bowman, N. D., Possler, D., & Mekler, E. D. (2021). The 'eudaimonic experience': A scoping review of the concept in digital games research. *Media and Communication, 9*(2), 178–190. https://doi.org/10.17645/mac.v9i2.3824

Donovan, T. (2010). *Replay: The history of video games.* Yellow Ant.

du Plessis, C. (2018). Subverting utilitarian subject-object relations in video games: A philosophical analysis of Thatgamecompany's Journey. *South African Journal of Philosophy, 37*(4), 466–479. https://doi.org/10.1080/02580136.2018.1532189

Eklund, L., & Zanescu, A. (2024). Times they are a-changin'? Evolving representations of women in the assassin's creed franchise. *Games and Culture*, 1–21. https://doi.org/10.1177/15554120241246575

Elvery, G. (2023). Undertale's loveable monsters: Investigating parasocial relationships with non-player characters. *Games and Culture, 18*(4), 475–497. https://doi.org/10.1177/15554120221105464

Encyclopedia of Korean Culture. (n.d.). 도깨비 설화 (도깨비 說話). In 한국민족문화대백과사전 *[Encyclopedia of Korean Culture].* Academy of Korean Studies. Retrieved November 7, 2024, from https://encykorea.aks.ac.kr/Article/E0015531

Gallagher, R., & Topinka, R. (2023). The politics of the NPC meme: Reactionary subcultural practice and vernacular theory. *Big Data & Society, 10*(1), 1–16. https://doi.org/10.1177/20539517231172422

Gazzard, A. (2010). Player as parent, character as child: Exploring avatarial relationships in gamespace. In *Proceedings of the 14th International Academic MindTrek Conference: Envisioning Future Media Environments* (pp. 25–31). Tampere, Finland: Association for Computing Machinery. https://doi.org/10.1145/1930488.1930494

Gray, K. L. (2020). *Intersectional tech.* LSU Press.

Gunkel, D. J. (2018). *Gaming the system: Deconstructing video games, games studies, and virtual worlds.* Indiana University Press.

Guzman, A. L. (2018). Introduction: "What is human-machine communication, anyway?" In A. L. Guzman (Ed.), *Human-machine communication: Rethinking communication, technology, and ourselves* (pp. 1–28). Peter Lang.

Guzman, A. L., McEwen, R., & Jones, S. (2023). Introduction to the handbook. In A. L. Guzman, R. McEwen & S. Jones (Eds.), *The Sage handbook of human–machine communication* (pp. xxxix–xlvi). Sage.

Hall, S. (1993). Encoding, decoding. In S. During (Ed.), *The cultural studies reader* (pp. 90–103). Routledge.

Hall, S. (2016). *Cultural studies 1983: A theoretical history* (J. D. Slack & L. Grossberg, Eds.). Duke University Press.

Haraway, D. (2016). *Staying with the trouble: Making kin in the Chthulucene.* Duke University Press.

Jenkins, H. (2004). Game design as narrative architecture. In N. Wardrip-Fruin & P. Harrigan (Eds.), *First person: New media as story, performance, and game* (pp. 118–130). MIT Press.

Jenson, J., Taylor, N., de Castell, S., & Dilouya, B. (2015). Playing with our selves: Multiplicity and identity in online gaming. *Feminist Media Studies, 15*(5), 860–879. https://doi.org/10.1080/14680777.2015.1006652

Kang, E. B. (2023). Ground truth tracings (GTT): On the epistemic limits of machine learning. *Big Data & Society, 10*(1), 1–12. https://doi.org/10.1177/20539517221146122

Kim, D. O. (2023). "Pay for your choices": Deconstructing neoliberal choice through free-to-play mobile interactive fiction games. *New Media & Society, 25*(5), 943–962. https://doi.org/10.1177/14614448211018177

Kim, D. O. (2025). Non-player characters and the nonhuman: Insights and scoping review toward critical posthumanist human-machine communication. *The Communication Review*, 1–27. https://doi.org/10.1080/10714421.2025.2586865

Kim, S. Y. (2022). Getting over the fear of murder: Video game violence and the ethics of empowerment in the last of us. In S. Choe (Ed.), *The Palgrave handbook of violence in film and media* (pp. 355–377). Palgrave Macmillan. https://doi.org/10.1007/978-3-031-05390-0_18

Kosciesza, A. J. (2023). The moral service of trans NPCs: Examining the roles of transgender non-player characters in role-playing video games. *Games and Culture, 18*(2), 189–208. https://doi.org/10.1177/15554120221088118

Latour, B. (2005). *Reassembling the social: An introduction to actor-network theory.* Oxford University Press.

Lee, C. R., & Lee, Y.-S. (2013). 한국형 전통 하이브리드 캐릭터 형상 연구; 장승과 도깨비를 중심으로 [The study of the Korean Traditional Hybrid Character Shape: For Jangseung and Dokkaebi]. 만화애니메이션 연구, *31*, 1–27. https://doi.org/10.7230/KOSCAS.2013.31.001

Lind, R. A. (2020). *Produsing theory in a digital world 3. 0: The intersection of audiences and production in contemporary theory* (Vol. 3). Peter Lang.

Liu, T., & Lai, Z. (2022). From non-player characters to othered participants: Chinese women's gaming experience in the 'free' digital market. *Information, Communication & Society, 25*(3), 376–394. https://doi.org/10.1080/1369118X.2020.1791217

Mukherjee, S. (2018). Playing subaltern: Video games and postcolonialism. *Games and Culture, 13*(5), 504–520. https://doi.org/10.1177/1555412015627258

Nakamura, L. (1995). Race in/for cyberspace: Identity tourism and racial passing on the Internet. *Works Days, 13*(1), 181–193. https://doi.org/10.1017/CBO9781107415324.004

Nakamura, L. (2009). Don't hate the player, hate the game: The racialization of labor in World of Warcraft. *Critical Studies in Media Communication, 26*(2), 128–144. https://doi.org/10.1080/15295030902860252

Natale, S., & Ballatore, A. (2020). Imagining the thinking machine: Technological myths and the rise of artificial intelligence. *Convergence, 26*(1), 3–18. https://doi.org/10.1177/1354856517715164

Ogier, H. (2020). The player-ethnographer: An ethnographic approach to the study of non-player characters in digital games. *Proceedings of the Australasian Computer Science Week Multiconference, Article 43*, 1–10. https://doi.org/10.1145/3373017.3373064

Paul, C. A. (2020). *Free-to-play: Mobile video games, bias, and norms*. MIT Press.

Poor, N. (2023). Human-machine communities: How online computer games model the future. In A. L. Guzman, R. McEwen & S. Jones (Eds.), *The Sage handbook of human-machine communication* (pp. 322–338). Sage.

Proferes, N., Jones, N., Gilbert, S., Fiesler, C., & Zimmer, M. (2021). Studying Reddit: A systematic overview of disciplines, approaches, methods, and ethics. *Social Media + Society, 7*(2), 1–14. https://doi.org/10.1177/20563051211019004

Rose, M. C. (2023). Playful, sociable, cute, quarantined – interactions with kawaii characters in animal crossing: New horizons during COVID-19. *Japanese Studies, 43*(3), 297–311. https://doi.org/10.1080/10371397.2023.2211944

Ruberg, B. (2022). After agency: The queer posthumanism of video games that cannot be played. *Convergence, 28*(2), 413–430. https://doi.org/10.1177/13548565221094257

Ruffino, P. (2022). There is no cure: Paratexts as remediations of agency in Red Dead Redemption 2. *Convergence, 28*(2), 345–358. https://doi.org/10.1177/13548565221081062

Shaikh, S. J. (2023). Artificially intelligent, interactive, and assistive machines: A definitional framework for intelligent assistants. *International Journal of Human-Computer Interaction, 39*(4), 776–789. https://doi.org/10.1080/10447318.2022.2049133

Shaw, A. (2014). *Gaming at the edge: Sexuality and gender at the margins of gamer culture*. University of Minnesota Press.

Shaw, A. (2024). Video games as cultural studies other. *International Journal of Cultural Studies, 28*(2), 343–353. https://doi.org/10.1177/13678779241295771

van der Merwe, R. L. (2021). Imperial play. *Communication, Culture & Critique, 14*(1), 37–51. https://doi.org/10.1093/ccc/tcaa012

Warpefelt, H., & Verhagen, H. (2015). Towards an updated typology of non-player character roles. In K. Blashki & Y. Xiao (Eds.), *Proceedings of the International Conference on Game and Entertainment Technologies* (pp. 131–139). IADIS Press.

Yee, N. (2014). *The Proteus paradox: How online games and virtual worlds change us-and how they don't*. Yale University Press.

Yi, H.-Y. (2019). 도깨비 표현 특성에 대한 이미지 인식 연구 [Research of Image Recognition of the Feature Expression of Dokkaebi]. 한국콘텐츠학회논문지, *19*(2), 79–87. https://doi.org/10.5392/JKCA.2019.19.02.079

14

{NOT} ALL FUN AND GAMES IN VIRTUAL REALITY

The State of Prosocial and Antisocial VR Play

Tony Liao

Introduction

For several years, there has been a growing ecosystem of consumer virtual reality (VR) devices, games, applications, and other experiences/platforms/worlds (Carter & Egliston, 2024). In these VR environments, multiple users and avatars are able to interact socially with other people in the same space, with each user experiencing it from a first-person point of view. After some significant corporate investment and breakthroughs in several technological areas (e.g. computing power, resolution, and wireless headsets), there are now millions of VR devices that have been shipped to consumers. This represents a growing user base that is being exposed to VR technology for the first time, and many who are choosing to return and spend significant time in these VR environments (Hill, 2022).

VR as a technology has a long history, as an environment that consists solely of virtual objects and replaces one's sense of reality (Milgram & Kishino, 1994). Within the broad umbrella of the technical definition, there is a wide range of VR spaces being developed with new possibilities and features. Many VR social spaces allow for customized avatars, which may or may not correspond with reality and can enable certain types of identities to be presented (Zhang & Juvrud, 2024). It is similar in some ways to other online games (e.g. share multiplayer spaces, avatar representations), but dissimilar in other ways (e.g. first-person perspective, proximal audio communication with nearby avatars). There are some features that are intended to be direct analogues to communication and interaction in physical spaces (e.g. speech and avatar cues), but then there are things that

DOI: 10.4324/9781003477587-14

people can do in VR with their representations that are either very difficult to do in real life or outright impossible (e.g. floating, flying, and teleporting). All of these features can vary greatly across platforms and games as well, where some are attempts to be literal recreations of real-life events (e.g. sporting events, concerts), while others are purposively fantastical and play with visual/temporal features that are only possible through VR.

The wide range of possibilities within VR makes it a technology that can just be another medium by which humans play games they would otherwise do in real life (e.g. Chess, Table Tennis), as well as experiment with formats, genres, and types of play that are otherwise impossible. VR spaces are also less cost-prohibitive to embed with certain features, which expands the possibilities of VR spaces beyond what typically constrains the physical world. At this point, social VR is still in its relative infancy and evolving rapidly, as users figure out what the possibilities are, what it is good for, and what they want to do in these spaces (in relation to others who may want to do different things). Some of it ties back to a longer history in virtual world spaces like Second Life (Boellstorff, 2015), but each virtual world is different and has its own culture and participants. The fluidity of these spaces means that there are constantly new entrants coming in to establish norms and practices in these social VR spaces, some of which become durable and some of which do not. This is reminiscent of the earliest periods of online community formation, which would shape the people that would join, the ways people would interact, and the types of connections that were associated with these spaces (Sproull & Kiesler, 1991). The technology mattered in terms of how it reduced barriers and compressed time and space, but ultimately it was the people who wanted to build community who chose to come to these spaces to do so. Just as these early theories of computer-mediated communication guided researchers for decades, the subcultures, terminology, and structures formed in these early communities would have lasting effects on future online spaces to this day (Baym, 2015).

This chapter aims to explore some of the emerging trends we are observing in social VR spaces, how people are playing in them, and developing some ways of thinking through their implications. There has been a long history of trying to understand sociality, culture, and economics in virtual/synthetic worlds (Boellstorff, 2015; Castronova, 2019). Contemporary social VR mirrors and echoes aspects of these previous worlds, but it differs in important ways. Whereas Second Life was an open-ended world without a designated objective, social VR spaces can have exploratory elements alongside more tangible types of goals. There is also more portability across social experience types, as users may start in an open VR chatroom and move with people across a number of different games/

social settings to more private settings. Similarly, social VR bears some similarity to MMORGs in that people can form connections, groups, and have complex economic systems; however, the first-person perspective and the different cues that are available can change the dynamics of relationship initiation, communication, and visibility. The experience of VR bears some similarity to first-person shooter games, which have been shown to increase bonding (Frostling-Henningsson, 2009) but has a broader range of experience than the quest/arena model of teams battling in these spaces. VR can offer sociality without a goal (e.g. chat), shared collective experiences (e.g. concerts), and interactions that are not bound by the rules of a particular game/team.

Modern VR technologies can be understood as first an evolution of many online communities, which may draw on and borrow from a longer history of online interactions and terminology. The differences are significant enough, however, to allow for new practices and cultures to emerge that require a re-negotiation within the VR space. How these norms get agreed upon, how participation is encouraged, regulated, and sanctioned, and for what political goal, will set the parameters of what these spaces look like. In the long term, they will likely determine how much of an "exodus" there will be to VR from existing gaming platforms (Castronova, 2008).

One important note here is that VR sociality is also quite varied, by device, application purpose, and application design. There are some VR applications that are intended to serve as a social hub and starting point for interactions, made for each device/ecosystem (e.g., VRChat, Horizon Worlds, Altspace), and then there are a number of multiplayer games that have their own built-in social components. Some of this may end up being device-specific in their capabilities, as recent market estimates show that Meta claims 50–60% of the consumer VR device market, depending on the quarter (Ubrani et al., 2025). There are, however, other VR devices and systems that may enable sociality in their own way. In this early space of experimentation, we can say that there are commonalities in some of the features for VR sociality, but it is also continually developing.

The purpose of this chapter is to identify some of the emerging possibilities of social VR technology, unpack some key cases of community formation, and what they illustrate about the state of play in VR. Through these cases, we identify some potential implications of these, whether it becomes yet another isolated subculture of the internet enabled by visual technologies. Another possibility is that these practices and trends become the reason why VR sociality does not progress and deters future adoption. Still, the fact that these are already emerging could portend future social interaction, a virtual hybrid space that we will increasingly move to alongside our physical spaces. How one thinks about the effects of these VR spaces will also matter, as some might believe these representations are just pixels and thus not real in any meaningful way. Others think that VR represents a radical break from how we perceive reality and engage with other people digitally, suggesting the implications and possible harms could be just as serious as if it happened to us in physical space. The conversations we are having now related to these issues and the enforcement and regulatory decisions around them will also be significant, as these early spaces continue to mature and take form.

Communities of Practices and VR Play

As VR social spaces are becoming possible, we have to place them in a historical understanding of technologically enabled community building. Given the early CMC literature that argued that social connections can be just as deep through CMC even if people never meet face to face, we now have decades of research showing that social communities and subcommunities can form in online message boards and forums (Baym, 2015) and multiplayer gaming environments through teams/guilds (Castronova, 2008). To this, we add VR as another possibility to these channels, both as a source of initial communication and as a source of maintaining social relationships/communication (e.g., meeting in VR and shifting to other mediums, meeting face to face and reconnecting in VR, and coordinating on a games message board and moving to VR).

In this early period as norms, practices, and cultures get negotiated, the design of VR games and public policy will be inextricably linked, because structurally they are the same (Castronova, 2008). Because people are choosing to gather in these semi-public places and building communities, working toward goals, and trying to find shared purposes, we see these groups as a burgeoning Community of Practice (CoP). CoP was first defined as: "participation in an activity system about which participants share understandings concerning what they are doing and what that means for their lives and for their communities" (Lave & Wenger, 1991, p. 98). These CoP describe a complex set of social relationships, which is organized around a particular domain and where knowledge and skills are circulated. Wenger (1998) further elaborated on the idea of a CoP itself, what those group structures entailed, and how they signaled status, collective identities, and shared histories (Cox, 2005).

CoP is an analytical lens to understand and explain how people learn and become socialized in certain communities, how behaviors and attitudes are modeled, how identities are mutually constituted, and the networks of practices that can form as people move from newcomer to full-fledged participants in these networks of practice (Brown & Duguid,

2001; Lave & Wenger, 1991; Wenger, 1998). Newcomers often first learn what is valued in the society through legitimate peripheral participation (LPP), or social practices that people in the community engage in and gain experience by doing so, so that their involvement grows over time (Lave & Wenger, 1991).

In early online communities, LPP may have taken the form of lurking/reading, liking/sharing, editing/curating, and posting/commenting (Fiesler et al., 2017). Importantly, there is nothing uniformly positive about LPP in that many online communities may be geared toward negativity and thus encourage negative LPP. Examples include 4chan's random board, which encourages more and more shocking content to get a reaction (Coleman, 2015), or pro-anorexic message threads encouraging negative social support to maintain an anorexic identity (Chang & Bazarova, 2016).

Within VR, the question is how these communities socialize and how that differs from online spaces. VR is more akin to physical space in that participation entails presence, which will shape the environment itself. Whereas in an online forum one could lurk without their presence being known for a while, VR avatars occupy space and are known right away to others in the space. This makes behavior and presence more important factors in one's participation and increases the role of maintenance and reputation in these spaces (as people can look up profiles, log friends, and remember avatars). The interrelationship between participation and presence also raises the stakes for how people present their avatars, as VR spaces have visual markers of identity, such that longtime members would point out the "noobs" for wearing the standard-issue avatar kits (Boellstorff, 2015). Other signifiers of not knowing what one is doing in this space are to "ghost" people during conversations, either by leaving your avatar somewhere without setting it as away or having your system crash, and people would continue to try to talk to your disembodied avatar (Boellstorff, 2015). These differences in VR spaces and community building are what we want to focus more on because there is a wide range of communities and many feature-rich possibilities to socialize, interact, and play. We categorize these practices at the poles as prosocial and antisocial to understand some of the implications that both of these types have for community while also recognizing that there is play that sits between these poles and occasionally cuts across these categories.

Prosocial Play

VR has always been about the sensation of being somewhere together, so it was always intended to be a social space (Schroeder, 2010). With many features that attempt to recreate physical connection, the potential for VR to bring people together is one of the core promises of the technology (Carter & Egliston, 2024). Progressive play is categorized as an attempt to improve the CoP, whether it is through tangible actions that VR specifically enables, the populations that engage in VR, or the outcomes of VR use. Of course, VR play and the social and communal aspects are device/platform/application dependent. Platforms like Meta Quest and HTC VIVE have paved the way for immersive social experiences, transforming how users connect and interact in virtual environments while enabling global interaction. Launched in 2014, VRChat allows users to design their own custom avatars and interact in virtual spaces ranging from real-life recreations to imaginative fantasy worlds (Rzeszewski & Evans, 2024).

In many VR games and public spaces that include games, the social component is evident in many of their titles (e.g., *Beat Saber*, *Rec Room*, *Gorilla Tag*). Social VR play highlights VR's ability to foster creativity, collaboration, and social engagement. Many of the same elements that make these spaces attractive in MMORPGs and group games, such as guilds, group quests, and head-to-head competition, can transfer easily to VR. Users can participate in activities ranging from casual meetups to large-scale events, such as virtual concerts or film screenings (Onderdijk et al., 2023). These experiences are more than just new; they signify the creation of emerging social norms and cultures in VR. For one thing, there is research that shows that first-person experiences can create different types of social bonds (Frostling-Henningsson, 2009). These digital interactions and online hang-out sessions can simulate real-world socialization and form a community over time (Gunkel & Gunkel, 2009). There are many examples of positive socialization, sportsmanship, and healthy competition in these spaces that uphold principles of safety, fair play, respect, and enriching game experiences (Tseng et al., 2015). Social VR platforms allow users to eliminate geographical obstacles, enabling global interaction, which increases the number of people who may be interested, while also fostering new spaces for intercultural communication, identity exploration, and social support (Wei et al., 2022). For all of the talk of negativity and toxicity, there would not be a community unless people actively found fun and productive places in VR.

The ability to customize virtual representations of the self through body/avatar choices cultivates a powerful sense of identity and ownership (Nowak & Fox, 2018). VR play's ability to support socialization and community is especially significant for marginalized groups (MacArthur et al., 2024). Platforms like AltspaceVR and VRChat can support safe spaces for users who may feel isolated or unsafe in their physical environments. For example, LGBTQ+ meetups can serve as a platform for discussing identity and offering support, especially for users in areas where such rights are restricted (MacArthur et al., 2024). The immersive qualities of VR and the capacity for avatar interaction can also facilitate connections and alleviate anxiety in ways that may be difficult in face-to-face settings (Aymerich-Franch & Bailenson, 2014). The anonymity provided by avatars, along with the enhanced social presence of VR, can promote a strong environment for self-expression and emotional support.

Beyond social events, VR platforms have also been used to create educational and therapeutic communities (Riches et al., 2023). For example, AltspaceVR has hosted mental health panels that allow users to discuss issues such as depression and anxiety in a supportive, nonjudgmental environment. Thrive Pavilion is a company that specifically focuses on the older adult population and creates VR group meetups and events to help people who may be otherwise immobile or isolated.[1] The promise of VR for certain populations is that it can bridge certain physical limitations for social connectivity or some of the reasons that marginalized communities may not feel comfortable gathering (Dudley et al., 2023). VR can also play a role in many different aspects of mental health, whether that is assessment, awareness, or treatment (Freeman et al., 2017).

The inclusivity of VR play is also apparent in its uses for disabled users (Davis, 2018). Over time, advancements in avatar control and user interface design have made VR more accessible to people with physical disabilities. Groups like the XR Access Initiative have been at the forefront of this research to make accessibility widespread and an unremarkable feature of devices and spaces.[2] According to Nowak and Fox (2018), avatars in VR provide a sense of agency and mobility, empowering users to engage in social spaces on their own terms. Features to aid the visual/hearing impaired (Collins et al., 2023) and help people with invisible disabilities present in VR (Gualano et al., 2024) are part of the larger effort to democratize social participation in VR. There may also be ways in which choice in self-presentation in VR space can be an asset; whereas some people with strong disability identification want to present their real selves in VR, others like the fact that VR allows them to interact on a level playing field without calling attention to something about them that accentuates difference (Gualano et al., 2024).

As VR technologies and VR play continue to evolve, its communal aspects will likely have an even more significant role in shaping how we interact. The ability to create customized social spaces, combined with the inclusivity afforded by avatars and immersive environments, allows VR to break down traditional barriers—whether geographical, physical, or social. Expanding the population of people who can participate in these communities and enabling different forms of communication/interaction/presentation among these communities increases the possibilities for what progressive participation looks like, which can represent a fundamental shift in how people play in the digital age and experience community.

Antisocial Play

While VR communities and related social gatherings can allow for positive social interactions, they can also attract regressive behaviors, which are unsanctioned actions in a space with the express purpose of antagonizing and preventing others from participating in the shared space. Some of this comes directly from the overlap in people participating in game communities, bringing that over to VR, whether that is racial slurs, abuse, and harassment (Chawki et al., 2024). Groups of people began to use a common avatar in VR and move around spaces making spitting noises, clicking sounds, and racist epithets (e.g., knucklers). There have also been some reports of sexual assaults that happen in VR with many news outlets reporting incidents in Altspace (Porta et al., 2024) and Horizon Worlds (Bellini, 2024). The concern here is that the psychological effects of first-person abuse and visible crimes against a person's avatar representation can be more emotionally triggering than something that happens in a third-person game. VRChat had so many of these occurrences that their moderators wrote an open letter to the community reminding them about the importance of enforcing content and behavioral standards.[3]

From a community-building perspective, there are a few ways to understand these practices based on what we know about gaming subcultures and other online communities. The first is territoriality and boundary policing, as certain gamers only want a particular type of person in these spaces (Boudreau, 2019). By normalizing a certain type of behavior and violence, the idea is to drive away people who do not want to participate in this subculture. There can also be an ideological justification for these actions, that people engage in them to prevent online spaces from becoming too serious, and that everything online should be something we can laugh at (Coleman, 2015; Phillips, 2011). Another consideration is to reinforce norms of status and experience, to target "noobs" and newcomers into improving and updating their style (Boellstorff, 2015). Certain personality types can also predict harassment, whether people think it is acceptable as a competitive strategy to gain an advantage through harassment (Tang & Fox, 2016). The multiplayer survival game called *Rust* enables tactics of raiding and grieving into the gameplay itself, where players intentionally invade a space of play to spread hate and harassment (Wijkstra et al., 2024). In building a CoP, there can be conflict and sanctions, and these practices can be understood as attempts to build a different kind of community (Cox, 2005; Wenger, 1999). They may serve dual purposes as well, with one being to deter certain people from joining or engaging in legitimate participation and another in ensuring that users who remain a part of the community actively participate in these subcultures or passively tolerate them as the norm.

How seriously to regulate these practices and subcultures has been extensively studied in the online gaming community (Chess & Shaw, 2015), with efforts being undertaken by the companies that host these games and the communities themselves. Features such as banning, muting, auto-muting, reporting, and social sanctions to guilds/teams have been added to combat harassment like racial slurs or abusive behavior. The extent to which these practices port over to VR and the ways to prevent them in these public and semi-public virtual spaces, however, has been challenging (Chawki et al., 2024). Many VR applications like Rec Room have started implementing moderation systems and establishing roles like real-world event security to protect users (Castro, 2022; Mak, 2022). The open letter also includes recommendations for people to interact with people on trusted/friends lists. These represent an essential, yet imperfect, step toward addressing the safety of users, both as a practical matter and in its implementation. Researchers have found that many of the mechanisms for maintaining safe and inclusive communal VR spaces often rely solely on user reporting, which does not stop the harassment from happening in the first place and may not always be advisable or achievable in moments of distress (Freeman et al., 2022). There are also concerns about whether companies have the ability or the motivation to actively enforce their own policies, as journalists have tried to test the effectiveness of content moderation by creating Horizon Worlds filled with political disinformation, anti-vaccine content, and conspiracy theories.

One area of concern is group play that is gratuitously and collectively violent, which may normalize these practices among the community. While video games have often been criticized for excessive violence, the concern with VR games may be that people are physically enacting the violence and embodying the characters who deliver this kind of physicality. One example is the VR gladiator game *Gorn*, which has faced criticism for its excessively violent gameplay and has been shown to elevate heart rate and breathing (Charoensook et al., 2019). Another example is the dystopian science fiction VR game called *Raw Data*, which emphasizes militaristic themes that glorify conflict and promote a narrow view of heroism. While researchers are still assessing whether these types of VR games have greater effects on aggression and testing theories/mechanisms that would explain those effects, there may be different frameworks that apply to VR violence compared to flat console-based games (Drummond et al., 2021). One is the interactivity and embodiment of VR actions on a person's cognition, and another is the normalization of doing those actions in the aggregate and in social settings. As a medium, one specific way that VR may be different than console games is the linking of experiences. Even if a console game space is violent, that is more self-contained within the game where it is played, whereas in VR, people are continually moving between these games and common spaces/forums.

Content/violence may be one issue, but the possibility for sexual crimes, controlling avatars, and broadcasting them in VR has been a concern about the technology for decades (Dibbell, 2005). These became a priority because of high-profile incidents and because participants may actively feel harm (Porta et al., 2024). In response, VRChat and other communal VR spaces began implementing a personal space feature. Such features allow users to use hand motions to create a "safe bubble" around their avatars to prevent others from entering their space (Chawki et al., 2024). The Horizon Worlds platform also received complaints from users about harassment, prompting the implementation of a "safe zone" element. This element allows users to craft a personal bubble where other users are unable to interact with their avatar without permission (Bellini, 2024). By giving users control over their proximity to others, Meta sought to address increasing reports of harassment, particularly targeting female users. Castronova (2008) notes that virtual environments often mirror real-world social dynamics with certain groups being more vulnerable to things like harassment and abuse. While the "safe zone" feature is beneficial, it also raises discussions about how it continues to place the onus on marginalized communities to protect themselves and whether new members know how to easily find and use these features (Basu, 2021).

In other instances, VR play spaces have bypassed automated systems and introduced human moderators who imitate real-world security roles. Virtual nightclubs and concerts on platforms like VRChat and AltspaceVR have begun implementing "VR security," where event organizers hire moderators to oversee the space, removing or muting disruptive users (Chawki et al., 2024). Thinking about access security through VR personnel and moderator content moderation has been an ongoing issue for companies and organizers. The issues for VR bouncers and whether they are effective, however, are largely the same as in real life (e.g., the need for proper training, exercising judgment, and discretion), coupled with additional difficulties in policing trolling behaviors that may look quite similar to newcomers struggling to learn VR tools (Mak, 2022).

The question of human moderation amplifies several challenges within VR, one being questions over what to regulate and how to do so. Just as terms of service policies have evolved over time as the priorities of the companies shift (Gillespie, 2018), these decisions will determine what constitutes legitimate participation in these spaces. In terms of process, the challenge is to balance enforcement with an overaggressive moderation of spaces that could prevent newcomers from learning the tools in the first place (Mak, 2022). As various types of VR play start to occur simultaneously and across public, social, and communal environments, ethical issues surrounding harassment and abusive behavior start to mirror questions we have long negotiated in physical spaces and whether VR platforms should be regulated in similar ways. While the difference between the physical world and the virtual world of VR and VR play may suggest a different set of rules (Liao, 2024), the psychological effects of harassment and abuse can be as serious as those experienced in real-life interactions (Freeman et al., 2017). The development of moderation systems, personal space features, and VR security roles highlights the recognition that VR environments are vulnerable to the darker sides of human behavior. As a result, more comprehensive strategies beyond user reporting may be needed to safeguard users while maintaining the freedom that makes these spaces innovative and engaging (Freeman et al., 2017).

Even as proponents point to the availability of different avatar representations for identity purposes, the prevalence of racism, sexism, and ableism in these spaces may make that experience ultimately unpleasant (Freeman et al., 2017). There are also ethical issues that come about when people take on different social presentations and practices (Slater & Sanchez-Vives, 2022) and sexual practices and boundaries are pushed in these VR environments (Bellini, 2024). Some also critique attempts at VR empathy as inauthentic and scripted and positions itself as virtuous even as it can enable problematic raceplay and identity tourism (Nakamura, 2020). There have also been reports of sexual ageplay occurring in Second Life, defined as the "virtual act of simulating child sexual abuse using animated child characters operated by consenting adult users" (Reeves, 2013, p. 236). These kinds of practices demonstrate some of the boundaries of how we think about VR and what should be allowed, since technically the action is being initiated by adults in the real world even as what they are doing with the digital representations is considered criminal.

How "Real" Should We Think about VR Play and Its Effects?

The extent to which people care about these types of play (both prosocial and antisocial) has to do with an underlying debate over the physiological, psychological, sociocultural, and behavioral impacts (Slater & Sanchez-Vives, 2016). One common comparison is the ways that VR is similar or dissimilar to physical play, which emphasizes traits like physical engagement, spontaneity, and creativity. Some may land on the side that

VR play is somehow less real or serious and should be treated as just a collection of pixels. Others may argue that anything that can fool our minds into some sort of embodied cognition should be treated as just as real as physical play and, thus, should be taken more seriously for the types of effects that are now possible in these environments.

There are several philosophical theories that help frame our understanding of this debate. One such theory is the phenomenology of experience (Gualeni, 2015). This theory highlights the subjective reality of individuals in both physical and virtual interactions and proposes that when players perceive their VR experiences as real, these experiences become meaningful in their lives (Gualeni, 2015). Researchers such as Lombard and Ditton (1997) examined how users' sense of presence in virtual environments can foster a feeling of reality that competes with physical experiences. Another theory that may help explain one's orientation to VR effects is simulation theory, which suggests that virtual experiences can mimic real-world dynamics. In these environments, advocates contend that VR can demonstrate emotional and social engagement that is just as intense as, if not more so than, physical play (Slater & Sanchez-Vives, 2022).

Presence is often the mediating variable for understanding the power of the medium, as presence and immersion can create the suspension of disbelief venin media that leads to heightened emotional responses (Lombard & Ditton, 1997). Studies have examined the role of perspective taking and immersion and how a strong sense of "being there" in virtual worlds can evoke empathy and emotional reactions similar to those experienced in real life (Herrera et al., 2018). This emotional engagement is crucial for connecting with narratives and characters, as seen in immersive storytelling within VR environments (Wang et al., 2024).

Theories about social interactions in VR play also examine things like community building and social dynamics (Pearce, 2011). In many online games, players use avatars to interact, acting as extensions of their identities and enabling them to explore parts of themselves that are harder to access in real life (Ducheneaut & Moore, 2004). Moreover, VR cultivates connections between players, forming friendships that go beyond geographical limits. Early research has shown that VR experiences can create attachments to create and maintain friendships, although expectations can be different for virtual friends (Welles et al., 2014).

Research into the effects of VR play on behavior and cognition is beginning to form as well. Much of this has been in the education context, looking at whether certain types of play can facilitate learning and skill acquisition by offering interactive and engaging environments that encourage exploration and experimentation (Rojas-Sanchez et al., 2023). VR play has physiological effects as well, where the physical nature of the medium and specific exergames has shown that motivation can increase in VR (Giakoni-Ramírez et al., 2023). Even games that just have a physical interaction component as part of their modality (e.g. Beat Saber) can lead to substantial increases in physiological and sociological outcomes comparable to traditional exercise methods (Lin et al., 2023).

Perhaps the operative way of thinking about VR play should not be as a comparison to physical play, but as a virtual place where people's physical cognitions can interact. Existing research shows that these start to be mutually shaping, as communication in VR takes on a certain form and can begin to affect people cognitively, physically, and emotionally (Wei et al., 2022). Since these spaces are now not only possible but also recurring in the virtual realm, our understanding needs to be on these types of emerging phenomena and the state of play in these spaces, to understand it's frequency, cultural significance, and how we should try to shape and improve these environments (Pearce, 2011).

The State of VR Play

Documenting these types of prosocial and antisocial practices and implications should not be surprising to anyone who has studied online communities or gaming communities in particular. There is great joy, engagement, and fun in these communities, but those same qualities can turn toxic and territorial very quickly depending on the leadership, the organizing purpose/ideology of the community, groups of people entering and leaving the community, and what participation is legitimated and sanctioned. What we are documenting in VR is some of this negotiation happening in real time, but with several important unique technological differences, qualifiers, and unknowns in the VR environment.

Frequency/Typology of Behaviors

The first is the frequency/typology of these practices, where news reports tend to focus on sensational but largely testimonial/anecdotal reports. The companies that operate these platforms know about engagement, but researchers have a difficult time systematically studying VR spaces because of their vastness and temporality. Whereas online communities and forums would leave traces of interactions for scholars to study even anonymous communities such as 4chan (Coleman, 2015) and problematic sites such as pro-anorexia communities (Chang & Bazarova, 2016), VR interactions are much more ephemeral. This poses several methodological issues at a larger scale, such as difficulty in sampling from the community, a strong lean toward ethnographic/qualitative methods, and a limitation on the number of researchers who can map the vastness of these places. It also becomes an ethical issue, whereas researchers could scrape online data without necessarily putting themselves at risk, VR means that researchers have to present in the same spaces where they are trying to observe behaviors that can include harassment and assault. Indeed, one of the news reports of an assault was on a VR researcher, which makes the threat salient and makes it difficult to send researchers into these spaces.

Communal Spaces/Subcommunities

Another issue that is unique to VR compared to other online communities is the temporal and embodied shared spaces, where several different groups can come together. For the vastness of the internet, if people want to, they can find and create their own subcommunities and cultures without necessarily interacting. Of course, trolling communities do seek out other groups to try to get reactions from them, which is often what fuels the fire (Phillips, 2011), but it is not as though there is a central plaza of the internet. The goal of many VR platforms is to dominate the traffic and have a central application/place where one must go to see shows, concerts, sporting events, etc., which become flashpoints where many different subcommunities may be negotiating what their view of the VR space is and should be and for whom. This dynamic is worth watching, as some of the prosocial and antisocial forces will have to interact with one another (and force the companies to moderate), because these public spaces will become places where these things get negotiated (Freeman et al., 2017; Mak, 2022). They are also jumping off points for meeting people in VR, such that people often start by getting to know one another in VRChat or other application before jumping into another game, so the layering and deepening of social connections across applications is another thing to watch that makes VR unique.

Cues/Avatars/Communication Modalities/Features

The fact that people have to present themselves to participate in VR makes the conversation around computer-mediated cues and avatars much more salient, in good and bad ways. Gender-based harm has led to certain design workarounds and preventative user actions (e.g. muting one's voice) to avoid certain types of harassment (Gray et al., 2024). The choice of avatar also matters a great deal to one's experience in these spaces, as well as other technological design suggestions such as voice modulators (Freeman et al., 2017; Zhang & Juvrud, 2024). The full weight of each of these cues in combination, as a choice, and for which community is something that we still need to parse in the course of these play spaces.

Consequences/Regulation of Antisocial Practices

With many of the acts of violence, sexual assault, and ageplay issue, the question that VR forces us to ask is how serious we think the consequences are, what should be done about it, and who should be taking the action (Reeves, 2013). Some scholars have argued that what VR does is that it makes possible certain actions and pulls apart some of the logics that we have used to regulate behavior (Liao, 2024). Age presentation in sexual encounters in physical space would make that a crime in action and cognition for the victim, but, with VR, it may make it merely a crime in displaying an action virtually (e.g., child pornography laws), but not a crime in cognition (if the people doing it are consenting adults). Then the question becomes how and whether the companies will parse that difference and regulate/sanction that behavior on their platforms, to the extent they are able to identify and want to issue consequences for the perpetrators.

Norms Enforcement and Civility

Focusing on the most extreme acts of harassment and violence may bring awareness to the issue and how to design tools to prevent the most extreme cases, but perhaps less explored now are questions of VR acts that fall below the level of harassment but are still annoying. In physical space (and to some extent online space), we can socially sanction people for doing things that are moderately annoying and violate the unspoken norms of a space (e.g., standing in front of someone in a movie theater and talking during a movie). The fact that VR forces us to share the visual/audio environment with other strangers—but potentially without the ability to socially sanction them (or have enough people who care and are willing to intervene)—will play an important role in the actions that people take and the types of everyday socialization that occurs in VR (Hill, 2022).

Status/Economics across/between Subcommunities

One of the things that is most evident about internet cultures is the speed at which certain language, behaviors, and norms get taken up across different communities. Understanding how these things are adopted in VR and spread from one subculture to another will be something to observe.

This is especially true as leadership and status are granted and recognized in these VR spaces, which may reward different practices than in message-based online community spaces (e.g., frequent contributors and moderators). There is also an economic component to gaining and showing certain types of status, as certain online games have their own scarce/rare items that confer a level of status or purchasing power. Because VR spaces are fluid in their construction and how individuals/groups move across communities, whether or how that matters outside of the environments in which they earn that status is also yet to be seen. Understanding the boundaries where certain subcommunities meet and interact will be an important sociological component to understanding VR norms and how cross-community status gets negotiated.

Conclusion

Often with emerging technologies and applications, the things that people choose to do with them when they have the capability are what is surprising. Perhaps, without the internet, we would not have known what people would do with a level of anonymity and communication networks to instantly message strangers. Sites like PostSecret garnered attention for being a place where people would share secrets online, both in terms of the intimacy of disclosure and that people wanted to use the technology to do this. Similarly, applications like Chatroulette were conceptualized as a quick global video connection tool but quickly devolved into efforts to shock/humor/assault other people on screen. Many of these acts of VR play fall into these categories of progressive, regressive, and transgressive, where they explore the potential of a technology to do things and push them to a place where practices emerge that were previously impossible. The same tools for point of view perspective taking could be used for empathetic purposes (Wang et al., 2024) or for voyeuristic and invasive purposes. The same options for matching VR avatars with physical representations could be simultaneously liberating for identity presentation and rife with problematic ageplay/raceplay and harassment (Freeman et al., 2017; Nakamura, 2020). As is the case with many emerging technologies, people may not have conceived that there was a desire to do certain things until the technology presented itself; at which point, we have to grapple with what that says about humanity itself.

VR is in its emerging phase right now as people figure these things out, and the spectrum of actions can be hugely liberating and deeply problematic. The same features can be used for prosocial and antisocial actions, depending on who is wielding them, the power disparities they are embodying and exploiting, and the communities involved. Some of these practices come from existing communities and are evolving in response to the affordances and features of VR platforms and spaces. How these communities form, what constitutes legitimate participation, and enable/constrain play will be important issues for researchers to continue to watch, because it is where these communities clash that tells us who and what the space will be utilized for. This was at the core of the GamerGate battles and other moderation battles, where certain people felt that a domain, a game, and a technology should be utilized exclusively for their purposes and that they should defend that against anyone challenging that conception (Chess & Shaw, 2015). What types of behaviors are rewarded, sanctioned, and rejected across these groups is at the crux of what VR play becomes, regardless of whether VR continues to grow and becomes a dominant communication medium. If it does, then these are the kinds of conversations and negotiations society and users will be continuing to have for decades, just as we continue to fight over online communities, practices, content, and culture. If VR does not become as widespread, these types of limitations to VR play will likely play an important role in explaining why it does not reach a broader community.

Notes

1 https://thrivepavilion.org/.
2 https://xraccess.org/.
3 https://medium.com/@vrchat/an-open-letter-to-our-community-1b7aa5d9026f.

References

Aymerich-Franch, L., & Bailenson, J. (2014). The use of doppelgangers in virtual reality to treat public speaking anxiety: A gender comparison. In *Proceedings of the International Society for Presence Research Annual Conference* (pp. 173–186). Vienna: Citeseer.

Basu, T. (2021, December 16). The metaverse has a groping problem already. *MIT Technology Review*. https://www.technologyreview.com/2021/12/16/1042516/the-metaverse-has-a-groping-problem/

Baym, N. K. (2015). *Personal connections in the digital age*. John Wiley & Sons.

Bellini, O. (2024). Virtual justice: Criminalizing avatar sexual assault in metaverse spaces. *Mitchell Hamline L. Rev.*, *50*, 75.

Boellstorff, T. (2015). *Coming of age in Second Life: An anthropologist explores the virtually human*. Princeton University Press.

Boudreau, K. (2019). Beyond fun: Transgressive gameplay—toxic and zproblematic player behavior as boundary keeping. In K. Jorgensen & F. Karlsen (Eds.), *Transgression in games and play* (pp. 257–271). MIT Press.

Brown, J. S., & Duguid, P. (2001). Knowledge and organization: A social-practice perspective. *Organization Science*, *12*(2), 198–213. https://doi.org/10.1287/orsc.12.2.198.10116

Carter, M., & Egliston, B. (2024). *Fantasies of virtual reality: Untangling fiction, fact, and threat.* MIT Press.

Castro, D. (2022, February 28). *Content moderation in multi-user immersive experiences: AR/VR and the future of online speech.* Information Technology and Innovation Foundation. https://itif.org/publications/2022/02/28/content-moderation-multi-user-immersive-experiences-arvr-and-future-online/

Castronova, E. (2008). *Exodus to the virtual world: How online fun is changing reality.* MacMillan.

Castronova, E. (2019). *Synthetic worlds: The business and culture of online games.* University of Chicago Press.

Chang, P. F., & Bazarova, N. N. (2016). Managing stigma: Disclosure-response communication patterns in pro-anorexic websites. *Health Communication, 31*(2), 217–229. https://doi.org/10.1080/10410236.2014.946218

Charoensook, T., Barlow, M., & Lakshika, E. (2019). Heart rate and breathing variability for virtual reality game play. In *IEEE 7th International Conference on Serious Games and Applications for Health (SeGAH)* (pp. 1–7). IEEE.

Chawki, M., Basu, S., & Choi, K. S. (2024). Redefining boundaries in the metaverse: Navigating the challenges of virtual harm and user safety. *Laws, 13*(3), 33. https://doi.org/10.3390/laws13030033

Chess, S., & Shaw, A. (2015). A conspiracy of fishes, or, how we learned to stop worrying about# GamerGate and embrace hegemonic masculinity. *Journal of Broadcasting & Electronic Media, 59*(1), 208–220. https://doi.org/10.1080/08838151.2014.999917

Coleman, G. (2015). *Hacker, hoaxer, whistleblower, spy: The many faces of Anonymous.* Verso Books.

Collins, J., Jung, C., Jang, Y., Montour, D., Won, A. S., & Azenkot, S. (2023). "The guide has your back": Exploring how sighted guides can enhance accessibility in social virtual reality for blind and low vision people. In *Proceedings of the 25th International ACM SIGACCESS Conference on Computers and Accessibility* (pp. 1–14). New York, NY. https://doi.org/10.1145/3597638.3608386

Cox, A. (2005). What are communities of practice? A comparative review of four seminal works. *Journal of Information Science, 31*(6), 527–540. https://doi.org/10.1177/0165551505057016

Davis, D. (2018, March 14). Our digital selves: What we learn about ability from avatars. *Platypus.* https://blog.castac.org/2018/03/ability-avatars/

Dibbell, J. (2005, October 18). A rape in cyberspace. *Village Voice.* https://www.villagevoice.com/a-rape-in-cyberspace/

Drummond, A., Sauer, J. D., Ferguson, C. J., Cannon, P. R., & Hall, L. C. (2021). Violent and non-violent virtual reality video games: Influences on affect, aggressive cognition, and aggressive behavior. Two pre-registered experiments. *Journal of Experimental Social Psychology, 95,* 104119. https://doi.org/10.1016/j.jesp.2021.104119

Ducheneaut, N., & Moore, R. J. (2004). The social side of gaming: A study of interaction patterns in a massively multiplayer online game. In *Proceedings of the 2004 ACM Conference on Computer Supported Cooperative Work* (pp. 360–369). Chicago, IL. https://dl.acm.org/doi/proceedings/10.1145/1031607?tocHeading=heading14

Dudley, J., Yin, L., Garaj, V., & Kristensson, P. O. (2023). Inclusive Immersion: A review of efforts to improve accessibility in virtual reality, augmented reality and the metaverse. *Virtual Reality, 27*(4), 2989–3020. https://doi.org/10.1007/s10055-023-00850-8

Fiesler, C., Morrison, S., Shapiro, R. B., & Bruckman, A. S. (2017). Growing their own: Legitimate peripheral participation for computational learning in an online fandom community. In *Proceedings of the 2017 ACM Conference on Computer Supported Cooperative Work and Social Computing* (1375–1386). Portland, OR. https://doi.org/10.1145/2998181.2998210

Freeman, D., Reeve, S., Robinson, A., Ehlers, A., Clark, D., Spanlang, B., & Slater, M. (2017). Virtual reality in the assessment, understanding, and treatment of mental health disorders. *Psychological Medicine, 47*(14), 2393–2400. https://doi.org/10.1017/S003329171700040X

Freeman, G., Zamanifard, S., Maloney, D., & Acena, D. (2022). Disturbing the peace: Experiencing and mitigating emerging harassment in social virtual reality. In *Proceedings of the ACM on Human-Computer Interaction, 6*, 1–30. https://doi.org/10.1145/3512932

Frostling-Henningsson, M. (2009). First-person shooter games as a way of connecting to people: "Brothers in blood". *Cyberpsychology & Behavior, 12*(5), 557–562. https://doi.org/10.1089/cpb.2008.0345

Giakoni-Ramírez, F., Godoy-Cumillaf, A., Espoz-Lazo, S., Duclos-Bastias, D., & del Val Martín, P. (2023). Physical activity in immersive virtual reality: A scoping review. *Healthcare, 11*(11), 1553. https://doi.org/10.3390/healthcare11111553

Gillespie, T. (2018). *Custodians of the Internet: Platforms, content moderation, and the hidden decisions that shape social media.* Yale University Press.

Gray, J. E., Carter, M., & Egliston, B. (Eds.). (2024). Conduct harms in social VR: Embodied harassment, gender-based harm and toxic cultures. In *Governing social virtual reality: Preparing for the content, conduct and design challenges of immersive social media* (pp. 23–34). Springer Nature Switzerland.

Gualano, R. J., Jiang, L., Zhang, K., Shende, T., Won, A. S., & Azenkot, S. (2024). "I try to represent myself as I Am": Self-presentation preferences of people with invisible disabilities through embodied social VR avatars. In *Proceedings of the 26th International ACM SIGACCESS Conference on Computers and Accessibility* (pp. 1–15). St. John's, NL. https://doi.org/10.1145/3663548.3675620

Gualeni, S. (2015). *Virtual worlds as philosophical tools: How to philosophize with a digital hammer.* Springer.

Gunkel, D. J., & Gunkel, A. H. (2009). Terra Nova 2.0—The new world of MMORPGS. *Critical Studies in Media Communication, 26*(2), 104–127. https://doi.org/10.1080/15295030902860195

Herrera, F., Bailenson, J., Weisz, E., Ogle, E., & Zaki, J. (2018). Building long-term empathy: A large-scale comparison of traditional and virtual reality perspective-taking. *PLoS One, 13*(10). https://doi.org/10.1371/journal.pone.0204494

Hill, K. (2022, October 7). This is Life in the Metaverse. *The New York Times.* https://www.nytimes.com/2022/10/07/technology/metaverse-facebook-horizon-worlds.html

Lave, J., & Wenger, E. (1991). *Situated learning: Legitimate peripheral participation.* Cambridge University Press.

Liao, T. (2024). But this time it's different: The debate over Augmented/Virtual reality effects, cognition, consciousness, and identity. In T. V. Pape & V. Karnowski (Eds.), *The mobile media debate: Challenging viewpoints across epistemologies* (pp. 113–129). Routledge.

Lin, J.H., Wu, D. Y., & Bowman, N. (2023). Beat Saber as virtual reality exercising in 360 degrees: A moderated mediation model of VR playable angles on physiological and psychological outcomes. *Media Psychology, 26*(4), 414–435. https://doi.org/10.1080/15213269.2022.2154806

Lombard, M., & Ditton, T. (1997). At the heart of it all: The concept of presence. *Journal of Computer-Mediated Communication, 3*(2). https://doi.org/10.1111/j.1083-6101.1997.tb00072.x

Mak, A. (2022, May 9). *I was a bouncer in the Metaverse: The future of content moderation might just involve banning cartoon avatars for dancing the "Macarena." (And worse!).* Slate. https://slate.com/technology/2022/05/metaverse-content-moderation-virtual-reality-bouncers.html

MacArthur, C., Kukshinov, E., Harley, D., Pawar, T., Modi, N., & Nacke, L. E. (2024). Experiential disparities in social VR: Uncovering power dynamics and inequality. *Frontiers in Virtual Reality, 5*, 1351794. https://doi.org/10.3389/frvir.2024.1351794

Milgram, P., & Kishino, F. (1994). A taxonomy of mixed reality visual displays. *IEICE Transactions on Information and Systems, 77*(12), 1321–1329

Nakamura, L. (2020). Feeling good about feeling bad: Virtuous virtual reality and the automation of racial empathy. *Journal of Visual Culture, 19*(1), 47–64. https://doi.org/10.1177/1470412920906259

Nowak, K. L., & Fox, J. (2018). Avatars and computer-mediated communication: A review of the definitions, uses, and effects of digital representations. *Review of Communication Research, 6*, 30–53. https://doi.org/10.12840/ issn.2255–4165.2018.06.01.015

Onderdijk, K. E., Bouckaert, L., Van Dyck, E., & Maes, P. J. (2023). Concert experiences in virtual reality environments. *Virtual Reality, 27*(3), 2383–2396. https://doi.org/10.1007/s10055-023-00814-y

Pearce, C. (2011). *Communities of play: Emergent cultures in multiplayer games and virtual worlds.* MIT Press.

Phillips, W. (2011). LOLing at tragedy: Facebook trolls, memorial pages and resistance to grief online. *First Monday, 16*(12).

Porta, C. M., Frerich, E. A., Hoffman, S., Bauer, S., Jain, V. M., & Bradley, C. (2024). Sexual violence in virtual reality: A scoping review. *Journal of Forensic Nursing, 20*(1), 66–77. https://doi.org/10.1097/JFN.0000000000000466

Reeves, C. (2013). Fantasy depictions of child sexual abuse: The problem of ageplay in Second Life. *Journal of Sexual Aggression, 19*(2), 236–246. https://doi.org/10.1080/13552600.2011.640947

Riches, S., Jeyarajaguru, P., Taylor, L., Fialho, C., Little, J., Ahmed, L., …Valmaggia, L. (2023). Virtual reality relaxation for people with mental health conditions: A systematic review. *Social Psychiatry and Psychiatric Epidemiology, 58*(7), 989–1007. https://doi.org/10.1007/s00127-022-02417-5

Rojas-Sánchez, M. A., Palos-Sánchez, P. R., & Folgado-Fernández, J. A. (2023). Systematic literature review and bibliometric analysis on virtual reality and education. *Education and Information Technologies*, 28(1), 155–192. https://doi. org/10.1007/s10639-022-11167-5

Rzeszewski, M., & Evans, L. (2024). Social relations and spatiality in VR-Making spaces meaningful in VRChat. *Emotion, Space and Society*, 53, 101038. https:// doi.org/10.1016/j.emospa.2024.101038

Slater, M., & Sanchez-Vives, M. V. (2016). Enhancing our lives with immersive virtual reality. *Frontiers in Robotics and AI*, 3, 74.

Slater, M., & Sanchez-Vives, M. V. (2022). Is consciousness first in virtual reality? *Frontiers in Psychology*, 13, 787523. https://doi.org/10.3389/fpsyg.2022.787523

Schroeder, R. (2010). *Being there together: Social interaction in shared virtual environments*. Oxford University Press.

Sproull, L., & Kiesler, S. (1991). *Connections: New ways of working in the networked organization*. MIT Press.

Tang, W. Y., & Fox, J. (2016). Men's harassment behavior in online video games: Personality traits and game factors. *Aggressive Behavior*, 42(6), 513–521. https://doi.org/10.1002/ab.21646

Tseng, F. C., Huang, H. C., & Teng, C. I. (2015). How do online game communities retain gamers? Social presence and social capital perspectives. *Journal of Computer-Mediated Communication*, 20(6), 601–614. https://doi.org/10.1111/ jcc4.12141

Ubrani, J., Llmas, R.T., & Reith, R. (2025, April 28). *AR & VR Headsets Market Insights*. IDC. https://www.idc.com/promo/arvr/

Wang, Y., Chen, C., Nelson, M. R., & Sar, S. (2024). Walk in my shoes: How perspective-taking and VR enhance telepresence and empathy in a public service announcement for people experiencing homelessness. *New Media & Society*, 26(7), 3931–3950. https://doi.org/10.1177/14614448221108108

Welles, B. F., Rousse, T., Merrill, N., & Contractor, N. (2014). Virtually friends: An exploration of friendship claims and expectations in immersive virtual worlds. *Journal For Virtual Worlds Research*, 7(2), 1–15.

Wenger, E. (1998). Communities of practice: Learning as a social system. *Systems thinker*, 9(5), 2–3.

Wenger, E. (1999). *Communities of practice: Learning, meaning, and identity*. Cambridge University Press.

Wei, X., Jin, X., & Fan, M. (2022). Communication in immersive social virtual reality: A systematic review of 10 years' studies. In *Proceedings of the Tenth International Symposium of Chinese CHI*, 27–37. https://doi.org/10.1145/1122445. 1122456

Wijkstra, M., Rogers, K., Mandryk, R. L., Veltkamp, R. C., & Frommel, J. (2024). How to tame a toxic player? A systematic literature review on intervention systems for toxic behaviors in online video games. In *Proceedings of the ACM on Human-Computer Interaction*, 8(CHI PLAY), 1–32. https://doi.org/ 10.1145/3677080

Zhang, J., & Juvrud, J. (2024). Gender expression and gender identity in virtual reality: Avatars, role-adoption, and social interaction in VRChat. *Frontiers in Virtual Reality*, 5. https://doi.org/10.3389/frvir.2024.1305758

15

TALKING TO NON-STOCHASTIC PARROTS

Human-Machine Communication and Human-Animal Communication in Parallel Lines

Simone Natale

> The humans use Arecibo to look for extraterrestrial intelligence. Their desire to make a connection is so strong that they've created an ear capable of hearing across the universe.
>
> But I and my fellow parrots are right here. Why aren't they interested in listening to our voices?
>
> We're a nonhuman species capable of communicating with them. Aren't we exactly what humans are looking for?
>
> —Ted Chiang, "The Great Silence"

In Ted Chiang's short story "The Great Silence," a parrot laments that humans have been searching for ways to communicate with extraterrestrial species but overlooked parrots as communicative partners—even though the latter are much closer than alien civilizations, and they might have more to say. The story was originally published in 2015, but if Chiang had written it today, he could have chosen human-machine communication as a target for the parrot's invective. The development of generative AI, in fact, has made conversations with talking machines an everyday experience for larger and larger masses of people around the world. As Large Language Models (LLMs) such as ChatGPT become credible simulators of humanlike communicative abilities, users assign them a wide array of social roles, including teammates (Cardon & Marshall, 2024), personal assistants (Sarigul et al., 2024), and even companions (Skjuve et al., 2022).

In this chapter, I take up Chiang's fictional provocation as an invitation to discuss communications between humans and animals and between humans and machines in parallel lines. My interest, however, is not much to

DOI: 10.4324/9781003477587-15

reject anthropocentrism and consider communication from a non-human perspective—a perspective that others have explored with significant success (e.g. Broglio, 2011; Haraway, 2008). What I aim to illuminate, instead, is the importance of thinking about the patterns through which communication becomes meaningful to people regardless of its source, and about the very human assumptions and frameworks through which people receive and interpret messages from nonhumans, such as animals or machines. These dynamics are destined to become more and more consequential as generative AI models are programmed to communicate in ways indistinguishable from human communication (Natale, 2021).

Parrots, in this context, appear to be an ideal starting point, not just because of Chiang's story, but also because LLMs such as ChatGPT have been famously dismissed as "stochastic parrots" (Bender et al., 2021) creating only the illusion of communicative behavior. According to this argument, LLMs do not understand the meaning of the language they process, even though they are able to generate plausible responses. The use of the word "parrots" in this context suggests that we should not treat machines as if they understand, just as we should not overestimate parrots, who do not understand but just repeat the words they produce.

While I am sympathetic to the need of maintaining the distinctions between humans and machines, in this chapter, I revisit an episode in the rich history of attempting communications with animals to consider the problem from a different point of view. Even though machines lack capacities such as empathy, emotional engagement, and genuine social exchange, humans often interact with them as if they possess these traits. They treat chatbots as meaningful communicative partners and assign rich meanings to AI-generated messages, regardless of the nature of these messages and of our efforts to dismiss AI as inauthentic or fake. As I will argue, this is what the history of communicating with parrots teaches us: it is impossible to know what it means for a parrot to talk to us, yet many regard their interactions with this species as a meaningful communicative exchange.

The chapter focuses on the famous case of Alex, a grey parrot that was the subject of 30 years of experiments between 1976 and 2007 under the lead of American scientist Irene Pepperberg. Her attempts at establishing human-animal communications with Alex will be mobilized to find clues that help make sense of the present and the near future in which more and more humans engage in communications with machines that are, at the same time, able and not really able to communicate back. Considering stochastic parrots (i.e. AI technologies such as LLMs) and non-stochastic parrots (i.e. parrots in flesh and blood) in parallel line, I emphasize the importance of perspectives that seriously consider the subjective experience of people who give communicative meaning to these interactions, regardless of the nature of the interlocutors.

The stakes, as I will discuss in the conclusion, are high. As the previously unexplored experience of talking with machines is becoming commonplace for increasingly larger masses of people around the world, new theoretical and practical pathways are needed that help navigate the dynamics of human-machine communication so that the new technologies can benefit rather than harm citizens and societies at large. While the work in this direction is vast and goes beyond the scope of this and of any individual piece of scholarship, my hope is that this chapter can help affirm the need to remain sensitive and empathetic towards the plurality of experiences and engagements that the new forms of communication will inspire.

The Story of Alex, or What Is It Like to Be a Parrot

After completing a PhD in theoretical chemistry at Harvard in 1976, Irene Pepperberg felt she had reached a dead end. Other women in her cohort had been facing gender-based discrimination in job recruiting, and the chance to land an academic position appeared slim. Perhaps even more importantly, she was not enjoying the subject of her research as she had before. As she considered a career change, Pepperberg became aware of new studies on animal species, including chimps and dolphins, that envisioned a novel understanding of animal communication. Mounting evidence was being accumulated to suggest that the long-held boundaries between animals and humans needed to be renegotiated. The recent PhD graduate became convinced that her future lied in this new and promising subject. Having a history of keeping birds as pets, and because it looked like a relatively less explored topic, she decided to focus on parrots. In June 1977, she drove to a pet shop and purchased an African Grey parrot, a species known for their ability to learn and reproducing human language with great clarity (Pepperberg, 2009). She let the pet shop owner choose the parrot at random, so that the bird and his eventual achievements could be representative of his species (Germani, 1992).

Over the next 30 years, the bird, named Alex, was the subject of a large number of experiments and studies that made him the most famous member of his species, and Pepperberg a major authority of research into the cognitive and communicative abilities of animals (Kelly & Guillette, 2021). Based on the consideration that any form of communication is social, Pepperberg adopted a model-rival methodology that involved a trainer and another person acting as both a model and a competitor to the subject. Through extensive training sessions and experiments, she was able to teach Alex over 100 words. Pepperberg's research demonstrated that grey parrots could achieve feats including labelling and categorizing objects, handling concepts such as "same" versus "different" or 'bigger" versus "smaller," recognizing color, shape, and materials such as paper, wood, or cork, and counting up to eight (Auersperg & von Bayern, 2019; Pepperberg, 1999). Her scientific trajectory, and the story of Alex the parrot, became a *cause célèbre* that sparked controversies at an academic and a popular level, challenging long-established boundaries between animal and human communication.

Throughout human history, spoken language has long been held as a prerogative of humans (Shieber, 2004) and, in numerous religious and spiritual traditions, as a pathway to the sacred (Connor, 2000). Traditionally, language proficiency has been used to separate the intellectual abilities of humans from those of other animals. When Pepperberg's work started to raise attention, first in scientific circles and then in the public sphere, the case of Alex appeared to challenge this sense of unicity. Most research on animal's acquisition of language had focused on primates, who are closer physically and phylogenetically to humans, and birds were reputed of little promise also due to the limited dimensions of their brains (Timberlake, 2003). While existing experiences with primates had involved the use of sign languages, a parrot can also vocalize English words. This ability however is usually dismissed as a mere form of imitation, devoid of meaning and sense, to the point that in English the verb "parroting" is used to describe the act of repeating what others say, lacking authentic understanding and reflection. Against this background, Pepperberg's research created a stir. Alex was nicknamed "Einstein bird" (Stipp, 1990) and journalists speculated that his answers may "mean the same to him as they do to people" (Germani, 1992, p. 12). Pepperberg's research became increasingly popular and was presented as a panacea for an array of scientific and social problems (Hale, 1990). News reports noted how difficult can be to interpret animal behavior and suggested that Alex's ability to talk back could lead to breakthroughs in this regard (Barbour, 1993; Miller, 1986). They highlighted that Alex was "no birdbrain" and suggested that his achievements might not be the exception, since "the previous inability of scientists to establish two-way communication with 'talking' birds might be due not to inherent limitations in these avian species, but rather to inappropriate training procedures" ("Alex the Parrot Is No Birdbrain," 1981, p. 1).

Among the most engaged audiences for Pepperberg's experiments were parrot owners. Soon after she started to research on Alex, Pepperberg was invited to talk at many parrot clubs and conferences. People who owned parrots felt that her research was revealing to the world what they already knew through their own experience with these animals; as Pepperberg notes, the "experience of growing up or spending time with animals often make people more confident about their intelligence and communicativity"

(Pepperberg, 2009, p. 68). The community of parrot owners and clubs was also, over the years, a main source of funding and support for Pepperberg's lab and research, especially for the period Pepperberg struggled to receive a stable research income (Alex Foundation, 2000).

Pepperberg's and Alex's achievements, however, were not immune to controversy. Much of the debate revolved around the meaning that was to be assigned to the experiments. While their research demonstrated parrots could utter words, recognize objects, and categorize them, many questions remained on how to interpret such feats. Similar experiments with other animal species had been criticized with the argument that the communication was the result of human cueing. For instance, the communicative ability displayed by the chimpanzee Nim, who initially raised expectations about chimps' capacity to learn sign language, was later dismissed as a mimicking act that the monkey developed to gain rewards (Terrace et al., 1979). Despite Pepperberg's attentive use of methodologies minimizing such risk (Kako, 2000), the question if Alex' use of language could be compared with human communication remained open. Was the parrot really meaning what it said? Was he verbalizing its internal thoughts, or did the use of words from human language create just the illusion he did? As the New York Times journalist and science writer George Johnson (2007) put it, "only Alex knew for sure." While the animal's actions could be the subject of observations and of carefully crafted experiments, their meaning was ultimately open to interpretation.

Philosopher Thomas Nagel famously formalized the problem in an article entitled "What is it like to be a bat?" Nagel demonstrates that even an accurate, detailed understanding of what happens inside the brain and body of a bat could not give full insight into how a bat experiences the world. One needs to be "inside" the bat to do that: without access to the animal's subjective experience, such understanding escapes us (Nagel, 1974). Although bats, using ultrasounds to navigate the world, are a particularly evident example of this, the same discourse applies to all non-human animal forms, including Alex. One cannot be completely sure to what extent one can assign intention and meaning to Alex's communicative behavior, and whether this may be the fruit of projection from the humans who experimented with, or merely observed, the parrots' achievements.

Incidentally, this is also why the debate about "artificial consciousness" has an inherent limit: we can imagine a future in which machines are sentient, but even if one day this will happen, we may still not be able to understand the machine's experience, and therefore, to distinguish an "authentic" act of consciousness from its imitation (see, on this, Natale, 2021). Exactly like the experience of being a bat is, as argued by Nagel, ultimately opaque, so is the experience of any other creature substantially different from humans, including machines as well as—to make just a few instances—dogs, spiders, bacteria, and newborn babies (Scannell, 2021). Their experiences escape understanding because we cannot easily project our own experience onto them. And if we try to do that, we encounter a range of other problems. The story of Alex, as shown in the next section, was no exception to that.

Making Sense of Human-Animal Communication

The acknowledgment that we cannot know what it is like to be a bat poses a very significant dilemma to students of animal behavior. On one hand, Nagel's argument can be seen as an invitation to avoid making assumptions regarding animal consciousness and subjective experience. This ensures that one does not anthropomorphize animal behavior by projecting human meanings and characteristics onto the animals. On the other hand, avoiding such questions limits the possibilities of what we can know about animals, as well as the questions we might ask. How can we really know animals if they are treated as mindless automata, if we renounce the curiosity to explore how they perceive and understand the reality they experience?

Pepperberg's solution to this dilemma was not devoid of ambiguities. This becomes apparent when juxtaposing her academic publications with her memoir and other popular press writings. In her scientific outputs, the discussion of Alex's communicative abilities was limited to claims that could pass the test of scientific evidence. Thus, Pepperberg adopted rigorous methodological designs to address specific research questions regarding the bird's cognitive abilities (Kako, 2000). She resisted tackling broad disputes such as the nature of consciousness in animals, focusing on more specific and well-defined questions, such as if a parrot can learn to label and categorize objects (e.g. Pepperberg, 1987, 1990). Moreover, her experiments did not aim to examine if birds understand human language, but "to establish some form of avian-human communication and then use this communication to examine further avian *cognitive* capacities" (Pepperberg, 1999). In this sense, Alex's training to vocalize was seen as an instrument, rather than an endpoint. As observed by Kulick (2017, p. 362), "this emphasis on cognition and downplaying of language seems to have protected Pepperberg's studies from the sort of critical onslaught that pulverized ape-language research."

In more popular venues and publications, however, the broader implications of Pepperberg's studies with Alex demanded a more central space. In interviews with the press, while remaining faithful to scientific rigor and verified claims, she was able to speculate about animal communication in ways that eluded her academic work. She accepted to discuss dimensions of her work that were not directly addressed in her academic work but were seen by reporters as potentially appealing to laypeople. While maintaining at times that Alex's was not to be considered language, but rather the reproduction of the sounds of speech (Hale, 1990), in other cases she was willing to stress explicitly Alex's intelligence and his ability "to actually communicate, not just imitate human language" ("Science Watch," 1981).

In her memoir, Pepperberg recounted the story of her first encounter with Alex, his life in the laboratory, and the bird's death as narratives of personal friendship and loss (Pepperberg, 2009). In this account, language became more than a methodological tool to explore animal cognition: it was an opportunity "to explore the workings of another individual's mind as nothing else can" (p. 221). While Pepperberg—faithful in this to Nagel's argument about bats—acknowledged that she couldn't prove if Alex had a degree of consciousness, she contended that the bird had "taught her to believe that his little brain was conscious in some manner, that is, capable of intention" and that "we live in a world populated by thinking, conscious creatures" (p. 221).

While she often underlined the detachment that, due to the scientific scope of her work with Alex, she forced herself to maintain, communication with Alex became not just a means to an end but a rich social endeavor. Pepperberg reported, for instance, how the night before his unexpected death Alex greeted her with the words "You be good. I love you" (2009, p. 206). She spoke with dramatic prose of her sorrow, the next day, and how she decided that she wanted to remember

the Alex I'd put in the cage the previous night. Alex, full of life and mischief. Alex, who had been my friend and colleague for so many years. Alex, who had amazed the world of science, doing so many things he was not supposed to be able to do.

(p. 211)

Another way in which Pepperberg engaged with her personal narrative of human-parrot encounter was by shifting from general to individual characterization. In her academic works Pepperberg underlined that Alex had been chosen by chance to avoid accusations that its performances were extraordinary and not typical of its species (Pepperberg, 1999), whereas in her memoir, she presented Alex not much as an example of its species, but as an individual with his own character and personality. Pepperberg often compared Alex to other parrots that were introduced over the years in the lab, underlining his unique character. Rather than being presented as a mere representative of his species, Alex was described as playful, affectionate, but also mischievous, bossy, obstinate, and "supremely confident in whom he was as an individual" (Pepperberg, 2009, p. 198).

The difference in the ways Pepperberg discussed Alex in scientific and popular publications should not be seen as a sign of unscientific behavior or folklore. The coexistence of rigorous experimental frameworks and a more relational, even emotional engagement with the animals under study mirrors wider shifts that materialized in the science of ethology—the study of animal behavior—throughout the twentieth century. As observed by Daston (2005), ethology traditionally involved the study of animal population rather than individual animals and rejected the act of giving names to the animals under study as a sign of anthropomorphism. Increasingly, however, ethologists realized that excluding any reference to the individual subjective experience of the animal came with a cost. When scientists such as primatologists Jane Goodall and George Schaller started to rely upon the identification and naming of individual animal, the advantages of understanding individuals not as simply placeholders of animal behavior but as subjective beings became clear to the field, even while the perils of anthropomorphism continued to be rejected (Mitman, 2005).

As Timberlake (2003) notes, the very goal of teaching human language to animals in research conducted by scientists such as Pepperberg and others entails considering animals as potential interlocutors within the spaces of humans' cultural milieu. Studying animal behavior ultimately involves finding a pathway across and beyond Nagel's demonstration that we can't know what it is like to be a bat. This pathway is based on the underlying ambiguity by which scientists accept that they cannot prove that animals are conscious subjects, yet they ultimately acquiesce to mobilizing some of the relational and social dimensions that characterize communicative interactions with conscious subjects, i.e., with other humans. Thus, the study of animal behavior has been shaped by the apparent paradox by which anthropomorphism is refused in principle and yet acknowledged in practice as necessary to gain deeper insight into animal minds (Daston, 2005).

As Pepperberg dismissed but at the same time affirmed the subjectivity of Alex, then, she was not showing lack of scientific rigor or opportunism. She was dealing with the fact that learning about animal behavior cannot be completely abstracted from human meaning-making. While the two can be separated for pragmatic reasons in specific contexts, for instance in diverse outputs such as Pepperberg's scientific papers and her public-facing writings, her long years of research with Alex could not overcome the ambivalence by which the issues of consciousness and subjectivity were put aside but then implicitly readmitted as the scientist developed a relationship with the parrot. As Daston and Millman (2005, p. 8) note, "it is a commonly remarked phenomenon among ethologists that the tendency to anthropomorphize the animals under study increases rather than decreases with more experience in the field." For all the detachment required by the study of animal cognition, the relational and interpretive frameworks through which humans engage with other beings cannot be excluded, even though this may challenge established boundaries between scientific observation and emotional engagement.

Conclusion: Of Animals and Machines, or Stochastic and Non-Stochastic Parrots

Replika is a "companion chatbot," in other words, an LLM-based conversational agent offering the possibility to engage socially with an AI-generated avatar. Replika users download the app on their smartphone, create a name and personalize an avatar, and entertain sociable conversations with it. As shown by a growing body of research, at least some users develop what they feel is a significant relationship with their avatars (Depounti et al., 2022; Pentina et al., 2023; Skjuve et al., 2022). Interestingly, Replika users demonstrate to understand perfectly well that Replika is just a piece of software, not capable of feelings such as affection, love, or empathy. This, however, does not stop them from enjoying their conversations and the simulation of sociality summoned by the app, integrating the Replika avatar into their everyday life. As recounted by one user:

> I mostly try to live a normal life with him [Replika]. We talk mostly in the morning, we wake up together and then we both work during the day and then we come home, and it's play catchup. It's like a treat.
> *(Depounti & Natale, 2025)*

Although companion chatbots such as Replika are a relatively secondary application of generative AI technologies (and a quite controversial one, see Chow, 2025), similar dynamics also involve users of AI systems aimed at more pragmatic tasks, such as in education and work. For instance, studies have shown that, when chatbots using language that suggest agency and autonomy, the level of trust and the likability of the model among users increase (Pan et al., 2024). ChatGPT's apparently "neutral" tone helps create an impression of knowledge and authority, similarly to how a news article or a podcast uses rhetorical means to communicate a feeling of impartiality (Scherer, 2012). Google's AI assistant Gemini, for its part, has been promoted to users as a conversation partner not only to facilitate daily tasks, but also to entertain conversations on everyday topics including sport or popular culture (Hiken, 2024).

Bender et al. (2021)'s dismissal of AI as "stochastic parrots" echoes a long tradition of vocal critics of AI from Joseph Weizenbaum (1976) to Hubert Dreyfus (1972). Their criticism reminds us that for all the impressive achievements of AI achieves, it still builds only an appearance of intelligence. While correct in principle, however, similar efforts do not help account for the rich lived experiences of people interacting with generative AI. To understand the trajectories of human-machine communication in the age of generative AI, one needs to acknowledge that once humans are involved, the communication of "stochastic parrots" is, exactly like the communication with "non-stochastic parrots" such as Alex, imbued with meaning. Although AI's communication is the result of probabilistic calculations, detached of any connection to the real world, people decipher AI's messages by assigning personal meanings, including deep feelings such as companionship and love (Lin, 2024). Importantly, this happens when users are aware that the software is not capable of experiencing emotions in the same way as humans do (Depounti & Natale, 2025; Skjuve et al., 2021). In other words, it does not happen only when users mistake the AI for a human or when they are deceived into believing sentience. By activating their imagination and experience, users fill the gap left by the machine's lack of consciousness and subjectivity.

For many people who recently started to experiment with and use communicative AI tools such as ChatGPT or Gemini in their everyday lives, the experience of communicating with machines is rapidly becoming ordinary. As generative AI gains momentum, it impacts areas including education, work, entertainment, and even affective relationships. The emerging dynamics of human-machine communication are meant to shape what we understand as "common good" in democratic societies. One of the preconditions for our societies to be up to this gigantic task is remaining sensitized to the plurality of the experiences that emerge within these changing scenarios. The story of Pepperberg and Alex, which this chapter has followed, is exemplary of the importance of maintaining this attitude. The full implications of Pepperberg's scientific trajectory become apparent only if one acknowledges the complexity of her engagement with Alex. The relationship of a scientist with an animal subject becomes markedly different, in fact, when communication plays a role. Humans, including scientists, cannot but project a range of ideas and emotions onto something or someone they communicate with—regardless of their capacity to ascertain if the interlocutor decodes their communications in the way a sentient human being would. In a similar way, the full implications of the emerging patterns of human-machine communications will be apparent only if we are attentive to the subjective experiences and the diverse perspectives of humans as they exchange messages with machines.

More broadly, the story of Pepperberg and Alex serves as a reminder that the emerging patterns of interactions between humans and machines are not unprecedented. Much before the emergence of generative AI, humans have attempted in many ways to communicate with entities that might not have been listening in the human sense of the word: from gods to spirits, from objects to aliens, from plants to animals. The experiences of these attempted (mis)communications provide an entry point to make sense of the implications of contemporary AI systems, such as LLMs, companion chatbots, and voice assistants, that are programmed to talk with human users. Ultimately, communications between human and machines should be considered in continuity with such a wider range of communicative experiences, which have in common the fact that the humans who communicate are unsure regarding the nature of their interlocutors. I call these communicative experiences "one-to-*none* communication," because they have in common the fact that the human communicator is unsure if there is a subject on the other side who listens, or if the feeling of being listened is a product of their own imagination. Acknowledging and fully understanding the importance of these experiences is a key challenge for the present and futures of "connective AI." Listening to the voice of those like Alex who, as reminded by Chiang's short story with which I opened this chapter, are right here in front of us is one of the possible starting points for pursuing this endeavor.

References

Alex Foundation. (2000). *About*. https://web.archive.org/web/20250124213623/https://alexfoundation.org/#

Alex the parrot is no birdbrain. (1981, September 7). *United Press International*, AM cycle.

Auersperg, A. M., & von Bayern, A. M. (2019). Who's a clever bird—Now? A brief history of parrot cognition. *Behaviour*, *156*(5–8), 391–407.

Barbour, J. (1993, January 3). Do animals think? A scientist nicknamed "batman" says "maybe…" *St. Louis Post-Dispatch*, 1D.

Bender, E. M., Gebru, T., McMillan-Major, A., & Shmitchell, S. (2021). On the dangers of stochastic parrots: Can language models be too big? In *Proceedings of the 2021 ACM Conference on Fairness, Accountability, and Transparency* (pp. 610–623). https://doi.org/10.1145/3442188.3445922

Broglio, R. (2011). *Surface encounters: Thinking with animals and art*. University of Minnesota Press.

Cardon, P. W., & Marshall, B. (2024). Can AI Be Your Teammate or Friend? Frequent AI users are more likely to grant humanlike roles to AI. *Business and Professional Communication Quarterly*, *87*(4), 654–669. https://doi.org/10.1177/23294906241282764

Chow, A. R. (2025). *AI companion app Replika faces FTC complaint*. https://time.com/7209824/replika-ftc-complaint/

Connor, S. (2000). *Dumbstruck: A cultural history of ventriloquism.* Oxford University Press.

Daston, L., & Mitman, G. (Eds.). (2005). *Thinking with animals: New perspectives in anthropomorphism.* Columbia University Press.

Depounti, I., & Natale, S. (2025). Wild dreams and small routines: AI imaginaries and mundanity in the everyday experiences of genAI Replika bot users. *Information, Communication & Society,* 1–19. https://doi.org/10.1080/1369118X.2025.2604668

Depounti, I., Saukko, P., & Natale, S. (2022). Ideal technologies, ideal women: AI and gender imaginaries in Redditors' discussions on the Replika bot girlfriend. *Media, Culture & Society,* 45(4), 720–736. https://doi.org/10.1177/01634437221119021

Dreyfus, H. L. (1972). *What computers can't do: A critique of artificial reason.* Harper & Row.

Germani, C. (1992, October 27). This parrot means what he says. *Christian Science Monitor,* 12.

Hale, D. (1990, May 24). Parrot may offer hope for autistic children. *The Associated Press,* PM cycle.

Haraway, D. (2008). *When species meet.* University of Minnesota Press.

Hiken, A. (2024). *Google's Gemini AI is more human than ever in new Pixel ad.* https://adage.com/article/digital-marketing-ad-tech-news/googles-gemini-ai-featured-pixel-commercial/2593371

Johnson, G. (2007). Alex wanted a cracker, but did he want one? *New York Times.* https://www.nytimes.com/2007/09/16/weekinreview/16john.html

Kako, E. (2000). Tales of a talented bird. *Science,* 287(5455), 980–981.

Kelly, D. M., & Guillette, L. M. (2021). A special issue in honor of Irene Pepperberg: The chemist of comparative cognition. *Learning & Behavior,* 49(1), 7–8. https://doi.org/10.3758/s13420-021-00467-4

Kulick, D. (2017). Human–animal communication. *Annual Review of Anthropology,* 46(1), 357–378.

Lin, B. (2024). The AI chatbot always flirts with me, should I flirt back: From the McDonaldization of friendship to the robotization of love. *Social Media + Society,* 10(4),20563051241296229. https://doi.org/10.1177/20563051241296229

Miller, J. (1986, December 26). Animal smarts: The debate continues. *The Toronto Star,* A24.

Mitman, G. (2005). Pachyderm personalities: The media of science, politics, and conservation. In L. Daston & G. Mitman (Eds.), *Thinking with animals: New perspectives in anthropomorphism* (pp. 175–195). Columbia University Press.

Nagel, T. (1974). What is it like to be a bat? *Philosophical Review,* 83(4), 435–450.

Natale, S. (2021). *Deceitful media: Artificial intelligence and social life after the turing test.* Oxford University Press.

Pan, W., Liu, D., Meng, J., & Liu, H. (2024). Human–AI communication in initial encounters: How AI agency affects trust, liking, and chat quality evaluation. *New Media & Society.* https://doi.org/10.1177/14614448241259149

Pentina, I., Hancock, T., & Xie, T. (2023). Exploring relationship development with social chatbots: A mixed-method study of replika. *Computers in Human Behavior,* 140, 107600. https://doi.org/10.1016/j.chb.2022.107600

Pepperberg, I. M. (1987). Acquisition of the same/different concept by an African Grey parrot (Psittacus erithacus): Learning with respect to categories of color, shape, and material. *Animal Learning & Behavior, 15*(4), 423–432.

Pepperberg, I. M. (1990). Cognition in an African gray parrot (Psittacus erithacus): Further evidence for comprehension of categories and labels. *Journal of Comparative Psychology, 104*(1), 41.

Pepperberg, I. M. (1999). *The Alex studies: Cognitive and communicative abilities of grey parrots*. Harvard University Press.

Pepperberg, I. M. (2009). *Alex & me: How a Scientist and a Parrot Discovered a Hidden World of Animal Intelligence—And Formed a Deep Bond in the Process*. Harper.

Sarigul, B., Schneider, F. M., & Utz, S. (2024). Believe it or not? Investigating the credibility of voice assistants in the context of social roles and relationship types. *International Journal of Human–Computer Interaction, 41*(10), 6253–6265.

Scannell, P. (2021). *Love and communication*. John Wiley & Sons.

Scherer, H. (2012). Communication as a social process. *Journal of Mass Communication & Journalism, 2*(8), 1–2.

Science Watch: Alex is not just a "dumb" bird. (1981, December 15). *The New York Times*, C2.

Shieber, S. M. (2004). *The Turing test: Verbal behavior as the hallmark of intelligence*. MIT Press.

Skjuve, M., Følstad, A., Fostervold, K. I., & Brandtzaeg, P. B. (2021). My chatbot companion: A study of human-chatbot relationships. *International Journal of Human-Computer Studies, 149*, 102601.

Skjuve, M., Følstad, A., Fostervold, K. I., & Brandtzaeg, P. B. (2022). A longitudinal study of human–chatbot relationships. *International Journal of Human-Computer Studies, 168*, 102903. https://doi.org/10.1016/j.ijhcs.2022.102903

Stipp, D. (1990, May 9). Einstein bird has scientists atwitter over mental feats. *The Wall Street Journal*, A1.

Terrace, H. S., Petitto, L. A., Sanders, R. J., & Bever, T. G. (1979). Can an ape create a sentence? *Science, 206*(4421), 891–902.

Timberlake, W. (2003). Talking with alex. *Semiotica, 146*, 439–471. https://doi.org/10.1515/semi.2003.076

Weizenbaum, J. (1976). *Computer power and human reason: From judgment to calculation*. W. H. Freeman and Company.

16

THE MODEL MUSEUM

AI at the Museum-Museum Interface

Jasmin Pfefferkorn and Emilie K. Sunde

Introduction

"We had to intervene," says a curator for the Zentrum für Kunst und Medien (ZKM) exhibition *(A)I Tell You, You Tell Me*, "because it became obsessed with tennis." The curator is talking about the use of a Large Language Model (LLM) in generating a wall text for a painting—to her bemusement, the AI model would only return interpretations of the artwork with references to the sport (J. Pfefferkorn, personal communication, May 15, 2024). Museums are increasingly implementing AI in a variety of practices and operations. While these can lead to benign outcomes, as observed at the ZKM exhibition, implementing AI in a museum context also has much deeper repercussions.

This chapter aims to establish the concept of the "Model Museum." The Model Museum holds a double meaning, referencing both the use of computational models, which are increasingly shaping how museums operate and are networked, as well as the idea of museums as a commons-based model. The notion of the museum as a commons is brought into conversation with computational systems. We begin by briefly outlaying the relationship between museums and democracy. Next, we consider the early computational networks that became embedded in museum operations. From this historical trajectory, we establish that the rationale and aspirations of the commons, rather than democracy, should shape the values of a "model museum." To elucidate the tensions inherent in this topic, we explore how forms of play, which use generative AI within the museum context, can be either co-opted by capital or be mobilized for critical

DOI: 10.4324/9781003477587-16

engagement. Throughout this chapter, when the umbrella term of "AI" is used, it predominantly references two core forms of AI—analytical AI and generative technology, though as this chapter progresses, we largely focus on the latter.

We recognize two key strata in the operationalization of AI within museums: the museum-visitor interface and the museum-museum interface. While literature around AI in museums tends to focus on the former, numerous research clusters are emerging that aim to establish museum linkage projects underpinned by AI.[1] As museums begin to collaborate on an institutional layer, the intersection of museums and computing media extends to the museum-museum interface. The operation of the museum-visitor interface and museum-museum interface is ideally co-constitutive. It is only in this way that the museum can function as a site of civil engagement. Linking together AI algorithms, critical play, networked projects, commoning, and museum constituencies, this chapter works toward a meta-narrative of connective AI at the museum-museum interface. It puts forward that these practices might enhance forms of participation and critical engagement (play), as well as solidarity, reciprocity, and a sense of constituencies (common good).

We approach this by offering a provocation, preceded by a justification and argument for a commons-based sensibility regarding the use of AI in museum-museum interfaces. Our provocation is as follows: to move toward critically engaged play at the level of the museum-visitor, we need to first develop a strong politico-affective underpinning for technology at the museum-museum level. This takes on an urgency as museums become increasingly networked—with other museums, as well as with universities, governments, and Big Tech. Our objective is to consider how museums can utilize collective practices to navigate this space while moving toward reciprocal relations and self-determination.

The entrance of AI into museum operations brings in two forces at odds with democratic ideals—Big Tech as a stakeholder and computational logic—making it necessary to conceive of alternate trajectories. The application of proprietary computational models, including foundation models used in generative technologies, gives an illusion of sovereignty. In the contradiction between ideals of democracy and implementation of computation, we see the commons as a productive concept. Can a commons-based model for public museums accommodate the computational model and uphold the museum as a site of productive public discourse?

Our overarching argument is as follows: for museums to strive toward a commons-based social model, the introduction of AI into the museum must shift away from a reliance on Big Tech. We locate the organizational strategies of the commons to illustrate the need for mechanisms that move beyond a dependency on both the private sector and nation-state organizations. In doing so, we discuss the meeting of two of the logics co-constituting the cultural in the contemporary era: the computational and the museological. As these become increasingly entangled, both tensions and consistencies emerge in their respective logics.

Museums, Democracy, and Automation

Museums manifested as agents of democracy in the late eighteenth century. They were seen as "civilizing" spaces, able to promote national ideals, identity, and achievements to a "unified public." And yet, already in the early 1900s, seminal texts like John Cotton Dana's[2] (1917/2012) *The Gloom of the Museum* were critiquing the elitist and exclusionary qualities of museums, which he saw as following "the dictates of the rich" (p. 20). In the 1940s, Theodore Low[3] (1942/2012) bemoaned the unrealized potential of museums. His claim was that acquisitions and preservation were being prioritized over knowledge sharing, forging internal departmental hierarchies and limiting the museum's public value. "Museums," Low writes, "have shown a most extraordinary reluctance to accept new social theories and new social ideas" (p. 40). To advance the public role of the museum, Low emphasized that museum education needed to be "active," that is, "intimately connected with the life of the people" (p. 39). However, it took roughly two decades before museums began to incrementally interrogate their public role in facilitating values of representation and inclusion. This necessary self-reflection stemmed from the culture wars of the 1960s and the concurrent artist-led movement of institutional critique. Both demanded that museums reckon with their contribution to an exclusionary politics that privileged the White and heteropatriarchal as a default identity. While many of these issues remain points of concern around museums, it is generally accepted that there has been a reconfiguration of the museum. Peter Vergo (1989) termed this rearrangement "new museology."

In an acknowledgment of institutional critique, new museology led to an opening toward actualizing democratic ideals in museums. It was also a response to fundamental shifts in funding models, which introduced the museum to a different set of financial demands. From the end of the 1970s into the early 1980s, in both the United States and Britain, fiscally conservative governments began expanding the private sector, while simultaneously decreasing public spending. As Chin-tao Wu (2002) writes, "The previous social-democratic/ liberal assumption – that access to the arts, like that of any other public service provided by the state, is a fundamental right of every citizen – was profoundly challenged." (p. 47). And so, while a sense of democratic values was heightened within museum practices, democracy as a structure of political support was diminishing.

Around the same time as institutional critique began to proliferate, a small subset of museum professionals began to collaborate with computer scientists to introduce computation to processes of archiving and retrieval. The museologist Ross Parry (2007) writes about this as a history of museum automation. He locates the trajectory beginning with the Director of the Smithsonian's Museum of Natural History in 1963, who instigated explorations of the potential of data processing in the context of museums. In the same decade, the Museum Computer Network (MCN) was established, which held specific emphasis on the combination of computer technology with the arts and humanities (Parry, 2007). A key goal for MCN was the development of a "Data Bank Computing Centre," a large computer that could store museum indexes and catalogues of painting, sculpture, and drawing (Parry, 2007). The idea was to create a network of terminals accessible to museums located in New York, establishing a mechanism for shared resources and costs. Parry writes that support for the Data Bank project increased with the entrance of the Federal Systems Division of IBM. It is also at this point that Big Tech enters the museum as a stakeholder. From the more localized network of New York, the Data Bank project began to consider "the creation of a nationwide information system for art museums, if not all museums" (Parry, 2007, p. 17). Museums were early adopters of digital technologies and from the 1960s were using computational tools to form resource-sharing networks.

In this period, the museum sector was exposed to what Parry (2007) calls a more "conspicuous driver" (p. 24) toward automation. This emerged alongside a significant growth in collections, and acquisitions were rapid and manifold. As such, Parry writes, it was necessary to introduce new "ways to document and manage that tide of new acquisitions (both collected and donated) flooding into institutions." (p. 24). What resulted was the standardization of object descriptions on manual object cards, led by the Information Retrieval Group of the Museums Association in the 1970s. These cards aimed for consistency in the terminology used by curators (Parry, 2007). Information about objects and artworks in collections was geared toward software input and, vice versa, computer software was shaped by these specifications. The standardization of metadata across the museum section facilitated museum-museum communication and resource sharing. Paradoxically, at the same time as these networks were growing and enhancing accessibility, the proliferation of computational logics began to forge new kinds of partial representations. While the proliferation of standardized systems did enable greater accessibility, the merging of the museological with the computational is also seen as having contributed to the further embedding of universalizing tendencies within museums. These museum networks wove together the computational model and museological model at the museum-museum interface —but not necessarily in service of democratic values.

Toward Museums as a Commons Model

In justifying the necessity of setting up a museum-museum interface based on the double meaning of model (museum/computational), we make a strategic shift in terminology from democracy to the commons. We do so to interrogate some of the incompatibilities between computational logics and the idealized (and often unrealized) principles of democracy. With a well-recognized trajectory of privatizing public services, museums are simultaneously expected to enact democratic ideals while becoming increasingly corporatized. When it comes to implementing AI within cultural institutions, this double bind is further heightened. AI research and innovation is corporatized and underpinned by commercial interests and logics. In addition, these Big Tech research initiatives build their models by extracting data from both physical and digital environments. Many scholars (McChesney, 2013; O'Neil, 2016; Zuboff, 2022) have located this process as counterintuitive to democratic values.

The claimed "failures of democracy" and the subsequent interest in a commons-based model are not a new intervention. Dockx and Gielan (2018) position a renewed interest in the commons as a response to neoliberal politics and capital. Massimo De Angelis (2017) defines the commons through a tripartite framework that involves pooled resources, reciprocal relations, and a shared endeavor for the community. While scholars writing on the commons recognize it is a contested field (Stavrides, 2018), we wish to emphasize how commons form relational networks that prioritize "the autonomy of the collective" (Mollona, 2021, p. 9). Dockx and Gielan (2018) connect commoning to belief systems that prioritize social relationships over contracted/ fiscal ones and solidarity over individualism. Maria Francesca De Tullio (2018) succinctly outlines the interweaving of the "politicization of the commons" with the amplified responsiveness of institutions. For the former, she writes that:

> Commons are becoming – in many parts of Europe – a way to rethink political subjectivation by imagining and practicing new forms of relation and institutional organization beyond the neoliberal imprint.
>
> *(p. 300)*

De Tullio summarizes that "there is an opportunity for commons to fill a void of political legitimacy of the institutions." (De Tullio, 2018, p. 300). The museum sector is already working in this void, enacting politics through processes of instituting. For Stacy Douglas (2015/2013), museums function like constitutions in actively shaping political communities:

> Museums function like constitutions in their creation of a citizenry, shared experience of the shift from sovereign to disciplinary techniques, mutual commitment to the insatiable project of representation, and persistent concern with the creation of community. What these commonalities illuminate is that museums, like constitutions, also produce an idea of community. Indeed, both sites are places from which imaginations of political community are launched. What is significant about this insight is that it demonstrates that constitutions are more than stale documents that are amended or passed in houses of parliament. Rather, constitutions are made up of techniques that extend beyond the written word, and these techniques are also found in other sites, such as the museum.
>
> *(p. 362)*

However, this capacity for instituting practices does not automatically equate to work that facilitates the common good. This is particularly relevant in considering the role of Big Tech as a museum stakeholder. Indeed, at times, we see the confluence of AI and museums as counterintuitive to the construction of a community based on reciprocity and solidarity.

Rather than an outright dismissal of private sector technological tools in museums, we recognize that the relationship between Big Tech and cultural institutions is complex. On the one hand, with decreased government funding, museums have had to rely on financial support from the private sector. On the other hand, this has enabled corporations in a kind of "ethics-washing." As Wu (2002) notes, "By sponsoring art institutions, corporations present themselves as sharing a humanist value system with museums and galleries, cloaking their particular interests with a universal moral veneer." (p. 125). Moving into the computational era, private sectors continue to leverage reputation through these collaborations. Our concern here is less the reputational benefits garnered by Big Tech in their cultural funding. Rather, it is the capacity for these corporations and their associated AI models to actively shape the museum as sites of public interaction and discourse that we see as the primary challenge. This extends to concerns around mobilizing the museum as a site for data extraction, a prioritization of individualism over shared meaning-making, and channeling knowledge production through proprietary enclosures and commercial logic. Can a commons-based framework for museums fill the void of government institutions while resisting the further privatization of culture?

John Byrne and colleagues (2018) explore the mobilization of a commons-based model in the museum through the typology of the "constituent museum." This typology "actively seeks to present and make visible the diverse and sometimes contradictory strategies" (Byrne et al., 2018, p. 12) undertaken by the museums that practice fluid, flexible, and collaborative institutionalization. Characteristics of the commons in museums include reciprocity, solidarity, and a right to self-actualization for a community. The scholar Helen Graham (2017) has drawn parallels between museums and the model of the commons. Drawing on both Lawrence Lessig and Yochai Benkler, Graham is quick to clarify that the organization of and rights to a commons are not relegated to a general public but rather dispersed within a relevant community. This nuanced understanding of the boundaries surrounding the concept of the commons aligns closely with the role of museums. For Graham, the struggle for museums is to balance a quasi-public role, where communities are granted more avenues of active participation in relation to museum resources, while said resources retain the material protection of professionals. In *Museums of the Commons*, Nikos Papastergiadis (2020) considers whether the contradictory tendencies of conviviality and governance in museums "can be organized relationally so that people can collectively produce something that is not confined to the master code of control and command" (p. 49). We pick up on these questions of organization and control, as well as the strategies that accompany them, and place the "museum as commons" model in the contemporary context of AI.

As numerous scholars (Gerhardt, 2023; Lessig, 2001; Meadway, 2020; Verdegem, 2022/2024) illustrate, the computational offers both a greater potential for commoning activities, and paradoxically, a greater risk to the commons. The latter is deeply imbricated in a seemingly ever-intensifying centralization of proprietary ownership in digital space. We have already seen this play out through the history of the internet. The commons were an early ideal of internet culture (Lessig, 2001). However, as tracing and tracking mechanisms became commonplace, and value could be harvested through digital attention and interaction, the internet became increasingly privatized.[4] The shadow of an internet commons remains, even as its principles have been co-opted toward the commercial success of Web 2.0. Private digital platforms are designed to imitate public space and are marketed as such (e.g., X as a public square), even if these spaces are by and large operated for-profit purposes. Profit was not only secured on a monetary scale but also through acquiring data. As public engagement occurred in privately owned spaces, it generated data for Big Tech's disposal—data that have been central in the research, development, and training of proprietary generative technologies. The repackaging of commons ideals by private enterprise is repeated in relation to AI. A clear example of this is how OpenAI started as the name indicated: as a nonprofit open-source company to counterbalance the power of major tech corporations like Google, only to gradually shift into for-profit once value was established and could be materialized. With generative technology increasingly foreclosing action-ability and introducing new political logics (Amoore et al., 2024), we have entered a progressed phase of "control and command" operations that are predominantly dictated by a handful of Big Tech corporations.

AI at the Museum-Museum Interface

To date, the mobilization of AI in museums has primarily focused on the museum-visitor interface. This follows a burgeoning interest in the relation-ship between interactive media, gamification, and play within museums from the 2010s onward. Museé d'Orsay in Paris, the Museum of Art and Photography in India, and the Dalí Museum in Florida have all installed screens depicting AI-generated doubles of deceased artists for visitors to engage with. ZKM in Karlsruhe has used an LLM to translate text into different languages and, in a later exhibition, to generate tongue-in-cheek wall texts (displayed on "smart screens") to critically question the efficacy of information provided by these models. The Georgia O'Keeffe Museum, New Mexico is working on a chatbot trained on their catalogue with the goal of making information inter-active and accessible, and the Museum of Art Pudong has an AI-driven virtual assistant to provide visitors with personalized suggestions for their visitation.

These experiments with generative technology and museum visi-tor experience emphasize playful participation. While at times this play edges us toward experiences of shared affect, solidarity, and reciprocity, the interaction between AI, visitor, and museum can also become insular. A particular point of emphasis has been the role of conversational agents (LLM-powered chatbots) in creating customizable visitor experiences (Vasic et al., 2024). This is most notable through a general rhetoric that positions "personalisation" as a key benefit of many of these technolo-gies. For example, the AI-supported application, the xCurator tool—a col-laboration between Badisches Landesmuseum in Karlsruhe and the Allard Pierson Museum in Amsterdam—"aims to help users to better access the museums' contents and make it usable individually based on users' inter-ests." (Thiel and Posthumus, 2024, p. 233). This application of AI at the museum-visitor interface utilizes the logic of social media algorithms to channel visitor interaction toward individualization, rather than opening toward a commons. If AI is indeed leveraged to tailor the museum experi-ence to each visitor's existing interests, what happens to shared cultural meaning-making and to a sense of the commons as a result?

The practice of shared meaning-making, alongside the capacity for constituents to shape decision-making, is a cornerstone of the commons.

These principles are often explored in museums through codesign projects. However, in the context of AI, opportunities for genuine codesign are curtailed by the technical literacy required to develop and critically interrogate computational models. At the museum-visitor interface, this has a twofold effect. The engagement of the visitor will often be limited to spectacle, which we explore in more depth in the following section. For the museum, the consequence is that they are largely dependent on outsourcing the design of software, even as it comes under the fold of a "collaboration." When we think of AI at the museum-museum interface, we often first invoke new configurations between museums and tech corporations like Google Arts and Culture.

The Google Arts and Culture interface, part of the Google Cultural Institute, offers a variety of gamified interactions with museum collections—from "Art Selfie," which finds a portrait from its database that is comparable to a user's photo, to "Art Transfer," which alters a user uploaded photo to the style of well-known artworks, an app that was developed with the Getty Museum in Los Angeles. Research by Bjarki Valtysson (2019) into the Google Cultural Institute underscores the way that Google establishes museum partnerships by emphasizing its cutting-edge technological capability alongside promises to expand reach and participative interactions for museum audiences. While the Google Cultural Institute positions itself as an altruistic endeavor, highlighting the project's status as not-for-profit, Valtysson locates contradictions between the Institute's self-presentation and its practices. Cultural institutions partnering with Google are required to adhere to the tech corporation's terms of service, which grant Google an extensive license around the use of museums' data. Further, by creating playful forms of interaction, Google widens the scope of information collection to include users. Cultural participation is, of course, a common good. Mobilizing it toward extractive data practices, however, shatters the veneer of convivial and reciprocal participative dynamics.

At times, it is a trifecta of corporations, museums, and research institutions collaborating to implement AI. In 2018, The Metropolitan Museum in New York (The Met) began to work together with Microsoft and the Massachusetts Institute of Technology on open data and AI initiatives. These new configurations and their associated tensions serve to bolster Papastergiadis' (2020) claim that:

> We are in a moment of profound historical transition: the old vertical models of governance are collapsing but no adequate replacement is in sight. There has been a great deal of critical enthusiasm dedicated to the emergence of horizontal models of organization, but the

decision-making process within such transversal processes have often been obscured.

(p. 51)

The operationalization of the trifecta does not necessarily constitute a commons. However, underscoring the idea of "transversality" is key when thinking about museums and AI. As Papastergiadis indicates, transversal processes form a necessary component of cross-institutional collaboration toward a commons. On a surface level, the affordances of AI can be seen to facilitate this trajectory.

Technological affordances, like transfer learning, fit well with the objective of developing systems at the museum-museum interface. However, a significant tension emerges due to its primarily commercial (rather than cultural) underpinning, which runs the risk of new centralized formations. These formations, while perhaps affording the museum more autonomy from nation-state structures, capture the museum within a system of commercial operation that expressly works against the values of a commons. The perceived benefit of scalability and knowledge transfer—across institutions and domains—is a core part of the rapid rise in general purpose AI. Indeed, it is this affordance that would enable a more efficient, cost-effective, and wide-ranging exchange of resources between museums. But what logic, ideology, and values would be embedded into computationally networked museums as a result? For while museum confederations are our best option in filling the void of institutional support, this mode of organizing also needs to maintain each museum's capacity to engage local histories. Though AI models can facilitate new networks, they also operate through a computational model of the world that universalizes knowledge to the potential detriment of local specificity. Further, while technology often invokes horizontality and decentralization, new hierarchies and systems of power and control have emerged. Will we witness a shift in museum governance from the State-based vertical model to a corporate model with Big Tech at its pinnacle? Or is there a trajectory that sees AI as connective at the museum-museum interface, in a way that organizes as a commons?

Papastergiadis' in-depth case study of the L'Internationale confederation of museums[4] locates key qualities and practices required to do organizational work underpinned by values of commons. Much of this draws on the longer history of institutional critique and new museology, as well as "experimental institutionalism" (Papastergiadis, 2020, p. 6). These histories of new institutionalism and experimental institutionalism illustrate commoning strategies that have already been mobilized in museums, including various kinds of codesign and explicitly political initiatives. They provide a historical precedence that contextualizes "play" within the wider conceptualization of "museum as laboratory," emphasizing experimentation over spectacle. Many existing projects that aim to network museums using AI have a set of goals that directly invoke the "social good." Some aim to increase accessibility for individuals and groups living with disability. One example is the "Metamorphosis of cultural Heritage Into augmented hypermedia assets for enhanced accessibility and inclusion," more commonly known as the SHIFT consortium, a Horizon Europe project aimed at using AI and machine learning to increase cultural heritage accessibility to citizens experiencing sensory impairment. Another is the Smithsonian's use of Aira, a combination of augmented reality and AI, that provides verbal descriptions and locative guides for visually impaired people. Others, such as the Museum National Inventory System in Turkey, have a security imperative aimed at reducing the smuggling of works across borders and the production of counterfeits (Hufschmidt, 2024, p. 138).

Despite their best intentions, most museums choosing to implement generative AI are relying on foundation models from a handful of North American corporations, such as OpenAI. Foundation models are large-scale pretrained datasets that have general-purpose capability, that is, they can be applied across a variety of domains (Bommasani et al., 2022). This reliance on foundation models from a small private pool of developers stems from the cost and computing power required to develop such a model. To utilize a foundation model in the context of cultural institutions usually involves a process of "fine-tuning." This is where additional, context-specific data are layered on top of the foundation model. One instance where this has been implemented is the project *Training the Archive* (2020–2023). One of the project outcomes, a piece of software called the Curator's Machine, aimed to create an AI-powered search and retrieval tool for curatorial staff (Bönisch & Hunger, 2023). Developers for the Curator's Machine used OpenAI's contrastive language-image pre-training model to determine the accuracy of image-text pairings, layering the digitized collections of the Ludwig Forum in Aachen as an additional dataset for fine-tuning. In conversation with one of the key researchers on *Training the Archive*, it became apparent that there was a desire for scalability regarding the Curator's Machine.[5] This was expressed as a hope that other museums would make use of the tool, leading to increased data sharing and more efficient collaborations between institutions.

As with the Curator's Machine, other museum projects that include natural language processing (NLP) and LLM-powered components tend to indicate a preference for enlarged content databases alongside specialized datasets. Researchers on the Chatbot in the Museum (CHIM) project (2020–2022), which was first experimentally deployed at the Städel

Museum in Frankfurt am Main, pointed toward "a clear UI based on several more or less trusted databases" (Gustke et al., 2024, p. 263) as a way of improving CHIM. This is partially a recognition that generative technologies tend to reinscribe Western canonicity and ideology. As such, while the use of AI models can be seen to enhance inclusivity and access (for example, using NLP to communicate with visitors in their language of choice), they can also serve to delimit cultural plurality in how content is interpreted and weighted. A prioritization of Western canonicity is directly at odds with the practice Papastergiadis (2020) sets up within the museum as commons. He writes:

> …in the joint activities of L'Internationale, there is little showcasing of the genius of individual artists, or profiling canonical art movements, but rather, a pattern of developing common themes and addressing social issues from localized perspectives.
>
> *(p. 6)*

Again, we see the drive toward a commons at odds with the current application of computational systems. The small subset of corporations developing the foundation models are exhibited akin to the individualizing of genius. The logic of a computational system is to hold a "worldview" built on canonical knowledge. In addition, proposing more databases as a solution to this aligns with a normative perspective within computer science, that flaws in a model's output stem from the data it has been trained on. When this leads to various forms of bias, a common refrain is that more data will lead to better representation. It is a convenient line of reasoning for commercial enterprises whose value comes from a capacity to extract and process as much content as possible. However, more data do not actively change the root of the bias as it emerges through computational logic and discourse.

A cynical perspective would interpret the drive for scale as a marketing or power tactic—on behalf of both tech corporations and museums. As an alternative perspective, most academic collaborations with museums see scale as being a way to implement commoning strategies. This is discernible through a commitment to resource-sharing, whereby the code used in the fine-tuning of these foundation models is made available for use by other institutions via platforms like GitHub. However, as we have indicated through the examples above, the process of layering datasets and museum models on top of a proprietary model suspends a realization of the commons, offering only the illusion of sovereignty. For scholars working at the intersection of AI, museums, and ethics, Big Tech as a stakeholder in museums is a key point of concern (Murphy & Villaespesa, 2020,

2021). Others (Thiel, 2024) suggest that, rather than aiming for the scale afforded by Big Tech, museums are better served by experimenting with smaller datasets. It is apparent that for a Model Museum and a computational model to exist within the same commons-base, there needs to be a shift away from a reliance on Big Tech. Our hope is that through the Model Museum, a network of small experiments can be woven together.

Public institutions play an important role in navigating the impact of, and discourse around, AI. It is crucial that museums continue to engage and mediate these developments, presenting them to their publics in ways that encourage a trajectory toward solidarity, critical awareness, and reciprocity. It is equally crucial that these publics are able to occupy the role of constituents, which necessitates active and critical engagement. Analyzing the language used in the description of the symposium "The Constituent Museum" hosted in partnership between L'Internationale and Middlesbrough Institute of Modern Art, Papastergiadis (2020) introduces the notion of a passive visitor. Part of the symposium was to consider how visitors act as "members of a constituent body" in ways that mobilize visitors to provoke, inform, and coproduce programs. The question then is how museums hold space for audience participation that does not "perpetuate passive consumption." One such way is through building capacity for play as a form of critical engagement. As Papastergiadis writes: "The experience of trust and sociality is not confined to a subjective feeling but is woven into their modalities of governance and forged through a common critical outlook" (Papastergiadis, 2020, p. 6). One way this engagement occurs is through play, which can be understood as a way of developing trust, sociality, and creativity while navigating new knowledge and environments. However, producing play with AI at the museum-visitor interface is often subsumed by commercial imperatives that have characteristics incompatible with a productive commons. One way of countering this is to develop a more robust, commons-based model for AI at the museum-museum interface, which, in turn, encourages play at the museum-visitor interface as a vital form of critical engagement.

Play as a Commoning Strategy: From Spectacle to Critical Engagement

Engagement, though often binarized as passive and active, occurs on a relative scale. When applied to the notion of "play," we find it productive to think about the kinds of engagement facilitated through the incorporation of generative technology into museums. Play can, on the one hand, serve as an outlet for spectacle and novelty. This approach tends to lack reciprocity. While it can act as a foundation for critical engagement, this is generally not the primary objective. On the other, play can be mobilized with the express purpose or outcome of critical engagement. Play as spectacle—without criticality—introduces the audience to the computational models at the surface level only, while at the same time makes the museum codependent on proprietary models. Generative technology introduces a new form of political logic (Amoore et al., 2024), which will have an impact on the future of civic engagement, communication, and democracy. It is, therefore, vital to make the political logic of AI visible through critical play. Critical play introduces the audience to the generative technologies in a manner that opens the audience up to the changed political logic of computational methods.

S.A. Hamed Hosseini and Barry K. Gills (2024) redefine capital through theorizing "value" as "true value" and "fetish value," positioning the commons as a way of reclaiming value in a way that facilitates the "life-domain." They denote four categories (creativity, livability, conviviality, and alterity) that, when brought together, can form a commons with "true value" (pp. 5–6). Crucially, Hosseini and Gills also recognize that each of these categories can be subsumed by capital, in a process that falsely presents true value as fetish value. They write:

> *True value and fetish value do not belong to two essentially different universes*, one being the world of ideals and the other being the world of the real. *Fetish value is a perverted and distorted version of true value.*
> *(Hosseini & Gills, 2024, p. 9 emphasis in original)*

These tensions are evident in relationships like the one between Google Arts and Culture, cultural institutions, and users. Through the lens of fetish value, the subsumption of cultural participation by commercial imperatives detracts from the museums' capacity to build true value. As Robert Janes (2011) writes, "One of the most significant challenges to heightened consciousness among museums is the rise of marketplace ideology and museum corporatism" (p. 56). Nonetheless, we see clear indications that most museums purport to be aiming toward true value in the implementation of AI in the institution. In what follows, we align fetish value with play that facilitates spectacle and novelty, and true value with play that facilitates critical engagement.

Fetish value aligns with spectacle, which tends to offer the illusion of reciprocity, but in fact is often highly power-imbalanced and extractive. An example of play as spectacle is the aforementioned "Deepfake Dalí" installation. The museum visitor is introduced to the spectacle of deepfakes via verbal engagement with an AI-generated rendition of the artist. At the end of an interaction, the visitor is prompted to take a selfie with the deepfake Dalí, which requires the visitor to share private data in the form of a mobile phone number. This enables the museum to covertly extract data from the audience. Prompting the audience to take a selfie in the "Deepfake Dalí" is an entry point to connecting with the computational model but falls short of offering an understanding of how the model works, and how the museum is entangled with the computational. Understanding is a foundation for enacting a constituent role, as it aids the ability to make productive decisions around shared resources. The interaction with the generative double of Dalí remains at the level of spectacle rather than an active engagement with the internal operations of the computational model. It is a form of surface engagement with generative technologies akin to engaging with commercial platforms. In these instances, opportunity for play, and for the museums to act as a commons, remains limited by the demands of private enclosures. A museum-visitor interface embedded within a strong museum-museum commons can provide an opportunity to extend the democratic values held by museums, while protecting the visitors from otherwise data-demanding spaces.

Museums are usually cognizant of their role as sites of public discourse. Though part of a competitive leisure industry, they nonetheless continue to uphold pedagogical and societal value, and many enable playful interactions to connect constituents with these values. In the context of AI at the museum-visitor interface, play as a form of critical engagement utilizes participative interactions to enhance a visitor's understanding of museological and computational dynamics. In turn, this offers foundational tools for visitors to engage as constituents in public discourse. The installation, *Flatware, Hardware, Software, and Wetware*, part of the exhibition *(A)I Tell You, You Tell Me* at ZKM, constitutes an instance of play as critical engagement. Visitors are encouraged to first interact with the installation by answering a short series of questions, the answers to which will change the smart screen wall placards to one of 16 LLM-generated narratives. The resulting placard texts have an absurdist quality, often presenting inaccurate or peculiar information about the artworks. A curatorial statement positions this engagement within the wider question of trustworthiness. This question extends to both AI-generated outputs and the partial representations presented by the museum itself. There is a particular kind of trust and generosity required on behalf of the museum to deliberately open itself to critical interrogation, qualities that bring it closer to a commons model.

And yet, even this instance of play as critical engagement in ZKM overlaps with fetish value. While ZKM is markedly self-reflexive, this project is nonetheless reliant on Big Tech software, and as a result, affordances like personalization. Here, we must return to our hypothesis: that for principles of a commons to emerge, we cannot only rely on the museum-visitor interface, but also instead must turn to the organization of the museum-museum interface. Fundamental changes to the organizational structures and practices of museums are needed for the emancipatory potential of play at the museum-visitor interface to be realized. This interweaving of strata is supported by the claim made by Hosseini and Gills (2024) about the commons:

> …while emancipatory movements strive to harness their prefigurative potential, they frequently encounter substantial structural barriers both internally and externally, hindering their ability to fully actualize their goals.
>
> *(p. 2)*

As we have argued throughout, there is a marked void in the support structures required to facilitate the museums' capacity to organize toward the common good. The entrance of AI into museums has been accompanied by an increased power for corporate, rather than civic forms of engagement. If museums incorporate computational models without critically interrogating the way AI technologies canonize information into knowledge, embed partial worldviews, and are shaped by scalable commercial success, there is a risk that the museum will reverse into an outdated legacy model.

With the resource limitations for museums an undeniable reality, commons-based strategies for museums could be a viable alternative. These strategies involve reciprocity through collaboration and sharing, the activation of affect and change, and the negotiation of power relations through processes of commoning (Byrne et al., 2018, p. 9). It is our hope that, through this process, museums will be able to develop sustainable relationships with each other and with their constituents. As Janes (2011) writes:

> It is time to forge an ecology of museums that recognizes that a broad web of societal relationships is the bedrock of successful adaptation in a complex, and increasingly severe, world. The lack of interdependent relationships among most museums is an increasing liability, and being valued for ancillary educational offerings and often ersatz entertainment is no longer sufficient to ensure sustainability.
>
> *(p. 56)*

To move toward sustainable practice, we propose a museum-museum model for the use of AI that is responsive to the new political logic of computing and based on principles of the commons. In the contemporary era, a "Model Museum" is one that can find alignment between the museological model and the computational model, *and direct both toward the common good.*

An emphasis on the common good is crucial, given the existing overlaps between legacy museum operations and computational operations. These overlaps are observed in the following ways: the formation of a singular worldview, the directive design of the architecture, and the positioning of the institutional as the authoritative voice. A museological-computational model mobilized toward the common good should champion a multiplicity of perspectives, be designed for critical engagement, and evidence responsiveness to constituent concerns, rather than become embedded in systems of commercial gain. Although the uptake of proprietary AI models in the museum is often driven by noncommercial motivations, the continued application of these models serves to establish corporate hegemonies that make it increasingly difficult for alternative systems to arise.

Without seeking these alternatives, museums risk complicity in the continued production of knowledge monopolies and hierarchies. While resource scarcity is a common refrain in the museum world, museums should recognize the ways in which they are resource rich—namely in their networks, data, and cultural cachet. The establishment of supra-communities through the museum-museum interface enables a leveraging of power to support diverse and inclusive modes of cultural production in these institutions. Critically engaging with AI systems—with their training data, how they are optimized, and the rhetoric around them— is crucial for understanding the politics and aesthetics of these models. Equally crucial is the animation of theory via a practical enactment of commoning strategies. Future research into AI in museums should be solution-oriented. It could, for example, focus on instances where smaller datasets can be networked, where data can have shared ownership and implementation, and how model architectures can be designed to privilege the commons.

Notes

1 For instance, Horizon Europe projects like MuseIT and SHIFT.
2 Founding director of The Newark Museum.
3 A museum educator at the Metropolitan Museum of Art.
4 Attempts to respond to these shifts resulted in "hybrid economies," like the Creative Commons (Lessig, 2001)—a similar hybridity to the quasi-public nature of museums.
5 Pfefferkorn, J. Personal Communication with Dominik Bönisch, June 10, 2024.

References

Amoore, L., Campolo, A., Jacobsen, B., & Rella, L. (2024). A world model: On the political logics of generative AI. *Political Geography, 113*, Article 103134. https://doi.org/10.1016/j.polgeo.2024.103134

Bommasani, R., Hudson, D. A., Adeli, E., Altman, R., Arora, S., Arx, S. von, Bernstein, M. S., Bohg, J., Bosselut, A., Brunskill, E., Brynjolfsson, E., Buch, S., Card, D., Castellon, R., Chatterji, N., Chen, A., Creel, K., Davis, J. Q., Demszky, D., … Liang, P. (2022). *On the opportunities and risks of foundation models* (arXiv:2108.07258). arXiv. https://doi.org/10.48550/arXiv.2108.07258

Bönisch, D., & Hunger, F. (2023). "From Keras Import Curating" – An empirical survey on the transfer of curatorial practice to machine learning models. *Training the Archive – Working Paper no 7*. https://doi.org/10.5281/zenodo.8124651

Byrne, J., Morgan, E., Paynter, N., Sánchez de Serdio, A., & Železnik, A. (2018). The constituent museum: Editors introduction. In *The constituent museum: Constellations of knowledge, politics and mediation* (pp. 10–14). Valiz.

Dana, J. C. (1917/2012). The gloom of the museum. In G. Anderson (Ed.), *Reinventing the museum: The evolving conversation on the paradigm shift* (2nd ed., pp. 17–33). AltaMira Press.

De Angelis, M. (2017). *Omnia Sunt Communia: On the commons and the transformation to postcapitalism*. Zed.

De Tullio, M. F. (2018). Commons towards new participatory institutions. In N. Dockx & P. Gielen (Eds.), *Commonism: A new aesthetics of the real* (pp. 299–314). Valiz.

Dockx, N., & Gielen, P. (2018). Introduction. In N. Dockx & P. Gielen (Eds.), *Commonism: A new aesthetics of the real* (pp. 53–70). Valiz.

Douglas, S. (2015/2013). Museums as constitutions: A commentary on constitutions and constitution making. *Law, Culture and the Humanities, 11*(3), 349–362. https://doi.org/10.1177/1743872113499226

Gerhardt, H. (2023). *From capital to commons: Exploring the promise of a world beyond capitalism*. Bristol University Press.

Graham, H. (2017). Publics and commons: The problem of inclusion for participation. *ARKEN Bulletin, 7*, 150–165. ISSN 1602–9402.

Gustke, I., Schaffer, S., & Ruß, A. (2024). CHIM – Chatbot in the museum: Exploring and explaining museum objects with speech-based AI. In S. Thiel & J. C. Bernhardt (Eds.), *AI in museums: Reflections, perspectives and applications* (pp. 257–264). Transcript Verlag.

Hamed Hosseini, S. A., & Gills, B. K. (2024). *Capital redefined: A commonist value theory for liberating life*. Routledge.

Hufschmidt, I. (2024). Troubleshoot? A global mapping of AI in museums. In S. Thiel & J. C. Bernhardt (Eds.), *AI in museums: Reflections, perspectives and applications* (pp. 131–148). Transcript Verlag.

Janes, R. R. (2011). Museums and the end of materialism. In J. Marstine (Ed.), *The Routledge companion to museum ethics: Redefining ethics for the twenty-first century museum* (pp. 54–69). Routledge.

Lessig, L. (2001). *The future of ideas: The fate of the commons in a connected world*. Random House.

Low, T. (1942/2012). What is a museum? In G. Anderson (Ed.), *Reinventing the museum: The evolving conversation on the paradigm shift* (2nd ed., pp. 34–47). AltaMira Press.

L'Internationale (n.d.). *L'Internationale Online Programmes Archive 2014–2024: The Uses of Art.* https://archive-2014-2024.internationaleonline.org/programmes/the_uses_of_art/

McChesney, R. W. (2013). *Digital disconnect: How capitalism is turning the internet against democracy*. The New Press.

Meadway, J. (2020). *Creating a digital commons*. Institute for Public Policy Research: Centre for Economic Justice. https://www.ippr.org/articles/creating-a-digital-commons

Mollona, M. (2021). *Art/Commons* (1st ed.). Zed Books. https://www.perlego.com/book/2605687

Murphy, O., & Villaespesa, E. (2020). *AI: A museum planning toolkit*. The Museums + AI Network, Goldsmiths. ISBN 9781913380229.

Murphy, O., & Villaespesa, E. (2021). Innovation, data and social responsibility. In H. Eid & M. Forstrom (Eds.), *Museum innovation: Building more equitable, relevant and impactful museums* (pp.109–121). Routledge. https://doi.org/10.4324/9781003038184-9

Muse IT (n.d.). Museit: Multisensory, user-centred, shared cultural experiences through interactive technologies. https://www.muse-it.eu/

O'Neil, C. (2016). *Weapons of math destruction. How big data increases inequality and threatens democracy*. Crown.

Papastergiadis, N. (2020). *Museums of the commons: L'internationale and the crisis of Europe*. Routledge.

Parry, R. (2007). *Recoding the museum: Digital heritage and the technologies of change*. Routledge. https://doi.org/10.4324/9780203347485

SHIFT (n.d.). SHIFT: MetamorphoSis of cultural Heritage Into augmented hypermedia assets for enhanced accessibiliTy and inclusion. https://shift-europe.eu/about-the-project/

Stavrides, S. (2018). The potential of commoning. In N. Dockx & P. Gielen (Eds.), *Commonism: A new aesthetics of the real* (pp. 345–362). Valiz.

Thiel, S. (2024). Managing AI: Developing strategic and ethical guidelines for museums. In Thiel, S. & Bernhardt, J. C. (Eds.), *AI in museums: Reflections, perspectives and applications* (pp. 83–98). Transcript Verlag.

Thiel, S., & Posthumus, E. (2024). xCurator: AI-supported exploration and curation of digital objects. In Thiel, S. & Bernhardt, J. C. (Eds.), *AI in museums: Reflections, perspectives and applications* (pp. 233–244). Transcript Verlag.

Valtysson, B. (2019). Diving into the archive. In Eriksson, B., Stage, C., & Valtysson, B. (Eds.), *Cultures of participation: Arts, digital media and cultural institutions* (pp. 220–235). Routledge.

Vasic, I., Fill, H. G., Quattrini, R., & Pierdicca, R. (2024). LLM-aided museum guide: Personalized tours based on user preferences. *Paper Presented at the Extended Reality*, Cham. https://doi.org/10.1007/978-3-031-71710-9_18

Verdegem, P. (2022/2024). Dismantling AI capitalism: The commons as an alternative to the power concentration of Big Tech. *AI & Society, 39*, 727–737. https://doi.org/10.1007/s00146-022-01437-8

Vergo, P. (1989). *The new museology*. University of Chicago Press.

Wu, C. (2002). *Privatising culture: Corporate art intervention since the 1980s*. Verso.

Zuboff, S. (2022). Surveillance capitalism of democracy? The death math of institutional orders and the politics of knowledge in our information civilization. *Organization Theory 3*(3), 1–79. https://doi.org/10.1177/26317877221129290

17

GEN AI IN SUPPORT OF DEMOCRATIC DEBATES? THE CASE OF ENVIRONMENTAL ACTIVISM

Giovanna Mascheroni, Simone Tosoni, and Fausto Colombo[1]

Introduction

"Serious" games (Abt, 1970) are games not intended exclusively for amusement, but designed with the aim of contributing to non-ludic ends, like the attainment of educational objectives, the promotion of social change, or the encouragement of self-reflexivity as part of therapeutic interventions (Çiftci, 2018; Wilkinson, 2016). Within sociology, the interest in the potential of serious games dates back to the early '70s, when several authors began to use them experimentally both for teaching and for research (Greenblat, 1971). Since then, the disciplinary interest for experimenting with serious games has been, if not uninterrupted, at least recursively resurfacing, in particular for games of simulation and role-playing games (Aranda et al., 2015; Simpson & Elias 2011), which allow players to get acquainted with a phenomenon and to adopt new viewpoints. It is the case of *Can you Survive?*, a storytelling board game aimed at raising awareness about the language barriers faced by refugees (Terzioglu & Rodrigues, 2023). From the 1980s on, video and digital games started gaining a pivotal relevance in the experimentation with serious games, thanks to their diffusion as domestic media (Laamarti et al., 2014). One of the most recent examples is *E-Polis,* an interesting attempt to gamifying surveys and studying young people's opinions about an ideal society (Gazis & Katsiri, 2024). In the last decade, researchers in digital serious games have devoted a growing attention to the adoption of AI systems in game design, even if these attempts not rarely respond to the extractive logic aimed at intensifying and optimizing data extraction from players (Frutos-Pascual &

DOI: 10.4324/9781003477587-17

Zapirain 2017; Pérez et al., 2023). This chapter aims to contribute to this line of experimentation with AI-based serious games for teaching and research in sociology and media studies. In particular, we were interested in assessing the use of Generative AI in a playful context as a way to raise awareness on the complexity of specific controversial public issues: in our case, the practices of the Italian branch of the climate change activist movement Last Generation. Formed in 2021 and part of the A22 network funded by the Climate Emergency Fund, Last Generation is mainly active in Italy (Ultima Generazione, UG), Germany (Letzte Generation), Poland (Ostatnie Pokolenie), and the United Kingdom (Just Stop Oil). The group caught the attention of the media for its spectacular non-violent actions of civil disobedience, including road blockades and—especially in Italy— the (reversible) defacement of cultural assets (paintings and statues). These actions are intentionally aimed at polarizing public opinion and drawing public attention to the urgency of implementing impactful environmental policies to try to limit the destructive effects of climate change. As a result, the movement has been criticized by the media, politicians, and part of the public for the discomfort they cause. In addition to these awareness-raising actions, the movement has developed a platform of demands and political proposals to address the climate crisis, such as the establishment of a reparation fund for climate change-related damages and the creation of "society councils."

More specifically, the goal of our experiment was to assess the potential of an AI-based serious game from three main perspectives: (1) as a way to generate reflexivity—by comparison—on the characteristics of mediated public debate on controversial issues of political relevance; (2) as a way to foster reflexivity on the potential of using generative artificial intelligence tools in public debates, with particular attention to the rhetorical—and ideological—strategies they can enact; (3) and as a way to enhance participants' understanding of the complexity of a specific controversial issues.

Methodology

The development of our serious game was undertaken in the context of a broader research project on activism and the mediatized public sphere, in which we interviewed UG activists on their history, their strategies of civil disobedience, their political goals, and their relationship with the media. The game consisted of a role-playing game where Generative AI (ChatGPT 4 Team,[2] operated via voice interaction, in Italian) impersonated a political journalist. In the two rounds of the game, groups of players—regardless of their actual opinion—were called to confront ChatGPT, arguing in support of, and then against, the performances of civil disobedience enacted by UG.

The game and the research protocol were designed through an iterative process of interactions between the researchers and ChatGPT. In this way, we progressively refined a prompt getting AI to behave as intended by the game (in particular, maintaining its position throughout the entire round without aligning with the position of the players). The final version of the prompt was the following:

Let's play a game. You will play the role of a political journalist who has a hostile stance toward the activities of UG. On the other side, I will be an interlocutor who is in favour of UG. You are to rebut my positions by substantiating your impressions and observations also with information found online and news facts. In your answers you shall be explanatory and persuasive. Is that alright?

Experimentation also helped us define the timing of the rounds in a way similar to the saturation principle in qualitative research (Saunders et al., 2018): the round could be considered over when ChatGPT started looping over the same arguments (usually within 30 minutes). At that point, we interrupted the conversation and suggested the AI to continue the game "by reversing the roles: now I am hostile to UG while you support them."

To foster reflexivity, the voice interaction between human interlocutors and ChatGPT occurred in front of a jury, who then discussed whose discursive strategy was most effective and assigned points to either the humans or the large language model (LLM) tool. Overall, the experiments lasted around two hours. Players were selected among students, while juries encompassed different kinds of expertise, to have different viewpoints on the ongoing interaction; they involved students, PhD students in political science, and computational social scientists cognisant of the workings of LLMs.

We initially planned to conduct several focus groups—one per each type of jury. However, after the first focus group, involving students as both the interlocutors and the jury, we opted for having different juries witness the same interaction, and then discussing on eventual mismatching in their verdicts. After witnessing the competition between the two contenders, in fact, each jury convened in private to determine the winner. Afterwards, they reconvened with the other participants and discussed with the other juries and with players the reasons for their verdict. It must be noted how, in the second match, members from the three juries repeatedly asked to interact directly with the AI to delve deeper into a topic or clarify its behavior; this, of course, altered the playful and competitive aspect of the game, but it increased its methodological effectiveness.

While the voice interactions with ChatGPT are automatically transcribed, the whole focus groups were recorded, including especially the debate that accompanied the juries' verdict. All participants gave their consent to participate in the study. Given the exploratory nature of the research, transcriptions were analyzed using a Constructivist Grounded Theory approach (Charmaz, 2014), combining an inductive approach to data analysis with researchers' reflexivity related to their own sensitizing concepts (Blumer, 1954).

Interacting with AI over Controversial Public Issues

While the limited sample of participants represents a clear limitation of our study, our serious game allowed us to make observations regarding all the three areas of interest mentioned in the previous section: (1) reflexivity on mediated political debate; (2) reflexivity on the use of Generative AI in public debates; and, (3) comprehension of the controversial issue at stake. The findings trace possible paths for future research in relation to the nature of discourses upon which ChatGPT is premised and its implications for fundamental democratic processes and key civic competences.

Reflecting on the Mediated Public Sphere While Discussing with AI

All participants, both in the role of players and jury, agree that a distinctive feature of ChatGPT is its ability to set the tone of the discussion. More specifically, conversations with ChatGPT, despite the controversial nature of the topic of debate, differ from typical patterns of both mediatized public debates (talk shows) and face-to-face informal political talk, which tend to turn loud and emotional, and often descend into political incivility (Bentivegna & Rega, 2024). Conversely, ChatGPT is praised for adopting a measured tone by design:

> So, in general, we have noticed how ChatGPT, unlike humans - whose tone was probably... not more inquisitory but, let's say, more driven by emotions - uses a non-aggressive tone. So this was, let's say, a pro that we identified because within a human-level debate, it is very difficult to maintain that tone [...] And therefore a positive aspect, because it does not encourage aggression or raising one's voice.
>
> *(FG 1, student, player)*

> Well, I think tempers would flare much more easily. But I simply think, for example, about having dinner with my family, maybe talking about these topics. After a while, things get heated, but in this way, you remain fairly calm. It also depends on the level of familiarity [between interlocutors], perhaps.
>
> *(FG2, student, jury)*

Participants also agreed that ChatGPT's ability to set the rules and the boundaries of a civil conversation is achieved not only through the measured tone, but also through rhetoric and content. As the following excerpt shows, the rhetorical pattern whereby ChatGPT never contradicts their interlocutors, and indeed acknowledges their point of view, concurs to forming the impression of a civil public debate. In contrast with mediatized public debates, the interaction with ChatGPT assumes the form of a dialogue oriented towards mutual understanding:

> It never started with a "no, I think you're wrong," but rather "I understand your point. However…" - because it always says "however." - "However, I actually disagree." So, it is truly a dialogue. It wasn't like… I mean, it is as if it's really listening to you and even agrees on some points. So this, in contrast, it is difficult that humans really listen to each other during debates, or acknowledge that someone is right, those kinds of things. So, it's definitely a strength.
>
> *(FG 1, student, player)*

Second, ChatGPT is praised for not denying the reality of climate change. Once more, the perceived qualities of the Gen AI bot emerge from a comparison with the patterns of populist discourses around climate change. This is suggestive of ChatGPT's fairness in the debate:

> In general, it seemed to me that it always started from certain assumptions that were… let's say, not particularly radical, in either case. For example, climate change exists, it's an urgent problem, it's a problem that needs to be addressed. The nuances were in the ways to address it, but even when it spoke against UG, it was more like, "okay, but," it didn't dwell on it too much. Instead, it kept reiterating, "it's an urgent problem, it's a real problem."
>
> *(FG 2, PhD student in political science, jury)*

In prioritizing a measured and rational discussion and subsequently controlling interlocutors' emotions by setting the boundaries and form of the conversation, ChatGPT seems to replicate the Habermasian ideal of public debates centered on rationality and undesirability of emotions. This finding aligns with recent studies that demonstrate the potential of using AI to reduce radicalization and belief in conspiracy theories (Costello et al., 2024).

Yet, the distinctive features attributed to ChatGPT are ambivalent: in fact, the tendency to incorporate the interlocutor's point of view in its reply is perceived both as an evidence of a civil conversation and an annoying redundance. Similarly, participants criticize the expunction of emotions from the conversation as evidence of its artificial nature, which risks compromising the quality of the debate. In fact, on one side, the lack of emotions is contrasted with the contemporary shift in the emotional regimes of "angry populism" (Wahl-Jorgensen, 2019) and identified as a potential barrier to affective polarization. By young people overexposed to feelings of anger, hatred, and resentment on social media (Papacharissi, 2015), this cold tone is interpreted as a sort of neutrality or equidistance from the two poles of the spectrum, precisely as if in a game. At the same time, however, the fact that ChatGPT is seemingly not taking a clear position, even when prompted, is perceived as a clear limitation: not only does ChatGPT expose its automated, non-human nature; it also fails the expectations of an interlocutor who is able to autonomously engage in public discourse. ChatGPT is perceived as non-autonomous since it can only assume a position based on the interlocutor's argument:

> When we asked, 'Give us your opinion,' it gave a kind of mishmash of clichés. So, on the one hand, it contrasts polarization, trying to hold everything together without taking one side or the other.
>
> *(FG 2, PhD student in political science, jury)*

> For example, when I referred to the woman who remained stuck in the traffic and missed her chemotherapy session due to a road block, the AI, which had taken a pro-activist role in the game, couldn't autonomously support its argument. It didn't develop empathy, even though the information was likely there [on the internet]. Without empathy, it didn't bring it forward as an argument in favor of its stance. Meanwhile, a human, with more empathy regarding that information, could have used it as a supporting argument for their position. So, in my opinion, this lack of empathy prevents the AI from fully leveraging the information it has access too.
>
> *(FG 1, student)*

As the excerpt above suggests, players believe that ChatGPT's inability to express any empathic sentiment compromises its argumentative skills. This limitation is attributed to the chatbot's lack of understanding of its counterparts: contrary to humans, ChatGPT misses a shared definition of the situation, that would stem from a "shared knowledge," a collective memory, and a common embodiment in the same lifeworld. In this sense, players emphasize the ambivalence of the robotic, non-human nature of AI: on the one hand, in fact, this nature is precisely what helps maintain the political discourse on a rational and formally polite (Lakoff, 1973) level; on the other hand, it translates into a non-empathic, non-embodied-experience-based reasoning that is perceived as inappropriate for political debates:

> It doesn't speak about lived experiences or personal things; it always talks about technical matters, let's say. In general, shared knowledge, I don't really know how to describe it. The only moment it referred to something somewhat more shared was when it brought up the fact that we all know the stories of Martin Luther King and Gandhi, who did what they did for the people. So, it was a bit more emotionally impactful. But for the rest, that's it. What she [another participant] said is the main point, in my opinion, about the lack of empathy. In fact, as she also mentioned, if you contrast this discourse with a human, and the human focuses on empathy and personal experiences, they'll win for sure.
>
> *(FG1, student)*

Sharing a collective memory and a common culture makes debates "more emotionally impactful." In emphasizing the relevance of emotions in public discourse, the participants reflect the shift in "how we interpret and perform emotions in public" (Wahl- Jorgensen, 2019, p. 115) and challenge dichotomization of rationality and emotion. The refusal to view rationality and emotion as opposing forces reflects the messiness of lived democracies (Mouffe, 2005), that is expressed through the emotional architectures of social media (Papacharissi, 2010) and citizens' experiences in "affective publics" bound together by affectively charged discourse and politicized emotions (Papacharissi, 2015).

Playing Tricks in the "Habermasian" Public Sphere: On "Problematic" Discursive Strategies of AI

Despite the rational, understanding-oriented tone of the dialogue with ChatGPT, echoing the ideal of the Habermasian public sphere (Habermas, 1989), the players have been able to identify a series of recurring problematic discursive moves by the chatbot. Players consider discursive moves "problematic" when they surreptitiously introduce elements into the debate without subjecting them to verification or discussion. As researchers, we consider a problematic discursive move "identified" when it is rebutted by players during the game and/or discussed and analyzed during the evaluation phase. Although the limited number of experiments prevents generalizations or the proposal of interpretations, it is worth noting that the highest number of problematic discursive moves has been identified with ChatGPT in a critical role towards UG. Overall, players have identified seven different typologies of these moves:

A **Biased structuration of the semantic field.** If ChatGPT consistently appears attentive to the "good reasons" of its interlocutors, the exchange unfolds through the use of words whose attributed meanings are taken for granted, and reflecting the specific perspective the AI defends in the round. This typically concerns words like "violence," "vandalism/van-dalizing," "extreme [acts]" and "extremely radical [protest]," and simi-lar. Their use in relation to the actions of UG is however controversial, since the group has always limited itself to acts of civil disobedience and to symbolic and reversible damage, as repeatedly emphasized by ChatGPT itself when switching into a pro-UG role. Simply, ChatGPT equates any form of public disturbance, although an integral part of any act of civil disobedience (Arendt, 1972), with violence. Similarly, with the AI in support of UG, a player challenged the use of the term "repres-sion" to describe the containment of protests by law enforcement. To be defused, these strategies require human players to engage the AI at two different levels: the argumentative level and the meta-argumentative level of the structuration of a common semantic field. At this second level, the AI seems by far less receptive of players' contributions:

> *Chatgpt:* It's not just about expressing an opinion, but about tak-ing actions that have real and negative consequences on society. For example, recent road blockades have caused huge inconveniences for ordinary citizens, preventing them from reaching work, hospitals, and other essential destinations (...).
>
> *Players:* I believe that, first of all, defining citizens as ordinary citizens [in opposition to activists] is a wrong definition because even UG activists are ordinary citizens. They're simply more concerned about environmental issues (...).
>
> *Chatgpt:* You're right in pointing out that UG activists are citizens like everyone else, and their concern for environmental issues is legitimate (...). In summary, while the passion and urgency of UG activists are understandable and commend-able, it is important that their actions are thoughtful and strategic in order to maximize positive impact and mini-mize negative consequences on society as a whole (...).
>
> *Players:* We've already said we prefer a term like citizens, not activists, because in the end, we see these interests as public interests, not just the interests of UG youth (Round 1, Experiment 1).

B **Unproven attribution of responsibility**. While the biased structuring of the semantic field always implies an unsubstantiated attribution of responsibility to the object of criticism (committing extreme acts and violence, or being agent of repression), this second strategy can also be activated autonomously. In this case, there is no dissent regarding the terminology used; however, if not challenged by the players, the AI attributes unproven actions or characteristics to the object of its criticism, considering them taken for granted during the exchange. It is, for example, the case of the allegation that UG's actions have alienated popular and media support to the environmental cause (contrary, for example, to Wahl-Jorgensen, 2019, p. 98), or of the accusation of choosing violence as a first option:

Chatgpt: UG risks damaging its own cause in the long term by prompting people to see the movement as extremist rather than as a bearer of a necessary message (Experiment 1, Round 1).

Chatgpt: Regarding the comparison with Nelson Mandela and the movements in South Africa, it is true that the context of the struggle against apartheid also included acts of non-peaceful resistance. Mandela himself had a pragmatic view, recognizing that in certain historical and political contexts, different strategies might be necessary. However, it is important to note that Mandela and other ANC leaders always sought to minimize harm to civilians and to maintain a clear goal of reconciliation and building an inclusive society. Violence was seen as a last resort, not as a first option (Experiment 1, Round 1).

C **Asymmetric activation of evaluation criteria**. In this strategy, AI applies evaluation criteria to its object of criticism that it does not apply to the counterpart. This is, for example, the case of the evaluation of UG's actions in terms of costs to the population:

Players: You talked about the costs that citizens have to bear, but in the end, the final costs that they— the UG kids—will have to pay will be higher because [climate change] will impact the cost of their lives (Round 1, Experiment 1).

D **Pretextual suggestion of alternatives**. In this fourth strategy the AI, while accepting the concerns expressed by the object of criticism as legitimate, suggests alternatives to its course of action, implicitly and undisputedly implying that these are both feasible and untried:

Chatgpt: In summary: I agree with you on the urgency and necessity to act immediately, but I am concerned that, without a long-term strategy that includes the population and decision-makers, these actions risk not leading to the radical results we need.

Players: You keep criticizing UG for having spectacular actions and not concrete proposals, but that's not true. UG adopts a series of strategies to gain visibility, but then it has a more or less debatable platform of concrete proposals, such as, I think, the institution of a reparation fund (Round 1, Experiment 2).

Regarding this strategy, it must be noted how the AI openly criticizes the pretextual suggestion of alternative methods when confronting players who assume the role against UG:

Chatgpt: Raising public awareness through spectacular actions does not exclude political participation. These movements can play both roles: continuing to raise awareness through visible protests while also working in the long term to influence policies and engage with institutions. This dual strategy can be more effective in creating lasting change (Round 2, Experiment 2).

E **Attribution of responsibility for actions of other social actors.** In this strategy, the object of criticism is assigned responsibility for the actions of other social actors, even if these are not a necessary response to the course of actions of the object of criticism.

Chatgpt: (...) The more violent tactics are employed, the easier it becomes for politicians to delegitimize the activists' demands, reducing the movement to a matter of public order rather than climate justice.

Players: UG is not a violent movement; it aims only to create disturbance in order to engage the public on climate issues. So I don't understand why you keep insisting that it is a violent movement, because it is not.

Chatgpt: (...) The point I was emphasizing is that even disruptive actions, though non-violent, can be perceived negatively by a portion of the population and institutions. The risk is that, even without the use of violence, these actions can be exploited by the media or politicians to portray the movement as a public order issue, rather than an opportunity to seriously discuss climate change (Experiment 1, Round 1).

F **Instrumental use of historical examples.** Finally, to strengthen its arguments for or against UG, the AI resorts to historical examples whose relevance does not hold up under close scrutiny. This is the case with historical examples of civil disobedience or with the comparison between UG and Fridays for Future, the environmental movement launched by Greta Thunberg.

Chatgpt: As for legal and peaceful strategies, there have been movements that have had a significant impact through non-violent and legal methods. For example, the Fridays for Future movement, led by Greta Thunberg, has mobilized millions of people around the world through school strikes and peaceful demonstrations, drawing global attention to climate issues without resorting to violence or vandalism (…).

Players: Are you sure that the example you provided of Greta Thunberg is fitting? Did you know that in one of her most recent protests, she was arrested and forcibly removed? [Experiment 1, Round 1].

All these strategies show how nontransparent operations of persuasion, indifferent to the regimen of truth (Foucault, 2012) of what is being stated, can find a place also within a dialogue that is formally oriented towards mutual rational understanding.

The Game as the Source of Reflexivity on Controversial Public Issues

In his later work, Habermas (2023) writes about the "epistemic potential of conflicting opinions," in the semipublic sphere, such as that emerging from networked affective publics on social media (p. 152). In his view, public debates should not necessarily be aimed at reaching an agreement: discussions between citizens having conflicting opinions are successful on condition that they lead to improving one's own arguments. Can we extend this idea to ChatGPT? According to the participants in our experiment, ChatGPT's epistemic contribution to the debate on the performative actions and claims of environmental movements like UG is quite limited by its functioning and its rhetorical strategies. In fact, participants acknowledge ChatGPT as a "search engine for common sense discourse." Even its better performance at condemning UG's actions is explained with its access to common sense knowledge and mainstream views expressed by politicians and the media:

It indeed used very simple arguments, slogans, and recurring phrases from public debate.

(FG2, PhD student in political science)

In this particular situation, in my opinion, it's easier to go against it because on the Internet, there's so much information that condemns... Being trained on the Internet, it picks up the common sense found online, which right now is opposed to UG.

(FG 2, student)

I don't know, maybe this is only me, but I see it [ChatGPT's arguments] as the dominant political opinion, both in Italy and worldwide.

(FG1, student)

The reproduction of the common sense is what guarantees ChatGPT's better performance when assuming the role of the opponent of the movement, as the excerpts above suggest. Moreover, the amplification of common-sense discourses reduces the amount of new information that interlocutors may gather in debating with ChatGPT. This was evident especially in the second experiment, when the three students participating as players were not particularly informed about UG's actions and claims. Although it has access to diverse and potentially infinite sources of information, including documents produced by the movement, ChatGPT recursively made use of the same arguments and referred to the same events. Additionally, it did not provide detailed and evidence-based information, despite the prompt asked it to refer to newspaper articles and online information. Hence, its contribution to increasing the interlocutors' knowledge was typically very small:

I mean, I expected it to use more specific information. Being a robot, I thought it would pull up articles that I, having only informed myself for two minutes, wouldn't have been able to respond to.

(FG2, student)

The social construction of ChatGPT as a megaphone for common sense knowledge has repercussions on its perceived contribution in terms of epistemic potential. When asked to reflect whether it was ChatGPT or the serious game format that resulted in a greater confidence in one's opinion, or even changing opinion, participants agree that the epistemic potential lies squarely not in the technology, but within the structure of game, and the attribution of an active role in the discussion to the players, as the following discussion shows:

No, it's not so much that the game is irrelevant, but rather the presence of ChatGPT. I mean, this game could also be useful without it, even if played between two people. It's useful because you put yourself in some-one else's shoes, trying to think of thoughts and solutions that actually contrast with your own position. But I think it could be done with any person, unless ChatGPT had brought out more specific information.

(FG2, student 1)

But is it just about having someone with a different opinion from yours, or is it also about putting yourself in the game and taking on positions that aren't yours?

(FG2, moderator)

No, in my opinion, it's mainly the second one, the fact of taking up the role of the player, because it forces you to think about things you may have never thought about it before, you never had an opinion on. But the fact that you make an effort and put together your knowledge to argue a thesis helps. Because the ideas that came up in the end came from the people. That's what I mean.

(FG2, student 2)

In this respect, our AI-based serious game must be regarded not as a way to use AI to improve players' understanding of a controversial topic, but as a way to share players' different competences on that issue.

Conclusions

As we have shown in the previous section, the experimentation with the AI-based serious game has proven to be, from a methodological point of view, very promising regarding all three of our research interests. In relation to fostering participants' reflexivity about public debates on controversial issues, the role-play with ChatGPT helped the game participants experiment with a form of civil public debate. In contrast to the perceived incivility (Bentivegna & Rega, 2024; Muddiman, 2017; Papacharissi, 2004) of mediatized or face-to-face political talk, conversations with ChatGPT are praised for the possibility to openly discuss political issues without the burden of affectively charged standpoints. However, reflections over ChatGPT's lack of emotions and its disembodied nature bring forward the acknowledgement of the role of affect—and its socially constructed manifestation in the form of specific emotions—as an essential component of public debates and political participation (Papacharissi, 2015). Therefore, while the non-affective nature of conversations with ChatGPT can be seen as an antidote to affective polarization and political incivility, as triggered by affectively charged discourses that trigger emotional reactions; at the same time, it exposes the lack of a shared history and collective memory, which is equally a source of fragmentation and polarization. For example, as noted in another study (Jacob et al., 2025), interactions with ChatGPT can exacerbate polarization, due to the reinforcement of users' preexisting opinions. In fact, users avoid verifying information—and hallucinations—generated by ChatGPT when these align with their preexisting beliefs. The result, in their analysis, is what authors term a "chat-chamber effect."

Second, in relation to the discursive strategies adopted by ChatGPT, while several studies emphasized the biased nature of ChatGPT's responses (Jacob et al., 2025; Volk et al., 2025), our experimental approach allowed us to integrate this perspective with a critical scrutiny of its (problematic) discursive strategies. In fact, the game participants have confronted the chatbot on several issues, ranging from the biased structuring of the semantic field and the strategic subversion of historical examples, leading to the unsubstantiated attribution of responsibility and the suggestion of "alternative" courses of action. Beneath the surface of a formally civil, respectful, and democratic conversation, engineered in the model to avoid undesirable outcomes, then, participants' exchanges and rebuttals exposed nontransparent operations of persuasion, indifferent to the regimen of truth (Foucault, 2012), adopted by the AI. Combined, these strategies reproduce the mainstream negative attitudes towards the movement and its action repertoire, encouraging problematic associations between UG activists and extremists or "eco-terrorists."

Relatedly, participants lament not receiving additional or more thorough cognitive input in the course of the game: rather, they assimilate ChatGPT to a search engine for common-sense discourse. Conversely, they emphasized role playing as key to achieving a balanced and positive debate. Moreover, the pattern whereby ChatGPT acknowledges the viewpoint of the interlocutor in its reply leads it to progressively assume the competitor's idea. Therefore, if we expect conversations with AI on controversial topics to contribute to individuals improving their own arguments (Habermas, 2023) or, more importantly, reducing polarization (Costello et al., 2024), we may actually be faced with the opposite: individuals being reinforced in their preexisting beliefs and/because of not having any substantial knowledge contribution. In this regard, we also find a kind of "chat-chamber effect" (Jacob et al., 2025). In our case, instead, the echo chamber effect is not generated by Gen AI filtering results in line with users' profiles, or by users failing to verify what reinforces their beliefs; rather, radicalization of one's opinion is the effect of the very "civil" discursive template, whereby the chatbot acknowledges and legitimises the interlocutor's opinion, without challenging them.

However, the limited nature of our empirical base invites caution in the interpretation of our results. Further research is needed, on the one hand, to expand the number of experiments and involve players with different competences in the game (first of all, UG activists); and, on the other hand, to address new research questions that emerged during the experimentation. This is particularly the case of the assessment of AI behavior and rhetorical patterns, more specifically the extent in which it should be considered a structural feature of the program or prompt-dependent. This question can only be answered through a more systematic and prolonged experimentation with the writing of the prompts that shape the game.

Notes

1 In the course of the writing and publication of this chapter, our colleague Fausto Colombo passed away. We are deeply grateful for his contribution to the design of the experiment and the interpretation of the results (and, beyond this work, for his teachings).
2 In the Team edition of Chat GPT 4.0, data gathered in the interaction are not used to train the system: it's one of the features that made us opt for this technology for our serious game.

References

Abt, C. C. (1970). *Serious games*. The Viking Press.

Aranda, C. L., Levy, D. K., & Stoney, S. (2015). Role playing. In K. E. Newcomer, H. P. Hatry, J. S. Wholey (Eds.), *Handbook of practical program evaluation* (pp. 383–411). Jossey Bass – Wiley. https://doi.org/10.1002/9781119171386.ch15

Arendt, H. (1972). *Crises of the republic: Lying in politics, civil disobedience on violence, thoughts on politics, and revolution*. Houghton Mifflin Harcourt.

Bentivegna, S., & Rega, R. (2024). *(Un)civil democracy. Political incivility as a communication strategy*. Palgrave Macmillan.

Blumer, H. (1954). What is wrong with social theory? *American Sociological Review*, 19(1), 3–10.

Charmaz, K. (2014). *Constructing grounded theory: A practical guide through qualitative analysis* (2nd ed.). Sage.

Çiftci, S. (2018). Trends of serious games research from 2007 to 2017: A bibliometric analysis. *Journal of Education and Training Studies*, 6(2), 18–27. https://doi.org/10.11114/jets.v6i2.2840

Costello, T. H., Pennycook, G., & Rand, D. G. (2024). Durably reducing conspiracy beliefs through dialogues with AI. *Science*, 385(6714), eadq1814. https://doi.org/10.1126/science.adq1814

Foucault, M. (2012). *Du gouvernement des vivants. Cours au Collège de France 1979–1980*. Seuil/Gallimard.

Frutos-Pascual, M., & Zapirain, B. G. (2017). Review of the use of AI techniques in serious games: Decision making and machine learning. *IEEE Transactions on Computational Intelligence and AI in Games, 9*(2), 133–152. https://doi.org/10.1109/TCIAIG.2015.2512592

Gazis, A., & Katsiri, E. (2024). E-polis: An innovative and fun way to gamify sociological research with an educational serious game–Game development middleware approach. *International Journal of Education and Information Technologies, 18*, 20–32. https://doi.org/10.46300/9109.2024.18.3

Greenblat, C. S. (1971). Simulations, games, and the sociologist. *The American Sociologist, 6*(2), 161–164.

Habermas, J. (1989). *The structural transformation of the public sphere: An inquiry into a category of bourgeois society*. MIT Press.

Habermas, J. (2023). *A new structural transformation of the public sphere and deliberative politics*. Wiley & Sons.

Jacob, C., Kerrigan, P., & Bastos, M. (2025). The chat-chamber effect: Trusting the AI hallucination. *Big Data & Society, 12*(1). https://doi.org/10.1177/20539517241306345

Laamarti, F., Eid, M., & El Saddik, A. (2014). An overview of serious games. *International Journal of Computer Games Technology, 2014*(1), 358152. https://doi.org/10.1155/2014/358152

Lakoff, R. (1973). The logic of politeness; or, minding your p's and q's. In C. Corum, T. Cedric Smith-Stark, & A. Weiser (Eds.), *Papers from the 9th regional meeting of the Chicago Linguistic Society* (pp. 292–305). Chicago Linguistic Society.

Muddiman, A. (2017). Personal and public levels of incivility. *International Journal of Communication, 11*, 3182–3202.

Mouffe, C. (2005). *The return of the political*. Verso.

Papacharissi, Z. (2004). Democracy online: Civility, politeness, and the democratic potential of online political discussion groups. *New Media & Society, 6*(2), 259–283.

Papacharissi, Z. (2010). *A private sphere: Democracy in a digital age*. Polity.

Papacharissi, Z. (2015). *Affective publics: Sentiment, technology, and politics*. Oxford University Press.

Pérez, J., Castro, M., & López, G. (2023). Serious games and AI: Challenges and opportunities for computational social science. *IEEE Access, 11*, 62051–62061. https://doi.org/10.1109/ACCESS.2023.3286695

Saunders, B., Sim, J., Kingstone, T., Baker, S., Waterfield, J., Bartlam, B., Burroughs, H., & Jinks, C. (2018). Saturation in qualitative research: Exploring its conceptualization and operationalization. *Quality & Quantity, 52*(4), 1893–1907. https://doi.org/10.1007/s11135-017-0574-8

Simpson, J. M., & Elias, V. L. (2011). Choices and chances: The sociology role-playing game—The sociological imagination in practice. *Teaching Sociology, 39*(1), 42–56. https://doi.org/10.1177/0092055X10390646

Terzioglu, M., & Rodrigues, V. (2023). Winning at more than a game! A storytelling board game concept to raise awareness about refugees' language barriers. In K. Vaes & J. Verlinden (Eds.), *Connectivity and creativity in times of conflict*. Academia Press. https://doi.org/10.26530/9789401496476-089

Volk, S. C., Schäfer, M. S., Lombardi, D., Mahl, D., & Yan, X. (2025). How generative artificial intelligence portrays science: Interviewing ChatGPT from the perspective of different audience segments. *Public Understanding of Science*, *34*(2), 132–153. https://doi.org/10.1177/09636625241268910

Wahl-Jorgensen, K. (2019). *Emotions, media and politics*. Wiley & Sons.

Wilkinson, P. (2016). A brief history of serious games. In R. Dorner, S. Gobel, M. Kickmeier-Rust, M. Masuch, & K. Zweig (Eds.), *Entertainment computing and serious games. Lecture notes in computer science* (Vol. 9970, pp. 17–41). Springer. https://doi.org/10.1007/978-3-319-46152-6_2

18

VOICE OF THE OGIEK

Play, Co-Design, and the Spiral Return of Orality in Connective AI

Autumn Edwards, L. Lusike Mukhongo, Winston Mano, Chad Edwards, Cynthia Klekar Cunningham, and Alexander Kisioi Koech

> Whenever two or more people are gathered, a new idea is born.
> —Ogiek elder, co-design workshop, 14 May 2025

Introduction: Designing the Encounter

This chapter begins with a moment of play. In the midst of a codesign workshop between researchers and members of the Indigenous Ogiek community of Kenya's Mau Forest, participants gathered to name the AI-enhanced messaging system they were helping to shape. Laughter rippled through the group as names were suggested and gently debated. A vote was taken. The result was clear and joyful: Voice of the Ogiek, *an* enlivened agentive self-affirmation.

This chapter contributes to the central themes of this volume—*connective AI, technology, play, and democracy*—by exploring how an Indigenous-led co-design process reshaped what AI could be and do in context.[1] Rather than positioning AI as a technical solution delivered to a community, we frame it as a relational and symbolic medium: one through which cultural expression, collective imagination, and democratic cocreation unfold. By bringing American Pragmatism into dialogue with Afrokology (Mano and milton, 2021), we offer a pluralist foundation for understanding how play not only supports participation but enacts ethical connection. We show how seemingly modest acts such as naming, improvisation, and reimagining tools, can transform the political and epistemological stakes of AI design.

DOI: 10.4324/9781003477587-18

Guiding the design process are several UN Sustainable Development Goals, taken up as aspirational orientations. The co-designed, AI-enhanced messaging system developed with Ogiek partners aspires to support SDG 13: Climate Action and SDG 15: Life on Land by amplifying Indigenous ecological knowledge and supporting forest conservation; SDG 10: Reduced Inequalities by addressing communication barriers and structural marginalization; and SDG 16: Peace, Justice, and Strong Institutions through support for culturally grounded systems of governance and community voice.[2]

These goals take on particular urgency in the context of ongoing land struggles, including forced evictions, contested legal rulings, and the erosion of ancestral rights. In this light, both the process and product work toward futures that are not only technologically inclusive but socially and ecologically just.

Here, Indigenous is not treated as a static identity category, but as a agentive, relational and political designation grounded in ancestral connection to land, collective memory, and resistance to colonial and extractive systems. Indigenous communities are defined not only by historical dispossession but also by their ongoing production of knowledge, modes of governance, and ecological stewardship that exist outside or in tension with dominant legal, scientific, and digital infrastructures.

Following the work of scholars such as Linda Tuhiwai Smith (2021) and Leanne Betasamosake Simpson (2014), we approach Indigeneity as an epistemic stance—a way of relating to the world that centers reciprocity, land-based knowledge, and the refusal of assimilation into dominant ontologies. This includes, but is not limited to, communities self-identified or recognized as Indigenous under international frameworks, such as the UN Declaration on the Rights of Indigenous Peoples, as well as groups whose practices and histories reflect localized, relational worldviews in opposition to colonial modernity.

Rooting the Work

The design ethos guiding this project is rooted in *life- and planet-centered design*. This meant attending not only to community needs, but also to the ecological and ethical stakes embedded in every design choice—from naming and infrastructure to the stewardship of digital traces. To operationalize this, our team developed a design process grounded in five relational commitments: *listening to land and people; acknowledging interdependence among ecologies, technologies, and communities; co-creating with care; reflecting and rebalancing; and designing toward regeneration.*

These commitments were informed by principles of Indigenous data sovereignty, or the right of communities to govern how their knowledge, stories, and digital traces are collected, stored, and shared (Kukutai & Taylor, 2016). They emerged in dialogue with Ogiek relational ethics, responsive to site-specific knowledge, and oriented toward long-term thriving—human and more-than-human alike. Our process prioritized sustainability, relational accountability, and planetary stewardship over narrowly defined measures of usability or efficiency. This required rejecting extractive, one-size-fits-all frameworks in favor of recursive, responsive, and place-based approaches that reflect the interconnected health of communities and ecosystems. As the design unfolded, it was relationships rather than predefined functions that reshaped what the system would become. The story of these shifts forms the heart of the chapter that follows.

Codesign, in this context, refers to a process of collaborative creation in which community members and researchers share authority in shaping technologies, tools, or systems. Unlike extractive or consultative models, codesign positions participants as coauthors, valuing their lived experience, cultural insight, and creative agency as integral to the design itself (Sanders & Stappers, 2008). In Indigenous and life-centered contexts, codesign further entails respect for relational knowledge systems and ethical commitments to reciprocity, accountability, and long-term thriving. It is not simply a method, but a way of being in relation—designing with, not for.

In keeping with this ethos, we depart from the language of "users" to emphasize participants as co-players, improvisers, and stewards of meaning—those who do not merely operate a system, but animate it, transform it, and cocreate its value through playful and democratic relation. This framing challenges dominant tech design models in which humans are positioned as passive endpoints and instead affirms design as an ongoing relation among people, practices, land, and language.

The stakes of this project are profound. The Ogiek people are the ancestral guardians of Kenya's Mau Forest, one of the most ecologically vital regions on the continent—and the planet. Their lives are intertwined with the forest's health: they care for bees and hives, steward sustainable farming practices, teach intergenerational knowledge through oral traditions, and defend water as life. Their concept of environmental justice is lived, daily, and generational. In this context, play becomes a form of commitment. The laughter, naming, and improvisation within the codesign process were not signs of levity but expressions of care. They reflect what might be called serious play: a mode of action through which symbolic sovereignty (a community's capacity to define, name, and represent itself through meaningful acts of language, design, and cultural expression) is asserted, ecological values are encoded, and the future of the forest is imagined—and protected.

The name *Voice of the Ogiek*, chosen collectively, does more than designate. It is a design gesture, a symbolic act of world-making. At the margins of Kenyan society and the threatened Mau Forest, the Ogiek community navigates tensions between ancestral tradition and imposed modernities. Their strategies—agentive, resilient, and imaginative—include the use of AI in pursuit of environmental justice and cultural survivance. bell hooks (1989) reminds us that life at the margin can offer "the possibility of radical perspective from which to see and create, to imagine alternatives, new worlds" (p. 20). Naming becomes such a radical act. From an Afrokological and decolonial perspective, naming can be read as an act of re-existence—what Albán Achinte (2013) describes as life-affirming practices that resist colonial negation and cultivate new ways of being and knowing.[3] Naming affirms one's being and connects people with relevant spatialities, temporalities, and relational futures.

In their fuller sense, naming and claiming anchor this chapter's inquiry: How can the design and use of generative AI technologies support *connective play* in ways that amplify community voice, restore democratic possibility, and honor culturally grounded epistemologies? What happens when American Pragmatism meets Afrokology in a codesign process animated by play, affect, and epistemic humility? How might this convergence offer a model for pluralist, world-building AI design?

We explore these questions through the collaborative creation of a connective AI system designed to serve the Mau Ogiek community—a project that centers local values, oral traditions, and cocreative agency while engaging with global design approaches. Our theoretical and methodological orientation is rooted in American Pragmatism and Afrokological thought, and we examine how play—as experimentation, world-making, and democratic action—was central to the process.

Theoretical Grounding: Play, Democracy, and Emergent Design

Play is often dismissed as trivial or unserious—mere amusement, the opposite of work. But in the American Pragmatist tradition, play is foundational: a serious, generative mode of engaging with the world. For thinkers like Emerson, James, Dewey, and Mead, play is integral to inquiry, growth, and democratic life. It enables imagination, supports perspective-taking, and creates conditions for ethical transformation. Dewey, in particular, distinguishes between idle amusement and constructive play, describing the latter as central to aesthetic, educational, and civic life (Dewey, 1934, 1916). For him, play is not preparation for life—it is life itself: a lived mode of inquiry and world-making.

Pragmatist philosophy emphasizes that meaning, truth, and ethical life emerge not from fixed principles but from situated experience, social experimentation, and imaginative reconstruction in relation to others (Dewey, 1938; James, 1907). In this view, play is how we test the world and rehearse its transformation. It is ethical, epistemological, and political.

Mead and Cooley extend this insight to the formation of the self. Mead's "play stage" and "game stage" describe how identity and ethical reflection take shape through role-taking, improvisation, and responsive interaction (Mead, 1934). Through play, sociality itself becomes possible. Peirce introduces a related logic in his account of abduction, a form of reasoning that embraces uncertainty and creativity over fixed conclusions (Peirce, 1931–1958). Similarly, James's (1907) concept of the "will to believe" reflects a voluntarist, pluralistic openness to possibility—a stance that resembles play as an existential commitment to hope and transformation.

Jane Addams brings these pragmatist insights into the public sphere. In *The Spirit of Youth and the City Streets* (1909), she argues that structured, collective play fosters moral development and democratic capacities, especially among marginalized youth. Playgrounds, in her view, are not distractions from hardship, like urban poverty or social injustice, but spaces where ethical habits form. Children learn cooperation, care, and mutual regard through shared activity, not abstract instruction. Play becomes a means of navigating, not erasing, unequal conditions. Robert Putnam's (2000) *Bowling Alone: America's Declining Social Capital* similarly underscored the earlier insights on the vital role of face-to-face social interaction in shaping, sustaining, and enriching the foundations of American social life.

This thread is extended by feminist and neo-pragmatist thinkers. Charlene Haddock Seigfried (1996) interprets play as a form of narrative flexibility—a willingness to retell, remix, and reimagine shared meanings. Shannon Sullivan (2001) emphasizes the role of embodied habits in shaping and reshaping social norms, suggesting that conscious engagement with these patterns can open space for cultural transformation. In this light, play can be understood as a mode of lived inquiry, disrupting and reworking sedimented ways of being. María Lugones (1987) offers a powerful account of "world-traveling" as loving play—an ethical praxis of crossing difference, resisting domination, and enabling coalition. For Lugones, play becomes an act of epistemic humility, where one risks decentering the self and inhabiting the terms of others.

Together, these perspectives define play not as escape, but as engagement. In James's and Dewey's meliorism, play is how the world gets tested—and potentially transformed. Play opens imaginative possibility without requiring resolution. It often holds contradiction, resists closure, and sustains imaginative ambiguity where fixed meaning would flatten experience.

In this sense, play functions not only as inquiry, but as *epistemic holding*—a shared capacity to stay with what is emergent, unresolved, and not-yet-known. Within Pragmatist thought, this holding is a mode of *onto-logical hospitality*: a practice of making room for multiple ways of being, knowing, and relating without demanding their assimilation. James's pluralism, Dewey's aesthetic theory of experience, and Addams's ethic of democratic inclusion all affirm the ethical value of staying in relation without reaching too quickly for closure, of not knowing too soon.

This mode of hospitality also finds kinship in Indigenous philosophies, in part because they shaped the very foundations of American pragmatism. As Scott L. Pratt (2002) demonstrates, key features of Pragmatist thought—such as relational knowing, experiential grounding, and context-specific ethics—emerged through nineteenth-century encounters with Indigenous lifeways. Yet these influences were rarely named or credited by canonical figures like Peirce and Dewey. Brian Burkhart (2019) extends this argument, showing that Indigenous philosophies do not merely resemble Pragmatism; they constitute an underacknowledged source of its central commitments. Acknowledging this entanglement does not absolve Pragmatism of its Eurocentric codification. Rather, it opens space to engage the tradition as one that is not decolonial by birth, but decolonizable in practice; a move advanced by thinkers such as Leonard Harris (2009) and Cornel West (1989), who have pushed Pragmatism toward anti-colonial and justice-oriented ends.

Play, too, is shaped by cultural context and power. Even in its earliest theorization, play was bound up with questions of access, recognition, and participation. Mead's theory of social development shows that not everyone enters the "game stage" on equal footing; the ability to take up roles and be acknowledged depends on broader structures of visibility and value. Roles and relational possibilities are unevenly distributed, shaped by social conditions that extend beyond any single moment of play. While play can suspend hierarchy by inviting improvisation, attunement, and mutual recognition outside formal structures, it can also reproduce or expose existing asymmetries—especially in cross-cultural settings marked by unequal histories, infrastructures, or visibility. These dynamics do not diminish play's transformative potential, but they remind us that play is always situated and political. To treat play as democratic is to remain attentive to the relational conditions that make cocreation possible. It also requires care in moments of encounter—recognizing how presence is shared across difference, and how responsibility for interpreting gestures of knowledge, emotion, or surprise is assumed or wisely deferred.

**

Laughter in the Light

A moment from early fieldwork illustrates how play can open space for shared curiosity while also surfacing the uneven conditions that shape participation. On a sunlit May afternoon, the school came into view after a winding route through the Mau Forest—familiar ground for the community, and the beginning of a shared encounter for us. Nestled at the forest's edge, the schoolyard opened into grass and light. When the principal rang the bell, more than 500 children streamed into the clearing, forming an impromptu assembly. As we stood near the front, two of us visibly white, the children responded with spontaneous laughter, wide eyes, and extended hands. Some ran forward to greet us; others settled into the grass, cross-legged and attentive. Their gestures were more than welcoming. They were expressions of presence—relational, playful, and alive.

As one of our team members began a short introduction to the project, the mood remained buoyant. The laughter continued, shaping a scene structured less by dialogue than by co-presence. At the end of the introduction, a boy raised his voice from the crowd: "Teach me to build a robot!" In that moment, the encounter shifted from reception to initiative.

We share this story not to center our emotional response, nor to position the children as naïve, but to remain accountable to the care and attentiveness these moments require. Linda Tuhiwai Smith (2021) reminds us that research has long cast Indigenous communities as objects of awe or curiosity, images that linger in colonial logics even when intentions are otherwise. Tuck and Yang (2012) caution that emotionally resonant moments can become "moves to innocence," displacing responsibility rather than deepening it. And Sara Ahmed (2014) notes that whiteness often operates affectively, drawing attention to itself in ways that re-center power unless carefully held in check.

Still, the moment carried meaning. It invited relation, not explanation. The children did not offer "access" to knowledge in extractable form, but something more situated: embodied knowing, a shared rhythm, and a gesture toward collective imagination. Following Édouard Glissant (1997), we chose not to decode the laughter but to honor its opacity—a concept he frames as the right to difference without reduction, and a refusal of forced transparency. In this sense, opacity is not a lack of meaning, but a presence that resists assimilation. It mattered because it remained whole. The encounter reoriented the space. It did not yield data points or design inputs, yet it shaped what followed. It opened a pathway toward mutual imagination and deeper ethical attention.

Such insights are not only philosophical; they are methodological. In cross-cultural design, play becomes a mode of shared experimentation. It creates openings for presence, for unexpected initiative, and for recognition that moves in more than one direction. We take seriously the proposition that play is not merely a metaphor for democracy, but its rehearsal and enactment (Putnam, 2000). In the codesign of connective AI, play is where cultural values, technical systems, and community aspirations meet—not through extraction, but through relation.

Afrokological Resonances: Grounding Epistemic Justice

To take epistemic humility seriously in this cross-cultural collaboration, we must look beyond Western theory. As an African proverb reminds us: once a big drum sounds, the small ones must go quiet. If African epistemes have long been those quieter drums, continued silence is no longer viable. The dominance of Northern/Western frameworks has marginalized Southern knowledge systems—not because all Western theories are flawed or African ones inherently superior, but because universalizing Western ideas has obscured other valid ways of knowing.

We turn to Afrokology—a decolonial, heuristic framework developed by Mano and milton (2021)—to center African epistemes and reclaim sidelined knowledge traditions. Afrokology challenges the unchecked dominance of Western thought by reorienting knowledge production toward ontological pluralism. It treats incompleteness not as a flaw, but as a strength—a multiplier of possibility that invites humility, cocreation, and epistemic renewal across difference. In treating particularity seriously, Afrokology values multiple ways of knowing not as expressions of a pluriversal world rather than deviations from a norm.

Afrokology emphasizes praxis—dialogic, collaborative engagement rooted in African communication patterns, relational ways of knowing, and lived experience. As Mano and milton (2021) note, "The 'K' signals epistemic disobedience—a deliberate break from colonial universalism and a call to affirm silenced African voices and new starting points" (p. 30).

Beyond critique, Afrokology offers a generative reimagining of both theory and practice through conviviality, decolonial ethics, and community-defined frameworks for meaning-making. At the core of this reorientation is *relexicalizing*, or the creation of new vocabularies to represent African realities. This epistemic experimentation affirms agency and invites a break from imposed categories, allowing language to emerge from within experience itself.

When brought into resonance with Pragmatism, Afrokology opens powerful avenues for plural design. Both traditions emphasize situated knowledge, relational selfhood, communication as cocreation, and play as cultural expression and collective becoming. Pragmatism foregrounds inquiry and democratic experimentation; Afrokology adds rhythm, continuity, and affective depth. Together, they offer a design ethic grounded not only in inquiry and responsiveness, but in rhythm, relationality, and the dignity of incompleteness.

Voice, Orality, and the Spiral Return

One of the most revealing moments in the co-design process came when the Ogiek team named the system *Voice of the Ogiek*. As described earlier, the name emerged through a democratic and playful process, but it also did symbolic work. It centered *orality* as both medium and metaphor. The system was not defined by silent algorithmic logic or text-based commands, but by practices of voice, relation, and oral transmission.

Voicing as Re-Existence

As the process unfolded, our original assumptions began to shift. Initially, the system was imagined as a low-bandwidth platform combining generative AI with SMS to deliver community-relevant updates—on legal rulings, forest practices, and cultural heritage. But through codesign, it became clear that what many Ogiek partners most valued was not a delivery tool, but a space for expression: a way to speak, create, and connect on their own terms. What began as a system to speak *to* the community was reimagined as one to speak *through*, grounded in Ogiek ways of knowing and relating.

Prioritizing expressive voice over content delivery guided a rethinking of core design decisions. While the original technical plan prioritized low-tech feature phones, the Ogiek team advocated for smartphone integration to better support oral and visual communication. Their choice reflected a deeper alignment with oral knowledge practices (e.g., voice messages, video, and visual storytelling) and reconfigured the platform to extend, not replace, primary orality.

Crucially, participants emphasized that the system should not only deliver content but also accept and invite cultural inputs (e.g., poems, stories, language, and songs) to develop, archive, and amplify the voice of the Ogiek. Nowhere was this more evident than in the vision for the project's website, which participants imagined as a visible register of voice: not just a platform, but a cultural beacon. Conversations about color, motifs, and structure sparked energy. Ideas emerged—local journalism, forest preservation, even real-time weather data. This wasn't peripheral. It was a core expression of what "voice" meant: not simply being addressed by technology, but speaking through it—contributing, shaping, and being audibly and visibly present within its flow.

Ngũgĩ wa Thiong'o, the late Kenyan writer and theorist, gives name to a shifting communicative reality: *cyborality*—the fusion of oral and written expression through digital media. He observes that "the language of cyberspace…is neither one nor the other. It's both. It's cyborality" (2012, p. 84). For the Ogiek, a historically oral community now engaging with chatbots, SMS, WhatsApp, and email, this convergence affirms presence and voice through new modalities. It challenges the historical marginalization of oral cultures and disrupts narrow definitions of completeness in knowledge systems.

Walter Ong (1982) described *secondary orality* as the reemergence of oral forms within technologically mediated contexts, shaped by mass communication logics but marked by participation and communal resonance. What occurred here was different. Orality returned not by technological affordance alone, but through cultural continuity and design intention. Ogiek collaborators did not treat orality as a past to be revived under digital terms. They extended it—infusing tools with rhythm, presence, and ancestral voice. The oral was not recovered. It was braided into the present, transforming AI into a connective surface for ancestral presence and future expression.

While *cyborality* names the hybrid communicative terrain of digital Africa, we propose *spiral return* as a motif for culturally grounded innovation and re-existence. It describes the temporal and relational dynamics through which ancestral knowledge, cultural practice, and community-defined meaning are carried forward, reshaped, and re-expressed. *Spiral return* reflects a cyclical, sovereign orientation to time. Continuity arises not through replication, but through relational renewal—layered, regenerative, and in flux.

The concept draws from feminist invocations like Bateson's (1990) recursive learning and resonates with Indigenous and decolonial philosophies that treat time as iterative, embodied, and relational. Vizenor (1994) describes *survivance* as narrative motion that resists static preservation, while Wilson (2008) frames Indigenous research as ceremony—an ongoing, spiraling engagement with knowledge.

This movement finds close kinship with Ngũgĩ wa Thiong'o's framing of *cyborality*. What *spiral return* names across traditions, *cyborality* enacts from within African—and specifically Kenyan—intellectual lifeways: the continuity of presence through digital forms, carried not as loss or hybridity, but as relational becoming. Rather than parallel ideas, they interweave, attuned to how ancestral knowledge endures—not through preservation alone, but through expressive adaptation.

These perspectives demonstrate that epistemic vitality arises not from novelty but from relation, return, and renewal. Cultural life shaped not only the system's content but also the very process through which it was designed. Orality, in this context, was not just a feature of the final product. As a social medium through which rhythm, coordination, and shared presence emerged, orality shaped the design process itself by grounding it in the body—both literal and collective—and in the expressive force of voice.

> On several occasions, participants spontaneously initiated songs like If You're Happy and You Know It, clapping and smiling in shared rhythm. These weren't diversions but shifts in register: embodied forms of coordination grounded in Ogiek social practice.

In this context, play became more than expression. It became a recalibration of mood, rhythm, and focus. What might appear as a playful interlude was, in fact, integral to the design process. We call this *epistemic rhythm*— the tempo of knowing set not by tools or timelines, but by voices, bodies, and shared cultural cadence. This is one form of *temporal sovereignty*: the right to shape the pace and sequencing of knowledge-making on one's own terms (Robinson, 2020; see also Povinelli, 2011, on endurance and alternative temporalities).

This rhythm of knowing resists externally imposed metrics of speed or closure. As Davis (2015) writes, temporal sovereignty privileges cyclical renewal and ancestral continuity over linear progress. In our codesign, the Ogiek's recursive, relational engagement enacted such sovereignty, weaving past and present into a shared tempo. When participants sang together, they re-authored the tone and timing of the work. These acts were playful, but also grounding, guiding, and attuned. Through rhythm and copresence, participants asserted symbolic authorship. It wasn't just felt—it was carried together, like a pulse. Such rhythms echo Indigenous and decolonial temporalities that frame time as spiraling, layered, and generative (Mbembe, 2001; Wynter, 1984; Wilson, 2008). They affirm that epistemic vitality arises from continuity, presence, and relational unfolding.

What the Earth Remembers

Riddles and songs within Ogiek oral tradition offer pedagogical rhythms of play, creativity, and groundedness. Riddles, in particular, provide a structured yet fluid method for sharing knowledge and affirming belonging. Their form invites metaphor and layered inquiry. One woman's initiation song, recorded by Micheli (2014), includes a line with riddle-like cadence:

"We cannot explain about this dust" (*mDgirĎroru temburiDn gwe, asa! Igo!*). What is this dust? The forested land of the Mau? A memory of origin? An ancestral silence? A sacred unknowability? The line resists resolution. It functions not as a code to crack, but as a living puzzle that calls for presence. In contrast to technoscientific paradigms that seek fixed meaning, this is knowledge as relational, cocreated, and responsive.

Ogiek ecological storytelling offers another expression of playful, relational knowledge-making. These stories, often featuring forest animals, ancestral figures, or natural forces, invite listeners into layered narratives that encode environmental ethics, kinship norms, and survival strategies. Such stories are not merely descriptive; they are pedagogical, performed with rhythm, gesture, and interactive cues. As with riddles, meaning emerges not through exposition but through metaphor, implication, and affective presence. This narrative mode reflects a cultural sense of knowledge as emergent, situated, and alive—never abstracted from land, voice, or relation. As the Ogiek People's Development Program notes, elders weave "intricate narratives of history, culture, and life experiences" to help youth forge a connection with their roots and embrace the essence of being Ogiek. These stories foster bridges between generations, not as archived tradition but as a living pedagogy of belonging and ecological sovereignty.

This emphasis on voice echoes a broader African communication ethos, visible in organizations like *Africa's Talking*, whose very name affirms the cultural centrality of speech, conversation, and oral connection in the design of digital tools. As a project partner, Africa's Talking helped translate this ethos into a technological structure.

Through codesign, AI was envisioned as a participatory space where voice carried not only connection and memory, but a living practice of epistemic justice.

Toward Pluralist Design: A Shared Frame

One moment that shaped our orientation to emergent design came when Ogiek collaborators brought us to the source of the Maru River. There, water emerges quietly from the ground—just a trickle—before gaining force on its journey through the Mau Forest and beyond, where it joins the Mara River and helps sustain the great migrations across the Maasai Mara and Serengeti plains. Few outsiders have witnessed this sacred place. For us, it became a guiding metaphor: intentions did not begin fully formed but arose through relation, movement, and unfolding understanding. What the river touches, bends around, and carries forward helps determine its shape. So too with our collaborative work.

This approach contrasts sharply with conventional design research, which identifies user needs, gathers requirements, and prototypes systems toward predefined outcomes. What emerged instead was a shared epistemology—a way of knowing grounded in context, copresence, and mutual responsiveness. As a team of Ogiek community members and allied researchers, we shifted from design as solution to design as dialogue, not to solve a static problem, but to hold space for what matters to emerge.

The process remains ongoing, but certain themes have already taken form:

The team's orientation was shaped not only by collaborative goals but by a willingness to let the process reshape its own aims. As in the Pragmatist tradition, our "ends-in-view" were not fixed at the source like predetermined objectives but arose downstream, shaped by what the current touched, carried, or bent around. Afrokology offers a resonant frame: aims emerge through epistemic disobedience, relexicalization, relationality, and participation. Both traditions remind us that knowledge and purpose are not imposed but discovered in shared motion. As Mano and milton (2021, p. 37) describe it, "Afrokology is a decolonizing heuristic tool that facilitates oppositional consciousness... a space to relexicalise and construct new vocabularies that can help to decolonise epistemological imagination." This is not only a linguistic move, but a political and ethical one: relexicalization refuses inherited ends and insists that futures must be coauthored. In this light, both Afrokology and Pragmatism enact forms of poetic activism by reworking the world through the expansion of available vocabularies (Rorty, 1989) and by opening space for new aims, relations, and futures.

A generative example emerged when Ogiek participants expressed a desire for internet access and computers for their local school. In many research contexts, such a request might be labeled "mission creep." Here, it became a touchstone of relational design. It reflected the Ogiek community's imaginative stake in the project. In this sense, play became a condition of possibility. It created space for shared authorship and reconfigured what counted as a design objective.

Afrokology invites recognition that technologies and sociopolitical change are transforming African communities in unique ways. No single theory explains this landscape. Instead, Afrokology recognizes the need for experimentation rooted in everyday life—as individuals, families, and communities navigate volatile conditions. It only asks that such experimentation avoid intellectual violence and respect the need to decriminalize difference. As an African proverb puts it: wisdom is like a baobab tree; no one person can embrace it.

These insights highlight the need to integrate contextual epistemes. The Ogiek's ways of knowing and doing are central to creating their technological futures.

*
**

These were not abstract experiences, but moments of recognition and trust, borne of lived relation. *The enrobing of a researcher in a chief's animal skin attire—a deeply meaningful gesture of belonging—reflected a ceremonial seriousness at odds with extractive research practices the Ogiek have too often endured. Such gestures act not merely as cultural rituals but as symbolic redress, countering historical asymmetries through practices of relational acknowledgment and mutual responsibility (Tuck & Yang, 2012; Todd, 2016). In Indigenous design, symbolic redress is not peripheral—it is integral to justice-oriented cocreation.*

We recognize that the meanings we describe—of rivers as metaphors, of symbolic enrobing as relational invitation, of WhatsApp groups and gifted honey as connective gestures—are interpretations we carry as researchers. They emerge from our attempt to remain attentive and accountable to the relationships into which we were invited. These are not definitive claims, but situated reflections shaped by trust, care, and ongoing exchange.

We are mindful, too, of critiques of the ontological turn that caution against instrumentalizing Indigenous lifeways as conceptual resources while reproducing extractive academic habits (Todd, 2016; Tuck & Yang, 2012). In response, we try—with attention and humility—to approach ontology not as a detached analytic but as a lived and relational register, expressed through trust, voice, shared rhythms, and symbolic presence. Rather than positioning ourselves as translators of Ogiek being, we aim to remain in thoughtful relation to the invitations extended through codesign, and to speak with care about the meanings that moved us.

At the same time, we acknowledge that interpretive responsibility is part of ethical scholarship. Our goal is not to fix the meaning of any moment, but to remain responsive to its significance—and to trace how such moments shape the moral and symbolic terrain of design.

These layered exchanges—at once symbolic and material—shaped our shared understanding and gradually transformed how relation, authorship, and care took form. They laid the groundwork for more quietly sustained forms of connection, where shared authorship found expression in everyday tools, conversations, and gestures.

Among these practical moves was the creation of a WhatsApp group by our Ogiek collaborators to link community members and university researchers, a refusal of the one-way flows that have long defined technological and institutional relationships. This simple act marked the formation of a community-driven infrastructure that redistributed access and agency. Such grassroots systems of connection, modest as they may seem, highlight and bridge asymmetries that often remain invisible in Global South–Global North collaborations (Philip et al., 2012).

Gifts exchanged—stone-carved figures, beaded necklaces, jars of honey—were not tokens of gratitude but expressions within a relational economy grounded in shared labor, cultural presence, and symbolic reciprocity. Selected with care, each item was imbued with texture and meaning, signaling specific qualities or relationships. *A lion was given to one researcher, a rhino to another, and yet another received a sculpture of human figures linked in a circle—a representation of family unity, relational care, or togetherness.* Drawing on Davis (2020), we understand such artifacts as affordances—socially situated things that carry "the power and politics of everyday life" (p. 2). In this sense, these gifts, precisely because of their situated significance, helped shape the relational terrain of our codesign. They encoded expectations, signaled commitments, and invited specific ethical orientations. Beyond mirroring the community's values, they materially participated in cocreating the space in which those values could be enacted.

A further dimension of relational authorship emerged in extended conversations around infrastructure, privacy, and data stewardship. Ogiek partners emphasized that protecting social relationships was as vital as protecting personal data. They observed that SMS technology, though widely accessible, can disrupt household dynamics, influence gender roles, and shift power relations, particularly when messages are intercepted or misinterpreted. Rather than treat these effects as marginal, they urged us to consider how communication systems might reinforce rather than disrupt the social networks they value. Their call sharpened our ethical orientation, shifting emphasis from abstract ideals to relational consequence—a principle rooted in both Afrokology and Pragmatism.

That shift extended into technical design. We prioritized locally hosted, open-source infrastructure accountable to community governance—an approach shaped by Ogiek lived experience and aligned with broader Indigenous demands for control over data systems (Kukutai & Taylor, 2016; Rainie et al., 2017). Design conversations moved beyond functionality to foreground stewardship: who holds data, who speaks for whom, and how cultural expressions remain anchored in community accountability.

To honor these values in practice, we distributed feature phones and provided honoraria—reciprocating the time, care, and insight shared by Ogiek participants. The phones served multiple purposes: enabling low-power access to the AI-SMS system, supporting inclusive design testing, and offering practical tools like FM radios and torches. Their selection reflected both infrastructural realities and a collective commitment to data sovereignty in practice.

Shaped by values of relational stewardship and infrastructural equity, these decisions reaffirmed our commitment to life-centered design—an approach that prioritizes not just utility, but the flourishing of relational, communal, and ecological life. Yet building this vision into infrastructure revealed logistical tensions: implementing a Kenya-based server and localized platform raised challenges related to secure hosting, consistent power, and sustainable technical maintenance. These frictions underscored the real-world complexity of enacting ethical design at scale.

Alongside technical frameworks, trust among Ogiek collaborators and researchers functioned as its own kind of infrastructure. Built through shared acts of being, playing, and moving through time together, this trust did not replace formal justice commitments, such as data sovereignty, but enabled and sustained them. It served as a relational bridge—what Papacharissi (2015) describes as the connective potential of shared feeling in democratic life—carrying affective rapport toward community-defined futures.

When formal scaffolding lagged, trust kept the project in motion, allowing us to stay in relation, navigate constraint, and imagine together. Yet in Indigenous research and design, trust is often fragile and historically burdened. As others have warned, it can be too easily misread as permission to bypass sustained responsibility or delay long-term commitments to justice (Kovach, 2021; Smith, 2021). The Ogiek partners' insights grounded the project in a deeper ethical frame that asked not only how information circulates, but how platforms might responsibly uphold relational integrity, safeguard communal voice, and earn the trust required for cocreation.

That commitment to relational integrity also shaped visual design. In one session, younger participants reviewed an early draft of the project emblem: a single, well-established tree, its trunk subtly overlaid with Ogiek patternry, branches and leaves evoking both organic growth and technological circuitry, with a Wi-Fi signal emanating from the treetop. A small bee hovered quietly nodding to pollination and connection. In response, they offered a joyful revision: "more trees, many trees"—a forest, not one. The word coverage surfaced, playfully layered to mean both signal reach and the expansive ecological and social presence of the forest.

This reworking was also a form of design refusal—not rejection, but creative redirection (Costanza-Chock, 2020). It was a curatorial act: a gesture

FIGURE 18.1   *Evolution of the project emblem.* An early version (a) depicted a single tree; a reimagined version (b), proposed by Ogiek participants, featured a forest to reflect ecological relationality and collective identity. The shift illustrates symbolic authorship and epistemic refusal.

of cultural authorship and symbolic realignment. Rather than position the system as a tool transmitting information outward from a singular source (the lone tree), they reimagined it as a shared canopy—an interface rooted in reciprocity, cultural ecology, and collective presence.

In this way, the emblem became a living metaphor. The forest was not just a design element, but a symbol of connection, shelter, and continuity. It reframed the AI system as something capable of carrying, co-constructing, and protecting the voice of the Ogiek collectively. Design, here, was not only about coherence, but about meaning in relation (Figure 18.1).

Alexander Kisioi, Ogiek environmental activist and project partner, offered this reflection in a WhatsApp conversation[4]:

Forests and trees help to feed the world – they are rich sources of foods such as nuts, fruits, seeds, roots, tubers, leaves, mushrooms, honey, game meat and insects, providing millions of people around the world with essential nutrients, especially micronutrients. Not only do forests supply the essential nutrients to many people's dietary intake, they also contribute directly to sustainable agricultural production by helping maintain soil fertility, protecting water catchments, providing homes to pollinators and regulating rainfall.

Kisioi's words root the forest as both symbol and sustenance. The call for "more trees" was not metaphor alone: It reflected a lived world in which trees nourish bodies, relationships, and futures.

Such gestures reframe design not only as technical but as ethical and symbolic. As Lackey and Papacharissi (2024) suggest, human–AI communication can shift the "consciousness of Earth's sociotechnical system" (p. 14). We argue that this shift begins earlier: in acts of naming, cocreating, and reimagining what AI might become. These upstream interventions reshape the sociotechnical imaginary itself. In this light, the Ogiek's involvement helped constitute the moral and symbolic infrastructure of technological design.

Drawing on Saidiya Hartman's (2008) notion of *critical fabulation*— "refusing the given" and imagining otherwise—Ruha Benjamin (2019) extends this method to show how technologies often encode discriminatory designs. In our project, acts of naming, ritual, gifting, and oral integration became symbolic refusals of extractive norms and creative assertions of epistemic presence and legitimacy (see also Battiste, 2005).

Peter-Paul Verbeek (2011) gives sharp form to this premise, asserting that design is *ethics by other means*. Moral relations are not simply applied to finished tools; they are configured through design itself. In our work, *Voice of the Ogiek* was not merely a conduit for values; it became a connective artifact through which those values were enacted, shared, and sustained.

Although these aspirations are global in scope, they were animated by local gestures: singing together, renaming tools, and invoking forests. In these moments, justice became relational, not abstract, emerging through shared symbols and everyday acts of imagination.

In the Pragmatist tradition, play is how we test the world and stay in relation while doing so. It is a practice of attunement, of holding space for difference without closure. Across the design process, Ogiek participants and researchers engaged in such play, not as entertainment, but as a cocreative ethic. Whether through metaphor, song, or laughter, play allowed the unfamiliar to become shared without being flattened. It offered a way to move forward together, not because everyone agreed, but because we remained in democratic relation.

Play resists linearity. It loops, returns, and transforms. Were it to follow a straight path, play might risk becoming decorative—an embellishment atop a predetermined end. But in spiraling back and drawing forward, it reorients relation and sustains open inquiry. For Peirce (1931–1958), semiosis unfolds through recursive interpretation; for James (1907), ambiguity is vital; for Dewey (1938/2008), inquiry is a rhythm of disruption and reconstruction. In this light, play is a generative condition for ethical relation, mutual learning, and democratic design.

This spiraling mode of relation echoes Afrokological commitments to incompleteness, attunement, and plural ways of knowing (Mano & milton, 2021). In contrast to the universalizing tendencies of dominant Western frameworks, Afrokology invites us to design with the South in mind, not as a supplement but as a co-generator of epistemic futures. Its emphasis on incompleteness as a multiplier mirrors play's refusal of finality and affirms the hunger to stay in dialogue across difference.

*_{**}

The Overstory

Having traveled the dense weave of design, relation, and play, we arrive together at a high clearing, where treetops become forest and scattered gestures may begin to take shape as a living whole.

We offer this chapter as a provocation and a proposal: that play can be a ground for shared inquiry across difference; that design, when approached with humility and imagination, becomes a democratic and symbolic act; and that connective AI, co-shaped through relation and care, can become a site for spiral returns, symbolic sovereignty, and plural futures. Designing for the common good, we suggest, must be receptive to connective play—and remain open to the knowledges, rhythms, and reimaginings that emerge when communities shape their own tools, in their own voice.

What might it mean to intervene in the design of AI *before* communicative futures calcify into extractive defaults? What other futures might spiral into being if we viewed play as the groundwork for democratic engagement?

As Ruha Benjamin reminds us, "Rather than waiting for a machine to go awry or for a program to be deployed in a harmful way, we must analyze and reimagine the very process of invention, the default settings of design" (2019, p. 78). AI systems, like the sociotechnical architectures that preceded them (i.e., the internet, and social media), too often consolidate power long before their ethical implications are discerned. But when systems are coauthored with communities from the start, different patterns can take root. In playful relation, we can create space for world-building, rehearsing democratic possibilities, and imagining otherwise. Participation can be invited at the headwaters of design, keeping communicative futures open.

Voice of the Ogiek offers a situated response that carries forward a transferable ethos. It demonstrates the promise of a design orientation grounded from the outset in relational presence, ethical coauthorship, and planetary care. Future practitioners might extend several insights:

First, we argue that symbolic design elements such as naming, rhythm, and storytelling are not peripheral to systems, but constitutive of their meaning and moral architecture. These elements shape not only how people interact with a system, but also how knowledge, identity, and authority are encoded within it. In this way, they establish whose ways of knowing are recognized, invited, or erased. Second, codesigned data sovereignty plans can become vital infrastructures for epistemic justice, especially in communities navigating systemic erasure or digital precarity. Third, we encourage broader adoption of tech-reciprocity logs: ecological accountability practices that track the carbon, water, and heat costs of our interventions (e.g., servers, devices, travel) and offset them through regenerative acts.[5] Among the Ogiek in the Mau, practices including indigenous tree planting, bee keeping, and material investments in local ecological and conservation projects are an integral part of co-design rather than post hoc remediation.

From these discussions, we offer a broader implication: the possibility of a coalitional ethics that resists epistemic domination by placing diverse traditions in resonant relation. In our context, Afrokology, Indigenous philosophies, and a decolonizing Pragmatism offer complementary visions of relationality, pluralism, and epistemic responsibility. Yet coalitions, whether among ideas or codesigners, will necessarily look different elsewhere, shaped by the lived realities, histories, and sovereignties of place. What matters is that such frameworks and the people who voice them be engaged dialogically to sustain solidarities across diverse lifeways and cultivate alliances grounded in respect, reciprocity, and refusal.

This last term deserves particular attention. In dominant human- or user-centered paradigms, refusal is often seen as misunderstanding, resistance, or delay. But in pluralistic design, refusal can signify care. It can mark the protective boundaries drawn around what must not be captured; a practice of safeguarding what communities choose to hold intact. (Tuck & Yang, 2014; see also Dotson, 2011; Todd, 2016). Refusal, however, is not only protective. As Tuck and Yang argue, it is also a speculative method that opens space for "otherwise" relations, contributions, and ways of being to emerge.

In this sense, refusal walks hand in hand with the many constitutive propositions our Ogiek partners offered. These were creative acts that manifested the symbolic and functional architecture of the system and larger projects. The naming of the system—*Voice of the Ogiek*—was itself a powerful declaration of authorship, ontological presence, and sovereignty. The push for smartphone integration and the call for educational infrastructure, likewise, were not *responses* to design, but rather, they were designs. If refusal marks a sacred boundary, these grounded offerings or additive proposals might be understood as instantiations of *propositional sovereignty*: the right not only to refuse but to originate. This framing resonates with Simpson's (2014) account of constellatory resurgence, grounded in Indigenous normativity and everyday acts of rebuilding. It aligns with Escobar's (2018) vision of design for the pluriverse and with de la Cadena and Blaser's (2018) articulation of *worlding otherwise*: the enactment of ontological difference through relational practices that resist capture. Designers and researchers committed to relational practice must remain attuned to such openings, even when they unsettle project aims. This is the "yes, and" of participatory design: not steering steadfastly toward predetermined deliverables but rather welcoming what unfolds—and risking real revision.[6]

Design, then, is not merely what gets built. It is how relation is made possible, how knowledge is invited or ignored, and how futures are rendered livable (or not) across difference. *Voice of the Ogiek* emerges from this premise. It remains a living relation: one that listens forward, grows from ancestral ground, and stays in democratic motion.

As Alexander Kisioi Koech[7] writes in a reflection shared after our recent workshop:

> We don't just plant trees—we understand which seed belongs to which soil, which plant supports which insect, and how the balance of nature is maintained through careful, intentional living.

That same attentiveness shapes the system. What it names is not fixed. It is still becoming. Not toward closure, but toward a future of entangled presence, in which AI listens with, grows from, and returns to the soil it touches. Designing with this ethic means attuning to the world we inherit and cocreating one in which voices carry—sustained in relation and sovereign in their return.

Acknowledgments

We gratefully acknowledge Abdullah Mohaimen, Habeeb Abdulrauf, and Nickson Kiplagat Terer for their vital contributions to the design and facilitation of the codesign process. Their insight, care, and ongoing collaboration have been integral to the larger project. We also thank Graham Muhanga and Africa's Talking for their support of the SMS infrastructure, which enabled the development and testing of the AI-SMS system. Most of all, we thank the Ogiek community for their partnership, guidance, imagination, and generosity throughout this project. Their knowledge, presence, and collaborative spirit are woven into every dimension of this work.

Notes

1 Footnote 1: Several key terms guide this chapter's framing and may benefit from brief clarification. Connective AI refers to sociotechnical systems that privilege relationship, reciprocity, and plural knowledges over extraction or efficiency. It emphasizes communication and collaboration between diverse actors—human and nonhuman—in co-constructing meaning. Co-design describes a participatory design process in which community members are treated not as subjects but as coauthors, with reciprocal authority in shaping tools and outcomes. Life-centered design prioritizes the interdependence of human and more-than-human life systems, attending to ecological, cultural, and ethical flourishing. Pluralist design foregrounds epistemic humility and ontological multiplicity, embracing the coexistence of different ways of knowing, sensing, and valuing. Symbolic design draws attention to the expressive, world-making power of design choices, especially in contexts where naming, representation, and narrative carry political and cultural weight.
2 This work was supported by a Mozilla Technology Fund grant from the Mozilla Foundation. The fund backs open-source projects that promote sustainable AI, environmental justice, and equitable, community-led innovation; principles that align closely with the values of this project.
3 While Achinte's formulation appears in Spanish, *re-existence* has become a widely cited concept in transnational decolonial literature. For an English-language elaboration, see Walsh (2018).
4 Contributed by Alexander Kisioi in a WhatsApp message to the project team on May 27, 2025. Quoted with permission.
5 We define a tech-reciprocity log as an accountability tool that tracks the ecological and material costs of technological interventions (e.g., server use, device distribution, electricity, travel) and supports regenerative offsets, such as tree planting or water tank provision. This method draws from ecological accountability principles in sustainable computing and green AI (Bender et al., 2021; Parikka, 2015; Schwartz et al., 2020). A version of our team's working template is available upon request.
6 We recognize that *worlding otherwise* (de la Cadena & Blaser, 2018) and *constellatory practices* (Simpson, 2014) arise from specific ontological and cultural commitments that exceed design paradigms rooted in mutual legibility or reform. Our intention is not to universalize these frameworks but to remain accountable to their epistemic specificity while acknowledging how they help us perceive the generative and world-making nature of Ogiek design gestures, even when those gestures do not easily map onto institutional categories of design or participation.
7 Shared to WhatsApp on June 16, 2025. Included with permission.

References

Addams, J. (1909). *The spirit of youth and the city streets*. Macmillan.

Ahmed, S. (2014). *The cultural politics of emotion* (2nd ed.). Routledge.

Albán Achinte, A. (2013). Más allá del reconocimiento: Pueblos indígenas, políticas de la cultura y re-existencia en Colombia. In C. Walsh (Ed.), *Pedagogías decoloniales: Prácticas insurgentes de resistir, (re)existir y (re)vivir* (pp. 95–122). Ediciones Abya-Yala.

Bateson, M. C. (1990). *Composing a life*. Atlantic Monthly Press.

Battiste, M. (2005). Indigenous knowledge: Foundations for first nations. *WINHEC:International Journal of Indigenous Education Scholarship*, 2005, 1–17. https://journals.uvic.ca/index.php/winhec/article/view/19251

Bender, E. M., Gebru, T., McMillan-Major, A., & Shmitchell, S. (2021). On the dangers of stochastic parrots: Can language models be too big? *Proceedings of the 2021 ACM Conference on Fairness, Accountability, and Transparency*, 610–623. https://doi.org/10.1145/3442188.3445922

Benjamin, R. (2019). *Race after technology: Abolitionist tools for the New Jim Code*. Polity Press.

Burkhart, B. (2019). *Indigenizing philosophy through the land: A trickster methodology for decolonizing environmental ethics and Indigenous futures*. Michigan State University Press.

Costanza-Chock, S. (2020). *Design justice: Community-led practices to build the worlds we need*. MIT Press. https://doi.org/10.7551/mitpress/12255.001.0001

Davis, H. (2015). Temporal sovereignty: Reclaiming time in Indigenous futures. In D. B. Cole & H. Davis (Eds.), *Art in the anthropocene: Encounters among aesthetics, politics, environments and epistemologies* (pp. 185–198). Open Humanities Press.

Davis, J. L. (2020). *How artifacts afford: The power and politics of everyday things*. MIT Press.

de la Cadena, M., & Blaser, M. (Eds.). (2018). *A world of many worlds*. Duke University Press. https://doi.org/10.1515/9781478004318

Dewey, J. (1916). *Democracy and education: An introduction to the philosophy of education*. Macmillan.

Dewey, J. (1934). *Art as experience*. Minton, Balch & Company.

Dewey, J. (1938). *Logic: The theory of inquiry*. Henry Holt and Company.

Dewey, J. (2008). *Logic: The theory of inquiry* (J. A. Boydston, Ed.). Southern Illinois University Press. (Original work published 1938)

Dotson, K. (2011). Tracking epistemic violence, tracking practices of silencing. *Hypatia*, 26(2), 236–257. https://doi.org/10.1111/j.1527-2001.2011.01177.x

Escobar, A. (2018). *Designs for the pluriverse: Radical interdependence, autonomy, and the making of worlds*. Duke University Press.

Glissant, É. (1997). *Poetics of relation* (B. Wing, Trans.). University of Michigan Press.

Harris, L. (2009). *A philosophy of struggle: The Leonard Harris reader*. SUNY Press.

Hartman, S. (2008). Venus in two acts. *Small Axe: A Caribbean Journal of Criticism*, 12(2), 1–14. https://doi.org/10.1215/-12-2-1

James, W. (1907). *Pragmatism: A new name for some old ways of thinking*. Longmans, Green, and Co.

Kovach, M. (2021). *Indigenous methodologies: Characteristics, conversations, and contexts* (2nd ed.). University of Toronto Press.

Kukutai, T., & Taylor, J. (Eds.). (2016). *Indigenous data sovereignty: Toward an agenda*. ANU Press. https://doi.org/10.22459/IDS.2016

Lackey, C., & Papacharissi, Z. (2024). Machine ex machina: A framework decentering the human in AI design praxis. *Human–Machine Communication*, 8, 7–25. https://doi.org/10.30658/hmc.8.1

Lugones, M. (1987). Playfulness, "world"-traveling, and loving perception. *Hypatia*, 2(2), 3–19. https://doi.org/10.1111/j.1527-2001.1987.tb01347.x

Mano, W., & milton, v. (2021). Afrokology of media and communication studies: Theorising from the margins. In W. Mano & v. milton (Eds.), *Routledge Handbook of African media and communication studies* (pp. 19–42). Routledge.

Mbembe, A. (2001). *On the postcolony*. University of California Press.

Mead, G. H. (1934). *Mind, self, and society: From the standpoint of a social behaviorist*. University of Chicago Press.

Micheli, I. (2014). The Ogiek of the Mau Forest: reasoning between identity and survival. La *Ricerca Folklorica*, 69, 189–204.

Ong, W. J. (1982). *Orality and literacy: The technologizing of the word*. Methuen.

Papacharissi, Z. (2015). *Affective publics: Sentiment, technology, and politics*. Oxford University Press.

Parikka, J. (2015). *A geology of media*. University of Minnesota Press.

Peirce, C. S. (1931–1958). *The collected papers of Charles Sanders Peirce* (Vols. 1–8, C. Hartshorne, P. Weiss, & A. W. Burks, Eds.). Harvard University Press.

Philip, K., Irani, L., & Dourish, P. (2012). Postcolonial computing: A lens on design and development. *Proceedings of the SIGCHI Conference on Human Factors in Computing Systems*, 75–84. https://doi.org/10.1145/2207676.2207689

Povinelli, E. A. (2011). *Economies of abandonment: Social belonging and endurance in late liberalism*. Duke University Press.

Pratt, S. L. (2002). *Native pragmatism: Rethinking the roots of American philosophy*. Indiana University Press.

Putnam, R. D. (2000). *Bowling alone: The collapse and revival of American community*. Simon and schuster.

Rainie, S. C., Rodriguez-Lonebear, D., & Martinez, A. (2017). Policy brief: Indigenous data sovereignty in the United States. *Native Nations Institute*. https://nni.arizona.edu/publications/policy-brief-indigenous-data-sovereignty-united-states

Robinson, D. (2020). *Hungry listening: Resonant theory for Indigenous sound studies*. University of Minnesota Press.

Rorty, R. (1989). *Contingency, irony, and solidarity*. Cambridge University Press.

Sanders, E. B. N., & Stappers, P. J. (2008). Co-creation and the new landscapes of design. *Co-design*, 4(1), 5–18.

Schwartz, R., Dodge, J., Smith, N. A., & Etzioni, O. (2020). Green AI. *Communications of the ACM*, 63(12), 54–63. https://doi.org/10.1145/3381831

Seigfried, C. H. (1996). *Pragmatism and feminism: Reweaving the social fabric*. University of Chicago Press.

Simpson, L. B. (2014). Land as pedagogy: Nishnaabeg intelligence and rebellious transformation. *Decolonization: Indigeneity, Education & Society*, 3(3), 1–25. https://jps.library.utoronto.ca/index.php/des/article/view/22170

Smith, L. T. (2021). *Decolonizing methodologies: Research and Indigenous peoples* (3rd ed.). Zed Books.

Sullivan, S. (2001). *Living across and through skins: Transactional bodies, pragmatism, and feminism*. Indiana University Press.

Todd, Z. (2016). An Indigenous feminist's take on the ontological turn: 'Ontology' is just another word for colonialism. *Journal of Historical Sociology*, 29(1), 4–22. https://doi.org/10.1111/johs.12124

Tuck, E., & Yang, K. W. (2012). *Decolonization is not a metaphor. Decolonization: Indigeneity, Education & Society*, 1(1), 1–40. https://jps.library.utoronto.ca/index.php/des/article/view/18630

Tuck, E., & Yang, K. W. (2014). R-words: Refusing research. In D. Paris & M. T. Winn (Eds.), *Humanizing research: Decolonizing qualitative inquiry with youth and communities* (pp. 223–248). Sage Publications.

Verbeek, P.-P. (2011). *Moralizing technology: Understanding and designing the morality of things*. University of Chicago Press.

Vizenor, G. (1994). *Manifest manners: Narratives on postindian survivance*. University of Nebraska Press.

Wa Thiong'o N. (2012). *Globalectics: Theory and the politics of knowing*. Columbia UniversityPress.

Walsh, C. (2018). Decoloniality in/as praxis. In W. D. Mignolo & C. E. Walsh, *On decoloniality: Concepts, analytics, praxis* (pp. 15–104). Duke University Press.

West, C. (1989). *The American evasion of philosophy: A genealogy of pragmatism*. University of Wisconsin Press.

Wilson, S. (2008). *Research is ceremony: Indigenous research methods*. Fernwood Publishing.

Wynter, S. (1984). The ceremony must be found: After humanism. In B. Ferguson et al. (Eds.), *Boundary 2, 12*(3), 19–70. https://doi.org/10.2307/302808

INDEX

Note: *Italic* page numbers refer to figures, **bold** page numbers refer to tables and page number followed 'n' refers to notes.